THE CHARTER AND ORDINANCES OF THE CITY OF PORTLAND,

TOGETHER WITH THE

ACTS OF THE LEGISLATURE,

RELATING TO THE CITY,

COLLATED AND REVISED BY AUTHORITY OF

A JOINT COMMITTEE OF THE CITY COUNCIL.

PORTLAND, ME.:
N. A. FOSTER, CITY PRINTER.
1868.

CITY OF PORTLAND.

IN BOARD OF MAYOR AND ALDERMEN,
APRIL 1st, 1867.

ORDERED, That a committee of two on the part of this Board, with such as the Common Council may join, be raised, who shall be hereby authorized and empowered to cause the ordinances of the city to be revised, collated and arranged, and to prepare the same for publication, together with the city charter and such statute laws as may be applicable to the proper administration of the municipal affairs of the city, and to prepare suitable abstracts and marginal notes to each section, with a copious index to the whole.

And said committee are further authorized to employ some person of suitable legal attainments to aid them in said revision, and they are required to report to the city council from time to time as said work is progressed with, and to complete the revision as soon as may be practicable.

Read and passed, and aldermen Bailey and Rice were appointed. Sent down.

Concurred, and joined Messrs. Colesworthy, Dow and Burgess.

Approved :

Attest : J. M. HEATH, *City Clerk.*

A true copy of records :

Attest : J. M. HEATH, *City Clerk.*

PREFACE.

The city government, the legal profession, and all others who have had occasion to refer to the municipal ordinances, have for a long time realized the imperative necessity of a new and carefully prepared edition.

In the year eighteen hundred and forty-eight, for the first time, we believe, the ordinances of the city were collected, arranged and published in a volume.

In the year eighteen hundred and fifty-five, a committee of the city council was appointed to revise and cause to be printed the city ordinances, which labor was performed in a full and very satisfactory manner.

Since that period, however, the rapid and steady growth of the city in population, commerce, buildings and general enterprise, has required a large amount of additional legislation to meet the pressing needs of the times. Especially has this been the case since the great fire of July 4, 1866, a calamity which demanded new ordinances in relation to the fire department, wooden buildings, the enlargement and straightening of streets, the location of new streets, and various other public and private interests growing out of the unprecedented state of city affairs.

The numerous ordinances, and amendments to ordinances, that have been passed, as well as the repeal of ordinances, since the year eighteen hundred and fifty-five, have been made known to the public only through the casual mode of newspaper advertisements and the annual municipal registers. These very soon became almost inaccessible. But added to this is the fact that, by the great fire, nearly every copy, both of revised ordinances and municipal registers, was destroyed. It has been, consequently, at times very difficult, in some cases, to decide precisely what the provisions of ordinances upon particular subjects were.

In view of these circumstances, the city council, by their order passed the first day of April, in the year eighteen hundred and sixty-seven, raised a committee " to cause the ordinances of the city to be revised, collated and arranged, and to prepare the same for publication, together with the city charter and such statute laws as may be applicable."

In accordance with the above authority, the present volume has been prepared.

The former volumes have contained the various special acts giving express powers to the town and city of Portland. As the act of the legislature passed in the year eighteen hundred and sixty-three, entitled " An act to confer certain powers on the city of Portland," incorporated within itself full powers, the prior acts are omitted as unnecessary and cumbersome.

It has been found somewhat embarrassing to determine what general laws of the State should be included in this volume. Great care and deliberation have been exercised in their selection ; but we may, nevertheless, have failed to insert some that are of importance. We have been restrained to a certain extent by the consideration that if all that seemed to have a bearing upon local municipal affairs were inserted, the volume would be too large.

The *revision* of the ordinances, as contemplated by the order of the city council, will be found to be of a very limited nature. The changes made are mainly verbal, besides such modifications as were necessary to conform to the provisions of the new city charter. The alterations in the fundamental law of the city made corresponding alterations in the municipal laws unavoidable. Where no changes seemed necessary, the ordinances have been printed from the official copy; but where there are several on one subject, they are combined into one ordinance, and numbered continuously; but in all instances the dates of their passage, or of amendments, are given in the margin.

CONTENTS.

LIST OF ORDINANCES

CONTAINED IN THIS VOLUME.

INDEX TO CITY CHARTER.

[The Figures refer to the Numbers of Sections.]

CITY CHARTER.

CITY CHARTER.

AN ACT TO CONFER CERTAIN POWERS ON THE CITY OF PORTLAND.

Be it enacted by the Senate and House of Representatives, in Legislature assembled, as follows:

SECTION 1. The inhabitants of Portland shall continue to be a body politic and corporate by the name of the city of Portland, and as such shall have, exercise, and enjoy all the rights, immunities, powers, privileges and franchises, and shall be subject to all the duties and obligations now appertaining to, or incumbent upon said city, or the inhabitants or municipal authorities thereof; and may ordain reasonable by-laws and regulations for municipal purposes, and impose penalties for the breach thereof, not exceeding one hundred dollars, to be recovered for such uses as the municipal authorities may appoint.

Corporate powers.

Power to make by-laws.

Penalties.

SEC. 2. The administration of all the fiscal, prudential and municipal affairs of said city, with the government thereof, shall be vested in one principal magistrate to be styled the mayor, and one council of seven to be denominated the board of aldermen, and one council of twenty-one to be denominated the board of common council, all of whom shall be inhabitants of said city; which board shall constitute and be called the city council; and shall be sworn or affirmed in the form prescribed by the constitution of the State for State officers.

Mayor.

Aldermen.

Council.

Duties of Mayor.

SEC. 3. The mayor of said city shall be the chief executive magistrate thereof. It shall be his duty to be vigilant and active in causing the laws of the State, and ordinances and regulations of the city, to be executed and enforced, to exercise a general supervision over the conduct of all subordinate officers, and to cause violations or neglect of duty on their part to be punished. He shall, from time to time, communicate to the city council, or either board, such information, and recommend such measures, as the interest of the city may require. He shall preside at all meetings of the mayor and aldermen, and in joint meetings of the two boards, but shall have only a casting vote. He shall be compensated for his services by a salary to be fixed by the city council, payable at stated periods, and shall receive therefor no other compensation, which salary, however, shall not be increased or diminished during his year of office.

Laws, &c., to be approved by Mayor.

SEC. 4. Every law, act, ordinance, resolve or order, requiring the consent of both branches of the city council, excepting rules and orders of a parliamentary character, shall be presented to the mayor for approval. If not approved by him he shall return it, with his objections, at the next stated session of the city council, to that branch in which it originated, which shall enter the objections at large on its journal and proceed to reconsider the same. If upon such reconsideration it shall be passed by a vote of two-thirds of all the members of that branch, it shall be sent, together with the objections, to the other branch, by which it shall be reconsidered, and, if passed by two-thirds of that branch, it shall have the same effect as if signed by the mayor. In case of vacancy in the office of mayor, when said law, act, ordinance, resolve or order be finally passed, the same shall be valid without approval.

Veto power.

Executive powers, in whom vested.

SEC. 5. The executive powers of said city generally, and the administration of police and health departments, with all the powers of selectmen, except as modified by this act, shall be vested in the mayor and aldermen. All the powers of establishing watch and ward, now vested by the laws of the State in the justices of the peace and municipal officers or inhabitants of towns, are vested in the mayor and aldermen, so far as relates to said city ; and they are authorized to unite the watch and police departments into one department and establish suitable regulations for the government of the same. The officers of police shall be one chief, to be styled the city marshal, so many deputy marshals as the city council may by ordinance prescribe, and so many watchmen and policemen as the mayor and aldermen may, from time to time, appoint. All other powers now or hereafter vested in the inhabitants of said city, and all powers granted by this act, as well as all powers relating to the fire department, shall be vested in the mayor and aldermen, and common council of said city, to be exercised by concurrent vote, each board to have a negative upon the other. Each board shall keep a record of its proceedings, and judge of the election of its own members ; and in case of vacancies, new elections shall be ordered by the mayor and aldermen.

Police.

Sec. 6. The compensation of all subordinate city officers whatsoever, shall be fixed by the city council. All officers of the police and health departments shall be appointed by the mayor and aldermen, and may be removed by them for good cause. All other subordinate officers, now elected by the mayor and aldermen or the city council, shall hereafter be elected by joint convention of the city council, and such officers may be removed for good cause, by concurrent vote passed in each branch by the assent of two-thirds of all the members thereof. Except as otherwise specially provided in this act, all subordinate officers shall be elected annually on the second Monday of March, or as soon thereafter as may be, and their term of office shall be for one year, and until others are qualified in their place. All vacancies may be filled by the board having authority to elect.

Compensation.

Appointments and removals.

Election of subordinate officers.

Sec. 7. No money shall be paid out of the city treasury except on orders drawn and signed by the mayor, designating the fund or appropriation from which said orders are to be paid, nor unless the same shall be first granted or appropriated therefor, by the city council; and the city council shall secure a prompt and just accountability by requiring bonds with sufficient penalty and surety or sureties, from all persons intrusted with the receipt, custody or disbursement of money; they shall have the care and superintendence of the city buildings and the custody and management of all city property, with power to let or sell what may be legally let or sold, and to purchase and take in the name of the city, real and personal property for municipal purposes to an amount not exceeding two hundred thousand dollars in addition to that now held by the city. And shall, as often as once a year, cause to be published for the information of the inhabitants, a particular account of receipts and expenditures, and a schedule of city property.

Powers of City Council.

Sec. 8. The assessors shall continue to be elected on the second Monday in March. At the first election thereof under this act, three persons shall be elected assessors, one of whom shall be elected for one year, one for two years, and one for three years, and at each subsequent election one assessor shall be elected for three years, each of whom shall continue in office until some other person shall have been elected and qualified in his place. The city council shall elect an assistant assessor in each ward, whose duty it shall be to furnish the assessors with all the necessary information relative to persons and property taxable in his ward; he shall be sworn or affirmed to the faithful performance of his duty. All taxes shall be assessed, apportioned and collected in the manner prescribed by the laws of this State relative to town taxes, except as herein modified; and the city council may establish further or additional provisions for the collection

Assessors.

Assistant Assessors.

thereof and of interest thereon. There shall be elected at the first election of subordinate officers under this act in March, twelve persons for overseers of the poor and workhouse, four of whom shall be elected for one year, four for two years, and four for three years; and all subsequent annual elections shall be for the term of three years. Overseers of Poor.

SEC. 9. The city council shall have exclusive authority to lay out, widen or otherwise alter, or discontinue any and all streets or public ways in the city of Portland, without petition therefor, and as far as extreme low water mark; and to estimate all damage sustained by the owners of land taken for that purpose; but all locations below high water mark shall be subject to the provisions of the laws relating to the commissioners of Portland harbor. A joint standing committee of the two boards shall be appointed, whose duty it shall be to lay out, alter, widen or discontinue any street or way in said city, first giving notice of the time and place of their proceedings to all parties interested, by an advertisement in two daily papers printed in Portland, for one week at least previous to the time appointed. The committee shall first hear all parties interested, and then determine and adjudge whether the public convenience requires such street or way to be laid out, altered or discontinued; and shall make a written return of their proceedings, signed by a majority of them, containing the bounds and descriptions of the street or way, if laid out or altered, and the names of the owners of the land taken, when known, and the damages allowed therefor; the return shall be filed in the city clerk's office at least seven days previous to its acceptance by the city council. The street or way shall not be altered or established until the report is accepted by the city council, and the report shall not be altered or amended before its acceptance. A street or way shall not be discontinued by the city council, excepting upon the report of said committee. The committee shall estimate and report the damages sustained by Streets.

Damages in laying out streets.

Appeals.

the owners of the lands adjoining that portion of the street or way which is so discontinued ; their report shall be filed with the city clerk seven days at least before its acceptance. Any person aggrieved by the decision or judgment of the city council in establishing, altering, or discontinuing streets, may, so far as relates to damages, appeal therefrom to the next court having jurisdiction thereof in the county of Cumberland, which court shall determine the same by a committee or reference under a rule of court, if the parties agree, or by a verdict of its jury, and shall render judgment and issue execution for the damages recovered, with costs to the party prevailing in the appeal. Such appeal shall be made to the term of the Supreme Judicial Court, which shall first be holden in the county of Cumberland, more than thirty days from and after the day the street is finally established, altered or discontinued, excluding the day of commencement of the session of said court. The appellants shall serve written notice of such appeal upon the mayor or city clerk, fourteen days at least before the session of the court, and shall at the first term file a complaint setting forth substantially the facts of the case. On the trial, exceptions may be taken to the rulings of the court, as in other cases. Co-tenants who are appellants shall join in their appeal or shall not recover their costs. If a street or way is discontinued before the damages are paid or recovered for the land taken, the land owner shall not be entitled to recover such damages, but the committee in their report discontinuing the same shall estimate and include all the damages, sustained by the land owner, including those caused by the original location of the streets, and in such cases, if an appeal has been regularly taken, the appellant shall recover his costs. The city shall not be compelled to construct or open any street or way thus hereafter established, until in the opinion of the city council the public good requires it to be done ; nor shall the city interfere with the possession of the land so taken by removing therefrom materials or otherwise, until they decide to open and construct said street. The city council may regulate the height and width of sidewalks in any public square, places, streets, lanes or alleys in said city; and may authorize posts and trees to be placed along the edge of said sidewalks. Nor shall the city be answerable for damages occasioned by telegraph poles and wires erected in its streets.

Sidewalks, &c.

SEC. 10. The mayor may on such terms and conditions as he may think proper, authorize and empower any person or corporation to place in any street, for such time as may be necessary, any materials for making or repairing any street, sidewalk, cross-walk, bridge, water-course or drain, or for erecting, repairing, or finishing any building or fences, or for laying or repairing gas or water pipes, provided that not more than one-half of the width of the street shall be so occupied. And such material so placed by virtue of any license obtained as aforesaid, shall not be considered an incumbrance or nuisance in such street; and the city shall not be liable to any person for any damages occasioned by such materials.

Obstructing streets.

Gas-pipes.

SEC. 11. The city shall remain divided into seven wards; and it shall be the duty of the city council, once in ten years or oftener, to revise, and if it be needful, to alter such wards, in such manner as to preserve, as nearly as may be, an equal number of voters in each. In each of said wards, at the annual municipal election, there shall be chosen by ballot, a warden and clerk, who shall hold their offices for one year from the Monday following their election, and until others shall have been chosen and qualified in their places. Said warden and clerk shall be sworn or affirmed to the faithful performance of their respective duties by any justice of the peace of the city; and a certificate of such oaths or affirmations having been administered, shall be entered by the clerk on the records of the ward. The warden shall preside at all ward

Wards.

meetings, with the powers of moderators of town meetings. If at any meeting the warden shall not be present, or shall refuse to preside, the clerk of such ward shall call the meeting to order and preside until a warden *pro tem.* shall be chosen. If both are absent, or shall refuse to act, a warden and clerk *pro tem.* shall be chosen. The clerk shall record all proceedings, and certify the votes given, and deliver over to his successor in office all such records and journals, together with all other documents and papers held by him in said capacity. The voters of each ward may choose two persons to assist the warden in receiving, sorting and counting the votes.

All regular ward meetings shall be notified and called by warrant from the mayor and aldermen, in the manner prescribed by the laws of this State for notifying and calling town meetings by the selectmen of the several towns.

Election of city officers.

SEC. 12. The mayor shall be elected by the inhabitants of the city, voting in their respective wards. One alderman, three common councilmen, a warden and clerk, and two constables shall be elected by each ward, being residents in the ward where elected. All said officers shall be elected by ballot by a majority of the votes given; and shall hold their offices one year from the second Monday in March, and until others shall be elected and qualified in their places. All city and ward officers shall be held to discharge the duties of the offices to which they have been respectively elected, notwithstanding their removal after their election out of their respective wards into any other wards in the city; but they shall not so be held after they have taken up their permanent residence out of the city.

Same.

SEC. 13. On the first Monday in March annually, the qualified electors of each ward shall ballot for mayor, one alderman, three common councilmen, a warden and clerk, and two constables, on one ballot. The ward clerk, within twenty-four hours after such election, shall deliver to the persons elected certificates of their election, and shall forthwith deliver to the city clerk, a certified copy of the record of such election, a plain and intelligible abstract of which shall be entered by the city clerk on the city records. If the choice of any such officers is not effected on that day, the meeting shall be adjourned to another day, (not more than two days thereafter,) to complete such election, and may so adjourn from time to time, until the election is complete. The board of aldermen shall, as soon as conveniently may be, examine the copies of the records of the several wards, certified as aforesaid, and shall cause the person who shall have been elected mayor by a majority of the votes given in all the wards, to be notified in writing of his election. But if it shall appear that no person shall have been so elected, or if the person elected shall refuse to accept the office, the said board shall issue their warrants for another election; and in case the citizens shall fail on a second ballot to elect a mayor, the city council in convention shall, from the four highest candidates voted for at the second election and returned, elect a mayor for the ensuing year; and in case of a vacancy in the office of mayor by death, resignation or otherwise, it shall be filled for the remainder of the term by a new election in the manner herein before provided for the choice of said officer. The oath or affirmation prescribed by this act shall be administered to the mayor by the city clerk or any justice of the peace in said city. The aldermen and common councilmen elect, shall on the second Monday in March, at ten o'clock in the forenoon, meet in convention, when the oath or affirmation required by the second section of this act shall be administered to the members of the two boards present, by the mayor or any justice of the peace after which the board of common council shall be organized by the election of a president and clerk. The city council shall, by ordinance, determine the time of holding stated or regular meetings of the board, and shall also, in like

Organization.

manner, determine the manner of calling special meetings and the persons by whom the same shall be called; but until otherwise provided by ordinance, special meetings shall be called by the mayor by causing a notification to be left at the usual residence or place of business of each member of the board or boards to be convened.

SEC. 14. After the organization of a city government and the qualification of a mayor, and when a quorum of the board of aldermen shall be present, said board, the mayor presiding, shall proceed to choose a permanent chairman who, in the absence of the mayor, shall preside at all meetings of the board, or at conventions of the two boards, and in case of any vacancy in the office of mayor, he shall exercise all the powers and perform all the duties of the office so long as such vacancy shall remain; he shall continue to have a vote in the board, but shall not have the veto power. The board of aldermen, in the absence of the mayor and permanent chairman, shall choose a president *pro tem.*, who shall exercise the powers of a permanent chairman.

Chairman of Aldermen.

His powers.

SEC. 15. In addition to the seven wards, the several islands within the city of Portland, are so far constituted a separate ward as to entitle the legal voters thereon to choose a warden, ward clerk, and one constable, who shall be residents on said islands. They shall hold their ward meetings on any one of the islands which a majority of the qualified voters residing on said islands may designate, and may, on the days of election, vote at the place designated for all officers named in the warrant calling the meeting. The warden shall preside at all meetings, receive the votes of all qualified electors present whose names are borne on the lists; shall sort, count and declare the votes in open meeting and in the presence of the clerk, who shall make a list of the persons voted for, with the number of votes for each person, and a fair record thereof, in presence of the warden and in open meeting, and a copy of the list shall

Island ward.

be attested by the warden and clerk, sealed up in open meeting and delivered to the clerk of ward number one, within eighteen hours after the close of the polls, to become a part of the record of said ward; and all votes thus thrown shall be deemed as thrown in and belonging to ward number one. All meetings of the voters of said island ward, for choice of municipal officers, shall, after the business of the meeting is transacted, stand adjourned for two days to determine whether an election has been effected; and adjournments may be had, not exceeding two days at any one time, until the election has been effected. If the warden or clerk of said island ward shall be absent at any election, a warden or clerk may be chosen *pro tempore*. Or in case of failure or omission to elect a warden or clerk, said officers may be chosen at any legal meeting duly called in said ward.

Powers of City Council.

SEC. 16. The city council, in behalf of the city, may offer rewards for the prevention of crimes or detection of criminals. They may remove all sunken wrecks in the harbor or its entrances, and dispose of the same to defray the expense of removal, and may at the expense of the city cause its harbor to be kept open and unobstructed by ice. They may also require all sail boats not under register or license, kept for hire in said harbor, to be examined and licensed for that purpose, and to be furnished with air-tight compartments; and may establish such regulations respecting such boats as they may deem expedient. They may also make and enforce by penalties, regulations respecting the enclosure of lots abutting on any street or way in the city, which may for want of such enclosure be dangerous to the public; and after notice to the owners or lessees of such lots, may, if the same are not enclosed in a reasonable time, cause the same to be enclosed at the expense of the owners or lessees. They may make regulations relative to the assize of bread sold, or offered for sale within said city. They may assess money for celebration of the anniversary of our national independence, and other public celebrations.

City clerk, his duties.

SEC. 17. The city clerk shall be clerk of the board of aldermen. He shall perform such duties as shall be prescribed by the mayor and aldermen or the city council, and shall also perform all the duties and exercise all the powers now incumbent on him by law. He shall give notice in two or more of the papers printed in said city, of the time and place of regular ward meetings; the time of such meetings when not fixed by law shall be determined by the board of aldermen. In case of the temporary absence of the city clerk, the mayor and aldermen may appoint a city clerk *pro tem.*

Meetings of citizens.

SEC. 18. General meetings of the citizens qualified to vote in city affairs may, from time to time, be held to consult upon the public good, to instruct their representatives, and to take all lawful measures to obtain redress of any grievances, according to the right secured to the people by the constitution of this State; and such meeting shall be duly warned by the mayor and aldermen upon requisition of sixty qualified voters. The city clerk shall act as clerk of such meetings, and record the proceedings upon the city records.

No compensation, &c.

SEC. 19. The aldermen and common councilmen shall not be entitled to receive any salary or other compensation during the year for which they are elected, nor be eligible to any office of profit or emolument, the salary of which is payable by the city; and all departments, boards, officers and committees, acting under the authority of the city, and entrusted with the expenditures of public money, shall expend the same for no other purpose than that for which it is appropriated; and shall be accountable therefor to the city, in such manner as the city council may direct.

SEC. 20. The treasurer of the city of Portland shall also be the collector for said city, with all the powers of collectors of taxes under the laws of this State. He shall be styled treasurer and collector, and shall give but one bond, said bond to be approved by the mayor and aldermen, for the faithful performance of his duties; and may appoint assistants and deputies as provided by law. All warrants directed to him by the assessors and municipal officers shall run to him and his successors in office, and shall be in the form prescribed by law, changing such parts only as by this act are required to be changed. The method of keeping, vouching and settling his accounts, shall be subject to such rules and regulations as the city council may establish. Said treasurer and collector shall collect all such uncollected taxes and assessments in whatever year assessed as may be collected during his term of office; and at the expiration of said term, his powers as collector shall wholly cease; all sales, distresses, and all other acts and proceedings, lawfully commenced by him as such treasurer and collector, may be as effectually continued and completed by his successor in office as though done by himself; and all unreturned warrants, which would otherwise be returnable to him, shall be returned to his successor in office. These provisions shall apply in all respects to the uncollected taxes of said city, assessed in the year eighteen hundred and sixty-three, but shall not in any way be construed to effect the collection of taxes assessed in other previous years.

Powers and duties of treasurer.

SEC. 21. The original location of all streets and ways in said city shall, once in ten years, or oftener, be ascertained by the city engineer, under the direction of the city council, as accurately as practicable, the location of different streets being ascertained by him from time to time, when expedient. He shall make a written report of his doings to the committee on new streets, which shall give twenty days notice, by advertisement in two or more public papers in the city, of the time and place at which it will act upon said report. Any person may appear and object to the report; and after a full hearing of all parties

Location of streets.

interested, the committee may accept, alter, or amend the report as it shall think right, and shall report their proceedings to the city council, who shall thereupon determine the lines for such streets and ways in said city, according to the original location thereof, and shall order the same to be designated anew by fixed and permanent boundaries, as and for the original boundaries; and a record of the location thereof to be made upon the city records; and a copy of the last record of such proceedings respecting any street, with evidence of the location of the boundaries therein designated, shall in all judicial proceedings, be *prima facie* evidence of the place of the original location of said street.

Passing of horses, &c., in streets.

SEC. 22. The mayor and aldermen of said city may on public occasions, by their order, forbid the passing, temporarily, of horses, carriages or other vehicles, over or through such streets or ways in said city, as they may deem expedient. No existing wharf in Portland shall be extended into the harbor a greater distance below low water mark than the same now exists, and hereafter no such new wharf shall be extended below low water mark into the harbor, without, in either case, the written assent of the mayor and aldermen. No wharf or incumbrance shall hereafter be erected or extended into said harbor beyond the harbor commissioners' line.

Extension of wharves.

Paving Sidewalks.

SEC. 23. The city council of Portland may require the owner of any lot of ground fronting on any street or way in said city, to cause the footway or sidewalk in front of said lot to be paved with bricks or flat stones, with suitable curb stones, the same to be done under the direction, and to the approbation, of the committee on streets. If the owner of such lot shall neglect to pave the same as aforesaid, and provide such curb stones, for the space of twenty days after he, or the tenant of such lot, shall have been thereto required in writing by the commissioner of streets, it shall then be the duty of said commissioner to procure the curb stones and pave the sidewalk or footway; and the city shall have a lien on the property for expense thereof, to be enforced as in the following section. The city council before requiring any such sidewalk or footway to be so paved, shall by a general ordinance assume a portion of said expense to an amount not less than one-half thereof, to be paid by the city in money or materials, but no owner or proprietor shall be required to construct as aforesaid, more than two hundred feet in length of sidewalk or footway, in any one street in front of any unimproved lots or parcels of land.

SEC. 24. The mayor and aldermen of said city may lay out, make, maintain and repair all main drains or common sewers in said city, and may assess upon the owners of the abutting lots and other lots benefited thereby, and who shall enter the same directly or indirectly, a proportional part of the charge of making such main drain or common sewer, to be ascertained and assessed by the mayor and aldermen of said city, and by them certified, after notice thereof given in writing to the party to be charged, or by public advertisement for seven days in two daily papers in said city; but not less than one-third part of the cost of such main drain or common sewer shall be paid by the city, and shall not be charged to the abuttors. All assessments so made shall constitute a lien on the real estate so assessed, for two years after they are laid. They shall be certified by the mayor and aldermen, under their hands, to the treasurer and collector of said city and his successors, with directions to collect the same according to law, and may, together with all incidental costs and expenses, be levied by sale of the estate by him or them, if the assessment is not paid within three months after a written demand of payment made by him or them, either upon the persons assessed or upon any person occupying the estate—such sale to be conducted in like manner as sale for non-payment of taxes on land of resident owners, and with a similar right of re-

Sewers and drains.

demption. Any person, who may deem himself aggrieved by any such assessment, may appeal to the Supreme Court in the same manner as is herein provided for appeals for damages for laying out streets, which court shall at the first term appoint three persons who may be inhabitants of said city, to settle and assess the share to be charged to such appellant; they shall make a return of their doings to said court and their decision, if accepted, shall be final. And in case the assessment made by the mayor and aldermen shall not be reduced on such appeal, the city shall recover costs, but otherwise shall pay costs. Any person who shall, directly or indirectly, enter any such main drain or common sewer without first obtaining a permit from the mayor therefor, shall be subject to a fine not exceeding one hundred dollars.

Repeal of prior acts.

SEC. 25. All acts and parts of acts inconsistent with this act are hereby repealed. *Provided*, *however*, the repeal of the said acts shall not affect any act done, or any act accruing, or accrued, or established, or any suit or proceeding had or commenced in any civil or criminal case before the time when such repeal shall take effect, and that no offence committed, and no penalty or forfeiture incurred, under the acts hereby repealed, and before the time when such repeal shall take effect, shall be affected by the repeal. And provided, also, that all persons who, at the time the said repeal shall take effect, shall hold any office under the said acts or ordinances of the city, shall continue to hold the same according to the tenure thereof, or until others are elected and qualified in their stead. And provided, also, that all the ordinances rules and regulations of the city of Portland, which shall be in force at the time when the said repeal shall take effect, shall continue in force until the same are repealed. No act which has been heretofore repealed shall be revived by the repeal of the above acts.

SEC. 26. This act shall be void unless the inhabitants of the city of Portland, at legal ward meetings called for that purpose, by a written vote, determine to adopt the same; and the qualified voters of the city shall be called upon to give in their votes upon the acceptance of this act, at meetings in the several wards, duly warned by the mayor and aldermen, to be held on the day of the next municipal election; and thereupon the same proceedings shall be had respecting the sorting, counting, declaring and recording the returns of said votes, as is herein provided at the election of mayor; and the board of mayor and aldermen shall within three days meet together and compare the returns of the ward officers; and if it appear that a majority of all the votes given on the question of its acceptance are in favor thereof, the mayor shall forthwith make proclamation of the fact, and thereupon this act shall take effect. And in case this act is so adopted and takes effect, the terms of office of all city officers which would otherwise expire in April, in the year of our Lord eighteen hundred and sixty-four, shall expire on the second Monday of March, in the year of our Lord eighteen hundred and sixty-four, or as soon thereafter as other persons are qualified in their places; subordinate officers shall be elected in April, eighteen hundred and sixty-three, at the time now fixed by law.

Vote of qualified voters on this act.

[*Approved March* 24, 1863.]

LAWS OF THE STATE,

AND

ORDINANCES OF THE CITY.

AGENTS OF THE CITY.

FOR SALE OF INTOXICATING LIQUORS.

1. The selectmen of any town, and mayor and aldermen of any city, shall immediately after this act shall go into effect, and on the first Monday of May annually thereafter, or as soon thereafter as may be convenient, purchase such quantity of intoxicating liquors as may be necessary to be sold under the provisions of this act, and shall appoint some suitable person, as the agent of said town or city, to sell the same at some convenient place within said town or city, to be used for medicinal, mechanical and manufacturing purposes, and no other; and such agent shall receive such compensation for his services, and in the sale of such liquors shall conform to such regulations, not inconsistent with this act, as the board appointing him shall prescribe, and he shall hold his situation one year unless sooner removed by them or their successors in office. Vacancies occurring during the year are to be filled in the same manner as original appointments are

Mayor and aldermen to purchase. Act 1858, ch. 33, § 5.

Agents to be appointed to sell for certain purposes.

—compensation and duty.

—term of office.

—vacancy, how filled.

Agents not to be interested. —may sell to municipal officers.

made. No such agent shall have any interest in such liquors, or in the profits of the sale thereof. Such agents may sell to such municipal officers intoxicating liquors, to be by said officers disposed of in accordance with the provisions of this act.

—shall have a certificate. Ib. § 6. —shall give bond, amount.

2. Such agent shall receive a certificate from the board by which he is appointed, authorizing him as the agent of such town or city to sell intoxicating liquors for medicinal, mechanical and manufacturing purposes only; but such certificate shall not be delivered to the person so appointed until he shall have executed and delivered to said board a bond, with two good and sufficient sureties, in the sum of six hundred dollars, in substance, as follows:

Form of Bond.

Know all men, that we,——, as principal, and——, as sureties, are holden and stand firmly bound to the inhabitants of the town of ——, (or city, as the case may be,) in the sum of six hundred dollars, to be paid them, to which payment we bind ourselves, our heirs, executors, and administrators, firmly by these presents. Sealed with our seals, and dated this——day of——A. D. ——.

Condition of bond.

The condition of this obligation is such, that whereas the above bounden——has been duly appointed an agent for the town (or city) to sell intoxicating liquors for medicinal, mechanical, and manufacturing purposes and no other, until the——of——A. D. ——, unless sooner removed from said agency. Now if the said ——shall in all respects conform to the provisions of the law relating to the business for which he is appointed, and to such regulations as now are or shall be from time to time established by the board making the appointment, then this obligation to be void; otherwise to remain in full force.

Liquors owned by towns or kept by agents, casks and vessels to be marked. Ib. § 28. —seized, bearing marks.

3. No such liquors owned by any city, town or plantation, or kept by any agent of any city, town or plantation, as is provided in this act, shall be protected against seizure and forfeiture, under the provisions of this act, by reason of such ownership, unless all the casks and vessels in which they are contained shall be at all times plainly and conspicuously marked with the name of such city, town or plantation, and of its agent. When any such liquors shall be seized, bearing such marks as are by this act required to be upon

liquors owned by cities, towns or plantations, if such liquors are in fact not owned by any such city, town or plantation, such false and fraudulent marking shall be conclusive evidence that the same are kept or deposited for unlawful sale, and render them liable to forfeiture under the provisions of this act. The liquors kept for sale by such agents shall not be adulterated or factitious, and shall not be protected from seizure and forfeiture by reason of being kept for sale by such agents, if so adulterated or made factitious and they have knowledge of the fact.

—false marks conclusive evidence, liquors forfeited.

—adulterated or factitious, not protected.

4. No person, authorized as aforesaid to sell intoxicating liquors, shall sell such liquors to any minor without the direction in writing of his parent, master or guardian, to any Indian, to any soldier in the army, to any drunkard, to any intoxicated person, or to any such persons as are described in the fourth section of the sixty-seventh chapter of the revised statutes, as being liable to guardianship, knowing them respectively to be of the condition herein prescribed; nor to any intemperate person, of whose intemperate habits he has been notified by the relatives of such person, or by the aldermen. And proof of notice so given by the aldermen, or by their authority, shall be conclusive of the fact of the intemperate habits of such person.

Agents not to sell to minors or others described.

Ib. § 29.

—notice by aldermen or relatives, sufficient evidence.

5. Any agent, authorized as aforesaid, who shall violate the law by illegal sale, shall be punished, on conviction, by a fine of twenty dollars for every such offence, and shall also be liable to a suit upon his bond; and it is the duty of the aldermen to cause the same to be put in suit, and prosecuted to the use of the city. And whenever conviction is obtained or judgment recovered on the bond, the authority of the agent is absolutely vacated; and it is the duty of the aldermen to revoke such authority, whenever they shall be satisfied of the violation of any of the conditions of the same.

Ibid. § 31.

Agents violating the law.

Duty of Aldermen to put bond in suit.

Agents authority to cease.

Aldermen to revoke authority.

6. The agents of the several cities, towns and planta-

City, town and plantation agents required to keep record of sales.

Act 1862, § 5.

tions of the State authorized by law to sell intoxicating liquors, shall keep a record in a book kept for that purpose, of the amount of intoxicating liquors purchased by them, specifying the kind and quantity of each, the price paid, and of whom purchased, and they shall also keep a record of the kind and quantity of the liquors sold by them, the date of sale and the price, the name of the purchaser, and the purpose for which it was sold; specifying in case such sale is made to the municipal officers of any other city, town or plantation, the name of such; which record shall be open to inspection. And if such agent shall fail to keep such a record, he shall forfeit and pay for every such offence a sum not less than ten nor more than twenty dollars, to be recovered on complaint or indictment before any court competent to try the same; which fine shall be paid into the treasury of the city, town or plantation where he may hold his agency, for the benefit of said city, town or plantation. And if any person shall knowingly misrepresent and falsely state to the said agent the purpose for which he purchases of said agent the intoxicating liquors, he shall for every such offence be fined twenty dollars, to be recovered on complaint or indictment before any court competent to try the same; which fine shall be paid into the treasury of the city, town or plantation where the offence may be committed.

—to be open for inspection.

—failure or neglect to keep, penalty for.

—how recovered.

Fines to whom paid.

False representation to agents.

Penalty for, how recovered.

ALIEN PASSENGERS.

STATUTES.

RULES AND ORDERS.

STATUTES.

Masters of vessels not to land passengers without consent; give bond or pay a sum per head.
R. S. chap. 24, § 39.

1. When a vessel, with passengers on board having no settlement in this State, arrives at any port or harbor within any town in the State, the master thereof shall leave a list of their names, and of the places from which they came first on board, with the overseers of the poor of such town, before they come on shore. He shall not land them without permission of the municipal officers, unless he gives bond to the town, with sureties approved by said officers, in a sum not exceeding five hundred dollars for each passenger, to save the town harmless from all expense on account of such passengers, as paupers, for

three years. The said officers, instead of such bond, may require payment of a sum not exceeding two dollars for each passenger.

Penalty.

If not paid, vessel may be sold.

Ib. § 40.

2. The master of such vessel, for a violation of any provision of the preceding section, forfeits two hundred dollars for each passenger coming on shore, to be recovered in an action of debt, by the municipal officers of the town, one-half to the use of the town, and the other to the use of the State; and there shall be a lien on such vessel to secure such penalties, which may be enforced by an attachment of the vessel within sixty days, though the defendant is not its owner; and it may be sold on execution like other personal property, and after deducting the amount of penalties and costs, the balance shall be paid to the owner on demand.

Towns may appoint officers to prevent passengers landing.

Ib. § 41.

3. A town accessible by vessels may appoint visiting officers, who, on the arrival of a vessel with passengers on board, are to go on board of her, and there remain until the provisions above mentioned are complied with; and they are to prevent the landing of any passenger in violation of such provisions; and to inform the municipal officers of any violation or attempt to violate such provisions. They are to be paid by the master a reasonable compensation to be fixed by said officers.

RULES AND ORDERS OF MAYOR AND ALDERMEN.

Form of receipt to be given by the visiting officer on receiving head money for alien passengers arriving at the Port of Portland.

PORT OF PORTLAND.[1]

Whereas, the———of———has arrived in the port of Portland, with alien passengers on board who were never before within this State; and whereas———of said vessel, desires in lieu of the bond required by the 39th section of chapter 24 of the revised statutes, to pay the visiting officer of the city of Portland, for the support of paupers, the sum of———for each alien, who———not in the

[1] Form of receipt substantially adopted by Mayor and Aldermen, January 5, 1854. See city records, vol. 6, page 426.

opinion of the visiting officer, a pauper, lunatic, or idiot, or maimed, aged, infirm or destitute, or incompetent to take care of himself, or herself, without becoming a public charge as a pauper.

Now be it known, that I,——visiting officer, have this day received of the said——the sum of——dollars in accordance with the act, and in pursuance of such——desire, and it is expressly understood and agreed by the said——that this payment or commutation is made at——request as voluntary, and never to be sued for, or recovered back in any process at law or in equity.

VISITING OFFICER.

$

PORTLAND.

AMUSEMENTS.

[INCLUDING THEATRES, CIRCUSSES, BOWLING ALLEYS, BILLIARD ROOMS, &c.]

STATUTES.

1. Penalty for exhibiting pageantry, &c., without a license.
2. Licenses for above, how granted; fee.
3. Penalty for keeping bowling alley without license.
4. Licenses for alleys and billiard rooms; fee.
5. Bond to be given.
6. Bond violated, to be revoked.
7. Penalty for violation.

1. If any person, for money or other valuable article, exhibits in this State any images, pageantry, slight of hand tricks, puppet show, circus, feats of balancing, wire dancing, personal agility, dexterity, or theatrical performances, without a license therefor as hereinafter provided, he shall forfeit, for every such offence, not more than one hundred, nor less than ten dollars; but this prohibition shall not extend to any permanently established museum.

Penalty for exhibiting pageantry, &c., without a license.

R. S., chap. 29, § 1.

2. The municipal officers of towns may grant licenses for any of the foregoing exhibitions or performances therein, on receiving for the use of their town such sum as they deem proper; twenty-four hours being allowed therefor; and they shall prosecute, by an action of debt, in the name and for the use of their town, all persons violating the provisions of the above section.

Licenses how granted; fee.

Ib. § 2.

Penalty for keeping bowling alley without license.

Ib. § 3.

3. No person shall keep a bowling alley or billiard room without a license, under a penalty of ten dollars for each day, to be recovered in an action of debt by any person suing therefor, one-half to his own use, and the other to the use of the town, where the offence is committed.

Licenses, how granted; fees.

Ib. § 4.

4. The municipal officers of towns may license suitable persons to keep bowling alleys and billiard rooms therein, in any place where it will not disturb the peace and quiet of a family, for which the person licensed shall pay ten dollars to the use of such town.

Bond to be given.

Ib. § 5.

Act 1862, chap. 82.

5. Every person licensed to keep a bowling alley, shall, at the time he receives his license, give a bond to such town with two good and sufficient sureties in a sum not less than one hundred dollars, conditioned that he will not permit any gambling, or drinking of intoxicating liquors in or about his premises, or any minor to play or roll in his alley without the written consent of his parent, guardian or master, or his alley to be opened or used from ten o'clock in the evening to sunrise.

Bond violated, license to be revoked, &c.

Ib. § 6.

6. If any person, so licensed, violates any of the conditions of his bond, the municipal officers, on being furnished with proof thereof, shall revoke the license and enforce the payment of the bond for the use of their town; and no person whose license is so revoked, shall afterwards be licensed in said town for such purpose.

Penalty for violations.

Ib. § 7.

Act 1862, chap. 184, § 2.

7. The keeper of any bowling alley or billiard room, who violates any of these provisions, shall forfeit ten dollars for the first offence, and twenty dollars for each subsequent offence; and any marshal, sheriff, police or other officer, may at any time enter said bowling alley or billiard room, or rooms connected therewith, for the purpose of enforcing this or any other law; and any person who obstructs his entrance shall forfeit not less than five, nor more than twenty dollars.

AUCTIONS AND AUCTIONEERS.

STATUTES.

1. License.
2. If refused, appeal to county commissioners.
3. To keep account of sales.
4. Penalty for allowing non-voter in the State to sell.
5. Penalty for receiving goods of minors, &c.
6. Sale of real estate in two towns. Penalty.
7. Penalty for permitting unauthorized persons to sell.
8. Exceptions of sales by sheriffs, &c.
9. Fines, how imposed and recovered.
10. Auctioneers may sell in any town. Pedlers not to sell.
11. When auctioneers need not deduct per centage.

ORDINANCE OF THE CITY.

No person to sell in streets of city, except in places assigned by mayor and aldermen. Penalty for violation.

1. The municipal officers of any town may license any suitable inhabitants of their county, by a writing under their hands, to be auctioneers for one year in such town and in any other town in said county, where there is no licensed auctioneer; and shall record every such license in a book kept by them for that purpose.

Municipal officers to license auctioneers and keep a record thereof.

R. S., chap. 34, § 1.

2. If such officers, after written application to them for a license, unreasonably refuse or neglect to grant it, the applicant, by giving them ten days notice and a bond to pay all costs arising thereafter, may appeal to the county commissioners, who, after a hearing of the parties, may grant the license if they judge it reasonable.

Appeal to county commissioners, in case of refusal.

Ib. § 2.

Auctioneers to keep account of goods sold, &c.

Ib. § 3.

(See § 11 of this chapter.)

3. Every person licensed shall keep a fair and particular account of all goods and chattels by him sold, stating of whom received, and to whom sold; and if said goods are sold voluntarily for the benefit of parties residing out of the State, he shall deduct two and a half per cent. from the gross amount of the sales for the use of the town, where the sale is made, and pay the same to the treasurer thereof within ten days after the sale; and in default thereof, he shall be liable to a fine of not less than fifty, nor more than three hundred dollars, and forfeit his license.

Penalty for allowing any one not a voter in the State, to act under him.

Ib. § 4.

Act 1860, chap. 188.

4. No auctioneer shall allow any person, not a legal voter in this State, to act for or under him in any sales by public auction, under penalty of fifty dollars for each offence; and any person so acting shall be subject to the same penalty.

Penalty for receiving goods of minors or servants, &c.

R. S. chap. 34, § 5.

5. If any auctioneer receives any goods for sale, at public auction, of any servant or minor, knowing him to be such, or sells any of his own goods, before sunrise or after sunset, at public auction, he shall forfeit a sum not less than fifty nor more than one hundred and seventy dollars for each offence.

Real estate, lying in two towns, how sold. Penalty.

Ib. § 6.

6. A parcel of real estate lying partly in one town and partly in another, may be sold by an auctioneer of either; but if any auctioneer sells or offers to sell any real or personal property at public auction in any other towns then those authorized by his license, or if any person sells without a license, he shall forfeit not exceeding six hundred dollars.

Penalty for permitting any person to sell contrary to law, &c.

Ib. § 7.

7. If the tenant or occupant of any building, having actual possession and control thereof, knowingly permits any person to sell any goods or chattels at public auction contrary to the provisions of law, in such building, or in any apartment, or yard appurtenant thereto, he shall forfeit not more than six hundred, nor less than one hundred dollars.

8. Nothing in the preceding sections shall extend to sales made by sheriffs, deputy sheriffs, coroners, constables or collectors of taxes, executors or administrators, or any other person authorized to sell goods, chattels, or lands, by order of any court or judge of probate.

Exceptions as to sales by officers.

Ib. § 8.

9. All fines imposed by this chapter may be recovered by indictment in any court proper to try the same; and it shall be the especial duty of city marshals and their deputies, sheriffs, constables and police officers, to make immediate complaint for every offence against the provisions hereof; and one-half of all fines shall be for the use of the prosecutor, and the other for the use of the town where the offence is committed.

Fines how recovered and appropriated.

Ib. § 9.

10. Any person duly licensed as an auctioneer in any town or city in this State shall thereby be authorized to sell at auction in any other town, city or place in this State in which there is no resident auctioneer, as fully as he could in the place where his license is obtained. This act shall not be so construed as to authorize hawkers and pedlers to sell at auction.

Auctioneers may sell in any town.

Act 1863, chap. 204.

Hawkers and pedlers forbidden.

11. The aldermen of any city, and the selectmen of any town, may license any person or persons to be auctioneers for one year in such city or town, and may exempt them from any liability to deduct two and one-half per cent. from the gross amount of sales, for the use of the city or town where the sale is made, when the goods sold by such auctioneers belong to, or are sold for the benefit of parties residing out of the State.

In what cases auctioneers may be exempted from liability to deduct two and a half per cent.

Act 1865, chap. 297.

ORDINANCE OF THE CITY.[1]

No person to sell at auction in streets of the city.

Mayor and Aldermen to assign places.

Penalty.

No person shall sell, or expose for sale at auction, any goods, wares, chattels, or other merchandise, in any street, alley, square, or other public place, or on any sidewalk in the city, except in such places as may be assigned by the mayor and aldermen for that purpose. And the mayor and aldermen are hereby authorized to assign such places for the purpose of selling goods at auction, as they shall think expedient. Any person who shall offend against the provisions of this ordinance, shall forfeit and pay a sum not less than five, nor more than twenty dollars.

[1] Ord. 1848, chap. 8, § 12.

BOATS AND LIGHTERS.

STATUTES.

1. Every boat or lighter employed in carrying stones, sand, or gravel, shall be marked at light water mark, and at least at five other places, with figures four, twelve, sixteen, twenty-four, and thirty, legibly made on the stem and stern post thereof, expressing the weight such boat or lighter is capable of carrying, when the lower part of the respective numbers touch the water in which it floats; and such marks shall be inspected yearly, and when found illegible in the whole or in part, they shall be renewed.

Lighters, carrying stone, sand or gravel, shall be marked, and marks inspected and renewed yearly.

R. S., chap. 36, § 18.

2. The master or owner, who uses without such marks, and any person, who falsely marks any such boat or lighter, shall forfeit fifty dollars, to be recovered by any person suing therefor in an action of debt.

Penalty for using lighters without marks or falsely marking them.

Ib. § 19.

3. The municipal officers of every town, where boats and lighters are employed for the purposes aforesaid, shall annually appoint, in April or May, some suitable person to examine and ascertain the capacities of all such boats and lighters, and mark them as above prescribed, who shall be duly sworn; and said officers shall establish and regulate the fees therefor.

Municipal officers to appoint inspectors, and regulate fees.

Ib. § 20.

When capacity of lighter has been altered, &c.
Ib. § 21.

4. When such inspector thinks that the burden or capacity of any such boat or lighter is altered by repairs or otherwise, he shall forthwith ascertain the same anew, and mark it accordingly.

Penalty for throwing ballast into any road, port or harbor, &c.
Ib. § 21.

5. No master of any vessel shall throw overboard any ballast in any road, port, or harbor, on penalty of sixty dollars ; and no person shall take any stone or other ballast from any island, beach, or other land, without consent of the owner, under a penalty not exceeding seven dollars for each offence, to be recovered in an action of debt by any person suing therefor, one-half to his own use, and the other to the use of the town, where the offence is committed.

BOUNDARY LINES.

STATUTES.

PERAMBULATIONS.

STATUTES.

Boundaries of the town of Portland.

Special laws of Massachusetts. Vol. 1, p 131, § 1.

1. By act of the general court of Massachusetts, passed July 4, 1786, incorporating the town of Portland, the boundaries of said town were described as follows, viz: Beginning at the creek that runs into Round Marsh, so called, thence north-east to Back Cove Creek, thence down the middle of that creek to Back Cove, thence across said Cove to Sandy Point, thence round by Casco Bay to Fore River,[1] thence up Fore River to the first bounds, together with all the Islands that now belong to the first parish in said Falmouth; and by section ninth of the same act, it was further enacted, that a certain tract of land within the limits of the town of Portland, and containing

[1] See act, locating a bridge across Fore River by which the limits of the city of Portland are extended, post, title "Vaughan's Bridge."

about one hundred and eighty acres, belonging to Samuel Dean, Joshua Freeman and Elizabeth Wise, and which descended to them from Moses Pearson, Esq., late of Falmouth, deceased, be annexed to the town of Portland and shall be considered as part thereof, and the lands granted to the first parish, in said Falmouth, for the support of the ministry there, are hereby annexed to said town of Portland, and shall be considered as part thereof.

Annexation of part of Westbrook to Portland.

Act 1845, chap. 279.

2. The southern half of that part of the old county road running northwardly from the city of Portland, which has the town of Westbrook on the easterly side, and the city of Portland on the westerly side, is hereby set off from the town of Westbrook, and annexed to the city of Portland.

PERAMBULATIONS.

Ancient boundaries continue.

R.S. chap. 1, § 1.

3. The bounds of towns continue as established, except as hereafter provided.

Perambulations, proceedings respecting them.

R. S. chap. 3, § 28.

4. The municipal officers of the most ancient town shall give ten days notice in writing to such officers of the adjoining towns of the time and place of meeting for perambulation; and the officers who neglect their duty in notifying or attending in person, or by substitutes, shall forfeit and pay ten dollars, two-thirds to the use of the town which complies with its duty, and the other third to any two or more of said officers of the town complying, to be recovered at any time within two years after the forfeiture is incurred; and the proceedings of such officers, after every such renewal of boundaries shall be recorded in their town books.

Monuments may be erected at angles.

Ib. § 29.

5. All towns, which, since the twenty-second day of March, eighteen hundred and twenty-eight, have perambulated, or hereafter perambulate their several lines as by law prescribed, and set up stone monuments, at least two feet high, at all the corners and several angles, and where the lines cross highways, or on or near the banks

of all rivers, bays, lakes, or ponds, which said lines cross, or which are the boundaries of said lines, shall be exempted from the duty of perambulating said lines, except once in every ten years, commencing in ten years from the time the stone monuments were so erected.

Disputed lines of towns, how settled.

Ib. § 30.

6. When a town petitions the supreme judicial court, stating that a controversy exists between it and an adjoining one respecting a town line or lines, and praying that it may be run by commissioners appointed by the court, the court, after due notice to all parties concerned, may appoint three commissioners, who shall, after giving notice to all persons interested of the time and place of meeting, ascertain and determine the line or lines in dispute, and describe them by courses and distances, and make, set, and mention in their return, suitable monuments and marks for the permanent establishment of such lines, and make duplicate returns of their proceedings; one of which shall be returned to the court, and the other to the office of the secretary of state; and such line or lines, shall be deemed in every court of law and for every purpose the true dividing line or lines between such towns.

Perambulation of line between Portland and Westbrook.

7. The aldermen of Portland[1] and the selectmen of Westbrook, on the 18th day of August, 1855, made a perambulation of the line between Portland and Westbrook, and renewed the bound marks between the city of Portland and the town of Westbrook, as follows:

Boundaries defined.

Commencing at center of channel at Deering's Bridge, thence westerly by said channel to east line of old county road; thence north-westerly, by the east line of said road, to where said line intersects the south line of road leading to Saccarappa; thence diagonally across said road to where the opposite lines of said roads intersect; thence north-westerly on west line of same road sixteen hundred

[1] Report of Committee appointed to perambulate the line between Portland and Westbrook, made to the mayor and aldermen, January 17, 1856. and recorded in city records.

and eighty-four feet, to a stone monument; thence on an angle to the west of sixty degrees fifty-two minutes, twelve hundred and eighty-four feet, to stone monument; thence on an angle of one hundred and thirty-eight degrees forty minutes to the south five hundred and thirty-three feet, to stone monument; thence on an angle of seventy-one degrees eight minutes to the west fifty-seven feet and six-tenths of a foot, to stone monument; thence on same line fifty-seven feet and three-fourths of a foot, to stone monument; thence on same line twenty-six hundred and six feet, to stone monument; thence south-easterly at right angles eight hundred and ninety-eight feet, to stone monument; thence at an angle of one hundred and five degrees to the west one hundred and fifteen feet, to stone monument; thence on same line one hundred and fifteen feet and one-half foot, to stone monument; thence on same line to center of channel in Canal Basin.[2]

[2] For explanation of above running, see plan made by A. P. Marshall, Esq., city engineer, January 17, 1856.

BREAD.

ASSIZE OF.

1. City council authorized to make laws in relation to assize of bread.

1. The city council of the city of Portland is authorized and empowered to ordain and publish such acts, laws and regulations, not inconsistent with the constitution and laws of this State, as shall be deemed by them to be needful and wise, in relation to the assize of bread sold or offered for sale in the city of Portland, so as best to guard against frauds in the sale of said article.

City council authorized to make laws in relation to assize of bread.

St. 1857, ch. 103.

BRIDGES.

STATUTES, &c.

1. Portland to support Pride's and Stroudwater Bridges.
2. Incorporation of the proprietors of Portland bridge. Name changed to Vaughan's bridge. Organization. Tolls, &c. Draw. Time allowed for building bridge. Location.
3. Act authorizing the county commissioner to locate a free bridge over the lines of Vaughan's bridge.
4. Draw, construction and regulation of.
5. Expense of constructing bridge, how paid. Bridge, territorial limits, regulations of. Additional powers of county commissioners.
6. Proceedings of county commissioners in regard to laying out said bridge.
7. Deering bridge laid out by Portland.
8. Back Cove bridge, incorporation of. Location. Restrictions.
9. Additional act. Draw and piers. Extension of time as a toll bridge.
10. Reduction of tolls. Further extension of time as a toll bridge.
11. Portland authorized to receive and maintain Back Cove bridge.
12. To be maintained as a free bridge.
13. City to have authority to construct said bridge for the purpose of a dam. May occupy flats.
14. Draw. Vessels to pass free of expense.
15. Assess a tax for support of bridge.
16. Portland bridge. Incorporation of proprietors. Location.
17. Draw. Piers. Vessels to pass free of expense.
18. Surrender of bridge to county of Cumberland by proprietors. Acceptance and establishment as a free bridge.
19. Powers given to county commissioners to establish a side passage to Canal street.

STATUTES.

PRIDE'S AND STROUDWATER BRIDGES.

1. In the act of the Massachusetts Legislature, incorporating the town of Portland, the following provision in regard to bridges in that part of Falmouth now called Westbrook, was enacted, viz:—"And be it further enacted that the inhabitants of the town of Portland shall from time to time amend and repair Pride's bridge on Presumpscot river and the great bridge, so called, (now called Stroudwater bridge,[1]) on Fore river, although the same be not included within the limits of Portland, aforesaid."

Town of Portland to support Pride's and Stroudwater bridges.

Mass. special laws, July 4, 1786, § 8.

VAUGHAN'S BRIDGE.

2. By an act passed by the Massachusetts Legislature, February 25, 1794, William Vaughan and others were constituted a corporation, under the name of the proprietors of Portland bridge, for the purpose of constructing a bridge from Portland to Cape Elizabeth. (A subsequent act, passed March 4, 1800, changed the name of the corporation to "the proprietors of Vaughan's bridge.") Provisions were made for organization, the rates of toll, (to be subject to the regulations of government after the term of thirty years,) and also, for the construction of a draw for the passage of vessels. It was further provided that the act should be void if the bridge should not be completed for the space of six years. The additional act passed March 4, 1800, extended the time for the completion of the same nine months. It was further enacted, that the bridge shall be built at a place called Bramhall's point in Portland, and land at or near Jacob Brown's farm in Cape Elizabeth, as may be determined by a majority of the proprietors.

Incorporation of the Proprietors of Portland bridge.

Ib. Feb. 25, 1794, § 1.

Ib. March 4, 1800, § 2.

Name changed to Vaughan's bridge.

Organization. Tolls, &c.

Draw.

Time allowed for building bridge.

Location.

[1]For articles of agreement defining the bounds of Stroudwater bridge made by the city council, and selectmen of Westbrook, see city records, vol. 6, page 213.

Act authorizing the county commissioners to locate a free bridge over the lines of Vaughan's bridge. 1854, 363, § 1.

3. By an act approved April 17, 1854, the county commissioners of the county of Cumberland were authorized to lay out and locate a free bridge and public highway across Fore river, in said county, commencing at the easterly end of Vaughan's bridge, in Portland, and extending on the line of said bridge to the westerly termination thereof, in Cape Elizabeth, if upon petition and hearing pursuant to the twenty-fifth chapter of the revised statutes, said commissioners shall judge said bridge and highway to be of common convenience and necessity.

Draw—construction and regulation of. Ib. § 2.

4. Said county commissioners shall cause to be constructed in such place in said bridge, as they may designate, a suitable and convenient draw, of not less than forty-two feet in width; and said draw shall be kept and maintained under such regulations as said commissioners may from time to time establish.

Expense of constructing bridge, how paid. Ib. § 3.

Bridge—territorial limits, regulation of.

Additional powers of county commissioners.

5. Three-fourths of the expense of constructing and maintaining said bridge, shall be paid by the city of Portland, and one-fourth by the town of Cape Elizabeth; and said commissioners shall have power to designate the sections of said bridge which shall be respectively built and maintained by said city of Portland, and said town of Cape Elizabeth, and to establish the lines of division between said sections, and if upon such division any part of said bridge required to be built and maintained by said city, shall extend within the present limits of said town of Cape Elizabeth, the territory covered by such part of said bridge shall be thereafter inclosed within the territorial limits of said city so long as said bridge shall be maintained; and said commissioners, in addition to the powers herein before granted, shall have powers in laying out and locating said highway and bridge conferred by the provisions of the twenty-fifth chapter of the revised statutes, relating to the location of highways, and the awarding of damages therefor.

6. At a meeting of the board of county commissioners

for the county of Cumberland, held May 29, 1854, a free bridge and public highway was laid out and located on the lines of Vaughan's bridge, in accordance with the provisions of the aforesaid act. It was determined that the bridge should be thirty-three feet in width, and twenty-five hundred and sixty-four feet in length, and that the section to be built and maintained by the city of Portland, should comprise fourteen hundred and eight feet; and that to be built and maintained by the town of Cape Elizabeth, eleven hundred and fifty-six feet. It was also determined that the city of Portland should build and maintain within her section a suitable and convenient draw, of not less than forty-two feet in width, for the passage of vessels, boats, &c.

Proceedings of county commissioners in regard to laying out said bridge.

Rep. C. C., June term, 1854, S. J. C.

It was also further determined that the city of Portland and town of Cape Elizabeth should be allowed the term of one year from the sixth day of June, 1854, to build said bridge.[1]

DEERING'S BRIDGE.

7. Deering's bridge, so called, was laid out by the town of Portland, as by the following extract from town records: "In town meeting, May 6, 1805:

Voted to raise one thousand dollars to build a bridge from high-water mark, in Green street, to the line that separates this town from Falmouth towards Reed's point."

Deering's bridge laid out by town of Portland.

Town Records, vol. 1, p. 400.

BACK COVE BRIDGE.

8. By an act passed by the Massachusetts Legislature, February 27, 1794, Thomas Smith and others were made a corporation under the name of the "Proprietors of Back Cove bridge," for the purpose of building a bridge from Sandy point, in Portland, to Secomb's point, in Falmouth. Similar provisions for organization and rates of toll were enacted as in the incorporation of Vaughan's bridge; and

Back Cove bridge. Incorporation of.

Mass. special laws, Feb. 27, 1794, § 1.

Location.

[1] See county commissioners' records, vol. 10, pp, 235, 236.

Restrictions.

it was also provided that the bridge should be so constructed as not to prevent the water flowing the flats westward of said bridge.

Additional act. 1825, 363.

9. By an act of the legislature of Maine, passed February 26, 1825, it was provided that the proprietors should build and ever after keep in repair, a convenient and sufficient draw or passage way, and also build and keep in repair a suitable pier upon each side of the bridge, and that vessels should pass and repass free from toll or expense; and also extending the time for the taking of tolls for the benefit of the proprietors for an additional term of ten years.

Draw and piers.

Extension of time as toll bridge.

Reduction of tolls. 1835, 583. Further extension of time as a toll bridge.

10. By an additional act, approved March 19, 1835, a reduction was made in the tolls; and the time for taking of tolls for benefit of proprietors, further extended for an additional term of two years.

11. By an act entitled "An act to relieve the public from the burden of tolls at Back Cove bridge," approved February 16, 1837, it was provided:

City of Portland authorized to receive and maintain Back Cove bridge. 1837, 257, § 1.

That the city of Portland be authorized and empowered to receive the bridge leading from Westbrook to Portland, called Back Cove bridge, from the proprietors thereof, and to support and maintain the same forever hereafter, and to relieve said proprietors from all responsibility on account of the same; *Provided*, that said bridge shall be and remain free from tolls from and after the nineteenth day of March next.

To be maintained as a free bridge. Ib. § 2.

12. Said city of Portland shall forever hereafter be bound to support and maintain said bridge as a free bridge, and shall have power and authority to do all things necessary and proper in maintaining the same.

City to have authority to construct said bridge for the purposes of a dam. Ib. § 3.

13. For the purpose of remunerating said city for the expenses of supporting and maintaining said bridge, said city shall have power and authority so to construct said bridge as to answer the purposes of a dam and basin, and shall have power and authority to erect and maintain, or

cause to be erected and maintained, such mills, factories, and machinery as shall be thought proper and expedient. And said city shall have a right to use and occupy so much land and flats as may be necessary for the above purposes, and if any person shall be injured thereby, he shall have the same remedy as is provided in the sixth section of the act to incorporate the city of Portland, passed February twenty-eighth, one thousand eight hundred and thirty-two.

May occupy flats.

14. Said city shall build and ever after keep in repair a convenient and sufficient draw or passage way over the channel of said river, for the passing and repassing of vessels through said bridge, and said draw shall be raised at all times without delay for vessels having occasion to pass or repass, free of expense.

Draw.

Ib. § 4.

Vessels to pass free of expense.

15. Said city hereby is authorized and empowered to assess and collect money from time to time for the purposes aforesaid, and to do all things necessary and proper respecting the same.

May assess a tax for support of bridge.

Ib. § 5.

PORTLAND BRIDGE.

16. The proprietors of Portland bridge were incorporated February 10, 1823. The corporators were authorized and empowered to construct a bridge from the northerly point of the farm of Elias Thomas, Esq., in Cape Elizabeth, to the nearest convenient point southwesterly of Robinson's wharf in Portland, and to purchase and hold such real and personal estate as may be necessary to carry the aforesaid object into complete effect.

Incorporation of proprietors.

Act 1823, 212, § 1.

Location.

17. It was further enacted that said proprietors should build and keep a convenient and sufficient draw or passage way, at least thirty-two feet wide, at some place in said bridge proper for the passing of vessels by day and by night through the same, and a suitable wharf or pier on each side of said bridge, and adjoining said draw, sufficient for vessels to lie at. And said draw shall be lifted for all

Draw.

Ib. § 4.

Piers.

Vessels to pass free of expense.

vessels without toll or pay, except for boats or vessels passing for pleasure; and all vessels intended to pass through said draw shall be free of charge at said wharf or pier until a suitable time shall offer for passing the same.

Surrender of bridge to county of Cumberland by proprietors. Act 1850, 197.

18. In accordance with the provisions of an act, approved August 28, 1850, entitled "an act relating to the surrender of toll bridges and turnpikes to public uses," authorizing the county commissioners to accept the surrender of bridges from the owners thereof, the proprietors of Portland bridge surrendered the same to the county of Cumberland, and at a meeting of the county commissioners, held at Portland, June 14, 1851, the same was accepted and established as a free bridge from and after that date.[1]

Acceptance and establishment as a free bridge.

Powers given to county commissioners to establish a side passage to Canal street. Act 1853, 95, § 1.

19. By an act, approved March 19, 1853, entitled "an act giving to the county commissioners of Cumberland county further powers in relation to Portland bridge," the county commissioners of Cumberland county were authorized, if they should adjudge the object contemplated by this act to be for the public convenience and interest, to alter Portland bridge in said county, by locating and establishing in addition to the present bridge, a side passage or branch, suitable for a public highway, leading from the western side of said bridge, and above low water mark, to Canal street, in Portland, to be constructed and maintained as a part of Portland bridge, as the same is now held and maintained, and in the manner and under the limitations provided in an act passed August twenty-eighth, eighteen hundred and fifty, entitled "an act relating to the surrender of toll bridges and turnpikes to public uses."

[1] See county commissioners' record, vol. 9, page 364.

BUILDINGS.

STATUTES.

1. City may make by-laws respecting wooden buildings.
2. Livery stables, &c., when prohibited.
3. Penalties.
4. Malicious mischief to buildings.

ORDINANCES.

1. Builders must give notice.
2. Wooden buildings, when prohibited.
3. Same, when removable as nuisances.
4. Buildings may be numbered. Penalty.
5. Cellar doors, &c., to be kept in repair.
6. Same, when to be lighted.
7. Penalty for defacing buildings, &c.
8. Posters not to be placed on buildings. Penalty.

STATUTES.

By-laws respecting erection of wooden buildings.

R. S., chap. 3, § 27, as amended by Act 1860, chap. 144.

1. Cities may make such by-laws or ordinances as they think proper, not inconsistent with the laws of the State, and enforce them by suitable penalties, respecting the erection of wooden buildings, or buildings the exterior of which shall be in part of wood therein, and defining their proportions and dimensions ; and any building erected contrary to a by-law or ordinance adopted under this specification shall be deemed a nuisance and dealt with accordingly.

Penalty for occupying tenements for sail maker, rigger or livery stable, except as municipal officers direct. Ib. § 11.

2. No person shall occupy any tenement in any maritime town for the business of a sail maker, rigger, or keeper of a livery stable, except where the municipal officers direct; and any person who offends against this section, shall forfeit ten dollars a month during the continuance of such occupancy, with costs.

Penalties. Ib. § 21. Ib. § 23.

3. The said penalties shall be appropriated, one-half to the use of the town where the offense is committed, and the other to him who shall sue for the same, with costs.

Wilful injuries to buildings, fixtures, goods or valuable papers of another. 20 Maine, 341. 33 Maine, 146. R. S., chap. 127, 9.

4. Whoever wilfully and maliciously destroys, injures, or defaces any building or fixture attached thereto, without consent of the owner, shall be punished by imprisonment less than one year, or by fine not exceeding five hundred dollars, and also be liable to the party injured, in an action of trespass, for three times the amount of injury so done.

ORDINANCES.

Notice shall be given of intention to build, &c. Rev. Ord., 1855, as amended by Ord., 1862.

1. All persons intending to erect any building, or to make alterations in the external walls of any building, or buildings, of any description, any part of which is to be placed upon or within ten feet of any of the public streets, squares, alleys, or lanes of the city, shall, before they proceed to build or erect the same, or lay the foundation thereof, or to make the said alteration, give notice in writing of such their intention, to the city engineer, specifying the dimensions of the proposed structure, the materials to be used, the number of the street, or precise location, fifteen days at least before doing any act for carrying such intention into execution, in order that the encroachment, or any other injury or inconvenience to the said public streets, squares, lanes, or alleys, which might otherwise happen, may be thereby prevented; and that the proper grade and line of the street may be ascertained. And all persons intending to erect, or make any alterations in any buildings as aforesaid, shall not pay any

fees of the city engineer, for giving the grade and line of the street, adjoining which the proposed building is to be placed.

2. No building, or buildings, the exterior walls of which shall be in part or wholly of wood, exceeding ten feet in height, shall hereafter be erected in this city without permission in each case from the mayor and aldermen.

Ord., 1867. Erection of wooden buildings forbidden.

3. It shall be the duty of the city marshal to cause to be removed at once, as nuisances, all buildings erected in violation of this ordinance.

When nuisances. Ib.

4. The mayor and aldermen shall have power to cause numbers of regular series to be affixed to or inscribed on all dwelling houses and other buildings erected or fronting on any street, lane, alley, or public court within the city of Portland at their discretion; and shall also have power to determine the form, size and material of such numbers, and the mode, place, succession, and order of inscribing or affixing them on said respective houses or other buildings. And any owner or occupant of any building or part of a building who shall neglect or refuse to affix to the same the number designated by the mayor and aldermen, or by some person by them duly authorized, or who shall affix to the same, or retain thereon more than one day, any number contrary to the direction of the mayor and aldermen, or person so authorized, shall forfeit and pay a sum not less than one dollar, nor more than twenty dollars, and a like sum for every subsequent offense.

Numbers of buildings. Rev. Ord., 1855.

Penalty for numbering contrary to directions.

5. Whenever any cellar door, or the platform thereof, shall project into any of the streets, lanes, alleys, public squares, or places, within the city, it shall be the duty of the owners and occupants of the buildings or estate to which the same belong, to keep the same in good repair, and if at any time the said cellar door or platforms are out of repair, so that in the opinion of the mayor and aldermen, the

Cellar doors and platforms to be kept in good repair. Ib.

safety of the inhabitants is thereby endangered, the mayor and aldermen are hereby authorized to notify the said owners and occupants of the fact; and if said owners or occupants neglect or refuse for the space of twenty-four hours to repair the same, the said mayor and aldermen shall forthwith cause the same to be repaired at the expense of said owners or occupants; and said owners or occupants shall, in case of such neglect or refusal as aforesaid, be further liable to a penalty of not less than one, nor more than twenty dollars, for each and every day that said cellar door, or the platform thereof, shall continue to be out of repair.

Cellar doors to be lighted when open at night.

Ib.

6. Whenever any of the cellar doors before mentioned are open, or the platform thereof removed at any time during the night, it shall be the duty of the occupant of the cellar to which the same belongs, to cause a sufficient light to be so placed that the opening of the said door or removal of said platform, shall at all times during the night be distinctly visible. And any person offending against the provisions of this section, shall forfeit and pay a sum not less than one nor more than twenty dollars.

Defacing buildings, &c.

Ib.

7. Any person or persons who shall be guilty of defacing any building or buildings, fence, sign, or other property, in the city, by cutting, breaking, daubing with paint, or in any other way defacing or injuring the same, or who shall throw any stones, chips, or any other thing against any building or buildings, with intent to injure the same, or to annoy or disturb any person who may be therein, shall forfeit and pay a sum not less than five dollars nor more than twenty dollars.

Posters or other bills not to be placed on buildings.

Ib.

8. No person shall post or stick up any poster or other bill, or any advertisement or notice of any kind, on any public building, or any building or fence, without the consent of the owners or occupants thereof, under a penalty of not less than one nor more than ten dollars.

CARRIAGES.

STATUTES.

1. Teams, to turn to the right; unable, to stop.
2. When stationary, or traveling slowly, allow others to pass.
3. Not to stand on way to obstruct it, nor be without a driver.
4. Bells on horses drawing runners.
5. Cities authorized to establish by-laws.

ORDINANCES.

1. Hackney carriage defined.
2. License required.
3. Same.
4. Mayor and aldermen may license and revoke.
5. Fee for license, city marshal to make quarterly report.
6. When licenses expire. Shall not be transferred without, &c.
7. Who shall be liable.
8. Neglect to take out license after it is granted.
9. Manner of marking and numbering.
10. No other number shall be used.
11. Shall not stand in any other place.
12. Shall not stand so as to obstruct.
13. Driver, &c., shall wear a badge.
14. Runners shall not be employed.
15. Mayor may give directions.
16. Rates of fare.
17. Shall be inspected by city marshal.
18. Carriage not to be driven by a minor, unless, &c.

OMNIBUSSES.

19. Time for starting.
20. Stopping.
21. Shall not leave the route.

STATUTES.

Teams about to meet, to turn to the right; when unable, to stop. 25 Maine, 39. R. S., chap. 19, § 2.

1. When persons traveling with a team are approaching to meet on a way, they are seasonably to turn to the right of the middle of the traveled part of it, so far that they can pass each other without interference. When it is not safe, or is difficult on account of weight of load to do so, a person about to be met or overtaken, if requested, is to stop a reasonable time, at a convenient place, to enable the other to pass.

When stationary or traveling slowly, to allow others to pass. Ib. § 3.

2. When a person with a team is stationary, or traveling slowly on a way at a place unsafe or inconvenient for passing him with a team, he is, if requested, to drive to the right or left, or to stop a reasonable time at a convenient place, to allow the other to pass.

Teams not to stand on ways to obstruct passage, &c. Ib. § 4.

3. No person is to leave his team stationary on a way so as to obstruct a free passage of other teams; or is to allow his team to be on a way without a driver.

Bells on horses drawing runners. Ib. § 5.

4. Three or more bells are to be fastened to one of the foremost horses drawing teams on snow without wheels.

5. Any city in this State shall have power to ordain and establish from time to time, all such rules and orders as the municipal government of such city may deem necessary and expedient, for the due regulation in such city, of omnibusses, stages, hackney-coaches, wagons, carts, drays, hand-carts, and all other vehicles whatever, used and employed wholly or in part in said city, whether by establishing their rates of fare, prescribing their routes and places of standing, or in any other respect, and may provide penalties not exceeding twenty dollars.

Cities authorized to establish rules and orders for the regulation of carriages.
R. S. chap. 3, § 27.

ORDINANCES.

1. Every hack, stage-coach, omnibus, chariot, coachee, barouche, landeau, or other vehicle, whether on wheels or runners, drawn by one or more horses, or other animal power, which shall be used in the city of Portland for the conveyance of persons for hire, from place to place within said city, shall be deemed a hackney-carriage within the meaning of this ordinance.

Hackney carriage defined.
Rev. Ord., 1855.

2. No person shall set up, use, or drive, in the city of Portland, any hackney-carriage for the conveyance of persons from place to place within said city, without a license for such carriage from the mayor and aldermen, under a penalty of not less than five nor more than twenty dollars every time such carriage is used.

License required.
Ib.

3. No person shall be permitted to drive any hackney-carriage in the city of Portland, unless he shall have first procured a license therefor from the mayor and aldermen. But the mayor shall have power to grant temporary permits to persons to drive hackney-carriages; which permits shall be valid only for two days after the meeting of the board of mayor and aldermen, next after the date of said permit. And if any person shall drive any hackney-carriage without being licensed or permitted as aforesaid, he shall forfeit and pay not less than five nor more than twenty dollars for every such offense—and the owner of

Same.
Ib.

the carriage so driven shall forfeit and pay the same penalty.

Mayor and aldermen may license and revoke.

Rev. Ord. 1855.

4. The mayor and aldermen will, from time to time, grant licenses to such persons, described in sections two and three of this ordinance, and upon such terms as they may deem expedient, to set up, use, or drive hackney carriages, for the conveyance of persons for hire, from place to place within the city, and they may revoke such licenses at their discretion; and a record of all licenses so granted shall be kept by the city marshal.

Fee for license. City marshal to make quarterly report.

Ib.

5. For every license so granted, there shall be paid to the city marshal, the sum of one dollar, for the use of the aldermen of the city, and the city marshal shall make a quarterly report to the mayor and aldermen, of all sums so received, and shall pay over the same to the aldermen.

When licenses expire shall not be transferred without, &c.

Ib.

6. All licenses granted as aforesaid, shall expire on the first day of July next after the date thereof; and no license shall be sold, assigned or transferred, without the consent of the mayor and aldermen, endorsed thereon by the city clerk.

Who shall be liable.

Ib.

7. The person in whose name the license for a hackney-carriage is taken out, as well as the owner, shall be liable for all forfeitures and penalties herein contained, unless upon the sale of said carriage, notice be given to the city marshal and the license delivered to him.

Neglect to take out license after it is granted.

Ib.

8. Any person who may be licensed as aforesaid, either as owner or driver of any hackney-carriage, who shall continue to use any such carriage, and shall neglect or refuse to take out and pay for his license within ten days after the same has been granted, shall be liable to a fine of not less than one dollar, nor more than twenty dollars, for each and every day thereafter, that he or they shall refuse or neglect to take out such license.

9. Hackney-carriages shall be marked and numbered in the manner following, viz: every hack or landeau

licensed, shall be marked upon the outside and upon each side, on the sill or rockers, immediately below the doors, with the number of the license, with white, gilded or plated figures, in the Arabic character, of not less than one inch and a half in size on a dark ground, or with a dark figure of the same size on a light ground, and no other figure or device within four inches of the same. Stage coaches shall be numbered in like manner, on the top rail of the doors. Omnibusses shall be numbered in like manner, on the lower pannel of the door. The name of the owner, and the number of the license, together with the date of inspection and rates of fare, shall be printed on a card of suitable size, and placed in all the hackney-carriages by the city marshal at the time of inspection in the most conspicuous place for the information of passengers. And if any owner or driver of any hackney carriage shall use or drive any such carriage, or permit the same to be used and driven, without complying with the foregoing requisitions, said owner and driver shall each be liable to a fine of not less than two nor more than twenty dollars for each offence.

Manner of marking and numbering.

Ord., 1867.

10. No owner or driver of any hackney-carriage shall use, or suffer such carriage to be used, with any other number upon the same than that assigned by the mayor and aldermen, nor place the number on any other part of such carriage than that designated in the preceding section, under a penalty of not less than five nor more than twenty dollars, every time such carriage is used.

No other number shall be used.

Rev. Ord., 1865.

11. No owner, driver, or other person having charge of any hackney-carriage, shall stand with such carriage in any place within the city, to be employed, other than the stand assigned to such carriage by the mayor and aldermen, under a penalty of not less than two nor more than twenty dollars for each offense.

Shall not stand in any other place.

Ib.

12. No owner, driver, or other person having charge of any hackney-carriage, shall stop his carriage abreast of

Shall not stand so as to obstruct.
Ib.

any other carriage in any street, square, lane, alley, or public place, so as to obstruct the same, or the sidewalk, flag stone, or crossing thereof, under a penalty of not less than two nor more than twenty dollars for each offense.

Driver, &c., shall wear a badge.
Ib.

13. Every owner, driver, or other person having charge of any hackney carriage which has a stand in any square or street, at any railroad station, steamboat landing, theater, museum, or other place of public entertainment, shall at all times when driving or waiting for employment, wear a badge on his hat or cap, with the number of his carriage thereon, in brass or plated figures of not less than one and a half inches in size, and so placed that the same may be distinctly seen and read; and he shall not wear upon his hat or carriage, the name of any public hotel, without permission of the proprietor of said hotel. Every person offending against the provisions of this section shall pay a penalty of not less than two nor more than twenty dollars for each offense.

Runners shall not be employed.
Ib.

14. No person except the owners or drivers of hackney-carriages, shall solicit or request, nor shall the owners or drivers of any hackney-carriage hire, employ, or permit any person to solicit or request any person or persons in the public streets, at places of public amusement, at railroad stations, steamboat landings, or any other public place in the city, to hire, engage or employ any hackney-carriage, under a penalty of ten dollars, to be recovered from such person, owner, or driver, any or either of them severally and respectively.

Mayor may give directions.
Ib.

15. In any street or square, or at any theater, museum, or other place of public amusement, where hackney-carriages attend for passengers, the mayor, or any person or persons by him authorized, may give directions respecting the standing of such carriages, while waiting for their passengers, and the route they shall go when going to or leaving any such place of entertainment; and if any owner, driver, or other person having charge of any such carriage,

shall refuse to obey such order or directions of the mayor, or other person or persons by him authorized, he or they shall be liable to a fine of not less than five nor more than twenty dollars for each offense.

16. The prices or rates of fare to be taken by, or paid to the owner, driver, or other person having charge of any hackney-carriages, except omnibuses, shall be as follows: that is to say, for carrying a passenger from one place to another within the city, not exceeding fifty cents at any hour of the day or night; for children between the ages of four and twelve years, if more than one, or if accompanied by an adult, half price only is to be charged for each child; and for children under four years of age, when accompanied by their parents or an adult, no charge is to be made. Every owner, driver, or other person having charge of any hackney-carriage, shall carry in addition to one trunk, two articles, such as a valise, saddle-bag, carpet bag, portmanteau, box, bundle, or other similar articles used in traveling, if he be requested so to do, without charge or compensation therefor; but for every additional trunk, or similar article he may carry, he shall be entitled to demand and receive not exceeding twenty-five cents. If any driver or other person shall demand or receive any greater sum for his services as specified in this section, or shall wilfully refuse to answer the demand of any person or persons for conveyance from one place to another within the city, he shall forfeit and pay for so doing a penalty not exceeding twenty dollars for each offense.

Rates of fare.

Ord., May 22, 1867.

17. The city marshal shall inspect all hackney-carriages before a license is granted for use of the same, and also upon the first Monday in July and January of each year. And the owners of licensed hackney-carriages shall cause them to be presented to the city marshal for inspection upon the days above mentioned, at such hour and place as the city marshal may appoint, and the city marshal shall cause public notice to be given of the hour

Inspected by city marshal.

Ib.

and place at which he will inspect such carriages, at least one week prior to the first Monday in July and January of each year. And if any owner of any licensed hackney-carriage shall neglect to present the same for inspection as above provided for, his license for the use of such carriage shall be suspended until such inspection is made. If upon such inspection any carriage is found in an unsuitable condition, either as regards strength, general good order, or cleanliness in any of its appointments for the safe and comfortable conveyance of passengers, the city marshal shall notify the owner thereof to place such carriage in proper repair, and the license of such carriage shall be suspended until the required repairs shall have been made to the satisfaction of the city marshal.

Carriage not to be driven by a minor unless, &c.

Rev. Ord., 1855.

18. No hackney-carriage used for the conveyance of passengers, shall be driven by a minor, unless he be specially licensed by the mayor and aldermen, under a penalty of not less than two nor more than twenty dollars for each offense.

OMNIBUSES.

Time for starting.

Ib.

19. Each license of any omnibus belonging to any line may specify the time that said omnibus shall leave the stand, and no omnibus shall leave the stand designated for it, until five minutes shall have elapsed after the departure of the one immediately preceding, under a penalty of not less than two nor more than twenty dollars for each offense.

Stopping.

Ib.

20. No owner or driver of any omnibus belonging to any line shall stop his omnibus on any part of the route assigned thereto, unless called by or to leave a passenger, and then for no longer time than may be sufficient for such passenger to take his or her seat, or leave such carriage, under a penalty of not less than two nor more than twenty dollars for each offense.

21. No owner or driver of any omnibus shall drive his omnibus, or permit the same to be driven, on any other route or street than that designated and established by the mayor and aldermen, under a penalty of not less than ten nor more than twenty dollars for each offense.

Shall not leave the route.

Ib.

TRUCKS, WAGONS, &C.

22. Every truck, wagon, dray, cart, sleigh, hand-cart, hand-sled, or other vehicle, which shall be used in this city for the conveyance from place to place within the city, of wood, coal, lumber, stones, brick, sand, clay, gravel, dirt, rubbish, goods, wares, furniture, merchandise, building materials, or any other article or thing whatsoever, shall be licensed as hereinafter provided, and shall have the number of the license placed on the outside of the same, in plain, legible figures of not less than one and a half inches in size, so that the same may be distinctly seen: And if the owner of any such vehicle shall use or suffer the same to be used, or if any other person shall use any such vehicle, without being licensed as hereinafter provided, or without having the number placed thereon, as aforesaid, he or either of them shall be liable to a fine of not less than three dollars nor more than twenty dollars for each offense.

License for trucks, wagons, &c.

Ib.

23. The mayor and aldermen will, from time to time, grant licenses to such persons as they may deem suitable, and upon such terms as they may deem expedient, to use and to drive any such vehicle as aforesaid, within the city of Portland, and they may revoke such licenses at their discretion; and a record of all licenses so granted shall be kept by the city marshal.

Mayor and aldermen may license and revoke.

Ib.

24. For every license so granted there shall be paid to the city marshal the sum of twenty-five cents, for the use of the aldermen of the city; and the city marshal shall make a quarterly report to the mayor and aldermen of all sums so received, and shall pay over the same to the aldermen.

Fees for license. City marshal to make quarterly report.

Ib.

When licenses shall expire. Shall not be transferred without, &c. Ib.

25. All licenses granted as aforesaid shall expire on the first day of July next after the date thereof, and no license of any vehicle shall be sold, assigned, or transferred without the consent of the mayor and aldermen, endorsed thereon by the city clerk.

Who shall be liable. Ib.

26. The person in whose name a license is taken out for any such vehicle shall, for all the purposes of this ordinance, be considered as the owner of the same, and be liable to the penalties herein contained, unless upon sale of any such vehicle notice thereof be given to the city marshal, and the license be delivered up to him.

Using for unlawful purposes. Ib.

27. Any person licensed as aforesaid, either as owner or driver of any of the before mentioned vehicles, who shall use or suffer to be used any such vehicle or vehicles for any unlawful purpose, shall pay a penalty of not less than ten nór more than twenty dollars, and his license shall be revoked by the mayor and aldermen.

Pace at which horses, &c., shall go. Ib.

28. All drivers or other persons having the care and ordering of any truck, cart, wagon, sled, or dray, passing in or through the streets, squares, or lanes of the city, shall drive their horses or beasts at a moderate foot pace, and shall not suffer or permit them to go into a gallop or trot; and such drivers or other persons shall hold the reins in their hands to guide or restrain such horses or beasts, or they shall walk by the head of the shaft, or wheel horse, either holding or keeping within reach of the bridle or halter of said horse or other beasts, and any person violating either of the provisions of this section shall be liable to a fine of not less than five nor more than twenty dollars for each offense.

To obey rules and regulations. Ib.

Penalty.

29. Every person licensed by virtue of the preceding sections shall be bound to obey and comply with all rules and regulations and ordinances that are or may be from time to time prescribed by the city council, or mayor and aldermen. One-half of any penalty that may be recovered by virtue of the provisions of the preceding sections, shall

accrue to the complainant, and he shall be entitled to receive the same from the city treasury when collected.

CARRIAGES IN GENERAL.

30. No carriage or vehicle of any description, whether of burden or pleasure, shall be driven through any part of the city of Portland, during any time that the snow or ice shall be upon, or cover the streets, squares, lanes, or alleys of the said city, unless there shall be three or more bells attached to the horse or horses, or some part of the harness or shaft thereof, under a penalty of not less than three nor more than twenty dollars for each offense.

Bells required in certain cases.

Ib.

31. No owner, driver, or other person having the care of any carriage, truck, cart, wagon, sleigh, sled, or other vehicle, whether used for burden or pleasure, shall stop or place such vehicle at or near the intersection of any street, lane, or alley, in such manner as to cross the footing or flag stones, or prevent foot passengers from passing the street, lane, or alley in the direction or line of the foot way or flag stone, on the side of such street, lane, or alley, under a penalty of not less than three nor more than twenty dollars; and any person who shall have so placed any such vehicle as aforesaid, and shall not immediately, on the request of any foot passenger, cause the same to be removed, or who shall absent himself so that such request cannot be immediately made and complied with, shall be liable to an additional penalty of not less than two nor more than ten dollars.

Carriages shall not stop so as to obstruct foot passengers.

Ib.

32. No truck, cart, or other vehicle shall be so placed in any street within the city by the owner, driver, or other person having the care or ordering thereof, as to prevent the passing of any other truck, cart, or carriage of any description; and no such vehicle shall be wholly or in part backed or placed across any street, square, lane, or alley, or upon any sidewalk or foot way of the same, unless it be for a reasonable time, not exceeding ten minutes, for the

How trucks, &c., shall be placed.

Ib.

Loading and unloading.
Ib.

loading or unloading of heavy articles. Any owner, driver, or other person having the care of any such vehicle, violating either of the provisions of this section, shall be liable to a penalty of not less than five dollars nor more than twenty dollars for each offense.

Mayor and aldermen to appoint stands, &c.
Ib.

33. The mayor and aldermen are authorized and empowered to appoint from time to time, as occasion may require, such and so many stands for trucks, carts, wagons, sleds, sleighs, hackney-coaches, and other vehicles, as may appear to them to be requisite; and no owner or driver of any such vehicle shall suffer the same to stand in any other place than has been or shall be designated, under a penalty of not less than three nor more than ten dollars.

Carts, &c., to be placed near sidewalks.
Ib.

34. Every owner, driver, or other person having the care or ordering of any cart, truck, wagon, sled, or other vehicle, shall place his horse and cart, truck, wagon, sled, or other vehicle, as near as possible to the post or abuting stone of the foot or sidewalk of the street in which he shall stand, and no more than one range of carts, trucks, or other vehicles shall stand in the street, nor shall any such vehicle so stand as to prevent the free passage of any other vehicle in the streets, squares, lanes, or other public places; and any person who shall violate the provisions of this section shall be liable to a fine of not less than three nor more than ten dollars.

Horses, &c., not to be fed on sidewalks.
Ib.

35. No owner or driver of any hackney-carriage, truck, wagon, dray, cart, sleigh, sled, or any other vehicle whatsoever, with horse or any other beast harnessed thereto, shall bait or feed any such beast on any sidewalk of the city under a penalty of not less than two nor more than ten dollars for each offense.

Riding upon outside of carriages, &c., forbidden.
Ib.

36. No person shall ride upon or take hold of any part of any chaise, coach, omnibus, or other carriage used for the purpose of transporting persons, while the same is passing, without the permission of the driver or person having the charge thereof, under a penalty of not less than one nor more than ten dollars.

CEMETERIES.

STATUTE.

ORDINANCES.

STATUTE.

Injury to monuments and places of burial.

R. S., chap. 124, § 27.

1. Whoever wilfully destroys or injures any tomb, gravestone, monument, or other thing placed or designed as a memorial of the dead, or any fence, railing or other thing placed about or inclosing the burial place of the dead; or wilfully injures, removes, or destroys any tree, shrub, or plant, within such inclosure, shall be punished by imprisonment less than one year, or by fine not exceeding five hundred dollars.

ORDINANCES.

Committee on cemeteries to be appointed.

Rev. Ord., 1855, as amended by city charter.

1. There shall be appointed annually, a joint committee of the city council, to be called the committee on cemeteries and public grounds, to consist of one member of the board of mayor and aldermen, and three members of the common council.

To have care and custody of cemeteries, promenades, &c.

Ib.

2. The said committee shall have the care and supervision of the cemeteries of the city; of Evergreen cemetery, belonging to the city, in the town of Westbrook; of the promenades, and all other public grounds of the city, subject to such rules, orders and regulations as the city council may from time to time adopt.

EVERGREEN CEMETERY.

Lands appropriated.

Rev. Ord., 1855.

3. The tracks of land situated in the town of Westbrook, purchased by the city of Oliver Buckley and William Stevens, by their several deeds, dated February 28, A. D. 1852, containing about fifty-five acres, are hereby set apart and appropriated for the burial of the

dead in this city, and the same shall be called and known by the name of Evergreen cemetery, according to the plan thereof made by Charles H. Howe, adopted and established by the city council on the second day of March, A. D. 1854.

4. The city treasurer, on the payment of the sum of twenty dollars for a lot in said cemetery by any inhabitant or non-resident tax-payer of this city, shall be, and hereby is required to execute and deliver to said person, his heirs and assigns forever, a certificate of said lot, signed by him, which may be in the following form, to wit:—

Lots, price of, &c.

Ord., April 16, 1866.

"Know all men by these presents, that the city of Portland, in consideration of twenty dollars paid by —— ——, hereby give and grant to the said —— ——, heirs and assigns forever, the right to occupy for the purpose of burial, lot number — of section — in Evergreeen cemetery, belonging to the city, situated in Westbrook, being the lot described by that number on a plan of the cemetery on file in the office of the city treasurer.

This right is granted, and is to be held and enjoyed subject to all such general regulations as have been or may be adopted by the city council or under their authority, for the management and care of the cemetery, and the due observance of order therein, and the same shall not be assigned or transferred without the consent of the city treasurer endorsed thereon.

In witness whereof this instrument is subscribed by —— ——, in behalf of the city, this —— day of ——, A. D. 18—.

—— ——, City Treasurer."

Any party, (except the city,) transferring a lot, purchased prior to the passage of this ordinance, shall pay into the fund [as provided by the following sections] the sum of ten dollars at the time of making such transfer.

5. One-fourth part of the amount received from the sale of lots in Evergreen cemetery, and all sums received from transfer of lots, together with all donations made by the holders of lots, or other persons, shall constitute a fund to be called "Evergreen fund," the interest of which shall be appropriated to improving and ornamenting the grounds and lots in said cemetery and keeping the

Evergreen fund.

Ord., June 28, 1867.

same in good order under the direction of the committee on cemeteries and public grounds. The payment of a sum not less than twenty-five dollars into the fund for each lot by the holder or any other person, shall entitle the donor to have the lot designated by him, kept in good order by the superintendent of said cemetery forever. And the said committee on cemeteries shall in their discretion cause such care and attention to be bestowed upon such lots as may be in accordance with the written request of the donors.

Ib.

6. The city treasurer shall have the care and custody of said fund, and such portion of the same as may not be wanted for immediate use in accordance with the provisions of this ordinance, may be loaned to the city on interest, or securely invested under the direction of said committee on cemeteries and public grounds, and all interests received, during each year, above the expenditures made, shall be added to the principal of the fund. The treasurer shall, at the close of each financial year, report to the city council the state of the condition of the funds.

City treasurer to keep record, &c.

Rev. Ord. 1855.

7. The city treasurer shall keep a record in which shall be entered all the lots of said cemetery, agreeably to the plan aforesaid, with their number and section, and with columns ruled for the names of the purchasers of each lot, the price, and date of sale. He shall, also, open a cemetery account, in a book kept for that purpose, in which shall be entered all moneys received on account of said cemetery; and he shall, annually, in the first week of April, report to the city council, a statement of all lots sold and assigned by him, with their number, and the names of the purchasers, and date of sale, and the amount received therefor. And all moneys so received shall be and hereby are constituted a fund to be appropriated exclusively for the purpose of improving and ornamenting said cemetery.

8. There shall be appointed by the mayor and alder-

men, annually, by nomination of the mayor and approval of the aldermen, a superintendent of Evergreen cemetery, who shall be, *ex officio* an undertaker, and who shall hold his office for one year, or until a successor is appointed and qualified.

Superintendent

Ib., as amended by Ord., May 15, 1856, and by city charter, § 6.

9. Said superintendent shall under the direction of the joint standing committee on cemeteries have the general supervision and care of said Evergreen cemetery, keep the fences, walls, gates and buildings in good repair, superintend all improvements and ornamenting of the grounds which may be directed by the committee, and have care of all carts and tools belonging to the city used on said grounds, and make report to the mayor annually in the month of February what property belonging to the city may be in his possession. He shall see that all the rights of the city are respected by artists, mechanics and laborers employed on the ground by holders of lots—that no encroachments are made upon any of the avenues, paths or lots reserved for ornamental purposes, and that all regulations with regard to interments, and that the construction of tombs and other structures, be duly complied with. He shall have power to remove from the cemetery improper and disorderly persons; also to abate nuisances and remove unnecessary incumbrances. It shall be his duty to acquaint himself with the lines and bounds of all lots in said cemetery assigned to purchasers, keep a plan of the ground on the premises for reference, and hold himself in readiness to give all necessary information and assistance to purchasers in the selection of lots.

Duties of superintendent.

Ord., April 18, 1866.

10. *Clause* 1*st*. No interment shall be made in or upon any lot for hire, nor without the written permission of the recorded holder of the lot in which the interment is to be made, or of his legal representative.

Of interments.

Ib.

Clause 2*d*. A space of not less than three feet in width shall be reserved for ornamental purposes on the front of all lots facing avenues, and of two feet in width on lots fronting paths, and no interments shall be made therein.

Space in lots fronting avenues.

Lots for tombs.

Clause 3d. Lots for tombs may be sold in places approved by the joint committee on cemeteries, but no tomb shall be erected wholly, or in part, above ground without permission of the committee, and all such must be furnished with shelves having divisions allowing interments to be separately made and perfectly sealed, so as to prevent the escape of unpleasant effluvia. Such portions as are above ground must be faced with granite or marble.

Monuments, trees, &c.

Clause 4th. The holder of each lot shall have the right to erect any proper stones, monuments, or sepulchral structures thereon, and also to cultivate trees, shrubs and plants on the same; but no tree growing within the lot or border shall be cut down or destroyed without the consent of the committee.

Roots, branches, &c., projecting, to be removed.

Clause 5th. If any trees or shrubs, situated in any lot, shall, by means of their roots, branches or otherwise, become detrimental to the adjacent lots, avenues or paths, or unsightly or inconvenient to passengers, it shall be the duty of the committee, and they shall have the right to enter the said lot and remove, or cause to be removed, the said trees or shrubs, or such parts thereof as are detrimental, unsightly or inconvenient.

Grading of lots.

Clause 6th. The grades of all lots will be determined by the committee, and all workmen employed in the construction of vaults, enclosing of lots, erection of monuments, &c., must be subject to the control and direction of the superintendent acting under the direction of the committee, in all matters appertaining to the general regulations of the cemetery.

Rubbish to be removed.

Clause 7th. Persons employed to work on lots must remove all the rubbish which they make, to such places of deposit as may be provided for the purpose, or if no places are provided, it must be removed from the cemetery. If they fail to do so, it may be removed by the superintendent at the expense of the holder of such lot or lots.

Clause 8th. All persons employed to work on or about

lots, wilfully violating or refusing to conform to the rules and regulations for the government of the cemetery, may be expelled from or prohibited performing any further work in the cemetery without permission from the committee.

Violations of rules to be expelled, &c.

Clause 9th. Holders of lots will not be permitted to erect wooden fences on the lots, or set up wooden head-boards or grave stones of slate. Live hedges are allowed. All foundations of monuments and other structures shall be made satisfactory to the superintendent, under the direction of the committee.

Wooden fences, &c., prohibited.

Clause 10th. All persons who shall be found within the grounds making unseemly noises, discharging fire-arms, driving at a rapid rate through the avenues, or otherwise conducting themselves unsuitably to the purposes to which the grounds are devoted, or in violation of these several regulations, will be required instantly to leave the cemetery, and upon refusal to do so, may be forcibly ejected by the superintendent.

Unseemly noises, &c., prohibited.

Clause 11th. Horses must not be left unfastened without a keeper; nor fastened, except at the posts provided for that purpose.

Horses not to be left unfastened.

Clause 12th. No member of the committee on cemeteries shall receive any compensation for services, or have any interest whatever in any work or materials furnished for any of the cemeteries.

Committee on cemetery not to receive compensation.

Clause 13th. No body shall be removed from the receiving tomb without the knowledge of the superintendent of the cemetery.

Body not to be removed from receiving tomb except, &c.

Clause 14th. All lots hereafter sold, shall be graded under the direction of the superintendent, at such price as shall be agreed upon with said superintendent. Any profits arising from said grading shall go into the fund for the preservation of the grounds and lots as before provided. And no person shall be employed to grade said lots except by consent and under the direction of the superintendent.

Superintendent to direct grading of lots.

11. No person shall cut down or remove any of

Standing trees not to be removed without permit.
Ord. Aug. 15, 1866.

the standing trees within Evergreen cemetery, except by written permit of the committee on cemeteries and public grounds, and any person violating this section shall be liable to a penalty of not less than ten, and not more than seventy-five dollars for each offense.

Superintendent of burials has charge of receiving tomb.
Ord., Jan. 5, 1864. § 1.

12. The superintendent of burials, under the direction of the committee on cemeteries and public grounds, shall have charge and control of the receiving tomb in Evergreen cemetery, and it shall be his duty to take care that said tomb is well secured by locks and bolts, and to keep a record of the name, age and residence of each deceased person who may be placed in said tomb, the time when so deposited, and the time of removal and the place of burial.

Of bodies deposited in tomb, &c.
Ib. § 2.

13. The superintendent of burials shall not allow the body of any deceased stranger, or any person not owning a plat or lot in said cemetery, to be deposited in said tomb without the permission of the committee on cemeteries in writing, nor until the price of a plat or lot in said cemetery shall have been deposited with the city treasurer; and no dead body shall be removed from said tomb without the permission of the superintendent of burials.

Temporary burials. Removal.
Ib. § 3.

14. All bodies that may be deposited in said tomb waiting burial, shall be removed therefrom by the undertaker depositing the same, before the fifteenth day of May in each year, unless suffered to remain by special permission of the committee on cemeteries.

Fees of undertakers.
Ib. § 4.

15. The undertakers shall be allowed to charge and receive for their services for attending a funeral and depositing the body of an adult in said tomb, six dollars, and for the removal and interment of said body in said cemetery, the further sum of two dollars; for attending

Same.

the funeral services of a child and depositing the same in said tomb, four dollars and fifty cents, and for the removal and burial of the same, one dollar, to be charged to the person or persons requesting said service.

FOREST CITY CEMETERY.

16. So much of the tract of land lying north-west of the fence of the Kennebec and Portland railroad, in the town of Cape Elizabeth, purchased by the city of Samuel Haskell, as per his deed, dated August 12, 1858, is hereby set apart and appropriated for the burial of the dead, and the same shall be called and known by the name of the "Forest City cemetery," according to the plan thereof made by Charles H. Howe, city engineer, and adopted and established by the city council on the seventeenth day of September, A. D. 1858.

Land appropriated for "Forest City Cemetery."
Ord., Dec. 17, 1858, § 1.

17. The city treasurer, on the payment of the sum fixed upon said lots, in the schedule of the same, on the aforesaid plan of Charles H. Howe, by any person, shall be, and hereby is required to execute and deliver to said person, his heirs and assigns forever, a certificate of said lot, signed by him, similar in form and upon the same terms as the certificate now given for lots in Evergreen cemetery.

City treasurer to execute deed.
Ib. § 2.

18. The city treasurer shall keep a record of all the lots sold in said cemetery, and an account of all the moneys received for the same, and shall annually report to the city council a statement of all lots sold, and assigned by him, with the names of the purchasers, and amount received by him therefor. And all moneys so received shall be, and hereby are constituted a fund, to be appropriated exclusively for the purpose of improving and ornamenting said cemetery.

City treasurer to keep record, &c.
Ib. § 3.

19. There shall be appointed by the mayor with the advice and consent of the aldermen, annually, a superintendent of Forest City cemetery, who shall be *ex officio* an undertaker, and who shall hold his office for one year, or until a successor is appointed and qualified, and his duties shall be the same in reference to the Forest City cemetery

Superintendent
Ib. § 4, as amended by city charter, § 6.

as those of the superintendent of burials, in reference to cemeteries within the city.

Committee authorized to exchange lots, &c.

Ib. § 5.

20. The committee on "cemeteries and public grounds" are hereby authorized, at any time, to exchange, free of cost, any lot in Forest City cemetery for a lot in the Eastern or Western cemeteries in this city, and the treasurer, upon the written request of said committee, shall make, execute and deliver, a certificate of such lot, free of charge, if so requested by said committee.

CITY AUDITOR.

ORDINANCES.

1. The city auditor elected annually.
2. To give bond.
3. Successor to be appointed in case of death, &c.
4. Expenditures to be vouched and drawn for.
5. Payments in advance, how made.
6. Committee on accounts to direct auditor, and examine bills.
7. Auditor to keep books.
8. Auditor to examine bills against city, &c.
9. Auditor to make annual estimates and statement of expenditure.
10. Auditor to open an account with treasurer.

1. There shall be elected annually, or at the time that may hereafter be fixed for the election of other subordinate officers, one person, possessing a practical knowledge of book-keeping, to be styled the city auditor of accounts, who shall continue in office during the year ensuing his election, and until another person has been elected and qualified in his place.

City auditor to be elected annually.
Ord., April 1, 1859, § 1, as amended by city charter.

2. Said auditor of accounts shall be sworn to the faithful performance of the duties of his office, and give bond, with surety or sureties, to be approved by the mayor and aldermen, in the penal sum of three thousand dollars, for the faithful performance of said duties, the true accounting for and payment over of all city moneys which

To give bond.
Ib. § 2.

shall come into his hands, and the delivery over to his successor, or to the city clerk, of all the books, accounts, papers, and other documents and property which shall belong to said office.

A successor to be appointed in case of death, &c.

Ib. § 2.

3. In case said office shall become vacant by death, resignation or otherwise, a successor shall forthwith, and in like manner, be appointed, who shall continue in office until the appointment and qualification of a successor.

Expenditures to be vouched and drawn for.

Ib. § 3.

4. No moneys shall be paid out of the city treasury unless the expenditures or the terms of the contract shall be vouched by the chairman of the committee of the board, under whose authority it has been authorized and made; nor unless the same shall be examined by the auditor, approved by the committee of accounts, and drawn for by the mayor.

Payments in advance, how made.

Ib. § 3.

5. In all cases where it is necessary for money to be paid in advance, for contracts made or for works begun, but not completed, the mayor may, upon being satisfied of such necessity, draw upon the city treasurer for the amount thus necessary to be advanced, which draft shall be paid by the city treasurer, provided the same be countersigned by the auditor; and it shall be the duty of the auditor to countersign all such drafts, not exceeding five hundred dollars, and to charge the same to the proper person and account; but the said auditor shall not countersign any such draft for any sum exceeding five hundred dollars, without the direction of the committee on accounts.

Committee on accounts to direct auditor, and examine bills.

Ib. § 4.

6. It shall be the duty of the committee of accounts to direct the auditor as to the manner in which the books, records and papers belonging to the department shall be kept, and the mode in which all bills and accounts against the city shall be certified or vouched, and as often as once in every month to examine, and if they see fit, to pass all bills and accounts against the city, which shall be certified by the auditor.

7. It shall be the duty of the auditor to keep, in a

neat, methodical style and manner, a complete set of books, under the direction of the committee of accounts, wherein shall be stated, among other things, the appropriation for each distinct object of expenditure, to the end that whenever the appropriations for the specific objects shall have been expended, he shall immediately communicate the same to the city council, that they may be apprised of the fact, and either make a farther appropriation or withhold, as they may deem expedient.

Auditor to keep books.

Ib. § 5.

8. The auditor shall receive all bills and accounts from persons having demands against the city, examine them in detail, cast up the same, and have them filed and entered in books, in such manner and form as the committee of accounts shall order and direct. When the auditor shall have any doubt concerning the correctness of any such bill or account presented against the city, he shall not enter the same in a book until he shall have exhibited the same, with his objections, to the committee of accounts, at their next meeting, for their consideration and final decision. And it shall also be the duty of the auditor to render any other services, from time to time, as the city council or the committee of accounts shall direct.

Auditor to examine all bills against the city, &c.

Ib. § 5.

9. It shall be the duty of the auditor of accounts to lay before the city council annually, at such time as the council may direct, an estimate of the amount of money necessary to be raised for the ensuing year, under the respective heads of appropriation; and shall also annually, at such times as the council may direct, make and lay before said council a statement of all the receipts and expenditures of the past financial year, giving in detail the amount of appropriation and expenditure for each specific object, the receipt from each source of income, the whole to be arranged as far as practicable to conform to the accounts of the city treasurer; and said statement shall be accompanied by a schedule of all the property belonging to the city, and an exhibit of the debts due from the city.

Auditor to make annual estimates and statement of expenditure.

Ib. § 6.

Auditor to open an account with treasurer.
Ib. § 6.

10. The auditor shall open an account with the treasurer of the city, charging said treasurer with the whole amount of taxes placed in his hands for collection, also the whole amount in detail of all bonds, notes, mortgages, leases, rents, interest and other sums receivable, in order that the value and description of all personal property belonging to the city may be at any time known at the office of the auditor.

CITY CLERK.

STATUTES.

ORDINANCE.

STATUTES.

1. All residents of this State intending to be joined in marriage, shall cause notice of their intentions to be recorded in the office of the clerk of the city, town or plantation in which they respectively reside, at least five days before a certificate of such intentions shall be granted; and the book in which said record is made shall be labelled on the outside of the cover thereof, with the words "Record of intentions of marriage," and be kept open to public inspection in the office of the clerk, and

Notice of intention of marriage, how to be recorded.

R. S., chap. 59, § 5, as amended by Act 1859, chap. 14.

Book of record to be labelled and kept open to inspection.

if there be no such clerk in the place of their residence, the like entry shall be made with the clerk of an adjoining town or plantation.

Clerk to give certificate.
Ib. § 6.

2. The clerk shall deliver to the parties a certificate, under his hand, specifying the time when notice of the intentions of marriage was entered with him, which certificate shall be delivered to the minister or magistrate, in whose presence the marriage is to be contracted, before he shall proceed to solemnize the same; *provided*, that no clerk shall issue such certificate to a male under twenty-one, or a female under eighteen years of age, unless the parties applying for said certificate shall first present to him the written consent of the parents or guardians of such applicant, if any they have residing within this State, that such certificate may issue; or to any town pauper, when the overseers of the poor of any town or city shall deposit a list of the names of the paupers of such town with said clerk.

Certificate not to be issued to minors without consent of parents or guardians.

Penalty if clerk violates.
Act, 1859, § 3.

3. If any town clerk knowingly delivers to any person a certificate of the intention of matrimony in violation of the provisions of the preceding section, or shall so deliver a certificate falsely stating the residence of either party named therein, he shall be fined twenty dollars.

Town clerk to record births and deaths.
R. S., chap. 59, § 20.

4. Every town clerk shall record all births and deaths, which occur in his town and come to his knowledge, stating the time of each, and the names of the parents, if known, for the fees allowed by law, to be paid by such town.

Parents and others to notify clerk.
Ib. § 21.

5. Parents, householders, masters of workhouses, alms houses, prisons, and vessels, shall give notice to the clerk of their town of the births and deaths, which take place in their families, houses, or vessels, and the elder person next of kin shall give notice of the death of his kindred.

Penalty for neglect.
Ib. § 22.

6. Any person, neglecting to perform the duty required of him in the two preceding sections for the space of six months, shall forfeit and pay one dollar for each

offence, to be recovered, on complaint, to the use of the town.

7. No mortgage hereafter made of personal property, to secure payment of more than thirty dollars, shall be valid against any other person than the parties thereto, unless possession of such property is delivered to and retained by the mortgagee, or the mortgage is recorded by the clerk of the town, plantation, or plantation organized for election purposes only, in which the mortgager resides. When a corporation makes a mortgage it shall be recorded in the town where it has its established place of business. When the mortgager resides in an unincorporated place other than a plantation organized for election purposes, the mortgage shall be recorded in the oldest adjoining town, plantation, or plantation organized for election purposes only, in the county. But a mortgage of personal property made to secure the payment of thirty dollars or less, may be recorded by the same clerk, in the same manner, and with the same effect as a mortgage of personal property made to secure the payment of more than thirty dollars.

Mortgages of personal property not valid except between parties, unless recorded or possession taken.

R. S., chap. 91. § 1, as amended by Act, 1865, chap. 287, and by Act, 1867, chap. 64.

8. When all the mortgagers of personal property reside without the State, and the mortgagee does not take possession, the mortgage shall be recorded on the records of the city or town in which the property is when the mortgage is made.

Certain mortgages to be recorded in city or town where property is. Act 1864, chap. 243, § 1.

9. Where there are two or more mortgagers, some of whom are residents within the State, the mortgage shall be recorded in the cities or towns in this State in which such mortgagers reside.

Mortgagers residing in State, mortgage to be recorded where they reside, &c. Ib. § 2.

10. When any personal property is attached, which by reason of its bulk or other special cause cannot be immediately removed, the officer may, within five days thereafter, file in the office of the clerk of the town, in which the attachment is made, an attested copy of so much of his return on the writ, as relates to the attachment, with

Attachment how preserved when property cannot be removed, &c.

18 Maine, 125. 19 Maine, 92, 435.

R. S., chap. 81, § 35.

the value of the defendant's property which he is thereby commanded to attach, the names of the parties, the date of the writ, and the court to which it is returnable; and such attachment shall be as effectual and valid, as if the property had remained in his possession and custody. The clerk shall receive the copy, and note thereon the time of his receiving it, and enter it in a book kept for that purpose, and keep it on file for the inspection of those interested therein, for which he shall be entitled to ten cents.

City clerk may appoint a deputy.

St. 1860, Mar. 17, § 1.

11. The town clerk of any town may appoint a citizen of said town, his deputy, who may, whenever the clerk is absent from his office, perform the duties of clerk, as set forth in section two of chapter ninety-one of the revised statutes, with the same effect as if performed by said clerk.

Appointment to be in writing.

Ib. § 2.

12. The appointment may be in writing, as follows:

I hereby appoint ——— to perform the duties of town clerk as set forth in section two of chapter ninety-one of the revised statutes, in the town of ——— during my absence from the clerk's office.

——— Clerk of the town of ———.

Deputy to be sworn.

Ib. § 3.

13. Before said deputy shall enter upon the duties of his office, he shall be sworn before a justice of the peace, faithfully to discharge the duties of his office.

ORDINANCE.

Duties of city clerk.

Rev. Ord., 1855.

1. The city clerk shall keep a full record of all the doings of the board of aldermen, and of all conventions of the city council, which record shall be subject at all times to the inspection of the mayor, or of any person or persons authorized thereto by the board of aldermen, or the city council. He shall notify all persons appointed to office by the mayor and aldermen, or by the city council, and he shall give notice to the chairman of all committees, the appointment of which shall originate in the board of aldermen, and shall transmit all papers to the common

council, when necessary for their convenience. He shall preserve all papers belonging to the city in suitable files, prepared for the purpose, and shall carefully keep all ordinances, after they have been finally passed, in a book or books to be inspected from time to time by the mayor and members of the city council. He shall procure all stationery and other necessary articles which may be needed by either branch of the city council, or any city officer, and keep an account thereof, to be laid before the city council. He shall draw bills and ordinances, when thereto required by any committee, and perform such other duties as may be prescribed by the board of aldermen or the city council.

CITY CONSTABLE AND MESSENGER.

ORDINANCES.

Duties of city constable and messenger.

Rev. Ord., 1855.

1. There shall annually be appointed by the city council, a suitable person to be styled city constable and messenger, who shall receive, deliver, and execute all notifications, summonses, warrants, and precepts, issued by the mayor, the city council, or either branch thereof, or by any committee of the same, and make due return of the same. He shall prepare and arrange the rooms and building in which the city council hold their sessions, and be in constant attendance on the city council when in session, and under the direction of the mayor, or city clerk, shall provide fuel, lights and other things necessary for the accommodation of both branches of the city council, or any committee thereof. He shall receive and deliver all notifications to officers elected by the city council, or by the mayor and aldermen, and he shall deliver all notifications to committees when thereto requested by the city clerk, or clerk of the common council.

He shall perform the duties of clerk of the market. He shall have the superintendence of the city hall and city government house, together with the furniture, and see that they are kept in good condition and ready for use. He shall also prepare and make ready the rooms which may be selected for ward meetings, and have the same cleaned and put in order, after said meetings are adjourned.

2. The city constable and messenger shall at all times be subject to such further orders as the city council may make. To be subject to orders of city council. Ib.

CITY COUNCIL.

ORDINANCE.

1. City council, stated meetings of.

1. Stated meetings of the city council shall be held on the first Monday evening of each month, at seven and a half o'clock. Special meetings of the mayor and aldermen, and of the city council, shall be called by the mayor, at such times as he may deem expedient, by causing a notification to be left at the usual residence or place of business, of each member of the board or boards, to be convened. Stated meetings. Ord., July 6, 1863.

[For powers and duties of the city council, see CITY CHARTER.]

CITY ENGINEER.

ORDINANCES.

1. City council to choose city engineer.
2. Duties.
3. Same.
4. Mean tide elevation to be a base line.
5. Description of streets, drains, sewers, &c., to be recorded.
6. To make plans of sewers.

City council to choose city engineer.

Rev. Ord., 1855, as amended by city charter.

1. There shall be chosen annually, and whenever a vacancy occurs, by the city council, a city engineer, who shall hold his office until a successor is chosen or he is removed. He shall be removable at the pleasure of the city council, and shall receive such compensation for his services as said council may from time to time determine.

Duties.

Ib.

2. The city engineer, under the direction and control of the mayor and aldermen, shall have charge of all the plans of streets belonging to the city; he shall make all surveys, admeasurements, and levels of streets in the city, and plans and profiles of the same, when thereto required as hereinafter mentioned, and perform such other surveying and engineering services as may be required by the mayor and aldermen or any committee of the city council. He may appoint assistants, subject to the approval of the mayor and aldermen, who shall receive such compensation as the city council may determine.

3. The city engineer, when required as aforesaid, shall take the angles contained between different street lines, and make a record of the same, as the true lines of the street, and those angles shall all have reference to a given base line. He shall also cause street monuments to be placed at the angles of the streets as well as at the points of intersection, on which monuments, the letter M shall be cut, and it shall be the duty of the commissioner of streets to put down such monuments when requested so to do by said engineer.

Same. Ib.

4. Mean tide elevation, (as obtained by the coast survey,) shall be adopted as a base line, from which all levels taken by the engineer shall be measured, and to which all grades of streets, sewers, drains, &c., shall have reference, and points shall be established in different parts of the city from which the grades can at once be accurately obtained.

Mean tide elevation to be a base line. Ib.

5. Said engineer shall record in a book, to be kept for that purpose, marked " street angles and distances," an accurate description of the angles, the points of beginning and ending of each street line, and the distances between said points. He shall also record in another book, marked "grades of streets, sewers, drains, &c.," an accurate description of all the grades of the streets, sewers, drains, &c., which books of record shall be certified by him, and be deposited among other city records.

Description of streets, drains, sewers, &c., to be recorded. Ib.

6. The said city engineer whenever any common sewer is ordered to be built or repaired, shall ascertain its depth, breadth, mode of construction and general direction ; with the dimensions of each lot of land benefited thereby, and a list of the owners of the same ; and take the plan thereof, and insert the same with all those particulars in a book kept for that purpose ; and shall ascertain and insert on such plan all entries made into such sewer.

City engineer to make plans of sewers. Ord., 1859, June 17.

[For duties of engineer in relation to drains and sewers, see chapter on DRAINS and SEWERS, post. Also, in relation to location of streets, &c., see CITY CHARTER.]

CITY (NOW MARKET) HALL.[1]

PROCEEDINGS OF TOWN MEETING.

1. Proceedings of the town of Portland relating to erection of town hall.
2. Use of part of same allowed to military companies.

ORDINANCE.

General charge of city hall to be with mayor.

Proceedings of the town of Portland relating to erection of town hall.

Town records, vol. 2, pp. 326, 335.

1. At a town meeting held Monday, April 25, 1824,—

Voted, That a committee be appointed to report what the buildings and lots of land which form the heater above the hay scales and adjoining the town's land can be purchased for, and also to report a plan, and the probable expense of erecting a suitable building there for a market and town hall. At a meeting held Monday, August 3, the committee made a report recommending the purchase of the lands and the erection of a building for said purposes, and the following vote was passed, viz:

Voted, To accept the report so far as relates to purchasing the land, and erecting a building for a town hall and market, agreeably to the plan mentioned in said report, of a building three stories high.

[1] This chapter is inserted for its historical interest. The city government building, burned at the great fire July 4, 1866, and rebuilt, takes the place of the old city hall for most public purposes.

Voted, To choose a committee to carry into effect the objects of the foregoing report by making the necessary purchases and contracts, and erecting the said contemplated building.

2. At a town meeting held March 27, 1826, it was

Use of part of same allowed to military companies.

Ib., p. 405.

Voted, That the third story in the town hall, (except for so much as has been appropriated for the use of the apprentices' library), be appropriated to the use of the several military companies in town, and that they have liberty at their own expense to fit up armories for the deposit of their guns, &c., the whole to be under the direction of the selectmen.

ORDINANCE.

General charge of city hall to be with mayor.

Rev. Ord., 1855.

The general charge of the city hall shall be lodged with the mayor, who may allow the free use thereof for any peaceable assembly of citizens, on application being made in writing by seven legal voters.

CLERK OF THE COMMON COUNCIL.

ORDINANCE.

Duty of clerk of common council.

Duty of clerk of common council.

Rev. Ord., 1855.

The clerk of the common council shall keep a full record of all the doings of the common council, which shall be subject to the inspection of the mayor, president of the common council, or any committee of the city council. He shall give notice to the chairman of all committees of the common council, and he shall transmit all papers to the board of aldermen when necessary for their concurrence. He shall preserve all papers, which properly belong to the common council, and shall perform all such duties as may be prescribed to him by the board of common council, or by the city council.

COURTS.

[SEE MUNICIPAL COURT.]

CONSTABLES.

STATUTE.

Wards to elect two constables each. Islands to elect one constable.

Section ten, chapter three, of the revised statutes, provides for the election of constables by towns at their annual meetings.

Qualified electors in each ward are authorized, at the annual election holden for the choice of mayor and aldermen, to elect two constables; and the inhabitants of the islands have power to elect one constable, who shall be a resident on some one of the islands.

Wards to elect two constables each.

City charter, §§ 12, 13, 15.

Islands to elect one constable.

[SEE POLICE.]

CONTRACTS AND EXPENDITURES.

ORDINANCES.

Deficiency of appropriation.

Ord., Jan. 2, 1865, § 1.

1. Whenever any committee or board is authorized to make any contract by the city council, or to expend any moneys appropriated by the city council for any purpose, and the estimates for such contract or expenditures shall exceed in amount the appropriation specifically made for the object thereof, or the sum specifically apropriated for any purpose shall have been expended by them, and for either reason a further appropriation is necessary, such committee or board shall report to the city council the fact of such deficiency of the appropriation, a statement of the cause or causes thereof, and an estimate of the amount necessary to be added to such appropriation, and the committee or board shall not conclude such contract, or make further expenditure in the premises, until they shall be authorized so to do by the city council.

Contracts not to be concluded when appropriations are deficient.

Committees limited in expenditures.

Ib. § 2, as amended by Ord., Jan. 6, 1868.

2. No joint or special committee of the city council or either branch thereof, or any board appointed by them, shall have power to make any expenditure from the appropriation provided by the city council, to an amount exceeding three hundred dollars, except where otherwise provided in the laws of the State or ordinances of the city, until an estimate of the expenditure proposed shall have been laid before the city council, and authority for such expenditure be first had and obtained from the city council.

COWS.

STATUTE.

Cities and towns authorized to regulate the going at large of cattle.

ORDINANCES.

1. Cows not to go at large.
2. Penalty.
3. City marshal to prosecute.
4. Cows to wear straps around the neck.

STATUTE.

Cities and towns are authorized to make by-laws to regulate the going at large of cows and other neat beasts, within their respective towns and cities, and may enforce them by penalties.

Cities and towns authorized to regulate the going at large of cattle, &c.
R. S., chap. 23, § 4.

ORDINANCES.

1. No cows shall be permitted to go at large, at any time, in any of the commons, streets, lanes, squares, or alleys of the city.

Cows not to go at large.
Rev. Ord., 1855.

2. If the owner of any cow shall suffer the same to go at large on any common, street, lane, square, or alley of the city, he shall forfeit and pay a sum not less than one nor more than five dollars for each offense.

Penalty.
Ib.

3. All informations and complaints for violation of the preceding sections shall be made to the city marshal, whose duty it shall be to collect forthwith any fine incurred

City marshal to prosecute.
Ib.

as aforesaid, or in default of payment thereof, to cause the owners of any such cow or cows to be prosecuted therefor.

Cows to wear straps around the neck.

Ib.

4. Every cow kept in the city shall at all times wear a strap around the neck, of not less than three inches in width, with the name of the owner and place of residence legibly painted or printed thereon. And for every cow found running at large without said strap, the owner of said cow shall forfeit and pay a sum not less than five nor more than ten dollars, to be recovered by complaint before the municipal court, one half for the use of the complainant, and the other half to the city.

CRIERS.

ORDINANCES.

1. License to be granted to common criers. Term of license.
2. Crying without license.
3. Criers to keep a list of matters cried, &c. Shall not cry libelous matter, &c.
4. Penalty for violation.

1. The mayor and aldermen may, from time to time, grant licenses to such, and so many persons as they may deem expedient, to be common criers in this city, and such licenses shall continue in force until the first day of May next after the date thereof, unless sooner revoked by the mayor and aldermen.

Licenses to be granted to common criers.

Rev. Ord., 1855.

Term of license.

2. No person shall be a common crier within the city of Portland, or cry any goods, wares, or merchandise, lost or found, stolen goods, strays, or public sales, in any of the streets, squares, lanes, or market places within the city, unless he shall be licensed as aforesaid.

Crying without license.

Ib.

3. Every person so licensed shall keep a true and perfect list of all the matters and things by him cried, and the names of the persons by whom he was employed, and subject to the inspection of the mayor and aldermen, whenever they shall demand the same; and no common crier shall publish or cry any abusive, libelous, profane or obscene matter or thing whatsoever.

Criers to keep a list of matters cried, &c.

Ib.

Shall not cry libelous matter, &c.

4. Any person who shall be guilty of a violation of this ordinance, or any part thereof, shall forfeit and pay for each offense a sum not less than one nor more than ten dollars.

Penalty for violation.

Ib.

DOGS.

STATUTES.

ORDINANCES.

STATUTES.

Towns may pass by-laws. Owners of dogs liable for double damages. R. S. ch. 30, § 1.

1. Towns may pass by-laws to regulate the going at large of dogs within them. When any dog does any damage to a person or his property, his owner or keeper, and also the parent, guardian, master, or mistress, of any minor or servant, who owns or keeps such dog, shall forfeit to the injured person double the amount of the damage done ; to be recovered by action of trespass.

Dogs may be killed that assault any person, or kill domestic animals. Ib. § 2.

2. Any person may lawfully kill a dog, that suddenly assaults him or any other person when peaceably walking or riding, or is found worrying, wounding or killing any domestic animals out of the enclosure or immediate care of the owner.

3. Whoever is assaulted, or finds a dog strolling out of the enclosure or immediate care of his master, may, within forty-eight hours thereafter, make oath before a justice of the peace that he really suspects such dog to be dangerous or mischievous, and notify his master by giving him a copy of said oath, signed by the justice; and if the master neglects for twenty-four hours thereafter, to confine or kill such dog, he shall forfeit five dollars to any person suing therefor; and if such dog is again at large out of the care of the master, any person may lawfully kill him.

Penalty for not confining or killing dangerous dogs, after notice.
R. S., Ib. § 3.

4. If a dog, after notice given as aforesaid, wounds any person by a sudden assault as aforesaid, or wounds or kills any domestic animals, the owner or keeper shall be liable to pay the person injured treble damages and costs.

Owner of dog assaulting person, &c., liable to treble damages.
Ib. § 5.

5. All dogs more than six months old, shall be taxed one dollar in the town where they are kept, on the first day of April in each year, to the owner or person who has them in possession at that time, provided that towns or cities shall so vote.

Tax imposed on dogs, if towns or cities so vote.
Act March 19, 1862.

ORDINANCES.

1. No dog shall be permitted to go at large or loose, in any street, lane, alley, court, or travelled way, or in any uninclosed or public place in this city, until the owner or keeper of such dog, or the head of the family, or the keeper of the house, store, shop, office, or other place where such dog is kept or harbored, shall have paid to the city marshal two dollars for a license for such dog to go at large.

Dogs not to go at large without license.
Rev. Ord., 1855.

2. The city marshal shall grant a license to any citizen for his or her dog to run at large, on the payment of two dollars; which license shall expire on the first day of May next after the same is given.

City marshal shall grant licenses.
Fee for same.
Ib.

City marshal to keep record of same. To make quarterly reports. To pay over moneys. Ib.

3. The city marshal shall keep a record of all licenses so granted, with the numbers of the same, and he shall make a report to the mayor and aldermen, once in three months, of all moneys so received, and shall pay over the same to the city treasurer for the use of the city.

License to be numbered.

4. Every license so granted shall be numbered, and the person named therein shall cause the same number to be legibly printed or engraved on a collar to be kept about the neck of the dog intended to be licensed. And no such dog shall be considered as licensed, unless the requisition contained in this section be complied with.

Dogs to wear collars. Ib.

City marshal to cause dogs at large without license to be destroyed. Ib.

5. It shall be the duty of the city marshal to cause all dogs to be destroyed which shall be found at large within the city, without a collar, as required by the fourth section of this ordinance.

Proceedings in case any dog shall disturb the quiet of any person by barking, &c. Ib.

6. On complaint being made to the mayor, of any dog within this city which shall by barking, biting, howling, or in any other way or manner disturb the quiet of any person or persons whomsoever, the mayor shall issue notice thereof to the person owning, keeping, or permitting such dog to be kept; and in case such person shall neglect to cause such dog to be forthwith removed and kept beyond the limits of the city, or destroyed, he shall forfeit and pay one dollar for every day during which such neglect shall continue after such notice; *provided*, that the justice before whom the complaint respecting such dog shall be heard and tried, shall be satisfied that such dog had in manner aforesaid, disturbed the quiet of any person in said city.

Proviso.

Penalty. Ib.

7. In case any dog shall be found loose or going at large, contrary to any of the foregoing provisions, the owner or keeper thereof, or the head of the family or keeper of the house, store, shop, office, or other place where such dog is kept or harbored, shall forfeit and pay a sum not exceeding ten dollars.

DRAINS AND SEWERS.

STATUTES.

1. City council may construct public drains. Damages how assessed.
2. Private drains. Regulation, how established. Application for permits.
3. If dissatisfied with price of permit, remedy.
4. Drains constructed before April 11, 1854.
5. Penalty for connecting private with public drains without permit.
6. Public drains to be kept in repair, &c. Penalty for neglect.
7. Records of permits to be kept.
8. Permit, when to be paid for.
9. Private drains, how repaired when neglected by owners.
10. Penalty for injuring public drains.
11. General authority over drains.

ORDINANCES.

1. Committee on drains, &c., to be appointed.
2. Sewers to be built in centre of street.
3. City engineer to supervise.
4. " " to keep account of expense, and list of persons benefitted.
5. Expenses apportioned between city and abuttors.
6. City engineer to report names of abuttors benefitted.
7. Private connecting drains, how built.
8. Drains not to be sunk under sidewalks, &c. Penalty.
9. Drains not to empty on surface. Penalty.
10. Water from roofs.

STATUTES.

City council authorized to construct public drains.

Act, April 11, 1854, chap. 77, § 1.

1. The city council of the city of Portland shall have authority to construct public drains or sewers through any of the streets of the city, at the expense of the city, and which shall be solely under the direction and control of the city council. Whenever it shall be necessary to provide a suitable out-fall for any such drain, at or near low water mark, the same may be located and constructed for that purpose, by the city council, over the lands of private persons; and such location shall be made, and damages assessed and paid therefor, in the same manner as is or may be provided by law for the location of streets in said city.

Damages.

Private drains.

Ib. § 2.

2. The abuttors upon the line of any such public drain, and the owners of private drains contiguous thereto, shall be allowed to enter and connect at suitable places, with such public drains, upon application as hereinafter provided, and paying such sum as the mayor and aldermen shall determine therefor; the mayor and aldermen shall also establish such other regulations and conditions as they may deem expedient, upon which the privilege of entering public drains in any case shall be granted and enjoyed; and shall give to the person applying and paying aforesaid, a written permit for such entrance. All applications for permits shall be in writing, and shall distinctly describe the land to which they are to apply. The privilege granted by such permit shall be available to the owner of the land described, his heirs and assigns, and shall run with the land, without any other or subsequent charge, or payment therefor.

Regulations, how established.

Application for permits.

Amount to be paid for permit, how determined in case of disagreement.

Ib. § 3.

3. If any person shall be dissatisfied with the sum which the mayor and aldermen shall require him to pay for permission to enter a public drain, and shall, within ten days after notice thereof, request in writing that the same may be determined by arbitration, the mayor and aldermen, at their next regular meeting, shall nominate six

persons, any two of whom selected by the applicant, together with a third person nominated by the applicant himself, shall be empowered to determine the sum to be paid; upon the payment of which by the applicant, together with the fees of the arbitrators, he shall be entitled to such a permit as was offered to be given by the mayor and aldermen for the sum determined by them.

Drains heretofore constructed, how maintained and managed. Ib. § 4.

4. All drains in said city, which have heretofore been constructed at the expense of the city, shall hereafter be maintained, managed, and controlled in the same manner as if they had been constructed under this act, subject to any rights which private persons may have acquired therein. And the privilege of entering such drains shall hereafter be granted and held upon the same terms and conditions as are herein provided in case of drains which may be constructed under this act.

Penalty for connecting private drains with public drains without permit. Ib. § 5.

Penalty for violation of permit.

5. If any person shall connect any private drain or sewer with any such public drain, or enter the same by any side drain, without a permit obtained therefor as herein provided, the mayor and aldermen shall be empowered forthwith to cause such connection to be broken and destroyed. If any person shall wilfully or negligently violate any of the conditions and regulations prescribed in his permit, the mayor and aldermen shall be empowered forthwith to cause his connecting drain to be disconnected from the public drain, and may declare his permit to be forfeited, in which case such person, his heirs and assigns, shall have no privilege of entering such public drain until a new permit shall be granted as herein provided. If any person, by the construction or use of any private drain, shall commit any public or private nuisance, he shall be liable to indictment or action for such nuisance, notwithstanding anything contained in this act.

Drains to be kept in repair, &c. Ib. § 6.

6. After any such public drain shall be constructed, and any person shall have paid for the privilege of connecting therewith, such public drain shall be constantly

maintained and kept in repair by the city, so as to afford sufficient and suitable flow for all drainage lawfully entitled to pass through it. But the same may be altered in its former course, or other public drains may be substituted therefor, so, however, that equally sufficient and suitable drainage shall be afforded. If the city shall not so maintain and keep in repair such public drain, any person lawfully entitled to the privilege of drainage through the same may have an action against the city to recover his damages occasioned thereby.

Penalty for neglect.

Records of permits to be kept.

Ib. § 7.

7. All proceedings of the mayor and aldermen under this act, shall be at legal meetings of that board. A suitable record shall be made and kept of all permits granted as herein provided, which record shall succinctly exhibit the persons and lands to which the respective permits apply. The mayor and aldermen shall have the exclusive direction, on behalf of the city, of all prosecutions under this act.

Amount for permit to be paid within 60 days.

Ib. § 8.

8. If any person, after the determination of the sum required to be paid by him for a permit, shall neglect to pay the same within sixty days after notice thereof, together with the fees of the arbitrators, if any, he shall have no benefit of such determination, nor of his application for a permit. The mayor and aldermen may determine the fees of the arbitrators in any case, and the same shall be paid, if required, in advance; the award of the arbitrators shall be by them returned to the city clerk, and recorded with the proceedings of the mayor and aldermen.

Fees of arbitrators, how determined, &c.

Private drains, how repaired in case of neglect of owners.

Ib. § 9.

9. If any private drain in said city, now existing, or which may hereafter be constructed, shall become so obstructed, decayed, or out of repair as to do injury to any street in which the same shall be laid, and the person or persons using such drain shall unreasonably neglect, after notice by the street commissioner, to repair such injury, the same shall be repaired by the city, and the expense thereof may be recovered to the use of the city,

by an action of the case against any one or more of the persons using such drains to whom notice as aforesaid shall have been given.

Penalty for wilfully or carelessly injuring public drains. Ib. § 10.

10. If any person shall wilfully or carelessly do any injury to any public drain constructed or maintained under this act, or to any street culvert leading into the same, or shall wilfully or carelessly obstruct any such street culvert, or the outlet of any such drain, he shall be liable to pay to the use of the city, to be recovered in an action of the case, double the amount of the injury and damages so done and caused, in addition to all the other penalties for such offense provided by law.

General authority. City charter, March 27, 1863, § 24.

11. The mayor and aldermen of said city may lay out, make, maintain and repair all main drains or common sewers in said city, and may assess upon the owners of the abutting lots and other lots benefited thereby, and who shall enter the same directly or indirectly, a proportional part of the charge of making such main drain or common sewer, to be ascertained and assessed by the mayor and aldermen of said city, and by them certified, after notice thereof given in writing to the party to be charged, or by public advertisement for seven days in two daily papers in said city; but not less than a third part of the cost of such main drain or common sewer shall be paid by the city, and shall not be charged to the abuttors. All assessments so made shall constitute a lien on the real estate so assessed, for two years after they are laid. They shall be certified by the mayor and aldermen, under their hands, to the treasurer and collector of said city and his successors, with directions to collect the same according to law, and may, together with all incidental costs and expenses, be levied by sale of the estate by him or them, if the assessment is not paid within three months after a written demand of payment made by him or them, either upon the person assessed or upon any person occupying the estate — such sale to be conducted in like manner as sale

for non-payment of taxes on land of resident owners, and with a similar right of redemption. Any person, who may deem himself aggrieved by any such assessments, may appeal to the supreme court in the same manner as is herein provided for appeals for damages for laying out streets, which court shall at the first term appoint three persons who may be inhabitants of said city, to settle and assess the share to be charged to such appellant; they shall make a return of their doings to said court, and their decision, if accepted, shall be final. And in case the assessment made by the mayor and aldermen shall not be reduced on such appeal, the city shall recover costs, but otherwise shall pay costs. Any person who shall, directly or indirectly, enter any such main drain or common sewer without first obtaining a permit from the mayor therefor, shall be subject to a fine not exceeding one hundred dollars.

[N. B. The statute of 1854, quoted above, is obsolete in part, the control of drains, &c., under the charter, being conferred exclusively upon the board of mayor and aldermen. See section 11, *ante.*]

ORDINANCES.

Committee on drains and sewers to be appointed. Rev. Ord., 1855, as amended by city charter.

1. There shall annually be appointed, a committee of the mayor and aldermen, to be called the committee on drains and sewers, to consist of three members of the board of mayor and aldermen.

Sewers to be built in centre of street. Ord., May 26, 1863, § 1.

2. All common sewers which shall be considered necessary by the mayor and aldermen in any street or highway, shall be laid, as near as possible, in the centre of such street or highway, shall be built by contract or otherwise at the expense of the city, of such dimensions, and of such materials, as the committee on drains and sewers or the mayor and aldermen shall direct.

City engineer to supervise. Ib. § 2.

3. The city engineer shall, under the direction of the mayor and aldermen, take general supervision of all common sewers, which are now or hereafter may be built

and owned by the city, or which may be permitted to be built or opened by its authority.

4. The city engineer shall keep an accurate account of the expense of constructing and repairing each public sewer, and shall report the same to the committee on drains and sewers, together with a list of the persons and estates benefited thereby, and the committee shall make out therefrom the assessments on the same, and report to the mayor and aldermen for their action.

City engineer to keep account of expense, and list of persons benefited.

Ib. § 3.

5. One-third part of the cost of all main drains or sewers, which shall be constructed under the direction of the mayor and aldermen, shall be paid by the city. The remaining two-thirds of the same shall be assessed upon the persons and estates deriving benefit therefrom, apportioning the assessment according to the number of square feet in each lot of land thus benefited. But no part of the cost of constructing the culverts required for such drain or sewer shall be charged to the abuttor. No sewer shall be built unless sufficient surety be given to the city by the owners of the abutting lands, that one-half of the assessments made shall be paid to the city within one year from the completion of such sewer, except in cases where the committee on drains and sewers shall decide that the direct interest of the city requires that a sewer shall be built.

Expenses apportioned between city and abuttors.

Ib. § 4.

6. The city engineer shall, from time to time, report to the mayor and aldermen the names of the owners of, and the descriptions of estates benefited by any public sewer which may be hereafter constructed, and who shall have entered the same directly or indirectly.

City engineer to report names of abuttors benefited.

Ib. § 5.

7. All private drains which shall hereafter enter into such public sewer shall be built of such materials as the mayor and aldermen shall direct, and shall be laid under the direction of the mayor and aldermen, or by some person by them appointed ; and they shall be laid in such direction, of such size, with such descent, and (where

Private connecting drains, how built.

Ib. § 6.

required) with such strainers as they shall require, and in such manner as they shall determine.

Drains not to be sunk under sidewalks.

Penalty.

Ib. § 7.

8. No person shall sink or lay any drain or aqueduct under any sidewalk, or nearer such sidewalk than the outer edge of the gutter of such street, under a penalty of not less than ten nor more than fifty dollars, provided that nothing herein contained shall prevent any person from constructing a sewer from his land or premises to the public sewer.

Drains not to empty upon surface.

Penalty.

Ib. § 8.

9. No person shall let out or empty upon the surface of any street, lane, or alley, any cellar drain, sink drain, or other drain, so that the water shall flow therefrom on to the street, lane or alley, under a penalty of ten dollars for each offense, and the further sum of ten dollars for each month that such drain shall be so continued to be let out or emptied as aforesaid.

Water from roofs.

Ib. § 9.

10. It shall be lawful for all persons having care of any buildings, at their own expense, to carry the rain water from the roofs of said buildings into any public sewer, free of any charge from the city, provided that the same be done by light water spouts or tubes under ground, and under the direction of the mayor and aldermen.

ELECTIONS.

STATUTES.

1. Qualifications of electors. Exceptions.
2. Electors exempt from arrest on days of election.
3. " " " military duty, when.
4. Time of State election.
5. Who are legal voters.
6. Assessors, when to prepare lists of voters.
7. Selectmen to prepare corrected lists.
8. Time, &c., of holding meeting to correct lists.
9. Of the entry of names in towns of one thousand or more voters.
10. Cities shall post lists, when.
11. Lists to be deposited with the clerk, and posted.
12. Names not to be added or stricken out, except, &c.
13. Papers of naturalization. Duties of selectmen.
14. Mode of warning meetings for election of governor, &c.
15. Time of opening polls.
16. What votes shall be on one list.
17. Check list required. Ballot box, one only allowed.
18. Votes to be on clean white paper.
19. Adjournment of meeting, when no choice of representative is effected.
20. Meetings for choice of certain officers, how regulated.
21. Result of ballotings, how ascertained.
22. Clerk to transmit returns to secretary of State.
23. County attorney to be notified, if return not received.
24. Loss of returns, how supplied.
25. Oath to be made to copy of record.
26. Certificate, how sealed and returned.
27. Vacancies, how filled.
28. Check lists to be preserved by clerks.
29. Ballot boxes, how constructed. Votes, how received.

ORDINANCES.

STATUTES.

Qualifications of electors. Exceptions. 7 Greenl. 497. Const., Art. 2, § 1.

1. Every male citizen of the United States of the age of twenty-one years and upwards, excepting paupers, persons under guardianship, and Indians not taxed, having his residence established in this State for the term of three months next preceding any election, shall be an elector for governor, senators and representatives, in the town or plantation where his residence is so established; and the elections shall be by written ballot. But persons in the military, naval or marine service of the United States, or this State, shall not be considered as having obtained such

Written ballot. 7 Greenl. 492, 497.

established residence by being stationed in any garrison, barrack or military place, in any town or plantation; nor shall the residence of a student at any seminary of learning entitle him to the right of suffrage in the town or plantation where such seminary is established.

Soldiers and seamen in the United States service.
Students at colleges and academies.

2. Electors shall, in all cases, except treason, felony, or breach of the peace, be privileged from arrest on the days of election, during their attendance at, going to, and returning therefrom.

Electors exempt from arrest on days of election.
8 Greenl. 187.
Const. Art. 2, § 2

3. No elector shall be obliged to do duty in the militia on any day of election, except in time of war or public danger.

And from military duty.
Ib. § 3.

4. The election of governor, senators and representatives, shall be on the second Monday of September annually forever.

Time of election.
Ib. § 4.

5. Every person, who is qualified by the constitution of this State to vote for governor, senators and representatives, in the town in which he resides, is entitled to vote in the election of all town officers, and in all the business affairs thereof.

Who are legal voters.
R. S., chap. 3, § 9.

6. In every town, where the selectmen are not the assessors, the assessors on or before the first day of August in each year, shall prepare a list of the persons they judge to be constitutionally qualified to vote therein in the election of governor, senators, and representatives, and deliver it to the selectmen for their information.

Assessors to prepare lists of voters and deliver to the selectmen.
R. S., chap. 4, § 1.

7. The selectmen of every town, on or before the eleventh day of August in each year, shall prepare a corrected list of persons qualified as aforesaid.

Selectmen to prepare a corrected list.
Ib. § 2.

8. The selectmen shall be in session at some convenient time and place, by them notified in the warrant for calling the meeting in such town, on the secular day next preceding the day of annual election of town officers in the month of March, or on the morning of the day of election, to hear and decide upon the applications of persons claiming to have their names entered upon said list;

Time and manner of holding meetings to correct list of voters.
Ib. § 12., as amended by Act Feb. 18, 1867.

and such session when held on a secular day preceding the day of election shall continue at least three hours, and when held on the day of election shall continue until the election of town officers required by law to be elected by ballot shall have been completed.

No names shall be entered on the list of voters in cities and towns, having one thousand or more registered voters, except on the three secular days preceding the election, &c.
Act, March 16, 1861.

9. In all cities and towns in this State having one thousand or more registered voters, it shall be the duty of the aldermen and selectmen of such cities and towns to receive applications of persons claiming a right to vote, on the three secular days next preceding the day of election, and no application shall be received after the hour of five of the clock afternoon on the secular day next preceding said day of election, and no name shall be added to the list of voters on the day of election by certificate or otherwise.

List of voters resident in wards, to be posted in cities having more than one thousand voters, &c.
Act, March 16, 1861.

10. In all cities having more than one thousand legal voters therein, it shall be the duty of the aldermen of each city to post up in some public place in each ward, a true printed or written list of the legal voters resident in said ward, such list to be posted at least seven days previous to the day of any election.

Lists to be deposited with clerk and posted.
R. S., chap. 4, § 4.

11. On or before the twentieth day of August annually, the selectmen shall deposit in the office of the town clerk, an alphabetical list of voters thus prepared and revised, and post up a similar list in one or more public places in the town.

Names not to be added or stricken out, except as provided.
Ib. § 5.

12. After such lists are thus prepared, deposited with the clerk, and posted up, the selectmen shall not add thereto, nor strike therefrom, the name of any person, except in open session on one of the days prescribed by law for receiving evidence of the qualifications of voters; nor shall they strike from said list the name of any person residing in the town, without notice first given to him that his right to vote is questioned, and an opportunity for a hearing on one of such days.

Names may be added at regular session on evidence.

But at any regular session for receiving such evidence, the selectmen shall place on the list of voters, the name of every person known by, or proved to them to be so qualified, whether he applies therefor or not.

13. When a person of foreign birth exhibits papers of naturalization, issued to him in due form by a court having jurisdiction, to the selectmen of his town, if satisfied of their genuineness, and that such person is entitled to vote, they shall approve such papers by a written indorsement thereon, with the date thereof, signed by one of them; register in a book kept for that purpose, the name of the person, the date of the papers, the date of approval, and the name of the court by which they were issued; cause the name of such person to be entered on the list of voters; and continue his name on the successive lists so long as he continues to reside there and is in other respects qualified to vote. If they are of opinion, that such papers are not genuine, or were not issued to the person presenting them, or that he is not for other cause a legal voter, they shall not approve them or perform the other acts required; but he shall not, by their refusal to approve his papers, or to enter his name, be deprived of his right to vote, upon satisfactory proof of it.

Selectmen, duties respecting papers of naturalization.
Ib. § 6.

14. The selectmen of every town, by their warrant, shall cause the inhabitants thereof, qualified by the constitution, to be notified and warned, seven days at least before the second Monday of September, annually, to meet at some suitable place to be designated in said warrant, to give in their votes for governor, senators and representatives as the constitution requires, and such meeting shall be warned in the manner legally established for warning other town meetings therein.

Mode of warning meetings for election of governor, &c.
Ib. § 14.

15. No such meeting shall be opened before ten o'clock in the forenoon on the day of election, unless the number of voters in such town exceeds five hundred; if it does, an earlier and suitable time in the day may be appointed by the selectmen.

Time of opening meeting.
Ib. § 15.

16. At every meeting for the choice of governor, senators, representatives, and other public officers re-

What votes shall be on one list.

R. S., chap. 4, § 20, as amended by Act, March 20, 1863.

quiring the like qualifications in the electors, the selectmen or other officer presiding shall require the electors to give in their votes for the officer or officers to be chosen on one list or ballot, or so many of such officers, as the voter determines to vote for; designating the intended office of each person voted for.

Check list required.

Rules prescribed.

Ib. § 21, as amended by Act, March 10, 1863.

One ballot box only allowed.

17. The selectmen or other officers presiding at any election shall keep and use the check list herein required at the polls during the election of any such officers; and have and use suitable ballot boxes to be furnished at the expense of the town, and no vote shall be received unless delivered by the voter in person, nor until the presiding officer or officers have had an opportunity to be satisfied of his identity, and shall find his name on the list and mark it and ascertain that his vote is single; nor shall more than one ballot box be used for receiving votes at any election at any one time.

Votes to be on white paper without marks.

R. S., chap. 4, § 22.

18. No ballot shall be received at any election of State or town officers, unless in writing or printing upon clean white paper without any distinguishing mark or figures thereon, besides the name of the person voted for, and the offices to be filled, but no vote shall be rejected on this account, after it is received into the ballot box.

When no choice of representative is effected, meeting shall be adjourned one week, and from week to week.

Ib. § 23.

19. When at a town meeting held for the election of representatives to the State legislature, by reason of two or more persons having an equal number of votes, a choice is not effected of any or all the representatives to which the town is entitled, the meeting shall be adjourned to the same day of the week following, and to the same hour and place at which the first meeting was called; and at such adjourned meeting, the voters shall give in their votes for so many representatives as are necessary to make up the number to which said town is entitled; and like adjournments shall be had until the full number is elected.

20. All town meetings, required to be held for the

election of county treasurer, of register of deeds, or of representatives to Congress, or of electors of president and vice-president of the United States, or for the determination of questions expressly submitted to the people by the legislature, as to calling, notifying and conducting them, shall be subject to the regulations made in this chapter for the election of governor, senators, and representatives, unless otherwise provided by law.

Meetings for choice of certain officers, and for determining questions.

Ib. § 24.

21. In order to determine the result of any election by ballot, the number of persons who voted at such election, shall first be ascertained by counting the whole number of separate ballots given in, which shall be distinctly stated, recorded and returned. Blank pieces of paper and votes for persons not eligible to the office shall not be counted as votes, but the number of such blanks and the number and names on ballots for persons not eligible shall be recorded and return made thereof. In case of representatives to Congress, and to the State legislature, registers of deeds, county and State officers, except where a different rule is prescribed in the constitution, the person or persons, not exceeding the number to be voted for at any one time for any such office, having the highest number of votes given at such election shall be declared to be elected. If by reason of two or more of the persons having the highest number of votes, receiving an equal number, the election of the requisite number of officers cannot be declared, without declaring more than the requisite number elected, no one of those having an equal number of votes shall be declared to be elected. In all other cases no person shall be deemed or declared to be elected, who has not received a majority of the whole number of votes counted as aforesaid; and if a number greater than is required to be chosen receive a majority of the whole number of votes so given, the number so required, of those who have the greatest excess in votes over such majority, shall be declared to be elected.

Result of ballotings, how ascertained.

Ib. § 25.

If the number to be elected cannot be so completed by reason of any two or more of such persons having received an equal number of votes, the persons having such equal number shall be declared not elected.

Clerk to transmit returns of votes to secretary of State.

Ib. § 26.

22. The clerk of each town shall deliver or cause to be delivered at the office of the secretary of State, the returns of votes given in his town, for governor, senators, representatives to the legislature, representatives to Congress, electors of president and vice-president of the United States, and for county officers, within thirty days next succeeding any meeting for their election, or shall deposit them, post paid, in some post office, directed to the secretary of State, within fourteen days after such meeting, to be transmitted by mail; and shall also forward, as soon as practicable, to such office a statement attested by him of the number of votes for said several officers, given at such election in his town, which shall be opened and filed by the secretary, and kept for the examination of the public.

County attorney to be notified if return not received.

His duty.

Ib. § 27.

23. If any such return is not received by the secretary of State within thirty days next after such meeting, he shall forthwith notify the county attorney of the county in which such town is situated, who shall give immediate notice thereof to the clerk of such town, and unless he receives satisfactory evidence, that said clerk has complied with the requirements of the preceding section, he shall prosecute for the penalty hereinafter provided.

Loss of returns, how supplied.

Ib. § 28.

24. When any such original return is in any way lost or destroyed, the selectmen and clerk of such town, on receiving information of such loss or destruction, shall forthwith cause a copy of the record of the meeting at which such vote was given, to be made with their certificate upon the same sheet, that it is a true copy of the record, that it truly exhibits the names of all persons voted for, for the offices designated, and the number of votes given for each at such meeting, and that said copy contains all the facts stated in the original return.

25. The selectmen and town clerk, who were present at the meeting and signed the original return, shall sign the certificate mentioned in the preceding section, designating their office against their names as in the original return, and make oath that said copy and certificate are true, before some justice of the peace of the county, who shall make certificate of such oath on the same paper.

Oath to be made to copy of record.

Ib. § 29.

26. Such copy and certificate shall then be sealed up, and directed to the secretary of State, with the nature of the contents written on the outside; and the clerk of such town shall cause the same to be delivered into the office of the secretary of State, as soon as may be.

Certificate, how sealed and returned.

Ib. § 30.

27. When the selectmen of any town, not classed with others as a representative district, by any means have knowledge that the seat of a representative thereof has been vacated by death, resignation, or otherwise, they shall forthwith issue their warrant, giving at least seven days notice, for a meeting of the electors of said town to fill such vacancy; and at such meeting the like proceedings shall be had, as at any meeting held on the second Monday in September for the like purpose.

Vacancies how filled in towns not classed for representatives.

Ib. § 31.

28. The clerks of towns shall preserve the check lists used at the September elections, for one year thereafter without alteration, and shall furnish to any person an exact and certified copy thereof within twenty days after demand and the payment or tender of the legal charges therefor, under the penalty provided in section forty-eight of chapter four of the revised statutes.

Check lists to be preserved by clerks of towns and to furnish certified copies.

Act, March 8, 1864, § 1.

29. The ballot boxes used at elections, shall be covered at the top with only a slide opening, and such slide shall not be opened till the name of the person offering his vote, is found and checked on the list, and then shall be shut till another voter presents himself, and his name is found and checked; and if the presiding officer or officers do not comply with these requirements, they shall be subject to the penalties provided in section forty-eight of chapter four of the revised statutes.

Ballot boxes, how constructed and used.

Votes, how received.

Officers, duties of.

Ib. § 2.

Penalties in certain cases.

— how recovered.

Ib. § 3.

30. Any penalty provided for in the two preceding sections hereof or in said chapter four of the revised statutes, in case the treasurer refuses or neglects for ten days after written request of any voter to commence a suit therefor, may be recovered by said voter in a suit in his own name to the same uses as specified in said chapter four.

Electors in cities to meet in wards.

R. S., chap. 4, § 33.

Warden to preside.

31. For all the purposes mentioned in chapter four, sections fourteen and twenty-four, of the revised statutes, the inhabitants of cities shall meet as the constitution requires, in ward meetings, to be notified and warned, as town meetings for similar purposes are. The warden shall preside; the clerk shall make such record as the constitution requires; and the city constables shall preserve order.

Warden pro tempore may be chosen.

Ib. § 35.

32. If the warden is absent from any such meeting, or refuses or neglects to preside, a warden pro tempore shall be chosen, and during such choice the ward clerk shall preside; and the warden pro tempore accepting the trust, shall be duly sworn, and have the power and perform the duties of warden of such meeting, and be liable to like penalties.

In cities, names of representatives on same lists as other officers.

R. S., chap. 4, § 37.

33. In voting for representatives to the State legislature in the wards of a city, the names shall be on the same ballot with the other officers to be chosen at the meeting by voters of like qualifications, unless the board of aldermen in their warrant notifying the meeting require a separate ballot or ballots, which they may do.

If no choice, further meetings.

Ib. § 38.

34. When a choice of any such representative is not effected, the aldermen shall call new meetings of the wards for the purpose, to be held at the same time, within two weeks after any former meeting; and the like proceedings shall be had at such meetings, as at the first, until a choice is effected.

35. In every city, the aldermen shall be in session on

each day of election when a list of voters is required, from nine o'clock forenoon to one o'clock afternoon, to hear and decide on the applications of persons claiming the right to vote; and on satisfactory evidence produced, they shall deliver to each such person a written paper by them signed, directed to the proper warden, requiring him to enter the name of such person on his list; and it shall be entered, and his vote received. For the purposes of this and the preceding section, three aldermen shall be a quorum. Notice of the times and places of all sessions, required by this and the preceding section, shall be given in the warrant for calling ward meetings. In all elections in cities, the polls shall be open until four o'clock afternoon and then be closed.

Aldermen, when to be in session to receive application of persons claiming a right to vote.

Three to be a quorum.

Notice of sessions to be given in warrant.

Polls to be closed at four o'clock.

Ib. § 40.

36. No qualified elector who has removed his residence from one ward to another in any city, within thirty days next preceding any election, shall vote at such election in the ward to which he has removed, but his name may be placed on the check list of the ward from which he has removed, as aforesaid, and he may vote therein.

Voting in wards regulated.

Act, April 4, 1859.

37. At the annual election for the choice of mayor and aldermen in the several cities of this State, the qualified electors in each ward shall by written ballot elect a warden and clerk, who shall enter on the duties of their respective offices on the Monday next following their election, and shall hold their offices for one year therefrom, and until others shall have been chosen and qualified in their places.

Wardens and clerks in cities, how elected.

— term of office of.

Act, March 20, 1863, § 1.

38. If any selectman, or other town, city, or plantation officer, or any such officer chosen pro tempore, wilfully neglects or refuses to perform any of the duties required of him, or wilfully does, authorizes, or permits to be done, any thing prohibited by the constitution or by law, he shall for each offense, forfeit not less than fifty, nor more than five hundred dollars, and be imprisoned in jail, not more than nine, nor less than three months, except where otherwise expressly provided.

Penalty for neglect to perform duties required of selectmen.

R. S., chap. 4, § 48.

10 Maine, 109.

Penalty for neglect of municipal officers to issue warrants for meetings for choice of officers.

39. If the aldermen of cities, selectmen of towns, or assessors of plantations neglect to issue their warrant as required by law for a meeting for the choice of State or county officers, representatives to the legislature, or to Congress, or of electors of president and vice-president of the United States, they shall each forfeit fifty dollars to their city, town, or plantation, to be recovered in an action of debt by the treasurer thereof, or by any citizen thereof when said treasurer is a member of the delinquent board.

Penalty how recovered, and by whom.

Ib. § 49.

Penalty for neglect of constable to summon voters.

40. If any constable or other person legally required to summon the voters of a city, town, or plantation to assemble at any meeting for the choice of any officers mentioned in the preceding section, neglect to do so, or to make due return of the warrant therefor, he shall forfeit twenty-five dollars to his city, town, or plantation for each offense, to be recovered as provided in the preceding section; but if he wilfully neglects or refuses to do so, he shall forfeit not less than fifty, nor more than two hundred dollars, half to the State and half to the prosecutor, to be recovered by indictment.

Penalty for wilful neglect to be recovered by indictment.

Ib. § 50.

Penalty for neglect to deposit and post lists.

Ib. chap. 4, § 51.

41. If the selectmen of a town or assessors of a plantation wilfully neglect to deposit a list of the voters with the town or plantation clerk, and to post up such lists, as are herein before required, they shall each forfeit not less than fifty, nor more than one hundred dollars; and for each day's neglect after the twentieth day of August, and until the election then next ensuing, they shall each forfeit thirty dollars.

Penalty for neglect to keep check lists, or to reject illegal votes.

Ib. § 52.

42. If such selectmen or assessors wilfully neglect or refuse to keep and use a check list, as provided in section twenty-one, chapter four, of the revised statutes, or wilfully receive any vote prohibited by section twenty-two, they shall each forfeit not less than fifty, nor more than one hundred dollars.

Penalties, how recoverable.

Ib. § 53.

43. The penalties in the two preceding sections may be recovered in an action of debt, in the name and to the

use of the town where the offense is committed, to be commenced and prosecuted to final judgment at the request of any voter therein, by the treasurer, unless he is one of the delinquent officers, and in that case, by one of the constables.

44. If any municipal officer strikes from the list of voters, after it is prepared and posted, the name of any person residing in the town, without the notice and opportunity for hearing provided by law, he shall forfeit not less than twenty, nor more than one hundred dollars, to be recovered in an action on the case by the person whose name was struck out.

Penalty for municipal officer striking names from list without notice.
Ib. § 54.

45. If any person wrongfully alters, erases, or mutilates any name on a list of voters, or fraudulently votes in the name of another, or under an assumed name, he shall forfeit the sum named in the preceding section, half to the use of the prosecutor, and half to the State, and be imprisoned not more than six months in jail.

Penalty for altering, erasing, or mutilating names on the check list, and for voting in the name of another.
Ib. § 55.

46. If any selectman or other officer of a city, town, or plantation, or any such officer chosen *pro tempore* wilfully neglects or refuses to perform the duties required by sections twenty-eight, twenty-nine and thirty of chapter four of the revised statutes, on notice of the loss and destruction of any return therein described, he shall forfeit not less than one hundred, nor more than five hundred dollars.

Penalty for neglecting to supply lost return.
Ib. § 56.

47. Any such selectman or other officer, *permanent* or *pro tempore*, who in such case makes a false certificate and makes oath to its truth, shall suffer the punishment provided against the crime of perjury, and be disqualified from holding any office under the constitution and laws of the State for ten years.

Penalty for making false certificate.
Ib. § 57.

48. If a person, to whom the returns of votes of any city, town, or plantation, for governor, senators, or representatives in Congress, are entrusted by the clerk thereof to be forwarded to the office of the secretary of State,

Penalty for neglect of persons to whom returns are entrusted to deliver them.
Ib. § 58.

wilfully neglects to use all proper means for their delivery within the time required, he shall forfeit not less than one hundred, nor more than five hundred dollars, or be imprisoned in jail not less than two, nor more than six months.

ORDINANCES.

Form of warrants of ward meetings.

Rev. Ord., 1855.

1. The form of warrants for calling meetings of the citizens of the several wards, shall be as follows, viz:

STATE OF MAINE.

[L. S.] CITY OF PORTLAND, SS.

To——— one of the constables of the said city of Portland,

GREETING:

In the name of the State of Maine, you are hereby required to warn and notify the inhabitants of Ward No. ——, in said city of Portland, qualified according to law, to meet at ——, in said Ward, on the ———— of ——— next, being the ——— day of said month, at ten o'clock in the forenoon, then and there to give in their votes for ——.

The polls on such day of election to remain open until four o'clock in the afternoon, when they shall be closed.

You are also required to give notice to said inhabitants, that the aldermen of said city will be in open session at ——— from nine o'clock in the forenoon to one o'clock in the afternoon on each of the three secular days next preceding such day of election, and from three o'clock to five o'clock on the afternoon on the last of said three secular days, for the purpose of receiving evidence of the qualification of voters whose names have not been entered on the lists of qualified voters, in and for the several wards, and for correcting said lists.

Hereof fail not, and have you there then this warrant with your doings thereon.

Given under our hands and seals, at the city of Portland, this —— day of ——, in the year of our Lord one thousand eight hundred and sixty-

MAYOR.

} Aldermen of the city of Portland.

To be served by constables and returned.

Ib.

2. All warrants for calling meetings of the citizens of the several wards which shall be issued by the mayor and

aldermen, shall be served by any constable of the city, who shall make his return on the warrant, stating the manner of notice and the time it was given, and return the same to the wardens of the several wards in said city, on or before the time of meeting of the citizens of said wards, therein specified.

3. The form of warrants for calling meetings of the inhabitants of the said city of Portland, shall be as follows, to wit:

Form of warrant for general meetings.

Ib.

STATE OF MAINE.

[L. S.] CITY OF PORTLAND, SS.

To——— one of the constables of the city of Portland,

GREETING :

Upon the requisition of sixty qualified voters of said city, you are hereby required, in the name of the State of Maine, to warn and notify the inhabitants of said city of Portland qualified to vote in city affairs, to meet at ——— in said city, on ——, the — day of —, at — o'clock in the —— noon, then and there to act upon the following articles, to wit :———

Hereof fail not, and have you there then this warrant, with your doings thereon.

Given under our hands and seals, at the city of Portland, this — day of —, in the year of our Lord ———.

MAYOR.

Aldermen of the city of Portland.

4. All warrants which shall be issued by the mayor and aldermen, for calling meetings of the inhabitants of the city, shall be served by any constable of the city, and returned to the mayor and aldermen on or before the meeting of the citizens therein specified.

To be served by constables and returned.

Ib.

5. It shall be the duty of the mayor and aldermen to fix the time when the poll shall close, as well as the time for opening thereof, in the election of all officers except ward officers, and insert the same in any warrant and notification to the inhabitants, of such election.

Time of opening and closing the polls shall be fixed by the mayor and aldermen, and inserted in the warrant.

Ib.

See CITY CHARTER, sections 8, 11, 12, 13, 14, 15.

EVERGREEN CEMETERY.

[SEE CEMETERIES.]

FERRIES.

STATUTES.

1. County commissioners; license ferries, establish tolls, take bond.
2. May establish them to be supported by towns; penalty for neglect.
3. Penalty for neglect to keep safe boat, and to give prompt attendance.
4. Person injured by neglect or default of ferryman may sue on his bond.
5. No ferry to be established within one mile of a steam or horse ferry.
6. Penalty for keeping a ferry, or transporting, contrary to law.
7. Ice to be leveled and way kept in repair in winter.
8. Penalty for neglect of it; liability for injuries.
9. Licensed ferrymen not to use steam or horse-boats.
10. At steam and horse ferries other boats may be used in times of danger.
11. Obstructions of ferry ways prohibited. Penalty.
12. Piers may be sunk at ferries to guide boats.
13. Property to be appraised on removal of ferryman.

1. County commissioners may license persons to keep ferries at such places and for such times, as are necessary, except where they are otherwise legally established ; may establish tolls for the passage of persons and property ; revoke such licenses at pleasure ; and shall take from the person licensed, a bond to the treasurer of State, with sureties, for the faithful performance of his duties.

County commissioners may license ferries, establish tolls, take bond.
8 Greenl., 365.
R. S., chap. 20, § 1.

2. They may establish ferries at such times and places as are necessary, and fix their tolls. When no person is found to keep them therefor, the towns in which they are established, are to provide a person to be licensed to keep them, and are to pay the expenses, beyond the amount of tolls received, for maintaining them. When established between towns, they are to be maintained by them in such proportions as the commissioners order. For each month's neglect to maintain such ferry or its proportion thereof, a town forfeits forty dollars.

They may establish ferries to be supported by towns; penalty for neglect.
Ib. § 2.

3. Every keeper of a ferry is to keep a suitable and safe boat, or boats, for use on the waters to be passed, and give prompt attendance for passage, according to the regulations established for the ferry. For neglecting to keep such boat, he forfeits twenty dollars, and for neglect of attendance, one dollar, to him who sues therefor in an action of debt ; and is liable in an action on the case to the party injured for his damages.

Penalty for neglect to keep safe boat, and for neglect of attendance.
Ib. § 3.

4. Any one injured in his person or property by the negligence or default of a ferryman, may commence a suit on his bond, in which the proceedings are to be similar to those in actions on the bonds of sheriffs.

A person injured by default of a ferryman may sue bond.
Ib. § 4.

5. When a ferry is established by the legislature to be passed by a steam or horse boat, no other ferry can be established on the same river within one mile above or below it.

Ferry not within one mile of steam or horse ferry.
Ib. § 5.

6. A person, who keeps a ferry contrary to the provisions of sections one and two, or without authority transports passengers or property across any licensed or established ferry for hire, forfeits four dollars for each day

Penalty for keeping a ferry or conveying passengers or property contrary to law.
Ib. § 6.

such ferry is kept, or for each time of transportation, and is also liable to the party injured and keeping the ferry at or near the place, for damages sustained by him, in an action on the case.

Ice to be leveled and way kept in repair in winter.

Ib. § 7.

7. When tidal waters, over which ferries are established, become so frozen that travelers may pass on the ice, the keepers of them are to level the ice and clear and repair the passage way from day to day, so that the same may at all times be safe and convenient for travelers with teams, sleds, and sleighs. Such way for passage may be made from a public landing sufficiently near to be connected with the opposite ferry landing. The commissioners are to fix a reasonable compensation therefor, to be paid from the county treasury. Or they may contract with another person to perform such duties, and give notice thereof to the keeper of the ferry before the river is closed; and during the continuance of such contract the liabilities of the keeper are transferred to the person contracting.

Penalty for neglect and liability for injury.

Ib. § 8.

8. The ferryman, or person so contracting, forfeits ten dollars for each day's neglect to perform such duty, and is liable in an action on the case, to pay damages to any person injured thereby.

Licensed ferrymen not to use horse boats or steam boats.

Ib. § 9.

9. A licensed ferryman, who uses at his ferry a boat propelled by steam or horse power, forfeits his license, and is liable to pay the damages occasioned thereby to any person or corporation.

At horse and steam ferries other boats used in times of danger.

Ib. § 10.

10. Persons required to use, at a ferry, steam or horse boats, when the passage by them is dangerous, may use other safe boats.

Obstructions to ferries prohibited; penalty.

Ib. § 11.

11. Any person, who places a wier or other obstacle, or without necessity, anchors or places a raft, vessel, or water craft, so as to obstruct the ordinary passage way of any boat at a ferry licensed or established, forfeits twenty dollars to the use of the proprietor of the ferry, to be recovered in an action on the case; unless such obstruction was inadvertently made, and removed within thirty

minutes, if practicable, after notice given of its improper position, or unless it was occasioned by hauling into a wharf, pier, landing, or dock, without any unreasonable delay or wilful misconduct.

12. The proprietors of a ferry, to guide their boats, may sink piers above and below and near their ferry ways, on each side of the river, not more than twelve feet in length or breadth, and not so sunk as to injure any wharf or landing, where vessels had previously taken or discharged freights.

Piers may be sunk to guide boats at ferries.
Ib. § 12.

13. Whenever the county commissioners remove a ferryman, they shall appraise the boat and other personal property used in running the ferry, at its fair value, and the person appointed shall purchase the same at said appraisal, if the person removed assents thereto.

Property to be appraised on removal of ferryman.
Act, March 9, 1860, chap. 147.

FINANCE.

ORDINANCES.

Committee on accounts to be appointed.

Duties.

Rev. Ord., 1855, as amended by subsequent ordinances and city charter.

1. There shall be appointed annually, by the city council, a joint committee on accounts, to consist of one on the part of the board of mayor and aldermen, and two on the part of the common council, whose duty it shall be to carefully examine all claims and accounts against the city, when certified by the auditor.

City treasurer's duties.

Ib.

2. It shall be the duty of the city treasurer and collector to collect and receive all rents which may be due to the city, and under the direction of the mayor and aldermen, to seal and execute all leases of city lands or buildings. He shall also receive all fines and penalties which may be paid to him from time to time. He shall proceed without delay to collect all accounts which may be delivered to him for collection, and in any case in

which he is unable to obtain a settlement of an account, he shall report the same to the mayor and aldermen, and follow such directions as they may deem it for the interest of the city to prescribe.

3. It shall be the duty of the committee on accounts to audit the accounts of the city treasurer, and of the auditor, at the close of each financial year, and as much oftener as they may deem expedient; and for this purpose they shall have access to all books and vouchers in their possession or in the possession of the city clerk, or any other officer of the city, and they shall in every case report to the city council the result of their examination.

Committee on accounts to audit the accounts of city treasurer and auditor.

Ib.

4. The city treasurer and collector shall give bond, with sufficient sureties, to the satisfaction of the mayor and aldermen, for the faithful performance of the duties of the said office of the treasurer and collector, and that he will truly and justly account for all moneys that may come into his hands.

City treasurer to give bond.

Ib.

5. The city treasurer shall make up his annual accounts to the first day of April, and the financial year shall begin on the first day of April, and end on the last day of March in each year.

Financial year —accounts to be made to.

Ib.

6. There shall annually be appointed a joint com mittee on finance, to consist of the mayor and two aldermen, on the part of the board of mayor and aldermen, and three members of the common council, whose duty it shall be, under the direction of the city council, to negotiate all loans made on account of the city, and to consider and report on all subjects relating to the finances of the city.

Committee on finance to be appointed.

Ib.

Duties.

7. It shall be the duty of the city clerk, the city marshal, deputy marshals, weighers of hay, and other officers of the city, authorized to collect moneys, to pay over to the city treasurer once in three months all moneys which they shall receive, belonging to the city.

City officers to pay over moneys to the treasurer.

Ib.

Surrender of the certificates of city debt by At. & St. L. R. R. Co.

Ord., June 28, 1864, § 1.

8. Whenever the Atlantic & St. Lawrence Railroad Company or its assigns shall deliver to the city treasurer, to be cancelled, any of the certificates of city debt issued in aid of said company, under the act of February 13th, 1852, together with all the coupons, paid or unpaid, belonging to the same, it shall be the duty of the city treasurer to surrender a corresponding amount of the mortgage bonds of said company, held by the city as collateral for such debt, and the certificates of city debt and coupons so delivered to the city treasurer shall be immediately cancelled by him.

Same subject.

Ib. § 2.

9. If the Atlantic & St. Lawrence Railroad Company, or its assigns, shall deliver to the city treasurer, to be the property of the city, any of the certificates of debt, or bonds of the State of Maine, payable by the State at any time not earlier than 1876, with the unpaid coupons belonging thereto, it shall be the duty of the city treasurer to receive the same and to surrender therefor a corresponding amount of the mortgage bonds of said company, held by the city as collateral for the debt incurred by the city in aid of said company under the act of February 13th, 1852; and such certificates or bonds of the State debt, shall be held by the city treasurer to meet the certificates of the city debt incurred under said act, or may be exchanged for the same, with any holder, whenever it can be done advantageously to the interests of the city, under the direction of the joint standing committee on finance; and in case any certificate of the city debt shall so be received by the city treasurer, he shall immediately cancel the same and the coupons belonging thereto.

Duty of committee on finance.

FIRE.

STATUTES.

1. Powers of fire department of Portland, in whom vested.
2. Towns may prescribe rules for care of engines, &c.
3. Officers chosen have powers of fire wards. Towns liable for acts of officers.
4. Inn-keepers to provide means of escape from fires, when.
5. Time allowed ; penalty for neglect.
6. Officers may demolish buildings, when.
7. Compensation for demolished buildings, when.
8. Larceny at fires.
9. Defective chimneys, &c., may be removed.
10. Lighted pipes, &c., in mills, &c.
11. Penalty for kindling fire on land without consent of owner.
12. " " " " with intent to injure another.
13. Lawful fires to be kindled at suitable time.
14. Penalty for selling, giving, or firing fire-works without license.
15. Towns may prohibit burning of bricks, &c. Penalty.

ORDINANCES.

GENERAL PROVISIONS.

1. Water not to be taken from reservoirs.
2. Bonfires, &c., not to be made. Penalty.
3. Penalty for carrying uncovered fire in the streets.
4. Penalty for discharging fire-arms.
5. Penalty for erecting or using brick-kilns without license.
6. Penalty for false alarm of fire.
7. Penalty for removing fire-ladders from place of deposit.
8. Penalty for setting fire to chimneys, &c.
9. Penalty for persons wearing badges, &c., falsely representing themselves as members of the fire department.

FOR THE GOVERNMENT OF THE FIRE DEPARTMENT.

1. Fire department, how organized. Election.
2. Organization of board of engineers.
3. Powers of engineers.
4. Engineers to cause combustibles to be removed.
5. " to demolish buildings at fires, when.
6. " may suspend companies, &c., when.
7. Engine companies, how composed.
8. Chief engineer, his powers and duties.
9. City council may form engine, hook and ladder, and hose companies, &c.
10. Foremen and clerks of companies; how chosen. Companies may make rules.
11. Meetings of companies.
12. Fines for absence.
13. Pay of members of companies.
14. Fires in adjoining towns.
15. Foreman, duties of.
16. Clerk, duties of.
17. Enginemen, their election and duties.
18. " their special duty to preserve engines, &c.
19. Repeal of prior ordinances, except, &c.
20. Compensation of officers and members.
21. " when paid.

RULES AND REGULATIONS OF ENGINEERS.

1. Orders of chief engineer, how given.
2. Duty of engineers.
3. Officers to report, on arrival at fire, for orders.
4. Of moving engines at fires.
5. Duties of foreman.
6. Same subject.
7. Duties of drivers of engines.
8. Absent members may be discharged, when.
9. Companies, &c., doing special duty.
10. Members leaving department, city property must be returned.
11. Board of engineers may temporarily make new regulations.
12. Chief engineer to furnish copies of ordinances, &c., to members, &c.

STATUTES.

1. All powers relating to the fire department are vested by the city charter, in the mayor and aldermen, and common council of the city of Portland, to be exercised by concurrent vote, each board to have a negative on the other.

Powers of fire department, in whom vested.

City charter, § 5.

2. Any city or town in this State, which has provided, or may hereafter provide, fire engines, hose, ladders, or other apparatus for the extinguishment of fires, or the preservation of life or property from destruction at fires, may by ordinances, or by-laws, passed by the city council of such city, or the inhabitants of such town, from time to time prescribe rules and regulations for the care and management of such apparatus in all particulars, for the employment, compensation and discharge of men for working the same, whether engine men or other persons; and for the appointment of officers to govern such men when on duty, and to take charge of such apparatus, as well as to prescribe the style, rank, powers and duties of such officers.

Towns may prescribe rules for care and management of fire engines and apparatus.

Act, March 5, 1860, § 1.

—for employment of men.

—for appointment of officers.

3. The engineers, or other officers chosen by any city or town under the provisions of any such ordinance or by-law, shall, within the limit of their respective precincts, have and exercise in addition to the powers and duties conferred upon them by such ordinance or by-law, all the powers and duties of fire-wards as defined in the chapter to which this is additional, except so far as the same may be limited or restrained by the provisions of the ordinance or by-law under which they may be chosen; and such cities and towns shall be responsible for the acts or orders of their said officers, to the same extent and in the same manner as towns are now by law liable for the acts or orders of fire-wards in similar cases.

Officers so chosen have powers of fire wards.

Towns liable for acts of officers.

Ib. § 2.

4. The aldermen of any city and the selectmen of any town are hereby authorized, whenever they deem it necessary, to require the owner, proprietor or keeper of any

Innkeepers to provide means of escape from fires, when required.

Act, March 24, 1858, § 1.

inn or public house, where strangers or travelers are lodged, within their respective cities and towns, to provide suitable and sufficient ladders and fire-escapes from the different stories of such inn or public house, easily accessible to each lodger in case of fire.

Time allowed.

5. If such aldermen or selectmen shall give notice to any such owner, proprietor or keeper, to provide such suitable and sufficient ladders and fire-escapes, sixty days shall be allowed to provide the same; but any such owner, proprietor or keeper, neglecting to provide the same after the expiration of said sixty days, shall forfeit and pay not less than fifty, nor more than three hundred dollars, for each and every month he shall continue so to neglect; to be recovered in an action of debt in the name and to the use of the inhabitants of said town or city.

Penalty for neglect.

Ib. § 2.

Officers appointed under special laws, may demolish buildings, when.

R. S., chap. 26, § 8, Act, 1831, chap. 134, establishing fire department of Portland.

6. The chief engineer, engineers, fire-wards, and other officers appointed for particular localities under the provisions of special laws, shall have the same power as to pulling down or demolishing any building to prevent the spreading of fires, and as to other things affecting the extinguishment thereof, as fire-wards now have by law; and the town to which they belong shall be liable to pay such compensation for damages consequent upon their acts, as other towns are liable to pay for similar damages; and the members of the fire department in such localities shall enjoy all the privileges, and be liable to all the duties of other firemen in the State; but nothing herein shall be construed to control the manner of their election.

Compensation for building demolished.

Exception.

Persons dissatisfied may apply to county commissioners.

7. If the pulling down or demolishing any building, except that in which the fire originated, is the means of stopping the fire, or if the fire is stopped before it comes to the same, then the owner of such building shall be entitled to a reasonable compensation therefor from the town; and if such town fails to make such compensation to his satisfaction, he may apply to the county commissioners at their next session; and after due notice to the

parties, they may confirm the doings of the town in estimating the amount of compensation, or in raising the money and paying the same, or alter them, as they judge proper, award costs to the prevailing party, and issue their warrant of distress to carry their judgment into effect.

Their powers. R. S., chap. 26. § 9.

8. If any person steals, carries away, or conceals any property not his own, at a fire, or exposed by reason thereof, and does not give notice of it to the owner or one of the fire-wards, he shall be deemed guilty of larceny and punished accordingly.

Plundering at fires declared larceny. Ib. § 10.

9. When any chimney, stove, stove-pipe, oven, furnace, boiler, or appurtenances thereto are defective, out of repair, or so placed in any building as to endanger it or any other building by communicating fire thereto, the municipal officers on complaint of any fire-ward, or other citizen, being satisfied by examination or other proof that such complaint is well founded, shall give written notice to the owner or occupier of such building, and if he unnecessarily neglects for three days to remove or repair the same effectually, he shall forfeit not less than ten, nor more than one hundred dollars.

Municipal officers to direct defective chimneys to be removed or repaired, under a penalty. Ib. § 12.

10. No person shall enter any mill, factory, machine shop, ship yard, covered bridge, stable or other building, having with him a lighted pipe or cigar, or shall light or smoke any pipe or cigar therein, under a penalty of five dollars, if a notice in plain, legible characters is kept up in a conspicuous position over or near each principal entrance to such building or place, that no smoking is allowed therein; and if any person defaces, removes, or destroys any such notice, he shall forfeit ten dollars.

Penalty for lighting or smoking pipe or cigar in mills, &c. Ib. § 13.

11. If any person kindles a fire by the use of fire arms in hunting or fishing, or by any other means, on land not his own, without consent of the owner, he shall forfeit ten dollars; and if such fire spreads and does any damage to the property of others, he shall forfeit a sum not less

Penalty for kindling fire on land without consent of owner, &c. Ib. § 14.

than ten, nor more than five hundred dollars and costs, according to the aggravation of the offense; and in either case, shall stand committed till the fine and costs are paid.

Penalty for kindling fire with intent to injure another, &c.

Ib. § 15.

12. If any person with intent to injure another, kindles or causes to be kindled a fire on his own or another's land, and thereby the property of any other person is injured or destroyed, he shall be punished by a fine of not less than twenty, nor more than one thousand dollars, or by imprisonment not less than three months, nor more than three years, according to the aggravation of the offense.

Lawful fires to be kindled at suitable time, &c.

Ib. § 16.

13. Whoever for a lawful purpose kindles a fire on his own land, shall do so at a suitable time and in a careful and prudent manner; and shall be liable, in an action on the case, to any person injured by his failure to comply with this provision.

Penalty for selling, giving away, or firing fire works without license.

R. S., chap. 128, § 2.

14. Whoever sells, offers for sale, or gives away any crackers, squibs, rockets, or other fire works, or fires or throws the same in any town, without the license of the municipal officers thereof, shall be punished by fine not exceeding ten dollars, to the use of such town.

Burning bricks in parts of a town prohibited by vote; nuisances.

R. S., chap. 17, § 5.

15. A town, at its annual meeting, may prohibit the burning of bricks, or the erecting of brick kilns within such parts thereof as they deem for the safety of the citizens or their property. And if any person, by himself or others, violates such prohibition, the municipal officers shall cause said bricks or brick kiln to be forthwith removed, at the expense of the owner thereof; and the offender shall be liable to a fine not exceeding two hundred dollars to the use of said town.

ORDINANCES.

GENERAL PROVISIONS.

1. If any person shall take any water from any reservoir or well where there is no pump, belonging to the city, for any purpose whatever, except for the extinguishment of fires or the use of the fire department, without first having obtained permission in writing from the mayor, he shall pay for each offense not less than five nor more than twenty dollars.

Water not to be taken from reservoirs.

Rev. Ord., 1855, as amended by Ord., Feb. 17, 1862.

No person, when authorized by the mayor and aldermen to encumber any street with materials for building, or under any circumstances, shall deposit any such materials or rubbish of any kind upon any city reservoir, or in any such manner as to interfere with the convenient use of such reservoir, under a penalty of not less than twenty dollars nor exceeding fifty dollars for each offense. If any such reservoir shall be so obstructed, the chief engineer shall at once cause the obstructions to be removed at the expense of the person or persons making such obstructions.

Ord., Aug. 10, 1867, § § 1, 2.

2. If any person shall make any bonfire, or other fire in any of the streets, squares, commons, lanes, or alleys, or on any wharf within the city, without the license of the mayor and aldermen, he shall be punished by a fine not exceeding twenty dollars.

Bonfires, &c., not to be made.

Rev. Ord., 1855.

Penalty.

3. No person shall carry fire from any house or place to any other house or place in the city, except in some covered pan or vessel, so as to secure the fire from wind and from being scattered by the way, under a penalty of not less than three dollars for each offense.

Penalty for carrying fire, except, &c.

Ib.

4. No person shall fire or discharge any gun, fowling piece, or fire arms within the limits of the city of Portland under a penalty for every such offense of not less than one nor more than twenty dollars; *provided*, however, that this section shall not apply to the use of such weapons at any

Penalty for discharging fire-arms.

Proviso.

Ib.

military exercise or review, or in the lawful defense of the person, family, or property of any citizen.

Penalty for erecting or using brick kilns without license. Ib.

5. No person shall erect, make, or fire, or cause to be erected, made, or fired, within any part of the city, any brick kiln or lime kiln, without license of the mayor in writing, designating the place of such kiln, under a penalty of not less than five nor more than twenty dollars, and a like sum for every week he shall continue such kiln, after notice to remove the same.

Penalty for false alarms. Ib., as amended by Ord., May 18, 1867.

6. If any person shall wilfully or maliciously give, or cause to be given, a false alarm or cry of fire by outcry or ringing an alarm bell, or striking an alarm at any box of the fire telegraph, he shall pay for each offense a penalty not less than twenty nor more than fifty dollars.

Penalty for removing ladders from places of deposit, except, &c. Ord., 1855.

7. If any person shall remove any ladder provided by the city to be used at fires, from the place of deposit, for any purpose but that of assisting in the extinguishment of fire, such person shall pay for each offense a sum not less than five nor more than ten dollars.

Burning chimneys, &c.

8. If any chimney, stove-pipe, or flue shall take or be set on fire, the owner or occupant of the building or tenement to which such chimney, stove-pipe, or flue appertains, shall forfeit and pay the penalty of two dollars for each offense; *Provided*, however, that any person may lawfully burn out or set fire to his chimney, stove-pipe, or flue, at any time between sunrise and noon, if the roofs of his own, and the buildings contiguous are thoroughly wet with rain, or covered with snow.

Proviso. Ib.

Persons not members of department prohibited from wearing badges or insignia. Penalty for so doing. Ord., July 30, 1858, § 5.

9. If any person not a member of the fire department shall, when the department is on duty, wear any badge or other insignia, representing himself as a member of the fire department, he shall, upon complaint of any engineer or officer of the fire department, pay a penalty of not less than two nor more than five dollars for each offense.

FOR THE GOVERNMENT OF THE FIRE DEPARTMENT.

1. The fire department shall consist of a chief engineer, four assistant engineers, and as many firemen, to be divided into companies, as the city council shall, from time to time, deem expedient. And the election of said engineers shall take place on the second Monday in March, annually; (but vacancies may be filled at any time;) and the said chief and other engineers shall, on their appointment, receive a written or printed certificate or warrant in the following words, viz:— Fire department, how organized. Election. Ord., Aug., 14, 1866, § 1.

"This certifies, that ——— ——— is appointed an engineer (or chief engineer,) of the fire department of the city of Portland, and is clothed with all the powers, and entitled to all the immunities belonging to said office.

Given under my hand this —— day of —— A. D. 18 .

——— ——— Mayor.

——— ——— City Clerk."

The respective rank of the engineers shall be determined by the city council; and the city council may at any time remove from office the chief engineer, or any of the other engineers, and may discharge all of them, if the interests of the city require such removal or discharge. Rank of engineers, how determined.

2. The engineers so appointed shall meet and organize; a majority shall form a quorum; in the absence of the chief, the engineer next in rank present, shall be the presiding officer, and shall at all other times in his absence perform his duties. They may appoint a secretary and other officers, and make such rules and regulations for their own government as they may deem expedient, subject to the approval of the city council. Organization of board of engineers. Ib. § 2.

3. The engineers shall, at all times, have the superintendence and control of all buildings, furniture and apparatus used for the purposes of the department, over the officers and members of the several companies attached to the department, and over all persons present at fires. And they may make such rules and regulations for the Power of engineers. Ib. § 3.

11

government of the department, and for the extinguishment of fires as they may, from time to time, deem expedient; the same not being repugnant to the laws of the State, and being subject to the approval of the city council.

To cause combustibles to be removed.

Ib. § 4.

4. It shall be the duty of the engineers, at such times as they may deem expedient, to examine or cause to be examined, premises where fire is at any time used, and where danger is apprehended therefrom; to examine into all places where shavings or combustible materials, or where ashes may be collected or deposited, and to direct such alterations, repairs, or removal to be made in such case as may be required, whenever in the opinion of any two of the engineers they may be dangerous to the security of the city from fire. And in case of the neglect or refusal of the owner or occupant of such building to make, or commence to make such alteration, repair, or removal, within forty-eight hours after notice, said engineers may cause the same to be done at the expense of said owner or occupant; and if such owner or occupant shall neglect or refuse to pay such expense, on demand of said engineers, he or she shall forfeit and pay not less than one nor more than thirty dollars, to be determined by the city council. And for such services the engineers shall receive such compensation as the city council may direct.

To demolish buildings at fires, when.

Ib. § 5.

5. Whenever it shall be determined at any fire, by any three or more engineers, one of whom shall be the chief engineer, (if present, or in his absence, the engineer next in rank who may be present,) or a majority of any greater number who may be present at such consultation, to be necessary to pull down or otherwise demolish any building, the same may be done by their joint orders. And they shall have the sole and absolute control of all streets, lanes, sidewalks and squares in the vicinity of such fire; and may close up or exclude persons or vehicles from passage through such places, for such length of time as may be necessary for the preservation of order and the extinguishment of fires.

6. A majority of the board of engineers shall have full power to suspend from duty any company that shall wilfully neglect or refuse to perform their duty, or shall be guilty of disorderly conduct, or of disobedience to the orders of either of the engineers, or for violation of any of the rules and regulations of the department. They shall also have full power at any time to suspend (for sufficient cause) any officer or member of the department, and whenever a company, officer or member of the department shall be thus suspended, they shall report the facts of the case to the city council for final action, unless they shall have reinstated such company, officer or member prior to the next meeting of the city council.

Board of engineers may suspend companies and officers for improper conduct.

Ib. § 6.

7. Engine companies shall consist of a foreman, clerk, engineman, fireman, and as many hosemen as the city council and board of engineers shall deem sufficient. And hook and ladder and hose companies shall consist of a foreman, clerk and steward, and as many hook and ladder men and hosemen as the city council and board of engineers shall deem sufficient.

Engine company, how composed.

Ib. § 7.

8. The chief engineer shall have control of all the engineers and other persons attached to the fire department; and shall direct all proper measures for the extinguishment of fires, protection of property, preservation of order, and observance of the rules and regulations. And it shall be the duty of said chief engineer to examine, or cause to be examined, the condition of the apparatus and buildings used by the department, and of the companies attached thereto, as often as circumstances may render it expedient, or whenever directed by the city council or the committee on fire department; and annually to report the same to the city council, and oftener if thereto requested: Also to cause a full description of the same, together with the name and age of the officers and members of the department, to be published annually, in such manner as the city council shall direct. And whenever the apparatus

Power and duties of chief engineer.

Ib. § 8.

used by the department requires repairs, additions or alterations, the chief engineer, under the direction of the committee on fire department shall cause the same to be made; and annually to report an account of the loss by fires, as near as can be ascertained, together with the names of the owners and occupants. He shall have the control of all reservoirs, and superintend the construction and repairs of the same under the direction of the committee on fire department, and visit the stores or shops of all licensed dealers in gunpowder, at such times as he may deem expedient, to see that the rules and regulations established by the mayor and aldermen in relation to gunpowder are complied with, and to prosecute all violations of the same in accordance with section 11 of said rules and regulations.

City council may form engine, hook and ladder, and hose companies, &c.

Ib. § 9.

9. As many engine, hook and ladder and hose companies shall, from time to time, be formed by the city council as they may deem expedient; the selection of members and enginemen for new companies to be made by the board of engineers, subject to the approval of the city council: And no person under the age of twenty-one years, shall be admitted a member of the department.

Foreman and clerk, how chosen.

Ib. § 10.

10. The foreman and clerk as provided for in section seven, shall be nominated by the members of the several companies, at meetings held on the first Monday of January annually, or at an adjournment of the same, to be held within one week of the annual meeting, and their names sent to the board of engineers; and being approved by them shall be sent to the city council for their approval. If approved, they shall each receive a certificate of appointment, signed by the mayor and city clerk, and shall hold their offices until removed or others are appointed in their places; and if rejected by the board of engineers other persons shall be nominated as aforesaid, and any company failing to nominate officers at their annual meeting, or an

adjournment thereof, the board of engineers shall appoint such officers as they may deem expedient, subject to the approval of the city council. The several companies may make rules and regulations for the internal government of their companies, subject to the approval of the board of engineers, a copy of which shall be deposited with said board.

Companies may make rules, &c.

11. On the first Monday evening of every month, (and no oftener except by order or permission of the chief or board of engineers or as provided in section 10,) the companies shall meet for the transaction of business; and whenever the chief or board of engineers shall consider it necessary, the companies shall meet for the purpose of working their respective apparatus, and in no case shall buildings used by them be occupied as places of general resort or rendezvous.

Monthly and other meetings of companies.

Ib. § 11.

12. The companies respectively shall charge to members a fine of fifty cents for non-attendance at any fire, and fifteen cents for non-attendance at any meeting of the company; and said fines shall be deducted by the city treasurer from the pay of each member, and refunded to the several companies.

Fines for absence.

Ib. § 12.

13. There shall be paid, semi-annually, in July and January, to each member of the respective companies, (except enginemen who may be paid oftener if expedient,) such sums as the city council may, from time to time, determine. And in case of the temporary absence of any member from the city, or inability to pérform his duties in consequence of sickness, he shall provide a substitute, who shall be at least twenty-one years of age, whose name he shall return to the foreman of the company for approval; failing in which, he shall be subject to all deductions that may accrue for his absence.

Pay of members of companies.

Ib. § 13.

14. When a fire occurs in any of the adjoining towns, not more than one engine shall be allowed by the chief engineer to go more than one-half mile beyond the limits

Fires in adjoining towns.

Ib. § 14.

of the city; but when a fire occurs within the above named limits, the chief engineer shall have discretionary power to send two engines.

Duties of foremen.

Ib. § 15.

15. The foremen shall certify to the correctness of the pay rolls, and keep, or cause to be kept, by the clerks of their respective companies, fair and exact rolls, specifying the time of the admission and discharge of each member, an account of all city property intrusted to their care, and fair records of the proceedings of the companies, in a book provided for that purpose by the city; which rolls or record books are always to be subject to the order of the board of engineers.

Duties of clerks.

Ib. § 16.

16. It shall be the duty of the clerks of each of the companies to report to the board of engineers, immediately after the annual meeting, the names of the newly nominated officers, also to return to the board of engineers, on the first day of July and January, a true and accurate list of the members of their respective companies, the length of time each has served; if he had a substitute, and how often; together with the amount of fines, (if any,) which are due from each member; and these returns, if approved by the board of engineers, shall be transmitted by them to the city treasurer. They shall also, within seven days after their monthly meetings, send to the board of engineers, the name of every person admitted to their respective companies at said meetings, and these persons, if approved, shall sign the following statement:

"The undersigned having been appointed members of the Portland Fire Department, hereby signify our agreement to abide by all the ordinances and rules and regulations of the city council and board of engineers. Any officer or member who shall neglect or refuse to sign the same, shall not be a member of said company, or entitled to any compensation whatever."

Election of enginemen.

17. The enginemen shall be elected annually by the city council, on the 2d Monday in March, but vacancies may be filled at any time. They shall, at all times, be in or about the engine house, and have charge of the engines

and all other city property committed to their care, and be held strictly responsible for its good condition for immediate service. They shall keep the engines and houses clean, and in good order, and perform all such other duties as may be required of them by the chief engineer. They shall also have the appointing of firemen from their companies, whose duty it shall be to assist them in the working of the engines, and to perform such other duties as may be required of them.

Their duties.

Ib. § 17.

18. It shall be the special duty of the enginemen to preserve their engines from injury as much as possible; to expose them to no unnecessary hazard; to cause them to be worked with judgment and skill, and not subject them to harsh treatment.

Their special duty to preserve engines from injury.

Ib. § 18.

19. All ordinances, rules and regulations, or amendments thereto, relating to the fire department, approved prior to the passage of this ordinance (excepting "an ordinance fixing the compensation of the officers and members of the fire department," approved July 13, 1864,) are hereby repealed; and this ordinance shall take effect and be in force from and after its approval by the mayor. [See sections 20 and 21, following.]

Repeal of ordinances, except &c.

Ib. § 19.

20. The annual compensation of the officers and members of the several fire engine and hook and ladder companies shall be as follows, viz;

Compensation of officers and members.

Ord., July 13, 1864, § 1.

To the first director of each company forty dollars. To the second director of each company thirty-five dollars. To the clerk of each company forty dollars. To the steward of each company forty dollars. To the fireman of each steam fire engine company forty dollars. To each member of the respective companies, other than the officers aforesaid, not exceeding thirty-six for each hand engine company, eleven for each steam fire engine company, and seventeen for each hook and ladder company, thirty dollars.

When paid.
Ib. § 2.

21. Said sums shall be paid to each officer and member individually, in semi-annual payments, during the months of January and July in each year for the six months next preceding said months of January and July: *Provided however*, that the said officers and members shall have faithfully performed their duties and complied with all orders, rules and regulations prescribed or established by the mayor and aldermen or board of engineers.

RULES AND REGULATIONS OF THE BOARD OF ENGINEERS, ADOPTED BY THE CITY COUNCIL, AUGUST 14, 1866.

Orders of chief engineer, how given.

ARTICLE 1. The orders of the chief engineer to the several companies of the department, will be communicated to the commanding officers, if convenient, who shall render prompt obedience thereto. When an engineer is charged with an order for any company, he will call the number in a distinct voice, which shall be responded to by any officer present, who shall immediately obey such order, without waiting to communicate with his superior, unless it can be done without delay. All members shall obey any order from an engineer.

Duty of engineers.

2. The engineers are to keep a watchful eye upon all parts of the fire, and report to the chief immediately all changes in the aspect of the conflagration, and these reports shall be as definite as possible, and the facts upon which they are supposed to be founded, should always be well ascertained. For these purposes the chief of the department will station himself at some point where the scene of operations can be overlooked, which shall be designated in the night time by a red signal lantern. It will in all cases be considered the duty of the assistant engineers to answer promptly the call of the chief engineer. And in case of disturbance at a fire, by any rude or riotous person, any engineer who may observe it, shall order the offender into the custody of the police, to be proceeded against by law.

3. In case of fire not more than one line of hose shall be run out without permission from an engineer. The officers in charge of the several companies immediately on their arrival at a fire shall report themselves, with the station of their apparatus, to the chief engineer, or his assistants. Those engines not immediately wanted will take convenient positions, their companies remaining by them under the direction of one of their officers, while the officer in command of such engine will report to the chief and remain there for orders.

Officers to report on arrival at fire for orders.

4. When in the progress of a fire it becomes necessary to move any engine, the movement will always be executed with as much expedition as possible. The companies so changing will use the same hose, unless otherwise ordered by an engineer, and the hosemen will hold themselves in readiness to render any assistance required of them by an engineer. No company attached to the department shall leave any fire, or take the apparatus of which they have charge therefrom, without the order or permission of the chief engineer.

Of moving engines at fire.

5. The foreman shall preside at all meetings of the company, and at fires or alarms have direction of the apparatus and all persons attached to the same. In his absence his duties shall be performed by the clerk. It shall also be the duty of the foreman to preserve order and discipline in his company, and require and enforce a strict compliance with the ordinances, rules and regulations, and the orders of the engineers, and at the annual meeting appoint two pipemen and four suction hosemen, who, after putting their hose in working order, shall assist the leading hosemen in the discharge of their duties.

Duties of foreman.

6. It shall be the duty of the foremen of the hook and ladder and hose companies to see that the fire apparatus of every kind of which they have charge, is kept clean and in good order for immediate use, and that no obstructions are placed at the entrances of the several buildings in which the apparatus is kept. They shall also appoint

Duties of foremen of hook and ladder and hose companies.

a steward, whose duty shall be to clear the snow from the sidewalk in front of the house, and generally to see that their apparatus is ready for immediate use.

Duty of drivers of engines.

7. It shall be the duty of the drivers attached to the engine and other apparatus connected with the department, to obey the orders of the foremen and enginemen and comply strictly with the rules and regulations and directions of the board of engineers. It shall also be their duty to see that the horses employed for the purpose of hauling the apparatus be in harness and ready for immediate use.

Absent members may be discharged, when.

8. Any member of the department absenting himself from one-third of the fires that occur in six months, may be discharged from the department, for neglect of duty, by the board of engineers, and any member neglecting or refusing to perform his duty, shall be immediately reported to the board of engineers.

Companies or members doing special duty by requirement of mayor, &c.

9. Any company or companies, or any member of the department, doing duty by requirement or invitation from the mayor, city council, committee on fire department, chief or board of engineers, shall act in strict conformity to the discipline as laid down in the ordinances and rules and regulations, and be subject to the penalties for noncompliance, and volunteer companies shall also be subject to the ordinances and regulations.

Members leaving the department, city property must be returned.

10. Whenever any members leave the department, it shall be the duty of the foreman to see that the property belonging to the city be returned; and failing to procure such articles, the company shall be held responsible for the same, if there is not a sufficient amount due the member from the city to protect the city from loss.

Board of engineers may temporarily institute new regulations.

11. Any regulation not expressed in these regulations for the government of the companies, may be instituted for the time being by the board of engineers, to be observed until the next meeting of the city council, when it shall be submitted to their consideration.

12. The chief engineer shall furnish every member in the department with a printed copy of these ordinances and regulations, and shall cause a copy of the same to be kept in all the houses of the department, and also to furnish each engine house with a list of the public wells, reservoirs and the location of each.

Chief engineer to furnish printed copies of ordinances and regulations to members, &c.

GUNPOWDER.

STATUTES.

RULES, &C., ESTABLISHED BY MAYOR AND ALDERMEN.

STATUTES.

Municipal officers to make regulations respecting gunpowder.

Penalty for violation,

R. S., chap. 26, § 19.

1. In every town, the municipal officers may make regulations in conformity to which all gunpowder in the town shall be kept, or transported from place to place; and no person shall keep it in any other quantity or manner, than is prescribed in such regulations, under a penalty of not less than twenty nor more than one hundred dollars for each offense; and all such gunpowder may be seized by any of said officers as forfeited, and within twenty days after such seizure, be libelled according to law.

Persons injured by explosion may recover damages. Ib. § 20.

2. A person injured by the explosion of gunpowder in possession of any person contrary to the regulations established as aforesaid, may have an action for damages against such possessor, or against the owner thereof, if conusant of such neglect.

Power of municipal officers to search for gunpowder.

Ib. § 21.

3. Any municipal officer, with a lawful search warrant, may enter any building or other place in his town to search for gunpowder supposed to be concealed there contrary to law.

Not lawful for any person to sell within the city of Portland, gunpowder without license.

Act, 1833, 337, § 1.

License to be in force one year.

May be renewed.

Proviso.

4. It shall not be lawful for any person or persons to sell any gunpowder, which may at the time be within the city of Portland, in any quantity, by wholesale or retail, without having first obtained from the mayor and aldermen of said city, a license to sell gunpowder; and every license shall be written or printed, and duly signed by the mayor, on a paper, upon which shall be written or printed a copy of the rules and regulations established relative to keeping, selling, and transporting gunpowder within the said city; and every such license shall be in force for one year from the date thereof, unless annulled by the mayor and aldermen, and no longer; but such license may, prior to its expiration, be renewed by an endorsement thereon by the mayor for the further term of a year, and so from year to year; *provided*, always, that the mayor and aldermen may rescind or annul any such license, if, in their opinion, the person or persons licensed have dis-

obeyed the law, or infringed any rule or regulation established by the mayor and aldermen.

Amount to be paid for license.

Ib. § 2.

5. Every person who shall receive a license to sell gunpowder, as aforesaid, shall pay for the same to the treasurer of the city, the sum of five dollars, and every person on having a license renewed, shall pay to said treasurer the sum of one dollar. And any person or persons, licensed to keep and sell gunpowder, as aforesaid, shall place and constantly keep in a conspicuous place over or at the side of the front door of the building in which powder is kept for sale, a sign, on which shall be inscribed in plain, legible letters, the words following, viz: "Licensed to keep and sell gunpowder."

Persons licensed to keep a sign over the door of the building in which gunpowder is sold, with the words thereon, "Licensed to keep and sell gunpowder."

Mayor and aldermen may establish rules and regulations for the sale of gunpowder.

Ib. § 3.

6. The mayor and aldermen of the city of Portland are authorized to make and establish rules and regulations, from time to time, relative to the times and places at which gunpowder may be brought to or carried from said city, by land or water, and the time and manner in which the same may be transported through said city, and prescribe the kind of carriage, boat or vehicle, in which the same may be brought to, transported through, or carried from said city. *Provided, however*, that said rules and regulations shall not be applied to any person or persons, excepting inhabitants of the city of Portland, until personal notice shall have been given of the existence of said rules and regulations.

Proviso.

Penalties.

Ib. § 4.

7. If any gunpowder, kept contrary to the provisions of this act, or contrary to the terms and conditions of any such license, or to any rules and regulations established or to be established, by the mayor and aldermen, as aforesaid, shall explode in any shop, store, dwelling-house, ware-house, or other building, or in any other place in said city, the tenant, occupant, or owner of said shop, store, dwelling-house, ware-house, or other building, or place, shall pay a fine not less than fifty nor more than three hundred dollars, one moiety thereof to the use of

the poor of said city, and the other moiety to the use of the person who may sue therefor, to be recovered by action of debt.

RULES AND REGULATIONS ESTABLISHED BY MAYOR AND ALDERMEN.

Mayor and aldermen to appoint keeper of powder magazine.
Adopted by mayor and aldermen, Dec. 31, 1855.
To give bond.

1. The mayor and aldermen shall annually, in the month of April, appoint a keeper of the city powder magazine, who shall be sworn to the faithful discharge of the duties of the office, and give bond with sureties to be approved by the mayor and aldermen in the sum of two hundred dollars for the faithful performance of his duties.

Duties of keeper of powder magazine.

2. It shall be the duty of the keeper of the city powder magazine to receive and safely keep in the city powder magazine, all powder brought thereto for deposit, and deliver the same to the owner thereof, or his order, when thereto requested, for such fees, to be paid to him by such owner, as may be established therefor, and shall only deliver powder in the manner prescribed in these rules and regulations.

No person allowed to keep or sell gunpowder without license.

3. No person shall keep or have in his shop, store, dwelling-house or other tenement, at any one time, a larger quantity of gunpowder than one pound, unless he is licensed by the mayor and aldermen to keep and sell gunpowder, which license shall expire in one year from its date.

No licensed person to keep over 75 lbs.
Ib., as amended in 1863.

4. No person licensed as aforesaid, shall have or keep in his store, shop, dwelling-house or in any other tenement, or place whatever, at any one time, a larger quantity of gunpowder than seventy-five pounds.

To be kept in copper chests.

5. Every person licensed as aforesaid, shall provide himself with a strongly made copper chest or box, with a copper cover well secured with hinges and lock of the same material; and the kegs or canisters in which said

powder may be, shall be kept in said copper chest or box, which shall, at all times, be placed near the outer door of the building in which it is kept, in a convenient place for removal in case of fire.

Chests to be placed near outer door.

6. No person shall haul unto or lay at any wharf, bridge or other landing place in this city, or bring within two hundred yards thereof any boat or vessel having on board any quantity of gunpowder exceeding twenty-five pounds, or land from or receive on board any boat or vessel, at any such wharf, bridge or landing place, any gunpowder exceeding the amount aforesaid without obtaining a permit from the mayor; and no boat or vessel with gunpowder on board in quantity exceeding twenty-five pounds, shall remain at any wharf, bridge or other landing place in the city more than six hours; nor shall any such boat or vessel be allowed to ground at any such place, or remain there after sunset.

Vessels not to land or receive over 25 lbs. without permit.

Not to lay at any wharf.

7. The mayor, or in his absence, the chairman of the committee on fire department, may grant permits to land gunpowder for immediate shipment or transportation, on either of the abutments near the draw of Tukey's bridge; they may also grant permits to land or ship gunpowder from canal boats or other boats on board vessels lying at or near the end of Smith's wharf or either of the wharves between said Smith's wharf and Portland bridge, provided that the consent in writing of the owner or agent, or wharfinger of such wharf shall first be delivered to the mayor.

Mayor and chairman of committee on fire department may grant permits to land or ship gunpowder.

8. The mayor, or in his absence, the chairman of committee on fire department, may grant permits for landing upon or shipment from any wharf in the city, of gunpowder in quantity not exceeding six kegs of twenty-five pounds each.

Same subject.

9. No gunpowder shall be conveyed from the magazine through any street in the city in any carriage other than the one provided for such purposes by the city,

How to be transported through the city.

excepting however that a quantity not exceeding six kegs of twenty-five pounds each may be conveyed through any street if the same be in tight casks and each of said casks put into a strong bag and remain in such bag while in any street. *Provided*, that the owners of powder mills may transport powder to the city powder magazine, or when the Cumberland and Oxford canal is closed, to the bridge or the wharves named in section seven, entering the city by Congress or Portland streets, along Vaughan, Brackett and Arsenal streets, to the city powder magazine, in their own carriages safely covered.

Proviso.

Streets through which gunpowder may be conveyed.

And the owners of powder mills may convey powder intended for shipment as in section seven, in their own carriages safely covered, through Vaughan, Danforth and Canal streets, to the wharves named in section seven, and in no case shall any vehicle in which powder is so conveyed, be allowed to stop in any street. *Provided*, however, that on and after the completion of Waldo street, said carriages, when transporting powder for shipment as aforesaid, shall pass through said Waldo, Canal and Commercial streets to the wharves aforesaid.

Proviso.

Persons licensed to keep sign over the door, with the words "Licensed to keep and sell gunpowder" thereon.

10. Every person licensed to sell gunpowder shall have and keep a sign board over the outside of the door or principal entrance to the building in which such powder is kept, on which shall be distinctly painted the words, "Licensed to keep and sell gunpowder."

Penalties.

11. Every person violating any of these rules and regulations will be liable to a fine of not less than twenty nor more than one hundred dollars, as provided in revised statutes, chapter twenty-six.

Mayor and aldermen to appoint persons to transport gunpowder.

12. The mayor and aldermen shall annually appoint one or more persons whose duty it shall be to transport all gunpowder in the city that may be required, and who shall have the custody of the vehicle provided for that purpose, whose compensation shall be such as the mayor and aldermen may determine.

HARBOR OF PORTLAND.

STATUTES.

1. The boundaries of the harbor of Portland defined.
2. Same subject.
3. Wharves, &c., not to be extended beyond said lines, or materials deposited in said harbor, or land removed.. Abatement of such erections, &c.
4. Receiving basins and reservoirs in said harbor defined, subject to control of commissioners. Erections, &c., therein, without permission, prohibited. Such permission to be deposited and recorded.
5. Prosecutions and punishment for violations of this act.
6. Appointment of commissioners. Term of office.
7. S. J. Court may issue writ of injunction, &c.
8. Commissioners' powers extended—restrictions and penalties.
9. Compensation of commissioners.

ORDINANCES.

1. Harbor master to be appointed.
2. " " his duties.
3. Stones, &c., not to be thrown in the harbor.
4. Rules for vessels in harbor.
5. Penalty for violating rules.
6. Of vessels anchored contrary to rules.

STATUTES.

RELATING TO PORTLAND HARBOR.

The boundaries of the harbor of Portland defined.

1. The harbor of Portland is bounded north-westerly by a line commencing at the eastern corner of the Gas Company's wharf, next above the Portland bridge, and extending straight to the southern corner of the end of

Act, 1856, chap. 654, § 1. Robinson's wharf, and along the end of it to the eastern corner; thence straight to the southern corner of the end of Central wharf, and along the end of it to the eastern corner; then straight to the southern corner of the end of Custom House wharf, and along the end of it to the eastern corner; thence straight to the southern corner of the end of Railway wharf, and along the end of it to the eastern corner; thence to the southern corner of the end of St. Lawrence wharf, and along the end of it to the eastern corner; thence parallel to the strait portion of the outside railroad track, to the shoals to the southward of Fish point, as defined on the plan of Portland harbor, made by the United States Coast Survey, in the year one thousand eight hundred and fifty-three.

Same subject. Ib. § 2. 2. It is bounded southeasterly by a line commencing at the end of the breakwater as it now is, and extending southwesterly to the easterly corner of the end of Ferry wharf; thence along the end of it to its westerly corner; thence in a straight line to Portland bridge, at a point of eight hundred and fifty feet from the point where the northwesterly line of the harbor touches said bridge, and nine hundred and seventy-five feet from the line of high water mark in Cape Elizabeth.

Wharves, &c., not to be extended beyond said lines, or materials deposited in said harbor, or land removed. 3. No wharf or incumbrance of any kind shall ever hereafter be erected or extended into said harbor beyond either of said lines. No stones or other materials shall be deposited in said harbor. No land within the same covered with water shall be removed without the written permission of the commissioners hereafter named. Every erection, incumbrance or material, erected, placed or deposited in said harbor, within the lines aforesaid, shall be deemed a public nuisance, liable to abatement.

Abatement of such erections, &c. Ib. § 3.

Receiving basins and reservoirs of said harbor defined. 4. The receiving basins and reservoirs of said harbor shall comprehend the tidal waters of Fore river and Back Cove, and those along the shore northeasterly to the easterly side of the mouth of Presumpscot river. They shall be and hereby are subjected to the control and regulation of the commissioners hereafter named. No erection, incumbrance or material, shall hereafter be placed or deposited in those waters, which will obstruct the flow and ebb of those waters, or diminish the volume thereof, without the written permission of said commissioners, or of a major part of them, therein describing the extent and character of the erection or deposit so permitted. Such permission by them subscribed shall be left with the clerk of the city of Portland, to be by him recorded before any such erection, obstruction or deposit is made. All erections, obstructions or deposits, made contrary to these provisions, are to be deemed public nuisances and liable to abatement.

Subject to control of commissioners.

Erections, &c., therein, without written permission of commissioners prohibited.

Such permission to be deposited and recorded.

Ib. § 4.

5. Any person who shall offend against any of the provisions of this act, shall be deemed guilty of a misdemeanor, and liable to prosecution therefor, by indictment in any court of competent jurisdiction, and on conviction, be punished by a fine not exceeding five hundred dollars; and he may also be sentenced to pay all expenses for an abatement or removal of such erection, obstruction or deposit made by him, and to stand committed until he shall pay the same, or give satisfactory security therefor.

Prosecutions and punishment for violations of this act.

Ib. § 5.

6. The governor shall nominate, and with the advice and consent of the council, appoint three persons commissioners of the harbor and tidal waters connected therewith, of the city of Portland. One of those first appointed shall continue in office one year, one for two, and the other for three years. At the expiration of each person's term of service, the same or another person shall in like manner be appointed to serve for three years. When a vacancy shall happen by death, resignation, or removal from the State, another person shall in like manner be appointed in his place to continue in service to the end of his term.

Appointment of commissioners.

Term of their office.

Ib. § 6.

7. Whenever on application of the mayor and aldermen of the city of Portland, or of the commissioners of the harbor of Portland, it shall be made to appear to the

S. J. Court may issue writ of injunction.

supreme judicial court at any term thereof holden in said city, or to any justice thereof out of such term time, that any person or persons are violating the provisions of an act to preserve the harbor of Portland, approved April third, eighteen hundred and fifty-six, [sections 4, 5, and 6 above] such court or justice may forthwith issue a writ of injunction to stay all proceedings adjudged to be in violation of said act until further order, and may on a hearing, dissolve, continue or make such injunction perpetual as justice may require, and may adjudge that the person or persons so violating the law shall pay all costs and expenses of such proceedings, and so much thereof as shall not be thus paid, shall be paid by the city of Portland.

May on hearing dissolve, continue or make injunction perpetual.

Costs of injunction by whom to be paid.

Act. 1858, chap. 151.

Commissioners' powers extended.

8. All the powers heretofore conferred upon the commissioners of the harbor of Portland, over the receiving basins and reservoirs of said harbor, are hereby extended over the tidal waters southerly and easterly of the lines of said harbor, so far as the jurisdiction of this State extends, including all channels and entrances into said harbor; and all acts forbidden to be done within the bounds of said basins and reservoirs, are forbidden to be done within the bounds, herein designated, under the like restrictions and penalties and with like modes of redress as provided by the former and present acts.

Restrictions and penalties.

Ib. chap. 161, § 1.

Compensation of commissioners.

St., 1856, chap. 654, § 7.

9. The commissioners shall be entitled to receive from the city of Portland a reasonable compensation for all services actually performed.

ORDINANCES.

Harbor master to be appointed.

1. There shall be elected annually, on the second Monday of the month of March, or as soon thereafter as may be, by the city council in convention, an able and discreet person, to be styled the harbor master, who shall hold said office until removed, or a successor appointed; and he shall be sworn to the faithful performance of his duty. He shall receive such compensation for his services as the city council shall establish, and shall be removed at

To be sworn.

Compensation.

their pleasure; and in case said office shall be vacant at any time, such vacancy shall be filled forthwith, in the manner prescribed.

Ord., March 29, 1850, and re-enacted in Rev. Ord., 1855.

2. It shall be the duty of the harbor master to take charge and see to the preservation of the harbor, within the limits of the city of Portland, and extending to low water mark on the shore of Cape Elizabeth, and to enforce all such rules and regulations as may be ordained or ordered by the city council or mayor and aldermen from time to time, with reference thereto, and to collect all penalties that may be incurred by a violation of the same.

Duties of Harbor master.

3. No person shall throw or deposit, or cause to be thrown or deposited, in said harbor, any stones, gravel, cinders, ashes, dirt, mud, or other substance which may in any respect tend to injure the navigation thereof. And any person violating the foregoing provisions of this section, shall for each offense be liable to a penalty of fifty dollars.

Stones, &c., not to be thrown into harbor.

4. The following rules are adopted for the regulation and management of vessels in said harbor, viz:

Rules for regulation and management of vessels.

I. All of said harbor west of what is called Hog Island Roads, shall be denominated the upper harbor, and all vessels in said upper harbor shall be anchored according to the direction of the harbor master.

II. All vessels entering the upper harbor, not intended to be hauled to some wharf immediately, shall be anchored on the south side of a line ranging with the red buoy, the Adams house, so called, on York street, at the foot of State street, and a staff on a gable roofed building on Robinson's wharf, up to abreast of the end of Main wharf, and from thence, on both sides of the channel to Portland bridge.

III. Outward bound vessels shall be anchored, between the first day of the months of May and November, north of a line ranging from the end of Atlantic depot wharf, to Little Hog Island; and between the first day of the months of November and May, north of a line ranging from the easterly corner of the coal-wharf of the Ocean

As amended by Ord., Dec. 16, 1859.

Steam Navigation Company, to the westerly corner of the fort on Hog Island Ledge.

IV. No vessel, either inward or outward bound, shall be anchored in the channel of the harbor, or the channel to the Great Eastern wharves.

V. All vessels lying at anchor more than seven days, with their inward cargo on board, shall rig in their jib-booms, and keep them in while so remaining at anchor.

VI. No vessel shall be allowed to lay at the end of any wharf, or in any dock, in such manner as to obstruct the free passage of other vessels coming in or going out, or being hauled from one wharf to another.

VII. All vessels at anchor in the harbor, shall keep a clear and distinct light suspended at least six feet above the deck, during the night.

VIII. No vessel shall, under any circumstances, be anchored in the track of the Ferry Boat, or so as to obstruct the passage of steamers to and from their respective places of landing.

Penalty for violation of preceding rules.

5. If any of the preceding rules shall be violated, the master or owner of the vessel, by means of which said violation shall occur, shall for each offense be subject to a penalty of twenty dollars.

Vessels anchored contrary to rules. Notice to be given to master, &c., of vessel.

6. If any vessel shall be anchored contrary to any of the rules prescribed in the preceding section, the harbor master shall forthwith give notice to the master or owner thereof, to remove said vessel at once; and if the same is not done without delay, or in case there is not a sufficient crew on board for that purpose, the harbor master shall cause such vessel to be removed at the expense of the owner or master thereof. And if the master or owner shall neglect or refuse to pay said expense on demand being made therefor by the harbor master, he shall be liable to a penalty of double the amount of such expense, in addition to the penalty provided in the preceding section.

Vessel to be removed at owner's expense.

Penalties.

HAWKERS AND PEDLERS.

STATUTES.

STATUTES.

1. No person, except as hereinafter provided, shall travel from town to town, or place to place, in any town in this State, on foot, or by any kind of land or water conveyance whatsoever, carrying for sale, or offering for sale, any goods, wares or merchandise, whole or by sample, under a penalty of not less than fifty nor more than two hundred dollars, and the forfeiture of all property thus unlawfully carried. But nothing in this act shall be construed as conflicting with the right of any commission merchant, or commercial broker, in any town or city in which he resides, from traveling from place to place in such town or city, and selling or offering to sell by sample or otherwise, any goods, wares or merchandise.

Pedling forbidden, except by license, under penalty.

Act, 1866, chap. 50, § 1.

2. The county commissioners may license for the purposes aforesaid, any person who proves to their satisfaction that he sustains a good moral character, and has

County commissioners may license.

Ib. § 2.

been five years a citizen of the United States, and such licenses shall expire one year from their date, and shall not be transferable ; and the person receiving such license shall pay therefor to the county treasurers, if he is to sell or offer to sell by retail, ten dollars ; if by wholesale, twenty-five dollars ; and said county treasurers shall pay all moneys received by them for such licenses into the treasury of the State ; but nothing herein shall prevent any citizen of this State from selling any fish, fruit, provisions, farming utensils or other articles lawfully raised or manufactured in this State.

License to be exhibited to magistrates, &c., when required; and penalty for refusal.

3. Every person who receives a license under this act, shall exhibit it at all times when required by any trial justice, constable or other peace officer, and upon refusal, he shall forfeit the sum of fifty dollars ; and the carriages, goods, wares and merchandise of such person, which he is then and there employing under such license, upon complaint before any justice of a police or municipal court, or any trial justice in said county, may be seized under his warrant, and detained in the custody of the officer until payment of said penalty or the discharge of the accused ; and in case of his conviction, if said property is not redeemed within twenty days thereafter, it shall be forfeited, and may be sold as if taken on execution, and the net proceeds distributed as hereinafter provided.

Seizure and sale of carriages, goods, &c., may be made upon complaint and conviction.

Ib. § 3.

Penalties and forfeitures, how recoverable, and to whose use accruing.

4. All penalties and forfeitures herein provided, may be recovered by indictment, or by action of debt, in the name of the prosecutor, one-half to the use of the town where the offence is committed, and the other to the use of the person prosecuting therefor ; and any trial justice or justice of police or municipal court, upon complaint for a violation of this act, may issue his warrant and cause the arrest of the accused and the seizure of the property alleged to be forfeited, and if upon examination he shall find there is probable cause to believe that the person charged is guilty, he may order him to recognize with

Arrests authorized, and recognizance for appearance before S. J. C. required.

sufficient sureties, to appear before the next supreme judicial court for said county, and in default thereof may commit him, and may order the detention of said property by the officer in whose custody it is, until trial in said court, and in cases of conviction said property shall be decreed forfeited to the uses aforesaid, and shall be sold as if taken on execution.

Commitment in case of default, and detention, forfeiture and sale of property.

Ib. § 4.

5. Every person licensed shall have painted on some conspicuous place on every carriage employed by him, in letters at least one inch wide, his name and the words, LICENSED BY C. C.

Provision respecting carriages.

Ib. § 5.

6. No charge shall be made for the licenses provided for in this act, to any soldier of this State, disabled in the service during the recent war for the suppression of the rebellion.

Disabled soldiers of this State exempted from license fees.

Ib. § 7.

7. It shall be the duty of the county commissioners of the several counties of this State to furnish the clerks of the several courts with a sufficient number of blank licenses signed by the board, or a majority of them, to meet all calls for licenses to peddle under the provisions of this act, which licenses, so signed, shall be charged to the clerks, who shall be held to account for licenses issued once in three months.

County commissioners to furnish blank licenses signed by them to clerk of courts.

Act, 1867, chap. 120, § 1.

8. All moneys paid for licenses under this act, shall be received by the clerks of courts, who shall pay over to the state treasurer, or deposit the same in the nearest bank where State funds are deposited, or such other place as may be mutually agreed on between the clerks and the treasurer of State, once in three months, except fifty cents for each and every license, taking receipts therefor, which receipts shall be received by the commissioners as payments for licenses signed by them; and all copies found in the hands of clerks at the expiration of three months, together with fifty cents for each license issued and recorded, shall be credited to such clerks.

Clerks to pay money received for licenses to State treasurer.

Ib. § 2.

HAY.

STATUTES.

ORDINANCES.

STATUTES.

Pressed hay in bundles, to be branded; unless branded, forfeited, &c.

R. S., chap. 38, § 35.

1. All hay, pressed and put up in bundles for sale in this State, shall be branded on the bands or boards enclosing it with the first letter of the christian and the whole of the surname of the person putting up the same, and with the name of the State and of the place where such person lives; and all pressed hay offered for sale or shipping, not thus branded, shall be forfeited, one-half to the use of the town where the offense is committed, and the other half to the person libeling the same.

How bales may be secured with boards, &c.

Ib. § 36.

2. Every bale of screwed or pressed hay may have four pieces of seasoned board not more than four inches wide or one inch thick to keep the hay in place; on one of which, or on one of the bands, shall be marked the

weight of the bale; and no sworn weigher of hay shall purchase any hay, but what is necessary for his own use.

3. If the master of any vessel takes on board pressed hay not branded as aforesaid, he shall forfeit two dollars for each bundle so received.

Penalty for master of vessel taking hay not branded.

Ib. § 37.

ORDINANCES.

1. There shall be chosen annually, on the second Monday of the month of March, or as soon thereafter as may be, by the city council, one or more weighers of hay, who shall have the care and control of the city hay scales, and whose duty it shall be to weigh all hay and straw brought into the city of Portland for sale, and such other articles as may be offered to be weighed. They shall give bonds to the city in such sum as the mayor and aldermen may require, for the faithful performance of their duty, and shall conform to such regulations as may from time to time be adopted by the city council, and shall receive such compensation as they shall deem just and reasonable, to be paid out of the monies received as fees for weighing hay and other articles.

Weighers of hay to be chosen. Their duty.

Bonds to be given.

Compensation.

Ord., Jan. 2, 1865, § 1.

2. No person shall sell or offer for sale any hay or straw without having the same weighed by the city weigher of hay, and a ticket signed by said weigher certifying the quantity each load, bale or parcel contains, on penalty of forfeiting the hay or straw so sold or offered for sale to the use of the city; or the owner or driver of such hay or straw shall forfeit and pay, to the use of the city, a sum not less than five dollars for each load of hay or straw sold or offered for sale without having complied with the provisions of this ordinance, at the discretion of the court before whom such case may be tried.

Hay or straw not to be sold without being weighed. Penalty.

Ib. § 2.

3. Any person not authorized as a weigher of hay in accordance with the provisions of the first section of this ordinance, who shall weigh any hay or straw brought into this city for sale, or shall permit or allow such hay or

Weighing hay without authority.

Penalty.

Ib. § 3.

straw to be weighed upon any scales belonging to him or them, shall forfeit and pay a sum not exceeding twenty dollars to the use of the city.

Fees for weighing.

Ib. § 4.

4. The weigher of hay shall be allowed to demand and receive from any person offering any hay, straw, or other article to be weighed upon the city hay scales, the sum of thirty cents for each load or other article so weighed, which sum shall include the weighing of the cart, wagon or other vehicle upon which a load has been weighed by said weigher.

Hay pressed and in bundles need not be weighed.

Ib. § 5.

5. The provisions of this ordinance shall not apply to hay pressed and put up in bundles or bales, as required by law, intended for shipment or for sale without being re-weighed in this city.

HEALTH.

STATUTES.

CONTAGIOUS DISEASES.

1. Precautions against infected persons; duty of municipal officers.
2. Precautions against persons arriving from infected places.
3. Restrictions on such persons; may be removed if refractory; penalty if they return.
4. Precautions authorized in border towns.
5. Process for removal or separate accommodation of infected persons.

6, 7. Process for securing infected articles.

8. Powers of officers in executing such process.
9. Expenses, how paid.
10. Compensation for men or property impressed.
11. Adjournment of courts because of danger from infection.
12. Removal of infected prisoners from places of confinement.
13. Order for removal, how returned. Such a removal not an escape.
14. Health committee, how chosen; their duties.
15. If no committee chosen, selectmen to perform the duties.
16. May order removal of private nuisances; proceedings thereon.
17. Masters, &c., of vessels may be examined on oath in certain cases.
18. Vessels with infected persons to anchor at a distance from towns.
19. Penalty for violation of this provision.
20. Selectmen may establish quarantine regulations. Penalty for breach thereof.
21. Duty of pilots to give notice thereof.
22. Punishment for violation or evasion of quarantine, after notice.
23. Selectmen to furnish signals, to be kept hoisted by master. Restriction of persons visiting vessels at quarantine.

UNWHOLESOME PROVISIONS AND DRINKS.

CONTAGIOUS DISEASES AMONG CATTLE.

ORDINANCES.

1. Mayor and aldermen constitute board of health.
2. City marshal to execute health laws.
3. City and consulting physicians.
4. Duty of city physicians.
5. " " consulting physicians.
6. No filth to be thrown in streets.
7. Penalty.
8. Who may remove filth.
9. Neglect to remove nuisances after notice.
10. Penalty.
11. Vaults, &c., restriction upon erection. Proviso.
12. Regulations as to cleansing vaults, &c.
13. Restrictions as to conveying contents of vaults; to be conveyed without city limits.
14. Fresh fish, where sold.
15. Same subject.
16. Offensive substances not to be thrown into wells.
17. Unwholesome provisions not to be sold.
18. Regulations respecting hog-sties. Penalty.
19. House offal.
20. City cart to collect offal.
21. Mayor and aldermen to appoint person to have charge of cart.
22. Offal to be delivered to person appointed. Penalty.
23. No other person to collect offal. Penalty.
24. Vaults, &c., in unhealthy condition to be cleansed.
25. Persons in tenements, where too numerous, or unprovided with vaults, may be removed. Penalty.
26. Hides or leather not to be exposed in streets. Penalty.

INTERMENT OF THE DEAD.

27. Superintendent of burials. Authority. Subject to regulations of mayor and aldermen.
28. Superintendent to be chosen annually. To give bonds and be sworn.
29. His duties.
30. Superintendent to have care of funeral cars.
31. Undertakers to be appointed and licensed. May employ porters. May be removed. Penalty for acting as undertakers without license.
32. No interments to be made without license. What time interments may to be made.
33. Undertaker's fees.
34. Depth of graves.

STATUTES.

CONTAGIOUS DISEASES.

Precautions against infected persons.

R. S., chap. 14, § 1.

1. When any person is, or has recently been infected with any disease or sickness dangerous to the public health, the municipal officers of the town where he is, shall provide for the safety of the inhabitants, as they think best, by removing him to a separate house, if it can be done without great danger to his health, and by providing nurses and other assistants and necessaries, at his charge or that of his parent or master, if able, otherwise, that of the town to which he belongs.

Precautions against persons arriving from infected places.

Ib. § 2.

2. When any infectious or malignant distemper is known to exist in any place out of the State, the municipal officers of any town in the State, by giving public notice therein, as they find convenient, may require any person coming from such place to inform one of them or the town clerk of their arrival and from what place; and if he does not, within two hours after his arrival, or after actual notice of such requirement, give such information, he shall forfeit one hundred dollars to the use of the town.

Restrictions on such persons; may be removed if refractory.

3. Said officers may prohibit a person, required to give such information, from going to any part of their town where they think his presence would be unsafe for the inhabitants; and if he does not comply, they may order him, unless disabled by sickness, forthwith to leave

the State in the manner and by the road they direct; and if he neglects or refuses so to do, any justice of the peace in the county, on complaint of either of said officers, may issue his warrant to any proper officer or other person named therein, and cause him to be removed out of the State; and if during the prevalence of such distemper, in the place where he resides, he returns to any town in this State without the license of the municipal officers thereof, he shall forfeit not exceeding four hundred dollars.

Penalty if they return.

Ib. § 3.

4. The municipal officers of any town near to or adjoining the line of the State, may appoint, by writing under their hands, suitable persons to attend at any places by which travelers may pass into such town from infected places in other States or Provinces, who may examine such passengers, as they suspect of bringing with them any infection dangerous to the public health, and if need be, may restrain them from traveling until licensed thereto by a justice of the peace in the county, or one of said officers; and any such passenger who without such license travels in this State, except to return by the most direct way to the State or Province whence he came, after he has been cautioned to depart by the persons so appointed, shall forfeit not exceeding one hundred dollars.

Precautions authorized in border towns.

Ib. § 4.

5. Any two justices of the peace may issue a warrant, directed to a proper officer, requiring him to remove any person infected with contagious sickness, under the direction of the municipal officers of the town where he is; or to impress and take up convenient houses, lodgings, nurses, attendants, and other necessaries for the accommodation, safety and relief of the sick.

Process for removal or separate accommodation of infected persons.

Ib. § 5.

6. When, on the application of the municipal officers of a town, it appears to any justice of the peace that there is just cause to suspect that any baggage, clothing, or goods of any kind within such town, are infected with any malignant contagious distemper, by a warrant directed to a proper officer, he shall require him to impress so many

Process for securing infected articles.

Ib. § 6.

men, as the justice thinks necessary, to secure such infected articles, and to post said men as a guard over the house or place where the articles are lodged, who shall prevent any person's removing or coming near such articles, until due inquiry is made into the circumstances thereof.

Justice may by warrant require officers to cause them to be removed to suitable places.

Ib. § 7.

7. He may by the same warrant, if it appears to him necessary, require said officers, under the direction of the municipal officers, to impress and take up convenient houses or stores for the safe keeping of such infected articles, and cause them to be removed thereto, or otherwise detained, until the municipal officers think they are free from infection.

Powers of officers in executing such process.

Ib. § 8.

8. Said officers, if need be, may break open any house, shop, or other place mentioned in the warrant where infected articles are, and require such aid as is necessary to execute it; and all persons at the command of either of said officers, under a penalty of not exceeding ten dollars, shall assist in such execution.

Expenses, how paid.

Ib. § 9.

9. The charges of securing such infected articles and of transporting and purifying them shall be paid by the owners thereof, at the price determined by the municipal officers.

Compensation for men or property impressed.

Ib. § 10.

10. When the officer impresses or takes up any houses, stores, lodging, or other necessaries, or impresses any man, as herein provided, the parties interested shall have a just compensation therefor, to be paid by the town in which such persons or property were impressed.

Adjournment of courts because of danger from infection.

Ib. § 11.

11. When a malignant infectious distemper prevails in any town wherein the supreme judicial court or court of county commissioners is to be held, said courts may be adjourned and held in any town in said county, by proclamation made in such public manner as the courts judge best, as near their usual place of meeting as they think safety permits.

12. When any person in a jail, house of correction, or workhouse, is attacked with any disease, which the municipal officers of his town, by medical advice, consider dangerous to the safety and health of other prisoners, or of the inhabitants of the town, they shall, by their order in writing, direct his removal to some place of safety, there to be securely kept and provided for until their further order; and if he recovers from such disease, he shall be returned to his place of confinement.

Removal of infected prisoners from places of confinement.
Ib. § 12.

13. If he was committed by order of a court or under a judicial process, the order for his removal, or a copy thereof attested by the municipal officers, shall be returned by them with the doings thereon into the office of the clerk of the court from which such order or process was issued. No such removal shall be deemed an escape.

Order for removal, how returned. Such removal not an escape.
Ib. § 13.

14. A town at its annual meeting, may choose a health committee of not less than three nor more than nine, or one person to be a health officer; who shall remove, at the expense of their town, all filth found in any place therein, which, in their judgment, endangers the lives or health of any inhabitant; and require the owner or occupant, when they think necessary, to remove or discontinue any drain or other source of filth.

Health committee, how chosen; their duties.
Ib. § 14.

15. If any town, at its annual meeting, omits to choose such committee or officer, the municipal officers shall be a health committee, and have all their powers and perform all their duties.

If no committee chosen, selectmen to perform the duties.
Ib. § 15.

16. When any source of filth, or other cause of sickness, is found on private property, the owner or occupant thereof shall, within twenty-four hours after notice from the said committee or officer, at his own expense, remove or discontinue it; and if he neglects or unreasonably delays to do so, he shall forfeit not exceeding one hundred dollars; and said committee or officer shall cause said nuisance to be removed or discontinued; and all expenses thereof shall be repaid to the town by such owner or occupant, or by the person who caused or permitted it.

May order removal of private nuisances; proceedings thereon.
Ib. § 16.

Masters, &c., of vessels may be examined on oath in certain cases.

Ib. § 17.

17. If a master, seaman, or passenger of a vessel, in which there is any infection, or has lately been, or is suspected to have been, or which has come from a port where any infectious distemper prevails, dangerous to the public health, refuses to answer, on oath, such questions as are asked him relating to such infection or distemper, by the municipal officers of the town to which such vessel comes, which oath either of said officers may administer, he shall forfeit not exceeding two hundred dollars, or be imprisoned not more than six months.

Vessels with infected persons to anchor at a distance from towns.

Ib. § 18.

18. When a vessel arrives at a port in this State, having on board any person infected with a malignant disease, the master, commander, or pilot thereof shall anchor it at some convenient place below the town of such port, at a distance safe for the inhabitants thereof and the persons on board other vessels in the port; and no person or thing on board shall be brought on shore, until the municipal officers give their written permit therefor.

Penalty for violation of this provision.

Ib. § 19.

19. For the wilful violation of the provisions of the preceding section, such master or commander shall forfeit not exceeding two hundred, and the pilot not exceeding fifty dollars for each offense.

Selectmen may establish quarantine regulations.

Penalty for breach thereof.

Ib. § 20.

20. The municipal officers of a seaport town may cause any vessel arriving there to perform quarantine at such place and under such regulations as they may judge expedient, when they think the safety of the inhabitants requires it; and whoever neglects or refuses to obey such orders and regulations, shall forfeit not exceeding five hundred dollars, or be imprisoned not exceeding six months.

Duty of pilots to give notice thereof.

Ib. § 21.

21. When such officers of a seaport town think it necessary to order all vessels, arriving there from any particular port or ports, to perform quarantine, they shall give notice thereof to the pilots of their port; who shall make it known to the master of all vessels which they board. If any pilot neglects to do so, or contrary thereto pilots any vessel up to said seaport town, he shall forfeit not exceeding one hundred dollars.

22. When the master or commander of a vessel takes it up to any seaport town, after notice that a quarantine has been so directed for all vessels coming from the port or place whence his vessel sailed, or by false declarations, or otherwise, fraudulently attempts to elude such directions; or lands or suffers to be landed from his vessel any person or thing, without permission of the municipal officers, he shall be punished as provided in section twenty.

Punishment for violation or evasion of quarantine, after notice.

Ib. § 22.

23. The municipal officers of every seaport town requiring vessels to perform quarantine shall provide, at the expense of such town, a suitable number of red flags at least three yards in length; and the master of every vessel ordered to perform quarantine shall cause one of them to be continually kept, during the term thereof, at the head of the mainmast of his vessel; and no person shall go on board such vessel during said term unless by permission of said officers; if he does, he shall be thereafter held liable to the same regulations and restrictions as those belonging to said vessel; and shall there be detained by force, if necessary, until duly discharged by said officers.

Selectmen to furnish signals.

Restrictions of persons visiting vessels at quarantine.

Ib. § 23.

24. In every seaport town where there is a health committee or officer, he may perform all the duties and exercise all the authority of the municipal officers in requiring vessels to perform quarantine.

Health committee may exercise authority of selectmen, relating to quarantine.

Ib. § 24.

25. All expenses incurred on account of any person, vessel, or goods, under quarantine regulations, shall be paid by him, or the owner of the vessel, or goods, as the case may be.

Quarantine expenses, how paid.

Ib. § 25.

26. A town may establish therein one or more hospitals for the reception of persons having the small pox or other disease dangerous to the public health; or its municipal officers may license any building therein as a hospital, to be under the control of said officers; but no such hospital shall be within one hundred rods of an inhabited dwelling house in an adjoining town without the consent of its municipal officers.

Hospitals may be established.

Restrictions as to location.

Ib. § 26.

Restrictions on inoculation with the small pox.
Ib. § 27.

27. If any person inoculates himself or any other person, or suffers himself to be inoculated with the small pox, unless at some lawful hospital, he shall forfeit not exceeding one hundred dollars for each offense.

Physicians and others liable to hospital regulations.
Ib. § 28.

28. When a hospital is so established or licensed, the physician, the persons inoculated or sick therein, the nurses, attendants, and all persons who come within its limits, and all furniture or other articles used or brought there, shall be subject to the regulations made by the municipal officers.

Hospitals to be provided on breaking out of infectious diseases; regulations.
Ib. § 29.

29. When the small pox or any other disease dangerous to the public health breaks out in a town, the municipal officers shall immediately provide such hospital or place of reception for the sick and infected, as they judge best for the accommodation and safety of the inhabitants; and such hospitals and places shall be subject to their regulations the same as established hospitals; and they shall cause such sick and infected to be removed thereto, unless their condition will not admit of it without imminent danger; in that case, the house or place where the sick is, shall be deemed a hospital for every purpose aforesaid; and all persons residing in or in any way concerned with it shall be subject to hospital regulations.

Precautions to prevent the spread of such diseases.
28 Maine, 255.
Ib. § 30.

30. When any disease dangerous to the public health exists in a town, the municipal officers shall use all possible care to prevent its spread and to give public notice of infected places to travelers, by displaying red flags at proper distances, and by all other means most effectual, in their judgment, for the common safety.

Penalty for violation of hospital regulations by persons subject thereto.
Ib. § 31.

31. If any physician or other person in such hospitals or places of reception, attending, approaching, or concerned therewith, violates any lawful regulation in relation thereto, with respect to himself or his or another's property, he shall forfeit not less than ten, nor more than one hundred dollars, for each offense.

32. When a householder or physician knows that a person under his care is taken sick of any such disease, he shall immediately give notice thereof to the municipal officers of the town where such person is; and if he neglects it he shall forfeit not less than ten, nor more than thirty dollars.

Householders and physicians to give notice of infectious diseases under their care.

Ib. § 32.

33. All forfeitures mentioned in the preceding sections, except otherwise provided, shall inure to the use of the town where the offense is committed.

Forfeiture, how recovered and appropriated.

Ib. § 33.

34. A town may choose a board of health of not less than three nor more than nine persons, who shall have all the powers, and be subject to all the duties, restrictions, liabilities, and penalties of the municipal officers, and health committee or officer.

Towns may choose a board of health; their powers.

Ib. § 34.

35. A town may provide for the inoculation of its inhabitants with the cow pox, under the direction and control of the health committee, health officer, or board of health; and raise all necessary sums to defray the expense thereof, or such part as they may think proper.

Vaccination may be at the expense of towns and plantations.

Ib. § 35.

36. Towns may establish by-laws for the preservation of health, and for protection against infectious diseases.

By-laws may be established.

Ib. § 36.

UNWHOLSOME PROVISIONS AND DRINKS.

37. Whoever sells any diseased, corrupted, or unwholesome provision for food or drink, knowing it to be such, without informing the buyer; or fraudulently adulterates, for the purpose of sale, any substance intended for food, or any wine, spirits, or other liquors intended for drink, so as to render them injurious to health, shall be punished by imprisonment not more than five years, or by fine not exceeding one thousand dollars; and whoever knowingly sells or offers for sale as food any veal killed before the calf was four weeks old, without informing the buyer, shall be punished by a fine of not more than twenty dollars, or by imprisonment not more than thirty days.

Selling unwholesome provisions and drinks. Penalty for selling veal of a calf less than four weeks old.

R. S., chap. 128, § 1.

SALE OF MEATS AND FISH.

Fresh meat and fish, cities have power to regulate sale of, &c. Act, Feb. 26, 1862, § 1.

38. Any city in this State shall have power to regulate the sale of fresh meat and fish within its limits; and may ordain and establish a locality or localities, where said articles may be offered for sale.

Penalties. Ib. § 2.

39. Such city may annex penalties for the breach of the provisions of any ordinance established to carry out the provisions of the preceding section.

CONTAGIOUS DISEASES AMONG CATTLE.

Cattle infected by contagious disease to be isolated. Act, March 19, 1862, § 1.

40. The mayor and aldermen of cities, in case of the existence in this State of the disease called lung murrain or pleuro pneumonia, or any other contagious disease among cattle, shall cause the cattle in their respective cities which are infected, or which have been exposed to infection, to be secured or collected in some suitable place or places, within such city, and kept isolated; and when taken from the possession of their owners, to be maintained, one-fifth to be paid by the city wherein the animal is kept, and four-fifths at the expense of the State; such isolation to continue so long as the existence of such disease or other circumstances renders the same necessary, or they may, at their discretion, direct the owners thereof to isolate such cattle upon their own premises, and any damage or loss sustained thereby shall be paid as aforesaid.

Maintenance.

Owners may be directed to isolate infected cattle.

Animals to be examined. Ib. § 2.

41. The mayor and aldermen shall, within twenty-four hours after they have notice of the existence of such disease, or have reason to believe it exists, cause the suspected animals to be examined by a veterinary surgeon or physician, by them selected, and if the same be adjudged to be diseased, they may, at their discretion, order them to be forthwith killed and buried at the expense of such city.

Infected cattle may be killed if necessary.

42. The mayor and aldermen shall cause all cattle which they shall so order, to be killed, to be appraised

by three competent and disinterested men, under oath, at the value thereof at the time of appraisal, and the amount of appraisal shall be paid as above provided.

Cattle killed to be appraised. Ib. § 3.

43. Said mayor and aldermen are authorized to prohibit the departure of cattle from any enclosure, or to exclude cattle therefrom.

Further powers to city officers. Ib. § 4.

44. Said mayor and aldermen may make regulations in writing to regulate or prohibit the passage from, to or through their respective cities or from place to place within the same, of any neat cattle, and may arrest and detain, at the cost of the owners thereof, all cattle found passing in violation of such regulations, and may take all other necessary measures for the enforcement of such prohibition, and also for preventing the spread of any such disease among the cattle in their respective towns and cities, and the immediate vicinity thereof.

Passage of animals, how regulated. Ib. § 5.

45. The regulations made by mayor and aldermen in pursuance of the foregoing section shall be recorded upon the records of their cities respectively, and shall be published in such cities in such manner as may be provided in such regulations.

Regulations to be recorded and published. Ib. § 6.

46. Any person who shall sell or dispose of any animal which is infected or known to have been exposed to infection within one year after such exposure without the knowledge and consent of said mayor and aldermen, shall be punished by fine not exceeding five hundred dollars or by imprisonment not exceeding one year.

Sale of infected animals prohibited. Ib. § 7. Penalty.

47. Any person disobeying the orders of the mayor and aldermen, made in conformity with the fourth section of this act or driving or transporting any neat cattle contrary to the regulations made, recorded and published as aforesaid, shall be punished by fine not exceeding five hundred dollars or by imprisonment not exceeding one year.

Disobedience of orders of mayor and aldermen. Ib. § 8. — how punished.

48. Whoever knows or has reason to suspect the existence of any fatal, contagious disease among the cattle in his possession or under his care, shall forthwith give

Knowledge or suspicion of disease to be reported. Ib. § 9.

Failure, how punished.

notice to the mayor and aldermen of the city where such cattle may be kept, and for failure so to do, shall be punished by a fine not exceeding five hundred dollars or by imprisonment not exceeding one year.

Neglect or refusal of city officers to comply. Ib. § 10. — penalty for.

49. Any city whose officers shall neglect or refuse to carry into effect the provisions of sections one, two, three, four, five, six and seven, shall forfeit a sum not exceeding five hundred dollars for each day's neglect.

Appraisals how made. Ib. § 11. — to whom cerfied.

50. All appraisals made under the provisions of this act shall be in writing and signed by the appraisers, and the same shall be certified to the governor and council and to the treasurer of the cities wherein the cattle appraised belong, by the mayors and aldermen respectively.

Further powers of cities. Ib. § 12.

51. The mayor and aldermen are authorized, when in their judgment it shall be necessary to carry into effect the purposes of this act, to take and hold possession for a term not exceeding one year within their respective cities, of any land, without buildings other than barns thereon, upon which it may be necessary to enclose and isolate any cattle; and they shall cause the damages sustained by the owners in consequence of such taking and holding, to be appraised by the assessors of the city wherein the land so taken is situated, and they shall further cause a description of such land, setting forth the boundaries thereof, and the area as nearly as may be estimated, together with such appraisal by the assessors, to be entered upon the records of the city.

Amount of appraisal, how paid.

The amount of said appraisal shall be paid as provided in the first section, in such sums and at such times as the mayor and aldermen respectively may order.

Owner dissatisfied, may maintain action.

If the owner of any land so taken shall be dissatisfied with the appraisal of said assessors, he may by action of contract, recover of the town or city wherein the lands lie, a fair compensation for the damages sustained by him; but no costs shall be taxed, unless the damages recovered in such action, exclusive of interest, exceed the appraisal of the assessors. And the State shall reimburse any city four-fifths of any sum recovered of such city in any such action.

Amount to be reimbursed.

52. Whenever such disease shall exist in any city in this State it shall be the duty of the mayor and aldermen of such city, forthwith to give notice thereof to the governor and secretary of the board of agriculture; *provided, however*, that if commissioners shall have been appointed as hereinafter provided, such notice shall be given forthwith to said commissioners.

Notice to governor and secretary of board of agriculture.

Ib. § 13.

— to commissioners in certain cases.

53. The governor is hereby authorized, whenever in his opinion the public good requires, to appoint commissioners who shall have full power to make all necessary regulations, and to issue summary orders relative thereto, for the treatment and extirpation of any contagious disease among cattle, and may direct the mayor and aldermen of cities to enforce and carry into effect all such regulations as may from time to time be made for that end; and any such officer or other person refusing or neglecting to enforce, carry out and comply with any regulation of the commissioners shall be punished by fine not exceeding five hundred dollars, or by imprisonment not exceeding one year for every such offence.

Commissioners may be appointed.

— powers of.

Ib. § 14.

— neglect or refusal to obey.

— how punished.

54. When said commissioners shall make and publish any regulations concerning the extirpation or treatment of cattle infected with, or which have been exposed to, the disease known as lung murrain or pleuro pneumonia, or other contagious disease, such regulations shall supersede the regulations made by the mayors and aldermen of cities, upon the same subject matter, and the operation of the regulations made by such mayors and aldermen shall be suspended during the time those made by the commissioners, as aforesaid, shall be in force. And said mayors and aldermen shall carry out and enforce all orders and directions of said commissioners to them directed as they shall from time to time issue.

Regulations made by commissioners to supersede all others.

Ib. § 15.

City authorities to enforce directions of commissioners.

ORDINANCES.

Mayor and aldermen shall constitute the board of health.

Rev. Ord., 1855.

1. The mayor and aldermen shall constitute the board of health of the city for all purposes, and shall exercise all the powers vested in, and shall perform all the duties prescribed to the health committee and selectmen of towns of this State, subject only to any limitations contained in the ordinances, regulations, and orders of the city council.

Execution of health laws and ordinances committed to city marshal.

Ib.

2. The execution of the laws and ordinances relating to the subjects of internal and external health, shall be under the superintendence of the city marshal and his deputies, and it shall be their duty, and they and each of them shall have the power, to enforce all laws, ordinances, regulations and orders relating to causes of sickness, nuisances, and sources of filth, existing within the city, within the harbor, or in any vessel within the said harbor, or on any island, subject always to the direction, authority and control of the mayor and aldermen.

City physician, and consulting physicians.

Ib., as amended by city charter, § 6.

3. The city council shall annually, on the second Monday in the month of March, or soon thereafter as may be, make choice of a city physician, and three consulting physicians of regular standing.

Duty of city physician.

Rev. Ord., 1855.

4. It shall be the duty of the city physician to give his professional attendance and services at the alms house, at the city hospital, and elsewhere, for patients under the care or at the charge of the city, whenever thereunto required by the overseers of the poor, master of the alms house, or mayor.

Duties of consulting physicians.

Ib.

5. It shall be the duty of the consulting physicians in case of alarm of any contagious or other dangerous disease occurring in the city or neighborhood, to give the mayor or to either board of the city council, all such professional advice and information as they may request, with a view to the prevention of such disease, and at all convenient times when requested, to aid and assist them with their counsel and advice in all matters that relate to the preservation of the health of the inhabitants.

6. No person shall throw or deposit, or cause to be thrown or deposited, in any street, court, square, lane, alley, or public place, any saw dust, soot, ashes, cinders, shavings, hair, shreds, manure, oyster, clam or lobster shells, waste or dirty water, or any animal, vegetable or offensive matter whatever. Nor shall any person or persons throw or cast any dead animal, or any foul or offensive matter in any dock or place between the channel and the shore, nor shall land any foul or offensive animal or vegetable substance within the city, nor shall cast any dead animal in the waters of the harbor or back cove.

No filth shall be thrown into streets.

Ib.

7. If any of the substances mentioned in the preceding section, shall be thrown or carried into any street, lane, alley, court, square, or public place, from any house, wood-house, shop, cellar, yard, or any other place, the owner or occupant of such house or place, and the person who actually threw and carried the same therefrom, shall severally be held liable for such violation of this ordinance, and all such substances shall be removed at the expense of the owner or occupant of the house or other place, whence the same were thrown or carried, within two hours after personal notice in writing to that effect given by the mayor, any alderman, the city marshal or deputy, or any health officer, duly appointed by the city council.

Penalty.

8. All dirt, saw dust, soot, ashes, cinders, shavings, hair, shreds, manure, oyster, clam, or lobster shells, or any animal or vegetable substance, or filth of any kind, in any house, warehouse, cellar, yard, or other place which the mayor, any alderman, city marshal or deputy, or health committee or officer, shall deem necessary for the health of the city to be removed, shall be carried away therefrom, by and at the expense of the owner or occupant of such house or other place where the same shall be found, and removed to such place as shall be directed, within four hours after notice in writing to that effect, given by the mayor, any alderman, city marshal, deputy, or health officer.

Filth, &c., may be removed by order of mayor, aldermen, or marshal.

Ib.

In cases of neglect to remove nuisances after notice.

Ib.

9. Whenever any person shall have been duly notified to remove any nuisance, or to perform any other act or thing which it may be his duty to perform for the preservation of the health of the city, and the time limited for the performance of such duty shall have elapsed, without a compliance with such notice, the city marshal shall forthwith cause such nuisance to be removed at the expense of the person so notified. And the mayor shall cause all persons who shall violate or disobey the health laws or regulations, to be forthwith prosecuted and punished. And if, in the opinion of the mayor and aldermen, or the city marshal, or deputy, it shall be for the health or comfort of the inhabitants of the city that any particular nuisance should be removed forthwith and without delay, it shall be their duty to cause the same to be removed accordingly. And if the said nuisance existed in violation of this ordinance, or of any of the laws, regulations, or ordinances relating to the health of the city, then the expense of removing the same shall be paid by the owner or occupant of the house or other place where the same was found, and if payment be refused on demand thereof, by the city marshal, it shall be sued for in the name of the city.

Penalty.

Ib.

10. Any person offending against the provisions of the preceding sections, shall forfeit and pay not less than one dollar nor more than twenty dollars for every offense; also the sum of one dollar for every hour that the nuisances or substances mentioned in the previous sections of this ordinance are suffered to remain after due notice thereof.

Vaults and privies, restriction upon erection.

Ib.

11. If any person shall erect or set up, or cause to be erected or set up, or shall continue any necessary or privy within nine feet of any street, lane, alley, court, square, or public place, or within a like distance of any adjoining lot, dwelling house, shop, or well, or any public building, such person shall forfeit and pay five dollars, and a further

penalty of five dollars for every month the necessary or privy shall continue and so remain. *Provided*, that these penalties shall not be incurred in any case where there is a necessary or privy already erected, or where one may hereafter be erected, with a vault under such necessary of the size of the same, eight feet deep, and enclosed with stone or bricks, well laid in water-proof cement.

Proviso.

12. No person shall open or empty a vault or privy within the city, except by the permission of the city marshal in writing, as is hereinafter ordered. When the surface of the contents of the vault of any privy shall be within twelve inches of the surface of the ground, the owner or occupant shall apply for permission to empty the same; and the city marshal shall give a permit directing the emptying of such vault, and the manner thereof. But no permit shall be given to empty the vault of a privy between the first day of July and the first day of September, unless the city marshal shall deem it necessary for the health or comfort of the inhabitants in the vicinity thereof, on inspection by himself or some other person by him appointed.

Regulations as to cleansing vaults and privies.

Ib.

13. No vault or privy shall be opened or emptied, or the contents, or any part thereof, conveyed into or through any part of the city except between the hours of ten o'clock in the evening and sunrise, in a vessel or vehicle that is water tight and closely covered. Nor shall any vessel or vehicle containing such contents be permitted to stand in any part of the city, except while loading, but the same shall be immediately removed to its place of destination and deposit, which place shall be without the limits of the city, or on the city farm, or other place remote from dwelling houses. And any person violating any of the provisions of this section, shall forfeit and pay not less than three nor more than ten dollars for each offense.

Contents not to be conveyed through streets except in water tight vessel.

Ib.

To be conveyed without city limits.

14. Fresh fish may be sold in any part of the city below high water mark; and no person shall sell fresh fish

Fresh fish, where sold.

Ord., Feb. 17, 1863.

in any other part of the city, except as hereinafter provided, under a penalty of five dollars for each offence. But the mayor and aldermen may assign places for selling the same *above* high water mark, under section second of chapter twenty-one of the revised statutes of 1857, or other like statutory provisions, and under such rules and regulations as said board may, from time to time, prescribe. Before, however, any place shall be so assigned, a written petition shall be presented to the board therefor, setting forth in detail the provisions proposed to be made for guarding against injury to the public health, and if the board is satisfied that such proposed arrangements are sufficient for such purpose, they shall personally inspect the premises named in the petition, and shall make no assignment until it appears to them that such provisions are secured. Whenever, in the opinion of said board, the public health requires the revoking such assignment, they shall at once revoke the same, with or without notice as they shall see fit.

Same.

Rev. Ord., 1855.

15. Nothing contained in the previous sections shall prevent any person from carrying and selling fresh fish, free from offal, in any part of the city during the year, in carts or vehicles suitably covered to preserve the fish from the sun, except that from the first day of June to the first day of September they shall not be carried and sold, as aforesaid, between the hours of nine A. M. and four P. M. under a penalty of five dollars for each offense.

Offensive substances not to be thrown into wells.

Ib.

16. No person shall throw, or cause to be thrown, into any well, cistern, or fountain, any stones, bricks, or part of bricks, dead animals, carrion, fish, offal, or any other substance whatever, under a penalty of not less than five dollars nor more than fifty dollars.

Unwholesome provisions not to be sold.

Ib.

17. No person shall knowingly sell or offer for sale within the city any unwholesome, stale or putrid articles of provisions, nor any meat that has been blown, raised or stuffed, nor any measly pork, nor any diseased meat of any kind, under a penalty of not less than twenty dollars nor more than fifty dollars for each offense.

18. If any person shall erect, place, or continue any hog-sty within one hundred feet of any street, square, lane, or alley, or of any dwelling house, such person shall forfeit and pay for every such offense, the sum of five dollars, and the further sum of five dollars for every week during which any hog or swine shall be kept or continued in such sty.

Regulations respecting hog-sties.

Rev. Ord., 1855.

19. All house offal, whether consisting of animal or vegetable substances, shall be deposited in convenient vessels, and be kept in some convenient place, to be taken away by such person or persons as shall be appointed by the mayor and aldermen for that purpose.

House offal.

To be taken away.

20. A city cart or other suitable vehicle shall be provided and furnished with a bell to give notice of its approach, which shall pass through all the streets, lanes and courts of the city, not less than twice in every week, to receive and carry away all such house offal as may have been accumulated in the vessels aforesaid.

City cart to collect offal.

Ib., as amended by Ord., May 12, 1863.

21. The mayor and aldermen shall appoint, annually, a suitable person to take charge of the cart or other vehicle mentioned in the preceding section, and to collect and carry away the house offal accumulated as aforesaid; and the person so appointed may appoint a deputy, when he may deem it necessary.

Mayor and aldermen to appoint person to have charge of cart.

Rev. Ord., 1855, as amended by city charter, 1863.

22. All persons shall promptly deliver the offal so accumulated on their premises to the person appointed as aforesaid to receive the same. And if any person shall neglect to provide suitable vessels for the deposit of such house offal, or shall in any way hinder or delay the person so appointed to receive it, in the performance of his duty aforesaid, he shall forfeit and pay a sum not less than two nor more than twenty dollars for each and every offense.

Offal to be delivered to person so appointed.

Rev. Ord., 1855.

23. No person shall go about collecting any house offal, consisting of animal or vegetable substances, or carry the same through any of the streets, lanes, or courts of the city, except the person appointed as aforesaid, or his

No other person to collect offal.

Ib.

Penalty.

deputy, under a penalty of not less than two nor more than twenty dollars for each and every offense.

Vaults and privies in unhealthy condition to be cleansed.

Ib.

24. Whenever any vault, privy, or drain, shall, in the opinion of the mayor or health officer, by its filth or dirt, become dangerous to the health, or prejudicial to the comfort of the citizens, the agent, occupant, or other person having charge of the land in which any vault, privy, or drain may be situated, the state and condition of which shall be in violation of the provisions of this ordinance, shall remove, cleanse, alter, amend, or repair the same, within a reasonable time after notice in writing to that effect, given by the mayor, any alderman, or the city marshal. In case of neglect or refusal for the space of five days, the mayor and aldermen shall cause the same to be removed, cleansed, altered, amended or repaired, as they may deem expedient, at the expense of the owner, agent, occupant, or other person, as aforesaid.

In case of neglect or refusal, to be done by mayor and aldermen at expense of owner.

Mayor and aldermen may remove persons from tenements where too numerous or unprovided with vaults.

Ib.

25. Whenever, upon due examination, it shall appear to the mayor and aldermen that the number of persons occupying any tenement or building in the city, is so great as to be the cause of nuisance and sickness, and the source of filth, or that any tenements or buildings are not furnished with suitable vaults, privies, or drains, they may thereupon issue their notice in writing to such persons, or any of them, requiring them to remove from and quit such tenement, or building, within such time as the mayor and aldermen shall deem reasonable. And if the person or persons so notified, or any of them, shall neglect or refuse to remove and quit, within the time mentioned in such notice, the mayor and aldermen are hereby authorized and empowered, thereupon forcibly to remove them, and to close up such tenement, and the same shall not be again occupied as a dwelling place under a penalty of not less than fifty dollars, to be recovered of the owner or owners, if they shall have knowingly permitted the same to be occupied.

Penalty.

26. No person shall hang or spread, or expose in any street, lane, alley, court or public place, any raw, dried, tanned, or dressed skins, hides or leather, under a penalty of not less than three nor more than ten dollars for each offense.

Hides or leather not to be exposed in streets.

Ib.

INTERMENT OF THE DEAD.

27. The department relative to the interment of the dead shall be placed under the control of one superintendent to be called the superintendent of burials, who shall ex-officio be an undertaker, whose duty it shall be, and he shall have power, to carry into execution all power and authority vested in the city council relative to the interment of the dead, the establishment of the police of the cemeteries and burying grounds, and the regulations of funerals and funeral processions, subject always to the authority and control of the mayor and aldermen; and it shall be the duty of said superintendent to carry into effect the ordinances of the city council and the laws of the State relative thereto.

Superintendent of burials.

Ib.

Authority.

To be subject to the regulation of mayor and aldermen.

To carry into effect city ordinances, &c.

28. Said superintendent shall be appointed annually, on the second Monday of the month of March, or as soon thereafter as may be, by the mayor, by the advice and consent of the aldermen, and he shall hold his office for one year, and until another be chosen, unless previously removed by the mayor, by the advice and consent as aforesaid, and in case of vacancy in said office on account of removal, death, or resignation, the mayor shall appoint a successor for the remainder of the year, and the said officer shall receive such compensation as the city council shall deem reasonable, and he shall be sworn to the faithful execution of his office, and shall give such bonds for the faithful performance of his duties, as shall be satisfactory to the mayor and aldermen.

Superintendent to be chosen annually.

Ib., as amended by city charter, § 6.

To be sworn.

To give bonds.

29. It shall be the duty of said superintendent to keep the fences, walls and gates of the several burying grounds

Duties of superintendent of burials.

Ib.

in the city in good repair, to take care that said burying grounds are well secured by locks and bolts, to designate the place, depth and width of every grave dug therein, to cause said graves to be dug in exact ranges and parallel with the lines as laid out in said cemetery, and as near to each other as he may think proper, and to take care that said graves be so filled and elevated that water may not remain thereon; and he shall record in a book to be kept for that purpose, the name, age and sex of each person interred, the family to which the deceased belonged, the disease of which he or she died, and whether resident or stranger, the time when interred, the number and range of the grave or tomb, &c., and report to the city council, in the month of February, annually, a list of such interments during the preceding year, specifying the particulars aforesaid as recorded.

Funeral cars to be in care of superintendent.

Ib.

30. All funeral cars used in and owned by the city shall be under the care of said superintendent, and shall be deposited for safe keeping in places provided for that purpose; and it shall be the duty of said superintendent to cause them to be kept clean and in good repair, and he shall not permit any person to use the same, except undertakers who are duly licensed.

Undertakers to be appointed and licensed by mayor and aldermen.

Ib., as amended by city charter, § 6.

May employ porters.

May be removed.

31. A sufficient number of undertakers shall annually, on the second Tuesday of March, or as soon thereafter as may be, be appointed and licensed by the mayor, by the advice and consent of the aldermen, who shall hold their offices one year, or until others are appointed in their stead, and who shall be responsible for the decent, orderly and faithful management of the funerals undertaken by them, and a strict compliance with the ordinances of the city in this behalf. Each undertaker may employ porters of decent and sober character to assist him, and shall be accountable to the mayor and aldermen for their conduct, and said undertakers and porters shall always be removable at the pleasure of the mayor. And all persons not licensed as

undertakers as aforesaid, are hereby forbidden and prohibited from undertaking the management of any funeral, under a penalty of not less than ten nor more than twenty dollars for each offense.

Undertakers not licensed, prohibited from acting as such.
Penalty.

32. No person shall bury or inter, or cause to be buried or interred, or deposit in the city tomb, any dead body, without first having obtained a license so to do, from the superintendent of burials, whose duty it shall be to grant the same to any licensed undertaker. And no person shall bury or inter, or cause to be buried or interred, any dead body, at any other time of the day than between sunrise and sunset, except when otherwise ordered by the superintendent of burials.

No interments to be made without license from superintendent of burials.
Ib., as amended by Ord., Dec. 18, 1857, § 2.
No interments to be made except between sunrise and sunset, except, &c.

33. The undertakers shall be allowed to charge and receive the following fees for their services, to wit: For services and interring an adult in Evergreen Cemetery, including hearse and porter's fee, seven dollars; and for a child five dollars. For interring in either cemetery in the city, including hearse and porter's fee, five dollars; and for a child four dollars.

Undertaker's fees.
Rev. Ord., 1855.

For opening church and carrying the body into the same for funeral services, an additional fee of two dollars. For taking up body from either cemetery within the city, and removing and interring the same in Evergreen Cemetery, five dollars; for every additional body taken up, removed and interred aforesaid at the same time, three dollars.

For taking up and removing the body of a child to Evergreen Cemetery, three dollars and fifty cents.

For services attending funeral and depositing the body of an adult in the city tomb, four dollars; for removing and interring the same in Eastern Cemetery, one dollar and fifty cents; in Western Cemetery, two dollars.

For attending funeral services and depositing a child in city tomb, three dollars; for removing and interring the same in Eastern Cemetery, one dollar; in Western Cemetery, one dollar and fifty cents.

Depth of graves.

Ib.

34. All graves for adult persons shall be dug not less than five feet deep; and the depth for children shall be left to the discretion of the superintendent. The corpse of every person of two years old and upwards shall be conveyed to the place of interment in a funeral car.

No body to be removed from city without permission of superintendent.

Ib.

Superintendent to attend to removal.

Ib., as amended by Ord., Aug. 26, 1859.

35. If any person shall be desirous to remove out of the city the body of a deceased person for interment, he shall make application to the superintendent of burials for permission so to do, and said superintendent shall grant such permission if no cause shall appear for withholding the same, and shall attend to such removal in person, or employ one of the undertakers of the city to attend thereto; and for a permit for such removal, the superintendent shall be entitled to receive the sum of twenty-five cents, provided that the provisions of this section shall not apply to interments made in Evergreen Cemetery, Forest City Cemetery, and Calvary Cemetery.

Undertakers to make returns to superintendent.

Rev. Ord., 1855.

36. Every undertaker shall within twenty-four hours after attending the interment of any deceased person, make a return in writing to the superintendent of burials, of the name, age and sex of the deceased, the names of parents when known, date of death, whether resident or stranger, and the date and place of interment.

Bodies not to be removed without permit of superintendent.

Ib.

37. No person shall remove any bodies or the remains of any bodies, from any of the graves or tombs in the city, or disturb or break up, or remove any body in any tomb or grave without special permission of the superintendent of burials.

Bodies in city tomb to be removed, except, &c.

Ib.

38. All bodies that are or may be deposited in the city tomb, waiting burial in any of the cemeteries belonging to the city, shall be removed therefrom, on or before the fifteenth day of May of each year, unless they shall be suffered to remain by special permission from the superintendent of burials.

Superintendent to remove bodies.

Ib.

39. If the requirements of the preceding sections are not complied with, it shall be the duty of the superintendent of burials to remove all such bodies from said tomb,

and properly inter the same, at the expense of the parties interested.

40. No person shall bury or inter, or cause to be buried or interred any dead body in either of the cemeteries within the city, except in family tombs, or lots, or plats that have heretofore been assigned for family burying-grounds, and in which there may be sufficient space for the interment of dead bodies.

Bodies not to be interred in city cemeteries, except, &c.
Ord., June 24, 1859, § 1.

41. Whenever the mayor and aldermen deem that any additional interments in any family tomb, lot or plat, in either of the cemeteries within the city would be injurious to public health, they are hereby authorized to order that such tomb, lot or plat shall be closed, and to forbid the same to be used thereafter for the purpose of interment.

Mayor and aldermen authorized to close tombs, &c.
Ib, § 2.

42. The mayor and aldermen are authorized to make and adopt any regulations in relation to the interment of the dead, which they may deem expedient, not inconsistent with the foregoing provisions.

Mayor and aldermen to make regulations, &c.
Rev. Ord., 1855.

43. Any person who shall be guilty of any violation of any of the provisions of this ordinance in relation to which a penalty is not prescribed, shall for each and every offense, forfeit and pay a sum not less than five nor more than twenty dollars, to be recovered by complaint before the municipal court, or by action in the name of the city.

Penalties for violation of foregoing provisions.
Ib.

[For duties of superintendent of burials relating to Evergreen and Forest City Cemeteries, see chapter on CEMETERIES, *ante*.]

HISTORIES OF CITIES AND TOWNS.

STATUTE.

Towns authorized to procure histories and raise money therefor.

Towns authorized to procure histories and raise money therefor.

Act, Feb. 15, 1859.

The inhabitants of cities and towns are hereby authorized and empowered to procure the writing and publication of the histories of their own cities and towns, and for this purpose, may raise such sums of money as may be necessary for the same, in the same manner as cities and towns are now authorized to raise money for necessary city and town charges.

HOUSES OF CORRECTION.

STATUTES.

STATUTES.

Town houses of correction and their object.

R. S., chap. 141, § 17.

1. Any town, at its own expense, may build and maintain a house of correction, or may appropriate in part or in whole any work-house owned by such town for such purpose; and any person belonging to or found in such town, liable to be sent by a justice of the peace to the county house of correction, may be sent to such town house by any justice of such town, and by the like process; but the provisions of this section shall not restrain such justice from committing any person so liable to the county house of correction; and the respondent party may appeal as in other cases.

Overseers thereof.

Ib. § 18.

2. The selectmen of any such town shall annually appoint three, five, or seven discreet persons, overseers of such house, and may establish, from time to time, such rules and orders not repugnant to law, as they deem necessary for governing and furnishing persons lawfully committed thereto.

Of work-houses for like uses. R. S. Ib. § 19.

3. When any work-house is so appropriated for a house of correction, the master thereof shall be master of the house of correction; but in other cases the overseers thereof shall appoint a suitable master, removable at their pleasure.

Compensation of overseers and master. Ib. § 20.

4. The overseers and master of such town house of correction shall have such compensation for their services as is annually voted by their towns.

Duties of the overseers. Ib. 21.

5. The overseers, from time to time, shall examine into the prudential concerns and management of such house, and see that the master faithfully discharges his duty.

Support of the prisoners. Ib. § 22.

6. Every person committed to such town house of correction shall be supplied by the keeper with a suitable quantity of bread and water, or other nourishment, as the overseers order; and all expenses incurred for commitment and maintenance, exceeding the earnings of the person confined, shall be paid by the parties liable for similar charges in the case of persons committed to a county house of correction.

Powers of overseers to commit persons. Ib. § 23.

7. The overseers of any such town house of correction may commit thereto, for a term not exceeding forty-eight hours, any person publicly appearing intoxicated, or in any manner violating the public peace, when the safety of the person intoxicated, or the good order of the community requires it, till such person can be conveniently carried before a magistrate and restrained by complaint and warrant in the usual course of criminal prosecutions.

Form of order for commitment. Ib. § 24.

8. The form of the order for commitment may be in substance as follows:

To A. B., master of the house of correction in the town of——: You are hereby required to receive and keep C. D. in said house of correction for the term of——hours, unless sooner discharged by our order.

E. F., G. H., } Overseers of said house of correction.

And any sheriff, deputy sheriff, constable or other person, to whom such order is given by said overseers, shall forthwith apprehend and convey such person to said house of correction, and deliver him to the master thereof, to be taken and kept agreeably to the order; and shall be entitled to receive from the town such fees for service and travel as are allowed for service of warrants.

INNHOLDERS AND VICTUALERS.

STATUTES.

1. Licenses to innholders and victualers, when and by whom granted.
2. Persons licensed to give bond; form thereof.
3. Licenses may be granted for a part of the year in certain cases.
4. Fee for license, and record of licenses.
5. Duty of innholders to provide entertainment.
6. Duty of victualers.
7. Innholders and victualers to keep up signs with their names and employments.
8. Not to keep instruments of gaming, or allow any gaming on their premises. Penalty for gaming in said premises.
9. Reveling, disorderly conduct and drunkenness prohibited in such premises.
10. Penalty for being a common innholder or victualer without a license.
11. Duty of licensing board to prosecute for all violations hereof. Penalties, how recovered and appropriated.

STATUTES.

Licenses to innholders and victualers, when and by whom granted.

R. S., chap. 27, § 1.

1. The municipal officers, treasurer, and clerk of every town shall annually meet on the first Monday of May, or on the succeeding day, or both, and at such time and place in said town as they appoint by posting up notices in two or more public places therein, at least seven days previously, stating the purpose of the meeting; and at such meeting may license under their hands as many persons of good moral character, and under such restrictions and regulations as they deem necessary, to be

innholders and victualers in said town, until the day succeeding the first Monday in May of the next following year, in such house or other building, as the license specifies.

Persons licensed to give bond; form.

Ib. § 2.

2. No person shall receive his license, until he has given his bond to the treasurer, to the acceptance of the board granting it, with one or more sureties, in the penal sum of three hundred dollars, in substance as follows, viz:

"Know all men, that we, ——, as principal, and ——, as sureties, are holden and stand firmly bound to——, treasurer of the town of——, in the sum of three hundred dollars, to be paid to him, or his successor in said office; to the payment whereof we bind ourselves, our heirs, executors, and administrators, jointly and severally by these presents. Sealed with our seals. Dated the—— day of ——, in the year 18—. The condition of this obligation is such, that whereas the above bounden——has been duly licensed as a——within the said town of——, until the day succeeding the first Monday of May next; now if in all respects, he conforms to the provisions of the law relating to the business for which he is licensed, and to the rules and regulations, as provided by the licensing board in reference thereto, then this obligation shall be void, otherwise remain in full force."

Licenses may be granted for a part of the year.

Ib. § 3.

3. The licensing board may, at any other time, at a meeting specially called, and notified as aforesaid for the consideration of any application therefor to them made, grant such license on the like conditions; but all such licenses shall expire on the day aforesaid.

Fee for license, and record of all licenses.

Ib. § 4.

4. Every person licensed shall pay to the treasurer, for the use of such board, one dollar; and the clerk shall make a record of all licenses granted.

Duty of innholders to provide entertainment.

Ib. § 5.

5. Every innholder shall, at all times, be furnished with suitable provisions and lodging for strangers and travelers, and with stable room, hay, and provender for their horses and cattle; and with pasturing, if required by the terms of his license; and he shall grant such reasonable accommodations as occasion requires, to strangers, travelers, and others.

Duty of victualers. 10 Maine, 438. 16 Maine, 121. Ib. § 6.

6. Every victualer shall have all the rights and privileges and be subject to all the duties and obligations of an innholder, except furnishing lodging for travelers, and stable room, hay, or provender for cattle.

Innholders and victualers to keep up signs. Ib. § 7.

7. Every innholder and victualer shall, at all times, have a board or sign affixed to his house, shop, cellar, or store, or in some conspicuous place near it, with his name at large thereon, and the employment for which he is licensed.

Not to allow gaming on their premises.

8. No innholder or victualer shall have or keep about his house, shop, or other buildings, yards, gardens, or dependencies, any dice, cards, bowls, billiards, quoits, or other implements used in gambling; or suffer any person resorting thither to use or exercise any of said games, or any other unlawful game or sport therein; and every person who shall use or exercise any such game or sport in any place herein prohibited, shall forfeit five dollars.

Penalty. 23 Maine, 43. Ib. § 8.

Reveling, disorderly conduct, drunkenness, prohibited, &c. Ib. § 9.

9. No innholder or victualer shall suffer any reveling, riotous, or disorderly conduct in his house, shop, or other dependencies; nor any drunkenness or excess therein.

Penalty for being a common innholder or victualer without a license. Ib. § 10.

10. No person shall be a common innholder or victualer without a license, under a penalty of not more than fifty dollars.

Duty of licensing board to prosecute. 12 Maine, 204. Ib. § 11.

11. The licensing board shall prosecute for any violations of this chapter, that come to their knowledge, by complaint, indictment, or action of debt, in any court of competent jurisdiction; and all penalties recovered shall be for the use of the town where the offense is committed.

INSPECTION OF FLOUR.

STATUTES.

STATUTES.

1. The mayor and aldermen of cities and the selectmen of towns, in this State, are hereby authorized to appoint annually, in their respective cities and towns, one or more suitable persons to be inspectors of flour for the period of one year from the date of appointment, but no one who is interested in the manufacture, or sale of flour, shall be so appointed.

Appointment of inspectors authorized; manufacturers and dealers not eligible.

Act, Feb. 23, 1866.

2. Every such inspector, before entering upon the duties of his office, shall be sworn to the faithful and impartial discharge of the same, before the clerk of the city or town in which he is appointed, and such clerk shall give him a certificate of his appointment and qualification, upon payment of a fee of fifty cents, which certificate shall be exhibited on the demand of any person interested in any inspection made by the holder of it.

Inspector to be sworn and receive certificate of appointment.

Ib. § 2.

Inspection, how made, and duty of inspectors defined.

Ib. § 3.

3. Inspection of flour in this State shall be for the purpose of ascertaining its soundness; every package of flour inspected under the provisions of this act, shall be opened sufficiently to allow a trier to be passed through it, and a sample of the whole length of the package shall be taken out and examined by the inspector, who shall mark upon each package with a brand, or stencil, the word SOUND or the word UNSOUND, as the quality of the flour contained in each shall be found, together with his name, residence, office, and the year of inspection. Every inspector shall keep a record of all flour inspected by him, in a book devoted exclusively to that use, which record he shall be required to exhibit to any person requiring it.

Inspectors to keep records and exhibit same.

Penalty for fraudulent marks, &c.

Ib. § 4.

4. Every inspector, who shall wilfully, falsely and fraudulently mark any package of flour with a mark indicating a quality different from the true quality, shall be punished by a fine of five dollars for each package so falsely and fraudulently marked, and shall also forfeit to any person injured thereby, three times the amount of damage to be recovered in an action of debt.

Penalty for alteration, &c., of inspection mark.

Ib. § 5.

5. Every person who shall, with intent to defraud and deceive, alter, obliterate or counterfeit, the inspection marks of any inspector, placed on any package of flour under the provisions of this act, and every person who, with intent to deceive and defraud, shall place upon any package of flour, marks which falsely purport to be inspection marks under the provisions of this act, shall, for every offence, be punished by fine not exceeding fifty dollars, and upon conviction of so altering, obliterating, counterfeiting or placing marks falsely purporting to be inspection marks, on as many as ten packages at one time, shall also be punished by imprisonment in the county jail not exceeding ten months.

Purchasers of flour may require inspection of same before delivery.

Ib. § 6.

6. Any person buying flour, may require the same to be inspected before it is delivered; the fees of the inspector shall be five cents a package, for lots of less than ten

packages ; for lots of more than ten and not exceeding twenty packages, two cents a package, and for any and every package exceeding twenty, one cent ; to be paid by the person demanding the inspection.

Fees for inspection, and by whom to be paid.

7. The inspectors of flour appointed under this act, shall, whenever required, in addition to the inspection of the soundness or unsoundness of the article examined, determine whether it conforms to and equals the sample furnished to them, and shall mark, with some distinct, and intelligible mark, the packages that are found like the sample, and for this service they may charge an additional compensation of one-half cent per package.

Duties of inspectors in relation to sample packages.

Ib. § 7.

8. Nothing contained in this act shall be held to prohibit, or render illegal, any contract for the manufacture, or sale of flour, which has not been inspected, when inspection is not required by the buyer or seller.

Provisions hereof, not applicable when inspection is not demanded.

Ib. § 8.

INTELLIGENCE OFFICES.

STATUTES.

Municipal officers may license intelligence offices.

Penalty.

R. S., chap. 35, § 6.

1. The municipal officers of any town may, upon payment of one dollar each, grant licenses to suitable persons for one year, unless sooner revoked after notice and for cause, to keep offices for the purpose of obtaining employment for domestics, servants, or other laborers, except seamen, or of giving information relating thereto, or of doing the usual business of intelligence offices; and no person shall keep such an office, without a license, under a penalty not exceeding fifty dollars for every day it is so kept.

Penalties, how recovered and appropriated.

Ib. § 2.

2. The penalty provided in this chapter may be recovered by complaint or indictment, in any court of competent jurisdiction, for the use of the State, when not otherwise appropriated.

JURORS.

STATUTES.

1. Board for preparing lists of jurors; towns may make alterations.
2. How the lists are to be prepared.
3. Persons exempted from serving.
4. Tickets of names to be kept in jury box; liable to be drawn once in three years.
5. Number required to be kept in jury box; names may be withdrawn in certain cases.
6. Commissioners to divide the county into jury districts, and furnish copy of division to clerk; how divided and numbered.
7. Rule by which the clerk shall issue venires.
8. Grand jurors to serve one year; venires for such to issue forty days before second Monday of September annually.
9. Grand and traverse jurors to attend on the first day of the term, unless, at a previous term, the court designates a different day.
10. Distribution of venires, and notice of meetings to draw jurors, &c.

11, 12, 13. Mode of drawing jurors; date of draft to be indorsed on the ticket.

14. Constables to notify jurors, and return venires.
15. Indorsement to be transferred, if ticket is renewed.
16. Penalty for neglect of municipal officers or clerk.
17. Penalty for neglect of constable or town.
18. Penalty for neglect of juror to attend.
19. Penalty for fraud by town clerk or municipal officer.

Board for preparing lists of jurors, &c.
R. S., chap. 106, § 1.

1. The municipal officers, treasurer, and clerk of each town constitute a board for preparing lists of jurors to be laid before the town for their approval; and the town, in legal town meeting, by a majority of the legal voters assembled, may strike out such names as they think proper from such lists, but shall not insert any other names.

How the lists are to be prepared.
Ib. § 2.

2. Such board, at least once in every three years, shall prepare a list of such persons, of good moral character, and qualified, as the constitution directs, to vote for representatives, under the age of seventy years, in such town, as they judge best qualified to serve as jurors.

Persons exempted from serving.
Ib. § 3.

3. The following persons shall be exempted from serving as jurors, and their names shall not be placed on the lists: the governor, councillors, judges and clerks of the common law courts, secretary and treasurer of the State, all officers of the United States, judges and registers of probate, registers of deeds, settled ministers of the gospel, officers of colleges, preceptors of incorporated academies, physicians and surgeons, cashiers of incorporated banks, sheriffs and their deputies, coroners, counsellors and attorneys at law, county commissioners, constables, and constant ferrymen.

Tickets of names to be kept in jury box., &c.
Ib. § 4.

4. After the list of jurors is approved by the town, the board shall write their names upon tickets, and place them in the jury box, to be kept by the town clerk; and the persons whose names are in the box shall be liable to be drawn and to serve on any jury, at any court for which they are drawn, once in every three years and not oftener, except as herein provided.

Number required to be kept in jury box, &c.
Ib. § 5.

5. Each town shall provide, and constantly keep in the box, a number of names ready to be drawn when required, not less than one, nor more than two for every hundred persons in the town, according to the census taken next before preparing the box; and the board shall withdraw from it the name of any person convicted of any scandalous crime, or guilty of any gross immorality.

6. Within one year after every new census, and oftener if a considerable change of population renders it proper, the county commissioners shall divide their county into not less than four, nor more than twelve districts numerically designated; and they shall place as many adjoining towns in each district, as will make the number of inhabitants in each, according to the last census, as nearly equal as may be, without dividing a town; and shall deliver a copy of such division immediately to the clerk of the courts in their county.

Commissioners to divide the county into jury districts, &c.

Ib. § 6.

7. The grand and traverse jurors shall be drawn from each jury district in such manner as to cause jurors, at each term of the court, to come from every part of the county as equally as may be, and, as far as practicable, from every town in rotation, having regard to the number of its inhabitants, taking not more than two grand jurors and two traverse jurors from the same town at the same time, unless from necessity, or some extraordinary cause, or to equalize the service; and the clerk of the courts shall issue venires to the constables accordingly.

Rule by which the clerk shall issue venires.

38 Maine, 200.

Ib. § 7.

8. Venires for grand jurors, to serve at the supreme judicial court, shall be issued at least forty days before the second Monday of September annually; and such jurors shall serve at every term of said court for the transaction of criminal business throughout the year.

Grand jurors to serve one year, &c.

Ib. § 8.

9. The grand and traverse jurors shall attend on the first day of the term for which they are drawn and summoned; unless the court at a previous term has designated a different day; and if so, the venire shall specify the day on which the jurors shall attend.

Jurors to attend on the first day of the term, &c.

Ib. § 9.

10. The sheriff on receiving venires for jurors shall immediately send them to the constables of the towns where directed, and each constable on receipt thereof shall notify the inhabitants of the town, qualified to vote for representatives, and especially the municipal officers and town clerk, by posting up notices in two public and con-

Venires, duties of sheriffs in relation to distribution of.

Constable shall notify inhabitants, &c.

—notice, how given. Ib. § 10, as amended by Act., 1861, chap. 7.

spicuous places in said town at least four days before such meeting, to assemble and be present at the draft of the jurors called for; which shall be six days at least before the sitting of the court to which the venire is returnable.

Mode of drawing jurors, &c. R. S., chap. 16, § 11.

11. The town clerk, or, in his absence, one of the municipal officers, shall carry the juror box into the meeting, which shall there be unlocked, and the tickets mixed by a majority of said officers present; and one of them shall draw out as many tickets as there are jurors required; and the persons whose names are drawn shall be returned as jurors, unless they have served on the jury within three years, or from sickness, absence beyond sea, without the limits, or in distant parts of the State, they are considered by the town unable to attend.

Same subject. Ib. § 12.

12. In either of said cases, or if a person is drawn who has been appointed to an office exempting him from serving, others shall be drawn in their stead; but any person thus excused, or returned and attending court, and there excused, shall not be excused on another draft, though within three years; and when all the persons, whose names are in the box, have served within three years, or are not liable to serve, the selectmen shall draw out the required number of those who have not served for eighteen months; and the clerk shall certify on the venire, that all persons whose names are in the box have served within three years, or are not liable to serve.

Date of draft to be indorsed on the ticket. Ib. § 13.

13. When a juror is drawn and not excused by the town, the municipal officers who drew his ticket shall indorse thereon the date of the draft and return it into the box.

Constables to notify jurors, and return venires. 5 Greenl. 333. Ib. § 14.

14. The constables shall notify the persons thus drawn four days at least before the sitting of the court, by reading the venire and indorsement thereon to them, or leaving at their usual place of abode a written notice that they have been drawn, and of the time and place of the sitting of the court where they are to attend; and

make a seasonable return of the venire with his doings thereon.

15. When a new list of jurors is made, the municipal officers shall transfer from the back of the old tickets to the new ones of the same persons, the minutes of the drafts made within the three preceding years.

Indorsement to be transferred, &c.
Ib. § 15.

16. If the municipal officers or town clerk neglect to perform their duties herein required, so that the jurors called for from their town are not returned, they shall be fined not less than ten, nor more than fifty dollars each.

Penalty for neglect of officers.
Ib. § 16.

17. Any constable, neglecting to perform his duties herein required, shall be fined not exceeding twenty dollars; and any town for a like neglect of its duties shall be fined not exceeding one hundred dollars.

Penalty for neglect of constable or town.
Ib. § 17.

18. Any juror, who, after being notified and returned, unnecessarily fails in his attendance, shall be fined as for contempt, not exceeding twenty dollars, unless he resides in Portland, and then not exceeding forty dollars.

Penalty for neglect of juror to attend.
Ib. § 19.

19. Any town clerk or municipal officer, who commits a fraud on the box previous to the draft, in drawing a juror or in returning a name into the box, which had been fairly drawn and drawing another in its stead, or in any other mode, shall be fined not exceeding two hundred dollars, half to the use of the State and half to the prosecutor.

Penalty for fraud by town officers.
Ib. § 20.

LAMPS AND LAMP POSTS.

STATUTE.

ORDINANCES.

STATUTE.

Injuries to monuments, guide boards, lamps, &c.

R. S., chap. 127, § 8.

Whoever wilfully and maliciously removes, defaces, or injures any lamp, or lamp post, or extinguishes any lamp on any bridge, street, way, or passage, shall be punished by imprisonment less than one year, and by fine not exceeding one hundred dollars.

ORDINANCES.

Committee on lamps and lamp posts to be appointed.

Rev. Ord., 1855.

To cause lamps to be set up at corners of streets.

1. There shall be appointed in the month of March, annually, a joint committee of the city council, to be called the committee on lamps and lamp posts, to consist of one member of the board of mayor and aldermen, and three members of the common council, and said committee shall cause to be set up and affixed lamps at the corners of such streets in the city as they may determine to be convenient and necessary.

Mayor and aldermen to make contracts, rules and regulations.

Ib.

2. The mayor and aldermen of the city, are hereby authorized and empowered to make all necessary contracts, rules, orders, and regulations respecting the said lamps, and the lighting and keeping the same in repair, and the regulation and preservation of the same, as they may deem most for the benefit of said city.

LEATHER.

STATUTES.

1. Manufacturer may stamp his name on leather, &c.
2. Inspectors of sole leather; their appointment; fees.
3. Mode of inspecting and stamping.

1. Every manufacturer of leather, and of boots and shoes, of any description, shall have the exclusive right of stamping them with the initials of his christian, and the whole of his surname; and such stamping shall be considered a warranty that the article is merchantable, and well made of good materials; and if any person fraudulently stamps any such articles with the name or stamp of any other person, he shall be punished by a fine not exceeding twenty dollars, or imprisonment not exceeding six months.

Manufacturer of leather, boots and shoes may stamp his name thereon, &c.

R. S., chap. 39, § 25.

2. The municipal officers of each town, when they deem it expedient, may appoint one or more suitable inspectors of sole leather, who shall be duly sworn, and receive such fees from their employer, as said officers establish; and when paid by the seller, to be repaid to him by the buyer; and when requested, shall go to any place in their town to inspect any sides of sole leather, which had not been inspected according to law in this State.

Appointment, oath, duties and fees of inspectors of sole leather.

Ib. § 26.

Mode of inspecting and stamping sole leather, &c.

Ib. § 27.

3. Each inspector shall provide himself with a proper apparatus, with which he shall weigh and stamp every side of sole leather inspected by him, with the weight thereof, his surname, and the name of his town; and on all sole leather made of good hides, and in the best manner, the word, "best," shall be stamped; on all made of such hides in a merchantable manner, the word, "good;" and on all other, the words, "second," or "third quality," "damaged" or "bad," according to the fact; and if any person counterfeits, alters or defaces such mark, he shall forfeit twenty dollars for each offense, half to the town and half to the person suing therefor.

LIBRARIES.

STATUTES.

1. Towns may establish libraries.
2. " may raise money therefor.
3. " may receive donations therefor.

1. Any town is authorized to establish and maintain a public library therein, for the use of the inhabitants, and provide suitable rooms therefor, under such regulations for its government as the inhabitants from time to time prescribe.

Towns may establish public libraries.

R. S., chap. 55, § 9.

2. Such town may appropriate, for the foundation and commencement of such library, a sum not exceeding one dollar, and for its maintenance and increase annually, a sum not exceeding twenty-five cents, for each of its ratable polls in the year next preceding that in which such appropriation is made.

May raise money therefor.

Ib. § 10.

3. Any town may receive, in its corporate capacity, and hold and manage, any devise, bequest, or donation, for the establishment, increase, or maintenance of a public library therein.

May receive and manage donations for that purpose.

Ib. § 11.

LUMBER.

STATUTES.

1. Towns to elect surveyors of boards, plank, timber, joist, shingles, clapboards, staves, hoops, and cullers of staves and hoops. Municipal officers may appoint surveyors of logs. All to be sworn.
2. All boards, plank, timber and joist to be surveyed before delivery on sale. Mode of measuring and marking same, and allowances. What kind of pine boards are merchantable, and what may be shipped out of the United States.

SHINGLES AND CLAPBOARDS.

3. Dimensions and quality of shingles Nos. 1, 2, and 3.
4. How shingles shall be split or sawed and packed. Forfeiture of shingles if deficiency of five in any bundle of No. 1, or if offered for sale before they are surveyed and branded.
5. Dimensions and quality of clapboards.

STAVES AND HOOPS.

6. Dimensions and quality of staves, and how enumerated.
7. Dimensions and quality of hogshead hoops; how packed and enumerated; and forfeiture of deficient bundles.
8. Not to be offered for sale, before surveyed and branded and certificate given, under a penalty. Forfeiture for master of vessel unlawfully exporting same, for first and second offence, and appropriation thereof.
9. Master or owner to produce surveyor's certificate before clearance, and affidavit thereto.
10. Penalty of surveyor or culler to neglect or refuse oath of office, and for neglecting or practicing fraud in his official duties.
11. Penalty and forfeitures, how recovered.

LOGS.

12. Duty of surveyors of logs.

1. Every town, at its annual meeting, shall elect one or more surveyors of boards, plank, timber, and joist; one or more surveyors of shingles, clapboards, staves and hoops; and every town containing a port of delivery, whence staves and hoops are usually exported, shall also elect two or more viewers and cullers of staves and hoops; and the municipal officers of any town may, if they deem it necessary, appoint not exceeding seven surveyors of logs, and all of said officers shall be duly sworn.

Towns to elect surveyors of lumber.

R. S., chap. 41, § 11.

2. All boards, plank, timber, and joist, offered for sale, shall, before delivery, be surveyed by a sworn surveyor thereof, and if he have doubts of the dimensions, he shall measure the same, and mark the contents thereon, making reasonable allowance for rots, knots, and splits, drying and shrinking; pine boards three-fourths of an inch thick when fully seasoned, and in that proportion when partly seasoned, shall be considered merchantable; and no pine boards, except sheathing boards, shall be shipped for exportation beyond the United States, but such as are square edged, not less than seven-eighths of an inch thick, nor less than ten feet long, under penalty of being forfeited to the town whence shipped.

Lumber to be surveyed before delivery.

Ib. § 12.

SHINGLES AND CLAPBOARDS.

3. All shingles, packed for exportation beyond the State, shall be sixteen inches long, free from shakes and worm holes, and at least three-eighths of an inch thick at the butt end when green, and if of pine, free from sap. They shall be four inches wide on an average, not less than three inches wide in any part, hold their width three-fourths of the way to the thin end, well shaved or sawed, and be denominated number one; but shingles intended for sale within this State, if of inferior quality or of less dimensions, may be surveyed and classed accordingly,

Dimensions and quality of shingles Nos. 1, 2 and 3.

Ib. § 13.

under the denominations of number two, and number three.

How shingles shall be split, or sawed and packed, &c.

Ib. § 14.

4. All shingles shall be split or sawed crosswise the grain; each bundle shall contain two hundred and fifty shingles, and if in square bundles, twenty-five courses, and be twenty-two inches and a half at the lay; and when packed to be surveyed as number one, or for exportation, if in any bundle there are five shingles deficient in the proper dimensions, soundness or number, to make two hundred and fifty merchantable shingles; or if any shingles are offered for sale, before they are surveyed and measured by a sworn surveyor of some town in the county where made, and the quality branded on the hoop or band of the bundle, unless the parties otherwise agree, they shall be forfeited to the town where the offense is committed.

Dimensions and quality of clapboards.

Ib. § 15.

5. All clapboards, exposed to sale or packed for exportation, shall be made of good sound timber, free from shakes and worm holes, and if of pine, clear of sap; and they shall be at least five-eighths of an inch thick on the back or thickest part, five inches wide, and four feet six inches long, and straight and well shaved or sawed.

STAVES AND HOOPS.

Dimensions and quality of staves, and how enumerated.

Ib. § 16.

6. Staves packed for sale or exportation shall be well and proportionably split, and of the following dimensions, viz.:

White oak butt staves, at least five feet in length, five inches wide, and one inch and a quarter thick on the heart or thinnest edge, and every part thereof;

White oak pipe staves shall be at least four feet and eight inches in length, four inches broad in the narrowest part, and not less than three-quarters of an inch thick on the heart or thinnest edge;

White or red oak hogshead staves shall be at least forty-two inches long, and not less than half an inch thick on the least or thinnest edge;

White or red oak barrel staves for a market out of the United States, shall be thirty-two inches long; if for use within the United States, thirty inches long; and in either case, half an inch thick on the heart or thinnest edge;

All white or red oak hogshead or barrel staves shall be at least, one with another, four inches in breadth, and no one less than three inches in breadth in the narrowest part; and those of the breadth last mentioned shall be clear of sap; and two staves shall be sold as one cast; fifty casts, one hundred staves; and ten hundred, one thousand.

Dimensions and quality of hogshead hoops; how packed, &c.

Ib. § 17.

7. All hogshead hoops, exposed for sale, or packed for exportation, shall be from ten to thirteen feet in length, and of oak, ash or walnut, and of good and sufficient substance, well shaved; if of oak or ash, at least one inch broad, and, if of walnut, three-quarters of an inch at the least end; the different lengths shall be made up in bundles by themselves; each bundle shall contain twenty-five hoops, four bundles make one hundred, and ten hundred, one thousand; and every bundle, packed for sale or exportation, found to be deficient in number or dimensions, shall be forfeited to the use of the town where exhibited.

The articles hereinbefore named, not to be offered for sale, &c.

Ib. § 18.

8. No person shall deliver on sale, or ship or attempt to ship for exportation, any boards, plank, timber, joists, shingles, clapboards, staves, or hoops, before they have been surveyed, measured, viewed or culled, as the case may be, and branded by the proper officer, and a certificate thereof given by him specifying the number, quality, and quantity thereof, under a penalty of two dollars a thousand, by quantity or tale, as such article is usually sold, one-half to the town where the offense is committed, and the other to the prosecutor; and in addition thereto, the master or owner of any vessel, exporting any of the articles aforesaid beyond the limits of the United States contrary to law, shall for the first offence forfeit two

hundred dollars for the use of the town whence said articles are exported; and if after conviction he commits a second offense in the same vessel, he shall forfeit the same sum, and the vessel, if found in this State, shall also be forfeited to the same use.

Master or owner to produce surveyor's certificate before clearance, &c.

Ib. § 19.

9. The master or owner of any vessel, having any of the lumber or other articles mentioned in the preceding section on board, for exportation as aforesaid, shall, before the vessel is cleared at the custom house, produce to the collector a certificate from the proper officer, that the same have been duly surveyed, measured, viewed, or culled, as the case may require; and such master or owner shall likewise make oath before the collector, or any justice of the peace, whose certificate shall be returned to the collector, that the articles so shipped for exportation are the same articles thus surveyed, measured, viewed or culled, that he has no others on board of the like description, and that he will not take any others.

Penalty for surveyor or culler to neglect or refuse oath of office, &c.

Ib. § 20.

10. If any person, duly elected a surveyor, measurer, viewer, or culler of any of said articles under the provisions of this chapter, neglects or refuses to take the oath of his office and to serve therein, he shall forfeit three dollars to the use of the town, and another person shall be elected to his place, who shall take the oath and serve as aforesaid under the like penalty; and the like proceedings shall be had, until the office is filled; or if any such officer duly qualified unnecessarily refuses or neglects to attend to the duties of his office when requested, he shall forfeit three dollars; and if he connives at or willingly allows any breach of the provisions hereof, or practices any other fraud or deceit in his official duties, he shall forfeit thirty dollars to the use aforesaid.

Penalties how recovered.

Ib. § 21.

11. All the pecuniary penalties aforesaid may be recovered by action of debt, indictment, or complaint, and all other forfeitures, by a libel filed according to law by the treasurer of the town interested therein, or by any inhabitant thereof.

LOGS.

12. Surveyors of logs may inspect, survey, and measure all mill logs floated or brought to market, or offered for sale in their respective towns and divide them into several classes, corresponding to the different quality of boards and other sawed lumber, which may be manufactured from them; and they shall give certificates under their hands, of the quantity and quality thereof to the person at whose request they are surveyed.

Duty of surveyors of logs.

Ib. § 22.

LUNATICS.

STATUTES.

Municipal officers to decide on cases and commit to hospital with certificate; keep a record of doings.

35 Maine, 402.

R. S., chap. 143, § 12.

1. All insane persons, not sent to any insane hospital, shall be subject to examination, as hereinafter provided. The municipal officers of towns shall constitute a board of examiners, and, on complaint in writing of any relative or justice of the peace of their town, they shall immediately inquire into the condition of any insane person therein; call before them all testimony necessary for a full understanding of the case; and if they think such person is insane, and that his comfort and safety, or that of others interested, will thereby be promoted, they shall forthwith send him to the hospital, with a certificate, stating the fact of his insanity, and the town in which he resided or was found at the time of examination, and directing the super-

intendent to receive and detain him till he is restored or discharged by law, or by the superintendent and trustees. And they shall keep a record of their doings, and furnish a copy to any interested person requesting and paying for it.

2. The officers, ordering the commitment of a person unable to pay for his support, may certify in writing to the superintendent that fact, and that he has not relations liable and of sufficient ability to pay for it; and if the superintendent is satisfied that such certificate is true, the treasurer of the hospital may charge to the State one dollar per week for his board, and deduct it from the charge made to the patient or town for his support.

May certify inability to pay for his support, and treasurer may charge State one dollar per week.

Ib. § 13.

EXPENSES OF SUPPORTING THE INSANE AT THE HOSPITAL.

3. The certificate of commitment to the hospital, after a legal examination, shall be sufficient evidence, in the first instance, to charge the town, where the insane resided, or was found at the time of his arrest, for the expenses of his examination, commitment, and support in the hospital; but when his friends or others file a bond with the treasurer of the hospital, such town shall not be liable for his support, unless new action is had by reason of the inability of the patient or his friends longer to support him; and such action may be had in the same manner, and before the same tribunal, as if he had never been admitted to the hospital.

Towns, where insane person resided or was found, pay for support, unless a bond given for it.

Ib. § 18.

4. The person or town, liable for the support of a person when lawfully committed to the hospital, shall be liable therefor, and for the expenses of his removal, when unlawfully committed and removed; but the expenses of such removal are not to exceed ten cents per mile from the hospital to the place of commitment.

Do so when unlawfully committed, and expense of removal.

Ib. § 19.

5. Any town, thus made chargeable in the first instance, and paying for the commitment and support of

Towns have remedy against the person, or those liable for his support as a pauper.

Ib. § 20.

the insane in the hospital, may recover the amount paid of the insane, if able, or of persons legally liable for his support, or of the town where his legal settlement is, as if incurred for the ordinary expenses of any pauper; but if he has no legal settlement in this State, such expenses shall be refunded by the State; and the governor and council shall audit all such claims, and draw their warrant on the treasurer therefor. No insane person shall suffer any of the disabilities incident to pauperism, nor be hereafter deemed a pauper, by reason of such support.

DISCHARGE OF THE INSANE.

Those liable for his support may apply for discharge.

Ib. § 21.

6. When any friend, person or town, liable for the support of any patient, who has been in the hospital six months, not committed by order of the supreme judicial court, nor afflicted with homicidal insanity, thinks he is unreasonably detained, he may apply to the municipal officers of the town where the insane resides, and they shall inquire into the case, and summon before them any proper testimony, and their decision and order shall be binding on the parties. They shall tax legal costs and decide who shall pay them. If such application is unsuccessful, it shall not be made again till the expiration of another six months.

Overseers of poor to remove when notified so to do.

Ib. § 22.

7. When the overseers of any town, liable for the support of a patient at the hospital, are notified by mail by the superintendent, that he has recovered from his insanity, they shall cause him to be removed to their town; and if they neglect it for fifteen days, the superintendent shall cause it to be done at the expense of such town.

GUARDIANS FOR SUCH AS ARE SENT TO THE HOSPITAL.

8. When any man or unmarried woman, of twenty-one years of age, is sent to the hospital for insanity, the municipal officers of the town where such insane resides, may apply to the judge of probate for the same county for the appointment of a guardian, when they think it for the interest of the insane and to prevent waste of his property, and the judge, on their certificate to that effect, without notice to the insane, shall forthwith appoint some suitable guardian of the same county, who shall give bond as in other cases, and have reasonable compensation for his services, to be allowed by the judge and paid out of the estate; but shall not be required to return any inventory, or exercise any other powers or duties of guardian for one year after his appointment, except to provide for the support of the insane and his family, and prevent waste of his property.

Judge of probate may appoint guardians for persons sent to hospital; their duties and compensation.

Ib. § 23.

9. Upon the discharge of any patient or inmate from the insane hospital, by the trustees at any annual or quarterly meeting under section four of chapter one hundred and forty-three of the revised statutes, or under the provisions of this act, the said trustees shall cause the selectmen of the town, or mayor of the city from which such patient or inmate was received, to be immediately notified by mail of such discharge; and on the receipt of such notice, it shall be the duty of the town or city so notified, forthwith to cause said inmate to be removed to said town or city; and if said town or city so notified, shall neglect to remove such inmate for the term of thirty days after said notice, said inmate may be removed to said town or city by the trustees or by their order, and an action at law shall lie in the name of the superintendent of the insane hospital to recover of said town or city, so neglecting, all the expenses which may necessarily be incurred in the removal of said inmate.

Trustees shall notify selectmen of towns and mayors of cities when patients are discharged by the board.

Act, March 15, 1861, chap. 43, § 1.

—town or city to cause inmate to be removed.

—if neglect after thirty days, trustees to cause removal.

Superintendent may bring action, &c.

Expenses of certain insane persons, how paid.

Act, Feb. 18, 1862, chap. 76, § 1.

10. In the case of persons committed by the municipal officers of cities and towns to the insane hospital, who have no legal settlement in this State, there shall be refunded by the State to the town made chargable in the first instance for their support in the hospital, all the expenses in each case, over and above one dollar per week.

MANUFACTURING ESTABLISHMENTS.

STATUTES.

1. Exempt from taxation, not exceeding ten years, provided, &c.
2. Exemption, how construed.

1. All manufacturing establishments, and all establishments for refining, purifying or in any way enhancing the value of any article or articles already manufactured, hereafter erected by individuals, or by incorporated companies, and all the machinery and capital used for operating the same, together with all such machinery hereafter put into buildings already erected, but not now occupied, and all the capital used for operating the same, are exempted from taxation for a term not exceeding ten years after the passage of this act, where the amount of capital actually invested shall exceed the sum of two thousand dollars; *provided*, towns and cities in which such manufacturing establishments or refineries may be located, or in which it may be proposed to establish the same, shall in a legal manner give their assent to such exemption, and such assent shall have the force of a contract and be binding for the full time specified; *and provided further*, that all property so exempted shall be entered from year to year on the assessment books, and returned with the valuations of the several towns and cities when required by the State for the purposes of making the State valuation.

Manufacturing establishments, &c. Act March 8, 1864, chap. 234, § 1.

—exempt from taxation, not exceeding ten years.

—capital.

Proviso.

Further proviso.

Act of 1864, chap. 234, § 1. how construed.

Act, Feb. 8, 1867.

2. Section one of chapter two hundred and thirty-four of the public laws of this State, of eighteen hundred and sixty-four, relating to manufactures, shall be understood and construed as giving towns and cities the power to exempt from taxation for the term of ten years from the date of the contract of said towns and cities, authorized according to the provisions of said section one of said chapter two hundred and thirty-four.

MUNICIPAL COURT.

STATUTES.

1. Court established, one judge.
2. Judge's jurisdiction as justice of the peace, concurrent or exclusive.
3. Not to act as counsellor or attorney, when, &c.
4. His jurisdiction in cases of larceny and offenses against city by-laws.
5. Houses of ill-fame.
6. Right of appeal.
7. Fines, how disposed of.
8. Jurisdiction though the penalty accrues to the city.
9. Court to be held on Monday.
10. Recorder, how appointed and qualified, his duties and fees; writs to be under seal of court.
11. Recorder's powers in absence of judge.
12. Justice of peace substituted in absence of judge and recorder.
13. Provisions when office of judge is vacant.
14. Restrictions on justices of the peace in Portland.
15. Exceptions under the laws of the United States.
16. When recorder may issue warrants.
17. Salary of recorder.
18. Costs, how to be taxed.
19. Recorder, during absence of judge, power in civil actions.
20. In case of vacancy of judge.
21. Judge, how elected; tenure of office.
22. Same subject.

1. There is hereby established a municipal court for the city of Portland, to consist of one judge, who shall be appointed, commissioned and qualified, in the manner provided by the constitution of this State. Court established. One judge. 1856, c. 204, § 1.

Judge's jurisdiction as justices of the peace, concurrent or exclusive.
1856, c. 204, § 2.

2. He shall, except where interested, exercise jurisdiction over all such matters and things within the county of Cumberland, as justices of the peace may exercise, and under similar restrictions and limitations; and concurrent jurisdiction with justices of the peace and quorum in case of forcible entry and detainer in said county; and exclusive jurisdiction where both parties interested, or the plaintiff and a person sued as trustee, are inhabitants of Portland.

Judge not to act as counsel in certain cases.
Act, 1862, chap. 151.

3. He shall not act as counsel or attorney in any case within the jurisdiction of said court, nor in any cause, matter or thing which may depend upon or relate to any cause cognizable by said court.

His jurisdiction in cases of larceny and offences against city by-laws.
Act, 1856, chap. 204, § 4.

4. The said court may take cognizance of simple larcenies, when the property alleged to be stolen shall not exceed in value twenty dollars, and on conviction award such sentence as is by law provided for such offenses; and have exclusive jurisdiction of all offenses against the by-laws of said city; and in prosecution on such by-laws, they need not be recited in the complaint, nor in allegations therein be more particular than in prosecutions on a public statute.

Houses of ill-fame.
Ib. § 5.

5. The same proceedings may be had in the same manner, against persons keeping houses of ill-fame, for the purposes of lewdness or prostitution, on complaint, as before a justice of the peace.

Right of appeal.
Ib. § 6.

6. Any person may appeal from a sentence or judgment against him, to the then next term, for civil or criminal business, as the case may require, of the court having jurisdiction within said county, by appeal from justices of the peace; and such appeal shall be taken and prosecuted in the same manner as from a sentence or judgment of a justice of the peace.

Fines to be accounted for.
Ib. § 7.

7. All fines and penalties awarded by said judge, shall be accounted for and paid over, as in case of those awarded by a justice of the peace.

8. The court shall have jurisdiction, though the penalty demanded in any action or prosecution accrues to the city of Portland.

Jurisdiction, though the penalty accrue to the city. St. 1856, chap. 204, § 8.

9. The municipal court shall be held on Monday of each week, at nine of the clock in the forenoon, and no civil process shall be returnable at any other time.

Court to be held on Monday, Ib. § 9, as amended by Act, 1859, chap. 57, § 1.

10. There shall be a recorder of said court, who shall always be a justice of the peace, and duly qualified as such, and he shall be appointed by the governor, by and with the advice of the council; he shall be duly sworn as recorder, and shall keep a fair record of the proceedings of the court, and deliver copies, when required, for the same fees which are allowed to justices of the peace. All writs issued by said court shall be under its seal and bear test of the judge, and shall be signed by the recorder.

Recorder, how appointed and qualified.

His duties and fees.

Writs to be under seal of court.

Act, 1859, chap. 57, § 2, as amending Act, 1856, chap, 204, § 10.

11. When the judge is absent, it shall be the duty of the recorder, and he shall have authority to exercise all the powers of the judge.

Recorder's powers in absence of judge. St. 1856, chap. 204, § 11, as amended by Act, March 26, 1863, § 1.

12. If the judge and recorder are both necessarily absent, the judge may designate some justice of the peace duly qualified, to perform the duties of his office; or if the judge should not so designate a justice of the peace, the recorder may do it.

Justices of the peace substituted in absence of judge and recorder. Act, 1856, chap. 204, § 12.

13. When the office of judge shall be vacant, the recorder shall finish the business pending before the court.

Provisions when office of judge is vacant. Ib. § 13, as amended by Act, March 26 1863.

14. No justice of the peace residing in the city of Portland, shall in any manner take cognizance of, or exercise jurisdiction over any crime or offense, or in any civil action, wherein the judge is not a party interested; nor accept or receive any fee or reward therefor; and any such justice of the peace, by violating this section, shall forfeit twenty dollars, to be recovered on indictment.

Restrictions on justices of the peace in Portland.

Ib. § 14, as amended by Act, March 26 1863.

15. But nothing in the preceding section shall be construed as prohibiting the justices of the peace, residing in Portland, from exercising at all times, all the power

Exceptions under the laws of the United States.

Ib. § 15.

and jurisdiction given them by any laws of the United States.

When recorder may issue warrants.

Ib. § 16.

16. When the judge is occasionally absent from the room or office in which the court is held, the recorder shall have power, on proper complaint, to issue warrants for the apprehension of persons charged with any criminal offense, or breach of the peace; and such warrants shall have the same authority as if issued by the judge.

Salary of recorder.

Act 1860, c. 172.

17. The recorder of the municipal court of the city of Portland, shall receive the annual salary of eight hundred dollars from and after the first day of January, in the year of our Lord eighteen hundred and sixty.

Costs how to be taxed.

Act 1859, c. 57, § 3.

18. The costs recoverable by parties in said court, shall be as follows:—The plaintiff, if he prevail, shall be entitled to recover one dollar for his writ, and the defendant, if he prevail, shall be entitled to recover an attorney fee of one dollar; and all other costs recoverable by either party, shall be taxed as before justices of the peace.

Recorder, duty of, in absence of judge.

Act, 1863, March 26, chap. 290, § 1.

19. During the temporary absence of the judge of the municipal court of the city of Portland, the recorder of said court is hereby authorized and empowered to try and determine civil actions and processes within the jurisdiction thereof.

— in case of vacancy of judge.

Ib. § 2.

20. In case of vacancy by death, resignation or otherwise in the office of judge of said court, the recorder aforesaid may try and determine all actions, civil and criminal, within the jurisdiction of said court, until a judge shall be appointed and qualified.

Judges how elected and tenure of office.

21. Judges of the municipal and police courts shall be elected by the people of their respective cities and towns, by a plurality of the votes given in at the annual meeting in March or April, and shall hold their offices for four years from the Monday following the day of their election.

Vacancies how filled.

Constitutional amendment, Art 9.

Vacancies in said office shall be filled by elections at the next annual meeting in March or April; and in the meantime, the governor, with the advice and consent of the council, may fill said vacancies by appointment, until the Monday following said annual meeting.

Election of municipal and police judges.

Rev. St. chap. 132, § 1.

22. The election of judges of municipal and police courts shall be effected and determined in cities as the election of mayor is; and in towns as the election of selectmen is. A plurality shall elect. The clerk shall notify the person elected who shall be duly sworn, and commence the discharge of his duties on the Monday following the day of his election. They hold their offices, and vacancies are filled, as provided in the constitution.

NUISANCES.

STATUTES.

Dangerous buildings may be adjudged nuisances; proceedings.

Act, 1860, chap. 177, § 1, as amended by Act, 1863, chap. 187.

Powers of aldermen and selectmen.

1. Whenever the mayor and aldermen of any city, or the selectmen of any town, after due notice in writing to the owner of any burnt, dilapidated or dangerous building, or publication in a newspaper in the county three weeks successively, or if no newspaper is published in the county, then in the State paper, and after a hearing of the matter, shall adjudge the same to be a nuisance to the neighborhood, or dangerous, they may make and record an order prescribing what disposition or alteration shall be made thereof, or such other provisions as they shall deem necessary, and thereupon it shall be the duty of the city or town clerk to deliver a copy of such order to a consta-

ble, who shall serve such owner, if resident within the State, with an attested copy thereof, and make return of his doings thereon to said clerk forthwith; if the owner or part owner is unknown, or resides without the State, notice shall be given by publication in the State paper, or in a paper published in the county three weeks successively, and no further service on such owner shall be required. If no appplication shall be made to the supreme judicial court, or a justice thereof, as is hereinafter provided, the mayor and aldermen of such city, or selectmen of such town, shall cause said nuisance to be abated, removed or altered in compliance with their order, and all expenses thereof shall be repaid to the city or town by such owner; if not paid within thirty days after demand, they may be recovered of such person by an action for money paid for his use.

Owner to be served with copy of order. Return of service. Nuisance may be abated. Owner to pay expense. Payment enforced.

2. Any owner aggrieved by any order passed under the provisions of the first section of this act, may apply to the supreme judicial court, if in session in the county in which such order is passed, or to any justice thereof, in vacation, for a jury, and such court or justice shall forthwith order a warrant for a jury to issue, to be empanneled by the sheriff in the same manner as is provided by section ten of the eighteenth chapter of the revised statutes in regard to the laying out of highways. Such application shall be made within five days after such order is served on such owner, and the jury shall be empanneled within seven days from the issuing of the warrant.

Owner aggrieved may apply to supreme court, or justice of, for a jury. Jury, how empanneled. Application, when to be made. Act, 1860, chap. 177, § 2.

3. The jury may find a verdict, either affirming or annulling the said order, or making alterations therein, as they may see fit, which verdict shall be returned forthwith to the justice issuing the warrant, for acceptance. He may accept or reject the same, and may, if rejected, order a new warrant, if he thinks reasonable. If the court is not in session, the action shall be entered on the docket of the court for the preceding term, exceptions

Verdict, what it may be. —return of. —may be accepted or rejected. Action, how entered.

Exceptions taken; proceedings. Verdict enforced. Ib. § 3.

taken by either party shall be allowed as of that term, execution may issue as of that term, and if the verdict is finally accepted, the justice may issue all proper process for enforcing the same.

Costs, how to be paid. Ib. § 4.

4. If the verdict shall affirm such order, costs shall be recovered by the city or town against such applicant. If the verdict shall annul such order in whole, costs shall be recovered by the applicant against such city or town, and in case such verdict shall alter such order in part, the court may render such judgment as to costs as to justice shall appertain.

Not applicable, unless by vote. Ib. § 5.

5. This act shall not be in force in any town or city, unless the inhabitants of the town, or the city council of the city, shall adopt the same at a legal meeting of said inhabitants, or city council called for that purpose.

Advertisements on fences, private property, rocks, or other natural objects, prohibited. Act, 1865, chap. 289, § 1.

6. All persons are hereby prohibited from advertising their wares or occupations, by painting notices of the same on, or affixing them to fences or other private property, or on rocks or other natural objects, without the previous consent of the owner, or if in the highway or any other public place, without the permission of the mayor of cities, selectmen of towns, or assessors of plantations.

Penalty. Ib. § 2.

7. Any person violating the provisions of this act shall be punished by a fine of ten dollars for each offense, to be recovered on complaint, one-half of which shall be for the use of the prosecutor and one-half for the use of the town in which the offense is committed.

Certain nuisances described. 37 Maine, 161. R. S., chap. 17, § 1.

8. The erection, continuance or use of any building or other place for the exercise of a trade, employment, or manufacture, which, by occasioning noxious exhalations, offensive smells, or other annoyances, becomes injurious and dangerous to the health, comfort, or property of individuals or the public; causing or suffering any offal, filth, or noisome substance to be collected, or to remain in any place to the prejudice of others; obstructing or impeding, without legal authority, the passage of any navigable river,

harbor, or collection of water; corrupting, or rendering unwholesome, or impure, the water of a river, stream, or pond; unlawfully diverting it from its natural course or state to the injury or prejudice of others; and the obstructing or incumbering by fences, buildings, or otherwise, the highways, private ways, streets, alleys, commons, common landing places, or burying grounds, shall be deemed nuisances within the limitations and exceptions hereafter mentioned.

Places to be assigned for unwholesome employments. 34 Maine, 36. Ib. § 2.

9. The municipal officers of a town, when they judge it necessary, may assign some place or places therein for the exercise of any trade, employment, or manufacture aforesaid, and forbid their exercise in other places, under penalty of being deemed public or common nuisances and liable to be dealt with as such. All such assignments shall be entered in the records of the town and may be revoked when said officers judge proper.

Proceedings when places so assigned become offensive. Ib. § 3.

10. When any place or building so assigned becomes a nuisance, offensive to the neighborhood, or injurious to the public health, any person may complain thereof to the supreme judicial court, and, if after notice to the party complained of, the truth of the complaint is admitted by default, or made to appear to a jury on trial, the court may revoke such assignment, and prohibit the further use of such place or building for such purposes, under a penalty not exceeding one hundred dollars for each month's continuance after such prohibition, to the use of said town; and may order it to be abated, and issue a warrant therefor, or stay it as hereafter provided; and if the jury on said trial, acquits the defendant, he shall recover costs of the complainant.

When buildings for the manufacture of gunpowder shall be deemed nuisances. Ib. § 4.

11. If a person carries on the business of manufacturing gunpowder, or of mixing or grinding the composition therefor, in any building within eighty rods of any valuable building erected when such business was commenced, the former building shall be deemed a public nuisance; and such person may be prosecuted accordingly.

Burning bricks in parts of a town prohibited by vote, nuisances. Ib. § 5.

12. A town, at its annual meeting, may prohibit the burning of bricks, or the erecting of brick kilns within such parts thereof as they deem for the safety of the citizens or their property. And if any person, by himself or others, violates such prohibition, the municipal officers shall cause said bricks or brick kiln to be forthwith removed, at the expense of the owner thereof; and the offender shall be liable to a fine not exceeding two hundred dollars to the use of said town; and if said bricks or brick kiln are not removed before a conviction, the court may issue a warrant for the removal thereof, or stay it as hereafter provided.

Stationary steam engine not to be used without license. Ib. § 13.

13. No stationary steam engine shall be erected in a town, unless the municipal officers have previously granted license therefor, designating the place where the buildings therefor shall be erected, the materials and mode of construction, the size of the boiler and furnace, and such provisions as to height of chimneys or flues, and protection against fire and explosion, as they judge proper for the safety of the neighborhood. Such license is to be granted on written application, and recorded in the town records, and a certified copy of it furnished, without charge, to the person or persons applying for the license.

Duty of town officers on application for a license. Ib. § 14.

14. When application is made for such license, said officers shall assign a time and place for its consideration, and give public notice thereof at least fourteen days beforehand as they think proper, at the expense of the applicant, that all persons interested may be heard before granting a license.

Such engine erected without license to be deemed a nuisance. Ib. § 15.

15. Any such engine erected without license shall be deemed a common nuisance without any other proof than its use.

[For additional laws and ordinances relating to nuisances, see chapter on HEALTH, *ante*.]

ORDINANCES AND BY-LAWS.

ORDINANCE.

1. Enacting style of city ordinances.
2. Ordinances to be published.
3. Time of ordinances taking effect.
4. Construction of ordinances, rules applicable.
5. Fines to enure to use of city, except, &c.

1. All by-laws of the city shall be denominated ordinances, and the enacting style shall be, "Be it ordained by the mayor, aldermen, and common council of the city of Portland, in city council assembled, as follows."

Enacting style of city ordinances. Rev. Ord., 1855.

2. The ordinances of the city council shall be published and promulgated by inserting the same two weeks successively in one or more newspapers published in the city of Portland; but this section is directory, merely, and a failure to comply with the same, shall not affect the validity of any order or ordinance.

Ordinances to be published. Ib.

3. Any ordinance enacted by the city council shall take effect and go into operation in ten days from and after the day on which it shall have been approved by the mayor, unless the provisions of any ordinance shall otherwise prescribe.

Time of ordinance taking effect. Ib.

4. In the construction of ordinances the same rules shall be observed so far as they may be applicable, as are provided in the revised statutes of this State, chap. 1, sect. 4, unless such construction would be inconsistent

Construction of ordinances, rules applicable. Ib.

with the manifest intent of the city council, or repugnant to the context of the same ordinance.

Fines to enure to use of city, except.
Ib.

5. All fines and penalties for the violation of any of the ordinances of the city council, or any of the orders of the mayor and aldermen, shall be recoverable by prosecution in the municipal court of Portland, or any court which may be established in place thereof, and when recovered, shall enure to the use of the city, and shall be paid into the city treasury, except in those cases where it may be otherwise provided by the acts of the legislature, or the ordinances of the city.

PAUPERS.

STATUTES.

Election of overseers of poor, city charter, 1863, § 8.

1. There shall be elected at the first election of subordinate officers, in Portland, under this act, in March, twelve persons for overseers of the poor and work house; four of whom shall be elected for one year, four for two years, and four for three years; and all subsequent annual elections shall be for the term of three years.

Settlement, how acquired, R. S., chap. 24, § 1.

2. Settlements, subjecting towns to pay for the support of persons on account of their poverty or distress, are acquired as follows:

Married women.

4 Greenl. 293.

I. A married woman has the settlement of her husband, if he has any in the State; if he has not, her own settlement is not affected by her marriage. When it appears in a suit between towns involving the settlement of a pauper, that a marriage was procured to change it by the agency or collusion of the officers of either town, the settlement is not affected by such marriage.

Legitimate children.

II. Legitimate children have the settlement of their father, if he has any in the State; if he has not, they have the settlement of their mother within it; but they do not have the settlement of either, acquired after they are of age and have capacity to acquire one.[1]

Illegitimate children.

III. Children, legitimate, or illegitimate, do not acquire a settlement by birth in the town where they are born. Illegitimate children have the settlement of their mother, at the time of their birth.[1]

Division of towns.

IV. Upon division of a town, a person having a settlement therein and absent at the time, has his settlement

[1] 2 Greenl., 194; 3 Greenl., 388; 4 Greenl., 47, 293; 7 Greenl., 90; 18 Maine, 376; 32 Maine, 60; 36 Maine, 390; 19 Maine, 441; 24 Maine, 281; 7 Greenl. 270; 10 Maine, 409; 11 Maine, 455; 35 Maine, 411.

in that town, which includes his last dwelling place in the town divided. When part of a town is set off from it and annexed to another, the settlement of a person absent at the time of such annexation is not affected thereby. When a new town, composed in part of one or more existing towns, is incorporated, persons settled in such existing town or towns, who had begun to acquire a settlement therein, and whose homes were in such new town at the time of its incorporation, have the same rights incipient and absolute respecting settlement, as they would have had in the town where their homes formerly were.[1]

Apprenticeship.

V. A minor who serves as an apprentice in a town four years, and within one year thereafter sets up such trade therein, being then of age, has a settlement therein.

Residence five years.

VI. A person of age, having his home in a town five successive years without receiving, directly or indirectly, supplies as a pauper, has a settlement therein.[2]

Residence March 21, 1821.

VII. A person having his home in a town on March twenty-one, eighteen hundred and twenty-one, without having received supplies as a pauper within one year before that date, acquired a settlement therein.[2]

Incorporation of towns. 11 Maine, 455. 21 Maine, 58, 266. 30 Maine, 452. 33 Maine, 580.

VIII. Persons having their homes in an unincorporated place for five years without receiving supplies as a pauper, and having continued their homes there to the time of its incorporation, acquire settlements therein. Those having homes in such places less than five years before incorporation, and continuing to have them there afterwards, until five years are completed, acquire settlements therein.

[1] 1 Greenl., 129; 13 Maine, 299; 19 Maine, 387; 20 Maine, 341; 21 Maine, 334; 23 Maine, 472; 31 Maine, 465; 35 Maine, 184; 39 Maine, 368; 37 Maine, 39.

[2] 10 Maine, 97; 13 Maine, 321; 17 Maine, 117; 18 Maine, 92; 21 Maine, 357; 23 Maine, 410; 24 Maine, 112; 34 Maine, 310; 15 Maine, 479; 18 Maine, 415.

Settlements remain, till new ones acquired. R. S., chap. 24, § 2.

3. Settlements acquired under existing laws, remain until new ones are acquired. Former settlements are defeated by the acquisition of new ones.

Revision of laws does not affect them. Ib. § 3.

4. Persons who have begun to acquire settlements under existing laws, are not to be affected by a repeal of them, and a re-enactment of their provisions in substance.

Duty of towns. Ib. § 4.

5. Towns are to relieve persons having a settlement therein, when on account of poverty, they need relief. They may raise money therefor as for other charges of the town.

Overseers' duties. Ib. § 5.

6. Overseers are to have the care of persons chargeable to their town, and are to cause them to be relieved and employed, at the expense of the town, and as the town directs, when it does direct.

Kindred liable. 23 Maine, 420. Ib. § 9.

7. The father, and mother, grandfather, and grandmother, children, and grand-children, by consanguinity, living within the State, and of sufficient ability, are to support persons chargeable in proportion to their respective ability.

Court on complaint may assess them. 5 Greenl., 324. Ib. § 10.

8. A town or any kindred, who have incurred any expense for the relief of a pauper, may complain to the supreme judicial court in the county, where any one of such kindred resides; and the court may cause such kindred to be summoned, and upon a hearing or default, may assess and apportion a reasonable sum upon such kindred, as are found to be of sufficient ability, for the support of such pauper to the time of such assessment; and may enforce payment thereof by warrant of distress. Such assessment is not to be made to pay any expense for relief afforded more than six months before the complaint was filed.

Children may be bound; terms and time. 18 Maine, 415. Ib. § 14.

9. The minor children of parents chargeable, or of parents unable in the opinion of overseers to maintain them, and such children chargeable themselves, may, without their consent, be bound by the overseers, by deed of indenture, as apprentices or as servants to any citizen

of the State, to continue till the males are twenty-one, and the females eighteen years of age or are married, unless sooner discharged by the death of their master. Provision is to be made in such deed for the instruction of males to read, write, and cypher, and for females to read and write; and for such further instruction and benefit within or at the end of the term, as the overseers think reasonable.

10. The overseers are to inquire into the treatment of such children, and to protect and defend them in the enjoyment of their rights in reference to their masters and others. They may complain to the supreme judicial court in the county, where their town is, or where the master resides, against such master for abuse, ill-treatment or neglect, of a child bound to him. The court is to cause him to be notified, and upon a hearing of the parties or on default, may, for sufficient cause proved, discharge the child with costs, or dismiss the complaint, with or without costs at discretion. Any child so discharged, or whose master has deceased, may be bound anew for the remainder of the time.

Overseers to inquire, may complain of master. Court may discharge child, who may be bound again.
Ib. § 15.

11. The overseers, by a suit on the deed of indenture, may recover damages for breaches of its covenants. The amount so recovered, deducting reasonable charges, is to be placed in the treasury of the town, to be applied by the overseers to the benefit of the child during his term, or be paid to him at its expiration. The court, on trial of such suit, for sufficient cause exhibited, may discharge the child. Such suit is not abated by the death of overseers or by the expiration of their term of office; but shall proceed in their names, or in the names of the survivors.

Suits on bond.

Damages for benefit of child.
Ib. § 16.

12. Overseers may set to work, or by deed bind to service upon reasonable terms, for a time not exceeding one year, persons having settlements in their town or having none in the State, married or not married, able of

Persons of age, may be bound for one year.
Ib. § 20.

body, upwards of twenty-one years of age, having no apparent means of support, and living idly; and all persons liable to be sent to the house of correction.

Person bound may complain to court. Ib. § 21.

13. A person so bound may complain to the court, in the county where he or the overseers reside, and the court, after notice to the overseers, and master, may, upon a hearing, dismiss such complaint, or discharge him from the master and overseers, and award costs to either party or against the town at discretion.

Overseers to relieve persons having settlements in other towns. 15 Maine, 363. 27 Maine, 489. 28 Maine, 289. 29 Maine, 313. 33 Maine, 453. 38 Maine, 472. Ib. § 24.

14. Overseers are to relieve persons destitute, found in their towns and having no settlement therein, and in case of decease, decently bury them; the expenses whereof and of their removal incurred within three months before notice given to the town chargeable, may be recovered by the town incurring them against the town liable, in an action commenced within two years after the cause of action accrued, and not otherwise; and may be recovered of their kindred in the manner before provided in this chapter.

Overseers where there is a jail, duties. Liability of creditor to pay. Ib. § 26.

15. Overseers of a town, in which there is a county jail, may, by their written order, set to work so far as necessary for his support, any debtor committed, and then chargeable to any town in the State for his support. The town where he has a settlement, is liable to pay the expenses incurred not so paid by him; and the town incurring them may recover the same of the creditor, at whose suit he was committed at the rate fixed by law for his support.

Notice to be given of relief to town liable. 15 Maine, 169. 21 Maine, 298, 443. 31 Maine, 124. Ib. § 27.

16. Overseers are to send a written notice, signed by one or more of them, stating the facts respecting a person chargeable in their town, to overseers of the town where his settlement is alleged to be, requesting them to remove him, which they may do by a written order directed to a person named therein, who is authorized to execute it.

Answer to be returned within two months.

17. Overseers receiving such notice are, within two months, if the pauper is not removed, to return a written

answer, signed by one or more of them, stating their objections to his removal; and if they fail to do so, the overseers requesting his removal may cause him to be removed to that town in the manner provided in the preceding section; and the overseers of the town to which he is sent are to receive him and provide for his support; and their town is estopped to deny his settlement therein, in an action brought to recover for the expenses incurred for his previous support and for his removal.

1 Greenl., 329. 3 Greenl., 197, 453. 4 Greenl., 298, 475. 5 Greenl., 31. 30 Maine, 211. Ib. § 28.

18. When a written notice or answer provided for in this chapter is sent by mail, postage paid, and it arrives at the post office where the overseers to whom it is directed reside, it is to be deemed a sufficient notice or answer.

Notice by mail sufficient. 21 Maine, 298, 443. Ib. § 29.

19. A person removed, as provided in this chapter, to the place of his settlement, who voluntarily returns to the town from which he was removed, without the consent of the overseers, on conviction thereof before a justice of the peace, may be sent to the house of correction as a vagabond.

Persons removed, returning may be sent to house of correction. Ib. § 30.

20. Overseers may make complaint, that a pauper chargeable to their town has no settlement in the State, to a justice of the peace, who may, if he thinks proper, by his warrant directed to a person named therein, cause such pauper to be conveyed, at the expense of such town, beyond the limits of this State, to the place where he belongs.

Foreign paupers may be removed. 8 Greenl., 71. Ib. § 31.

21. Towns are to pay expenses necessarily incurred for the relief of paupers by an inhabitant not liable for their support, after notice and request to the overseers, until provision is made for them.

Towns liable to individuals. 20 Maine, 442. 36 Maine, 376. 37 Maine, 9. Ib. § 32.

22. When a person in their town, notoriously subject to habits of intemperance, is in need of relief, the overseers are to make complaint to a justice of the peace in the county, who is to issue a warrant and cause such person to be brought before him, and upon a hearing and proof of such habits, he is to order him to be committed

Overseers to complain of persons intemperate. Ib. § 33.

to the house of correction, to be there supported by the town where he has a settlement, and if no such town, at the expense of the county, until discharged by the overseers of the town in which the house of correction is situated, or by two justices of the peace and quorum.

Towns may recover of paupers. 4 Greenl., 258. 22 Maine, 445. Ib. § 34.

23. A town, which has incurred expense for the support of a pauper, whether he has a settlement in that town or not, may recover it of him, his executors, or administrators, in an action of assumpsit.

Overseers take possession of property of paupers deceased. 8 Greenl., 315. Ib. § 35.

24. Upon the decease of a pauper then chargeable, the overseers may take into their custody all his personal property, and if no administration on his estate is taken within thirty days, may sell so much thereof, as is necessary to repay the expenses incurred. They have the same remedy to recover any property of such pauper, not delivered to them, as his administrator would have.

May prosecute and defend. Ib. § 36.

25. For all purposes provided for in this chapter, its overseers, or any person appointed by them in writing, may prosecute and defend a town.

Penalty for bringing paupers into a town. 2 Greenl., 5. Ib. § 38.

26. Whoever brings into and leaves in a town where he has no settlement, a poor person, knowing him to be so, with intent to charge such town with his support, forfeits a sum not exceeding one hundred dollars, to be recovered, to the use of such town, in an action of debt.

Masters of vessels not to land passengers without consent, give bond or pay a sum per head. Ib. § 39.

27. When a vessel, with passengers on board having no settlement in this State, arrives at any port or harbor within any town in the State, the master thereof shall leave a list of their names, and of the places from which they came first on board, with the overseers of the poor of such town, before they come on shore. He shall not land them without permission of the municipal officers, unless he gives bond to the town, with sureties approved by said officers, in a sum not exceeding five hundred dollars for each passenger, to save the town harmless from all expense on account of such passengers, as paupers, for three years. The officers, instead of a bond, may take two dollars for each passenger.

PAWNBROKERS.

STATUTES.

1. License and removal of pawnbrokers, and penalty for acting without license.
2. To keep an accurate and particular account of all business done, under a penalty.
3. Rate of interest fixed at twenty-five per cent. on loan of twenty-five dollars, and six on larger.
4. Time and mode of selling pawned property, and notice thereof, fixed under a penalty.
5. Penalty for not paying over proceeds of sale, after deducting amount due on loan.

1. The municipal officers of any town may grant licenses to persons of good moral character, to be pawnbrokers therein for one year, unless sooner removed by said officers for a violation of law regulating their business; and any person carrying on said business without a license, shall be liable to a penalty not exceeding one hundred dollars.

License and removal of pawnbrokers, &c.
R. S., chap. 35. § 1.

2. Every pawnbroker shall keep a book, in which he shall enter the date, duration, amount and rate of interest, of every loan made by him; an accurate account and description of the property pawned, and the name and residence of the pawner, and, at the same time, deliver to said pawner a written memorandum signed by him, containing the substance of the above entry, and, at all reasonable times, submit said book to the inspection of any of the officers aforesaid; and for every violation of this section he shall forfeit twenty dollars.

To keep an account of all business done, under a penalty.
Ib. § 2.

Rates of interest fixed.
Ib. § 3.

3. No pawnbroker shall directly or indirectly receive any rate of interest greater than twenty-five per cent. a year on a loan not exceeding twenty-five dollars, nor than six per cent on a larger loan made upon property pawned, under a penalty of one hundred dollars for each offense.

Time and mode of selling pawned property, and notice thereof, fixed under a penalty.
Ib. § 4.

4. No pawnbroker shall sell any property pawned, until it has remained in his possession three months after the expiration of the time for which it was pawned; and all such sales shall be at public auction by a licensed auctioneer, and after notice of the time and place of sale, the name of the auctioneer, and a description of the property to be sold are published in a newspaper in the town, where the property is pawned, if any, and if not, posted in two public places therein at least two weeks before the sale; and all sales of such property otherwise made, shall be wholly void, and the pawnbroker, undertaking to make the same, shall forfeit twenty dollars for every such offense.

Penalty for not paying over proceeds of sale, &c.
Ib. § 5.

5. After deducting from the proceeds of any sale as aforesaid the amount of the loan, the interest then due, and the proportional part of the expenses of sale, such pawnbroker shall pay the balance to the person entitled to redeem such property if no sale had been made; and if not so paid on demand, he shall forfeit double the amount so retained, one-half to the use of the pawner, and the other to the use of the State.

PERMITS.

ORDINANCES.

Fee for permits.

Whenever a permit shall be granted to any person, under the authority of any order or ordinance, the applicant shall pay to the officer granting the same the sum of twenty-five cents, except in cases otherwise specially provided for.

Fee for permits.
Rev. Ord. 1855.

PETROLEUM, INSPECTION OF.

STATUTES.

1. Inspectors appointed. Their duties.
2. Casks, how to be marked. False marks, how punished.
3. Casks must be inspected. Penalty for neglect.
4. Oil not to be sold unless inspected. Penalty.
5. Penalties, how enforced.
6. Duty of mayor, &c.

Inspectors appointed.

1. In every city and town in this State containing two thousand inhabitants or more, the mayor and aldermen or the selectmen shall, on or before the first day of May, annually, appoint one or more persons to be inspectors of petroleum and coal oils and burning fluids, who shall be sworn to the faithful discharge of their duties. And it shall be their duty, when requested, to inspect such oils and burning fluids, by applying the fire test with some accurate instrument, to ascertain the igniting or explosive point thereof in degrees of Fahrenheit's thermometer; and they shall cause every vessel or cask thereof by them so inspected to be plainly marked by the name of such inspector, the date of inspection, and the igniting or explosive point of the contents thereof.

Their duties.

Act, March 1, 1867, § 1.

Casks, how to be marked.

2. Whenever any cask or vessel of such oil or fluid will not bear the fire test of at least one hundred and twenty degrees Fahrenheit, without ignition or explosion, the same shall be marked as aforesaid, and shall also be marked—unsafe for illuminating purposes. And if any inspector shall knowingly put false marks upon any such casks or vessels of such oils or fluids inspected by him, he shall be punished by a fine of not exceeding five hun-

False marks, how punished.

Ib. § 2.

dred dollars, or by imprisonment for the term of six months in the county jail.

Casks must be inspected.

3. Every person and corporation engaged in manufacturing, in any city or town in this State, any such petroleum or coal oil or burning fluid, shall cause every cask or other vessel thereof to be inspected and marked as aforesaid, by a sworn inspector. And if any person, or the agent or the officer of any corporation, shall manufacture and sell within this State any such oil or burning fluid, without first causing it to be inspected and marked as aforesaid, or that has been so inspected and marked as unsafe for illuminating purposes, he shall be punished by a fine of not exceeding five hundred dollars, or by imprisonment six months in the county jail.

Penalty for neglect.

Ib. § 3.

Oil not to be sold unless inspected.

4. No person shall sell any such oil or burning fluid without first causing each cask or vessel of the same to be duly inspected and marked as aforesaid, unless it has already been so inspected and marked in this State or elsewhere; and if any person shall sell such oil or burning fluid that has not been so inspected and marked, or that has been so inspected and has been marked as unsafe for illuminating purposes, he shall be punished by a fine of not exceeding five hundred dollars, or by imprisonment in the county jail six months.

Penalty.

Ib. § 4.

Penalties, how enforced.

5. All prosecutions under the second, third and fourth sections of this act shall be by indictment.

Ib. § 5.

Duty of mayor, &c.

Ib. § 6.

6. The selectmen of towns, and the mayor, aldermen and police of cities, or any one of them, shall have the right at all times to examine all such oils and fluids kept in their respective cities, and towns, for sale, and to cause the same to be inspected and tested; and it shall be their duty to do so in all cases where they are informed or believe such oils or fluids are kept for sale in violation of law; and whenever they shall find any person keeping or selling any such oil or fluid in violation of the provisions of this act, it shall be their duty to cause such persons to be prosecuted therefor.

PILOTS.

STATUTES.

1. Appointment of pilots.
2. Board of Trade of Portland to appoint pilots for said city.
3. Their duty. Master may pilot his own vessel.
4. Fees, &c.
5. Liabilities of pilots.

Appointment, oath and bond of pilots.
R. S., chap. 36, § 1.

1. The governor, with advice of council, may appoint pilots for any port, in which a majority of the ship owners and masters apply in writing therefor and recommend suitable persons, and give to each of them branches or warrants for the execution of the duties of their office; and they shall, before entering upon the same, be duly sworn, and give bond to the treasurer of State in the sum of five thousand dollars for the faithful performance thereof.

Board of Trade of Portland to appoint pilots for said city.
Act, 1854, chap. 232, § 2.

2. By the provisions of "an act to incorporate the Board of Trade of Portland," approved March twenty-second, eighteen hundred and fifty-four, power was given to said board to appoint such number of pilots for the harbor of Portland, as they may deem necessary for the safety and convenience of the commerce of said port; and also to fix such compensation for the services of said pilots as said board may deem just and reasonable.

Their duty.

3. Such pilots are authorized and directed to take charge of all vessels, drawing nine feet of water and upwards, bound into, and of all such vessels, except coasting and fishing vessels, bound to sea out of any of said

ports, and shall pilot them into or out of the port assigned them, first showing to the master thereof their branch and informing him of their fees; but any master may pilot his own vessel without being subject to pay therefor.

Master may pilot his own vessel.
R. S., chap. 36, § 2.

4. The governor and council may fix the fees of pilotage; specify the same in the warrant of each pilot; transmit to each collector of customs in said ports a schedule thereof, to be hung up by him for public inspection; hear and determine all complaints against such pilots for misconduct, and suspend or remove them and appoint others in their room.

Governor and council to fix fees, hear complaints, and suspend or remove.
Ib. § 3.

5. If any vessel, while under the charge of such pilot, is lost, run aground, or cast away, through his fault, he shall be liable to pay the owner or insurer a just compensation for any damage thereby sustained.

Liable for damage caused by their fault.
Ib. § 4.

POLICE.

STATUTES.

1. Administration of police of city vested in mayor and aldermen.
2. Cities authorized to establish police regulations.
3. Police officers authorized to act as constables in certain cases.
4. Criminals and fugitives from justice may be arrested without a warrant.
5. Aid may be required by officer. Penalty for refusing.

ORDINANCES.

1. City marshal to be appointed. To give bonds. To be sworn.
2. Duties of city marshal. To carry into effect laws and ordinances.
3. Duty to prosecute offenders. To lay before mayor and aldermen a statement of prosecutions, &c. To render to mayor and aldermen, annually, an account of moneys received. To pay over once in three months. To comply with rules and regulations.
4. Deputy marshals to be appointed. To act as captains of city watch. Compensation.
5. Duties of deputy marshals. To assist the marshal. To obey and execute orders of mayor and marshal. To serve warrants and subpœnas. To obey rules, &c.
6. Deputy marshals invested with power, &c., of captains of the watch. To assign to night police limits. To receive reports. In case of sickness or absence the mayor to appoint a deputy marshal.
7. Policemen, how appointed. Compensation. Duties. To arrest and commit to watch house, offenders. To obey rules, &c. To obey orders of mayor or marshals.
8. Watchmen may be appointed. Their duties. To be subject to rules, &c.
9. Policemen and watchmen subject to be called upon for extra services. Compensation.
10. Penalty for resisting police in discharge of duties.
11. Police uniform.

STATUTES.

1. By section five of the charter of the city of Portland, the executive powers of said city generally, and the administration of police and health departments, with all the powers of selectmen, except as modified by the charter, are vested in the mayor and aldermen. All the powers of establishing watch and ward, vested by the laws of the State in the justices of the peace and municipal officers or inhabitants of towns, are vested in the mayor and aldermen, so far as relates to said city; and they are authorized to unite the watch and police departments into one department and establish suitable regulations for the government of the same. The officers of police shall be one chief, to be styled the city marshal, so many deputy marshals as the city council may by ordinance prescribe, and so many watchmen and policemen as the mayor and aldermen may, from time to time, appoint.

Powers of mayor and aldermen over police.

Police, how constituted.

City charter, 1863, § 5.

2. Cities may establish such police regulations as they may deem necessary for the prevention of crime, the protection of property, and the preservation of good order, not inconsistent with the laws of the State.

Cities may establish police regulations.

R. S., chap. 3, § 27.

3. Police officers, duly appointed in any city, shall have all the powers of constables in all criminal matters, or relating to the by-laws of their city.

Police officers of cities have powers of constables in certain matters.

R. S., chap. 80, § 46.

4. The city marshal of Portland, or other persons legally qualified to execute criminal process within said city, shall have power, without warrant, to arrest and detain any person found in said city, upon information that such person has committed a crime in another State or country, or in any city or town within this State, and is a fugitive from justice or is about to escape, and the person so arrested may be detained by such officers for a reasonable time, until such person can be delivered into proper or legal custody on a warrant or otherwise, according to the nature of the case.

Criminals and fugitives from justice may be arrested without a warrant.

Act, 1853, chap. 167, § 2.

Aid may be required by officer.

5. Any officer aforesaid, in the execution of the duties of his office in criminal cases, for the preservation of the peace, for apprehending or securing any person for the breach thereof, or in case of the escape or rescue of persons arrested on civil process, may require suitable aid therein; and any person, so required to aid, who neglects or refuses so to do, shall forfeit to the use of the county not less than three, nor more than fifty dollars; and if he does not forthwith pay such fine, the court may punish him by imprisonment not exceeding thirty days.

Penalty for refusing.

R. S., chap. 80, § 48.

ORDINANCES.

CITY MARSHAL.

City marshal to be appointed.

1. The mayor, by and with the advice and consent of the aldermen, shall in the month of March, annually, appoint a city marshal, who shall hold his office until another be appointed and qualified in his stead. And the city marshal, before entering upon the duties of his office, shall give bonds, with sureties to be approved by the mayor and aldermen, in such sums as they may prescribe, and shall be sworn to the faithful performance of the duties of his office.

To give bonds.

To be sworn.

Rev. Ord., 1855, as amended by city charter.

Duties of city marshal.

2. It shall be the duty of the city marshal, from time to time, to pass through every street, alley, court, square, and public place of the city, to observe nuisances, obstructions, or impediments therein, to the end that the same may be removed, according to law; to notice all offenses against the laws; to be vigilant and active in detecting any violation or breach of any law or city ordinance, taking the names of the offenders, to the end that they may be prosecuted; to receive all complaints made for any breach of the laws, and for that purpose shall attend daily at his office, and at stated times. It shall be his duty to enforce and carry into effect, to the utmost of his power, all and each of the city ordinances according to

To carry into effect laws and ordinances.

Rev. Ord., 1855.

the true intent and meaning of the same, and to obey and execute all the commands and orders of the mayor and aldermen.

3. It shall be the duty of the city marshal to prosecute all offenders against the laws of the State and ordinances of the city, within one week after detecting or ascertaining the offense or offenses by them respectively committed; to attend regularly and punctually at all trials of offenders prosecuted in behalf of the city, and to use all lawful means for their effectual prosecution and final conviction; to lay before the mayor and aldermen a correct statement of all prosecutions by him instituted before the municipal court, within one week after their final determination. And it shall be his duty annually, to render to the mayor and aldermen an account of the names of all persons from whom he may have collected fines, and for what offense, and the sums so collected from each, during his term of office; and as often as once in three months, he shall pay over to the city treasurer all monies which he may have received belonging to the city; and he shall further perform all such other additional duties, and comply with all such regulations as may at any time be prescribed to him by the mayor and aldermen.

Duty to prosecute offenders.

To lay before mayor and aldermen a statement of prosecutions, &c.

To render to mayor and aldermen, annually, an account of monies received.

To pay over once in three months.

To comply with rules and regulations. Ib.

DEPUTY MARSHALS.

4. The mayor, by and with the advice and consent of the aldermen, shall in the month of March, annually, appoint two deputy marshals, who shall discharge all the duties of captains of the city watch, and they shall devote all their time to the discharge of the duties of their office, and they shall be entitled to receive for their services such compensation as shall be determined by the city council.

Deputy marshals to be appointed.

To act as captains of city watch.

Compensation.

Ib. as amended by city charter.

5. It shall be the duty of said deputy marshals to act through the week, Sundays included, as the day police, to assist the marshal in the discharge of his official duties, to

Duties of deputy marshals.

To obey and execute orders of mayor and marshal.

To serve warrant and subpœnas.

To obey rules, &c.

Ib.

obey and execute all orders of the mayor and the city marshal, to officiate for the city marshal in his absence, to serve all warrants and subpœnas in criminal matters which they may receive from the city marshal or municipal court, to endeavor to prevent all disturbances and violations of law, and to arrest and detain for further proceedings every person found by them violating any of the laws of the State, or ordinances of the city, and they shall obey all rules and regulations of the mayor and aldermen.

Deputy marshals invested with power, &c., of captains of watch.

To assign to night police limits.

To receive reports.

6. Said deputy marshals are hereby invested with all the powers and authority of captains of the watch, and they shall, every other night, by turns, discharge the duties of that office, and act throughout the night as captain of the watch. The captain of the watch shall each night assign to the night police their respective limits, and be present at the office, at the hour appointed by the mayor and aldermen for their discharge, to receive their reports and discharge them from further duty, unless in his opinion, it shall be expedient to continue the whole, or any number of them, on duty through the night, which at any time he is authorized to do; he shall also each night, unless his attendance is required at the watch-house, ascertain by his personal investigation when practicable, whether the policemen and watchmen are faithful in the performance of their duties, and report the next morning to the mayor the officer who shall be found unfaithful. In case of sickness or inability of either of the deputy marshals to perform the duties incumbent on him, the mayor shall have authority to appoint another deputy marshal in his stead, so long as his services may be required.

In case of sickness or absence, the mayor to appoint a deputy marshal.

Ib.

Policemen, how appointed.

7. The mayor, by and with the advice and consent of the aldermen, shall also appoint, from time to time, such numbers of persons as they shall deem expedient, to constitute a police of the city, who shall be placed on duty at such hours and serve for such time as the mayor and

aldermen shall determine; and they shall be entitled to such compensation for their services as the city council shall determine. It shall be incumbent on the police, during the hours they shall be on duty, to patrol constantly throughout their respective limits, to endeavor to prevent all violations of law, and arrest and commit to the watch house all persons found by them violating any of the laws of this State, or ordinances of the city; they shall obey all rules and regulations established by the mayor and aldermen, and the orders of the mayor, marshal, or deputy marshals, and shall be subject to removal by the mayor, whenever in his opinion it shall be deemed expedient.

Compensation.

Duties.

To arrest and commit to watch house, offenders.

To obey rules, &c.

To obey orders of mayor, &c.

Ib. as amended by city charter.

8. The mayor, by and with the advice and consent of the aldermen may, from time to time, appoint such number of watchmen as they may deem expedient, who shall be sworn and shall perform such duties and be subject to such rules and regulations as are or may be established by the mayor and aldermen.

Watchmen may be appointed.

Their duties.

To be subject to rules, &c.

Rev. Ord., 1855, as amended by city charter.

9. Said policemen and watchmen shall at all times, either by day or by night, be subject to be called upon by the mayor or city marshal, to assist in quelling any riot or disturbance, or arresting any offenders, or to perform any other duties of policemen that may be required of them, for all which extra services they shall be paid such compensation as the city council shall determine.

Policemen and watchmen subject to be called upon for extra services.

Compensation.

Ib.

10. If any person shall resist the police in the discharge of their duty, or any member thereof, he shall pay a fine of not less than ten nor more than fifty dollars for each and every offense; and if any person shall neglect or refuse to aid and assist the police, or any member thereof, when called upon so to do, he shall forfeit and pay not less than five nor more than twenty dollars.

Penalty for resisting police in discharge of duties.

Ib.

POLICE UNIFORM.

Uniform of police; order of mayor and aldermen. April 20, 1860.

11. *Ordered*, That the dress of the officers and members of the Portland Police Department, when on duty, shall be in conformity to the schedule described as follows:

City marshal to wear blue dress coat with police buttons, black pantaloons, merino vest, black hat with gold star in a rosette on the same.

Deputy marshals to wear blue frock coat with police buttons, dark blue pantaloons, blue cloth cap with glazed covering. This dress to be dispensed with on detective duty.

Police to wear dark blue frock coat, dark blue pants, black silk or satin vest. In spring and fall, black cloth vest. In winter, single breasted, made to button up to the top, except a loop across the top under the chin; black silk or satin neck stock. The buttons on the frock coat to be worn in the usual manner, and the usual number, and to be fastened with a ring through the eye, so that the same can be removed and their places supplied by buttons of a different pattern, when the officer is permitted to lay aside his uniform, or when he leaves the department; blue cloth cap of uniform style and shape, made with glazed covers.

Marshal, deputy marshals and policemen shall wear dark blue overcoats, cut in uniform style, single or double breasted as the marshal shall decide, and of the same shade of color, and supplied with the police buttons, to be worn in the same manner as the buttons to be worn on the frock coat, at such seasons of the year as the marshal may direct.

On public occasions, so much of the police uniform shall be worn as the marshal may direct or determine.

Nothing in the adoption of the uniform dress, shall prevent the city marshal from ordering such dress for officers detailed for special duty, as he may think proper.

PORTLAND & FOREST AVENUE RAILROAD.

ORDERS AND ORDINANCES OF THE CITY.

1. Location of tracks.
2. Routes of road. Turn outs.
3. Tracks to be laid in or near centre of streets. Grades and curves.
4. Construction of tracks. Snow and ice. Rules and regulations.
5. Additional location.
6. Obstructions.

Location of tracks.

Order May 26, 1863.

1. *Ordered*, That the tracks of the Portland and Forest Avenue Railroad Company shall be located in the city of Portland as follows; but upon the express condition to the location, that said railroad company shall, at all times after the rails are laid down, keep in good order and complete repair, at their own expense, that portion of all streets through which the said rails are or may be laid, lying between the rails, and also that portion of the street lying outside of the rails and adjacent thereto, extending one foot and a half from and outside of each rail, throughout the whole length of said railroad in the streets of the city of Portland; and also that the work of laying down the tracks and rails of said road shall be done under the direction and to the satisfaction of the municipal officers, and also the form and kind of rail, to be used shall be satisfactory to said municipal officers and approved by them.

Routes of road.

2. Said location beginning at or near the depot of the Atlantic & St. Lawrence railroad, and thence extending with one track over the following streets, viz: up India

street to its junction with Middle, thence from the junction of India and Middle streets up Middle to the head of Preble street, thence from the head of Preble street over Preble street to Portland street, thence from the junction of Preble and Portland streets over Portland street to its junction with Parris street, thence from the junction of Portland and Parris streets over said Parris street, to its junction with Kennebec street, thence from the junction of Parris and Kennebec streets over said Kennebec street to Green street, thence from the junction of Kennebec and Green streets over Deering's bridge, to the line of Westbrook. And diverging from this route in Congress street near the head of Preble street, and extending therefrom by two tracks over said Congress street to the head of High street, thence from the junction of Congress and High streets with one track over High street to Spring street, thence from the junction of High and Spring streets over Spring street to Clark street, thence from the junction of Spring and Clark streets over Clark street to Pine street, thence from the junction of Clark and Pine streets, over said Pine street to Congress street, thence from the junction of Pine and Congress streets over Congress street to the head of High street, so as to connect with the tracks hereinbefore specified, and extending to the head of Preble street, and thence by one track from the junction of Congress and Preble streets over said Congress street to Atlantic street; also diverging from Congress street in front of the new city building at the head of Exchange street, and extending over said Exchange street to Middle street, with such turn outs as may be necessary for the safe and convenient operation of said road, and for reaching their car houses, as may be approved by the municipal officers.

Turn outs.

Tracks to be laid in or near centre of streets.

3. The tracks of said railroad shall be laid in or near the centre of the streets above named and to such grades as shall be determined by the municipal officers; and the

curves around the corners of all streets shall be located by the city engineer under the direction of the municipal officers, with the co-operation of the directors of said railroad company. Grades and curves.

4. And this location is granted upon the express condition that in the construction of said tracks, blocks of stone of the alternate length of eighteen and twenty inches, measuring from the rail outward, and otherwise of such quality, form and size as the municipal officers may direct, shall be laid down outside of each rail; and upon the further condition, that said railroad company, shall, at their own expense, pave between their double tracks, wherever double tracks are laid, and also between their rails throughout the whole length of said railroad in the streets of the city; said pavement to be, until otherwise ordered, fair quality round beach paving stone, and to be laid to the satisfaction of the municipal officers; and upon the further condition that whenever there shall be snow or ice in said streets to the depth of six inches or less, said railroad company may remove the same from their tracks, by shovels or by using such kind of snow plough as the street commissioner shall approve of, provided they level it off and grade outside of their rails, so as to allow sleighs and other vehicles to pass along said streets and over their rails with safety and convenience. But whenever there is solid snow or ice exceeding the depth of six inches in said streets, then said railroad company shall not be allowed to remove the same from their rails without first obtaining the consent of the street commissioner, approved by the municipal officers, and then only upon condition that they haul it off and grade the streets wherever said snow or ice is so removed, to the satisfaction of the street commissioner. But if their consent for removing said snow or ice is refused, then said railroad company is authorized to use a sufficient number of sleighs, or mount their cars on runners, to convey passengers over their road until the cars can be used on their tracks.

Construction of tracks.

Snow and ice.

And upon the further condition that said railroad company shall faithfully observe and obey the following rules and regulations in using their road, viz:

Rules and regulations.

First—That no car shall be drawn at a greater speed on their road than six miles an hour.

Second—That while the cars are turning the corners from one street to another, the horses shall not be driven faster than a walk.

Third—The cars driven in the same direction shall not approach each other within a distance of three hundred feet, except in case of accident or at stations.

Fourth—That cars running in different directions shall not be allowed to stop abreast each other except at stations.

Fifth—That no cars shall be allowed to stop on a cross walk nor in front of an intersecting street, except to avoid collisions or prevent danger to persons in the street.

Sixth—That in case the conductor of any car is required to stop at the intersection of two streets to receive or land passengers, the car shall be so stopped as to leave the rear platform slightly over the last crossing.

Seventh—That the conductor and driver of each car shall keep a vigilant watch for all teams, carriages, persons on foot, and especially for children, and upon the least appearance of danger to such teams, carriages, persons or children, the car shall be stopped in the shortest time possible.

Eighth—That the conductors do not allow ladies or children to enter or leave the cars while in motion.

Ninth—That no salt or other articles shall be used in removing snow or ice from their tracks, which may prove injurious to sleighs or other vehicles crossing them, without the consent of the municipal officers.

Tenth—That a printed copy of these rules and regulations shall be put up and kept in a conspicuous place inside of every car used on their road:

And also upon the further condition that said railroad company shall accept the location hereinbefore specified, and agree to the several provisions, conditions and regulations connected with the same, within one month from March 1st, 1863, and said company shall file in the office of the city clerk, a duly certified copy of the vote agreeing to this location, with its conditions and regulations, within said one month, and make and complete, and put in running order said railroad in two years from said date, otherwise such portion as is not then made shall be null and void :

And also upon the further condition that said railroad company shall comply with and obey any and all other rules, regulations, orders, ordinances, or requirements which have been adopted, or may be adopted at any time hereafter by the municipal officers of Portland in relation to said railroad, or to the streets through which the tracks thereof are laid, not inconsistent with the rights herein granted :

And upon the further condition that any similar corporation hereafter incorporated, which shall construct its railroad in any of the streets of the city of Portland, where the Portland and Forest Avenue railroad company have no track, may enter upon and connect with and use the track of said Portland and Forest Avenue railroad company for such rates of compensation as may be mutually agreed upon, and in case of disagreement of the directors of said companies, three disinterested persons shall be appointed by a judge of the supreme court, upon the application of either party and due notice to the other, who shall upon hearing, fix said rates of compensation and determine all matters in dispute between said companies, and the services of said commissioners shall be paid in equal proportions by said companies.

And it is expressly understood that the municipal officers reserve all the rights and powers granted them by the second, third, and seventh sections of the act incorporating said company; and that none of said rights or powers so granted shall be deemed to be in any way waived, limited or qualified by anything contained in this order.

Additional location.

Order, Dec. 7, 1863.

5. *Ordered*, That the Portland & Forest Avenue Railroad Company be, and they are hereby authorized to extend the location of their railroad from their present terminus on Clark street, over and upon Spring street to Bowdoin street, upon the same terms and conditions, and with the same restrictions and limitations as are now granted by the terms of the original location of said road.

Obstructions.

Ord., Sept. 5, 1864.

6. Any person wilfully placing an obstruction of any kind upon the rails of the Portland and Forest Avenue railroad, in the streets of this city, shall be punished by fine not exceeding twenty dollars.

NOTE.—The conditions of acceptance by the company, were complied with by the properly attested papers received and placed on file at city clerk's office, March 23, and April 24, 1863.

PUBLIC BUILDINGS.

ORDINANCES.

1. Committee on public buildings to be appointed.
2. To have care and custody of public buildings, except, &c Proviso.
3. To lease buildings belonging to city, subject, &c.
4. Committee to prepare plans, &c., of buildings to be erected, repaired, &c.
5. To publish notice of time and place for exhibition of same.
6. Proposals for work to be sealed. How opened. Not to be disclosed till contract is made. Proviso.
7. Contracts exceeding $500 to be in writing, and signed by the mayor. Not to be altered, unless, &c.
8. Expenditure not to exceed appropriations.
9. Purchases of land for erecting buildings, to be made under direction of committee.
10. No building or land appurtenant to be sold without an order from city council.
11. Repairs, &c., to be done under committee on public buildings.

1. There shall be appointed, annually, a joint committee of the city council, to be called the committee on public buildings, to consist of two members of the board of mayor and aldermen, and three members of the common council.

Committee on public buildings to be appointed. Rev. Ord., 1855.

2. The said committee shall have the care and custody of all buildings belonging to the city, and of the erection, alteration and repair thereof, except as is otherwise provided in this and other ordinances of the city, and subject to such rules, orders and regulations as the city council may from time to time adopt: *Provided*, that the

To have care and custody of public buildings, except, &c. Ib.

Proviso.

school committee shall have the care and custody of the school houses belonging to the city.

To lease buildings belonging to the city, subject, &c.

Ib.

3. The said committee are authorized to lease any building belonging to the city, which is not otherwise appropriated, for any period not exceeding three years, and upon such terms and conditions as they may deem expedient, subject, however, to the approval of the mayor and aldermen; and in such case the lease shall be signed and executed by the city treasurer.

Committee to prepare plans, &c., of buildings to be erected, repaired, &c.

Ib.

4. Whenever any building for the use of the city shall be erected, altered, or repaired, the expense of which may exceed the sum of five hundred dollars, it shall be the duty of the committee that may have charge of the same, to prepare or cause to be prepared the requisite plans and specifications of the work to be done.

To publish notice of time and place for exhibition of same.

Ib.

5. The said committee shall give notice in the newspapers in which the ordinances of the city are published, of the time and place of the exhibition of such plans and specifications as may be necessary to enable contractors to make their estimate of the proposed work.

Proposals for work to be sealed.

How opened.

Not to be disclosed till contract is made.

Proviso.

Ib.

6. No proposal shall be received by the said committee, from any person offering to contract for such work, unless the same is sealed, and no proposal shall be opened except in committee actually assembled, and the contents of no proposal shall be made known to any person not a member of the committee, until after a contract shall have been made, provided, always, that if any such proposals shall be offered by persons who, in the judgment of said committee, shall be incompetent to perform their contracts in a workmanlike manner, or irresponsible in respect to their means of faithfully executing the same, the said committee may in their discretion reject any such proposal, notwithstanding the same be at a lower rate than other proposals offered for the same work.

Contracts exceeding $500 to be in writing, and signed by mayor.

7. In all cases where the amount of any contract shall exceed the sum of five hundred dollars, the contract shall be in writing, and signed by the mayor on the part of the

city, and after being signed by the parties, no such contract shall be altered in any particular, unless a majority of the said committee shall signify their assent thereto, in writing, under their respective signatures, indorsed on the said contract.

Not to be altered, unless, &c.
Ib.

8. The amount of expenditures for the foregoing purposes, in any one year, shall never exceed the appropriations made by the city council for the same, and no expenditure exceeding two hundred dollars shall ever be made in the alteration or repair of any building, without an express vote of the city council authorizing the same.

Expenditures not to exceed appropriations.
Ib.

9. Whenever the city council shall order the purchase of land, for the purpose of erecting any building thereon, such purchase shall be made under the direction of the said committee on public buildings.

Purchases of land for erecting buildings, to be made under direction of committee.
Ib.

10. No building, or land appurtenant thereto, shall be sold by any committee of the city council, without an order from the city council authorizing such sale.

No building, &c., to be sold without order of city council.
Ib.

11. All repairs, alterations or enlargements of any of the public buildings belonging to this city, necessary or requiring to be made, shall be done under the direction of the joint standing committee on public buildings, and no bill shall be allowed or paid by the city for any labor or materials used in repairs upon any building belonging to the city, unless the same shall have been approved by said committee.

Repairs, &c., to be done under committee on public buildings.
Ord., Feb. 9, 1865.

[See chapter on CONTRACTS AND EXPENDITURES, p. 116, *ante*.]

REBUILDING OF BURNED DISTRICT.

STATUTES.

1. Bonds of city; amount and when payable.
2. Commissioners to negotiate loan.
3. " may loan on mortgages of real estate.
4. Interest upon loans.
5. Sinking fund. Moneys on hand, how to be invested.
6. Vacancies in board of commissioners, how filled. Removals, how made. Succession in management of property.
7. Duties of city treasurer.
8. Accounts, records and reports, how and when made.
9. Acceptance of act by citizens.

ORDER OF CITY COUNCIL.

1. Relating to bonds.

STATUTES.

Bonds of city, amount and when payable.

Acts, 1867, chapters 373, 390.

1. For the purpose of aiding in rebuilding said city, so much of which was recently destroyed by fire, the city of Portland is authorized to issue its bonds to an amount not exceeding two millions of dollars, payable in not exceeding twenty years from their date, and bearing an interest at the rate of six per centum per annum, payable at the option of the commissioners in any place in the United States, or payable in England in sterling.

Commissioners to negotiate loan.

2. A board of four commissioners, citizens of said city, shall be appointed by the mayor and aldermen of said city. Each of said commissioners shall give bond to the city, in such sum as the mayor and aldermen shall determine,

conditioned for the faithful discharge of his duty as commissioner. They shall receive such compensation for their services as shall be established by the mayor and aldermen. The bonds issued by virtue hereof, shall be negotiated by said commissioners, under the direction of the mayor, and delivered by the city treasurer upon the warrant of the commissioners.

Their compensation and duties.

Act, 1867, chap. 373.

3. The said commissioners, under such general regulations as shall be established from time to time by the mayor and aldermen of said city, shall loan the proceeds of said bonds in a safe and judicious manner, upon mortgages of real estate, for the purpose of building dwelling-houses, stores and buildings, in said city of Portland.

May loan upon mortgages of real estate.

Acts, 1867, chapters 373, 390.

4. Upon all loans made by said commissioners under this act, they are hereby authorized to charge, take or reserve, a rate of interest not exceeding seven and three-tenths per centum per annum.

Interest upon loans.

Act, 1867, chap. 373.

5. For the purpose of the payment of the bonds issued under this act, a sinking fund shall be established, to be under the direction of said commissioners. All payments of loans, all receipts of interest above interest paid, after payment of necessary expenses, and all other moneys received, excepting from the sale of said bonds, shall be placed to the credit of said sinking fund. The commissioners shall from time to time at their discretion, invest the moneys on hand, securely, so that they shall be productive; and the same may be loaned on mortgages of real estate, as provided in section three of this act, or invested in the bonds issued under this act, or any other bonds of the city of Portland, or of the State of Maine, or of the United States, which securities shall be held for the increase of the sinking fund. And the commissioners may, from time to time, sell or transfer any of said securities.

Sinking fund.

Moneys to be invested in securities, how held and conveyed.

Ib.

6. Vacancies in the board of commissioners shall be filled by the remaining or surviving commissioners. Said

Vacancies, how filled.

Removals, how made.

commissioners, or any of them, shall not be removable from office, except by the supreme judicial court, in their discretion, upon complaint of the mayor and aldermen of said city, which court is hereby empowered to adjudicate upon said complaint according to the course of proceedings in equity, and to pass all proper decrees touching the same. Vacancies thus created shall be filled as above provided; and as often as any new commissioner or commissioners shall be appointed, the management of the property then held shall rest by operation of law in such new commissioner or commissioners, jointly with the prior commissioners.

Succession in management of property.

Ib.

Duties of city treasurer.

Ib.

7. The city treasurer shall have the care and custody of all moneys received from the sale of bonds, or from any other sources, and shall be responsible on his official bond to the city for the safe keeping of the funds thus entrusted to him. He shall also have the care and custody of, and be responsible for, all the securities of the sinking fund. He shall pay out and deliver any of said moneys or securities only upon the warrant of the commissioners.

Accounts, records and reports, how and when made.

Ib.

8. The said commissioners shall keep a true record of all their proceedings, and an account of all sums received from the sale of bonds or from any other sources, and the payments made of the same. They shall, annually, in the month of January, report to the city council their proceedings for the year. And their records and accounts, and the accounts and securities of the sinking fund, shall at all times be open to inspection by the finance committee of the city council.

Acceptance of Act by citizens.

Ib.

9. This act shall not take effect unless accepted by the legal voters of said city, at ward meetings duly called, and at least two thirds of the votes cast at said meetings, shall be necessary for the acceptance of the act.[1]

[1] The act was accepted March 15, 1867, and March 20, 1867, Woodbury Davis, Eben Steele, Ambrose K. Shurtleff and Weston R. Millikin were appointed commissioners.

ORDER.

PASSED MAY 6, 1867.

1. *Ordered*, That in accordance with the act of the legislature of this State, approved February 28, 1867, entitled "An act to enable the city of Portland to aid in rebuilding said city," the treasurer be, and he is hereby authorized to issue the bonds of the city in sums of not less than one thousand dollars each, from time to time, as may be required by the commissioners appointed under said act, to an amount not exceeding the sum authorized by said act, at the rate of interest of six per cent. per annum, payable in twenty years from this date, both principal and interest payable in lawful money of the United States of America, and at the option of the said commissioners at any place within the United States. Each bond aforesaid shall be signed by the treasurer, countersigned by the mayor, attested by the city clerk with the seal of the city, and also countersigned by one or more of the commissioners under said act; but the coupons shall be signed by the treasurer only.

Relating to bonds.

RIOTS.

STATUTES.

STATUTES.

Unlawful assembly and riot. 18 Maine, 346. R. S., chap. 123, § 2.

1. If three or more persons assemble in a violent or tumultuous manner to do an unlawful act, or, being together, make any attempt or motion towards doing a lawful or unlawful act in a violent, unlawful, or tumultuous manner, to the terror or disturbance of others, they

shall be deemed guilty of an unlawful assembly; if they commit such acts in the manner and with the effect aforesaid, they shall be deemed guilty of a riot, and be punished, in either case, by imprisonment less than one year, and by fine not exceeding five hundred dollars; and in case of a riot, each offender shall also suffer such punishment as he would be liable to if he had committed such act alone.

2. Any person, engaged in an unlawful assembly or riot, may be indicted and convicted thereof alone, if it is alleged in the indictment and proved at the trial that three or more were engaged therein, and if known, they must be named, but if unknown, that fact must be alleged.

One person may be convicted, without the others.

Ib. § 3.

SUPPRESSION OF MOBS BY OFFICERS AND ARMED FORCE.

3. When twelve or more persons, any of them armed with clubs or dangerous weapons, or thirty or more, armed or unarmed, are unlawfully, riotously, or tumultuously assembled in any town, it shall be the duty of each of the municipal officers, constables, and justices of the peace thereof, and of the sheriff of the county and his deputies, to go among the persons so assembled, or as near to them as they can safely go, and in the name of the State, command them immediately and peaceably to disperse; and if they do not obey, such magistrates and officers shall command the assistance of all persons present in arresting and securing the persons so unlawfully assembled; and every person refusing to disperse, or to assist as aforesaid, shall be deemed one of such unlawful assembly, and punished by a fine not exceeding five hundred dollars, and imprisonment less than one year; and each such magistrate or other officer, having notice of such unlawful assembly in his town, and refusing or neglecting to do his duty in relation thereto as aforesaid, shall be punished by a fine not exceeding three hundred dollars.

Duty of magistrate and officers to disperse unlawful assembly, &c.

Ib. § 4.

When rioters refuse to disperse, &c.
Ib. § 5.

4. When persons, so riotously or unlawfully assembled, neglect or refuse, on command as aforesaid, to disperse without unnecessary delay, any two of the magistrates, or officers aforesaid, may require the aid of a sufficient number of persons in arms or otherwise, and proceed in such manner as they judge expedient, to suppress such riotous assembly, and arrest and secure the persons composing it; and when an armed force is thus called out, they shall obey the orders for suppressing such assembly and arresting and securing the persons composing it, which they receive from the governor, any judge of a court of record, the sheriff of the county, or any two of the magistrates or officers mentioned in section four.

If any person is killed or wounded, officers held guiltless, &c.
Ib. § 6.

5. If, in the efforts made as aforesaid to suppress such assembly, and to arrest and secure the persons composing it who refuse to disperse, though the number remaining is less than twelve, any such persons, or any persons present as spectators or otherwise, are killed or wounded, said magistrates, officers, and persons acting with them by their order, shall be held guiltless and justified in law; if any of said magistrates, officers, or persons thus acting with them, are killed or wounded, all persons so unlawfully or riotously assembled, and all other persons who refused, when required, to aid such magistrates and officers, shall be held answerable therefor.

PUNISHMENT AND REMEDY FOR INJURIES BY MOBS.

Punishment for pulling down houses or premeditated personal injuries.
Ib. § 7.

6. If any persons, thus unlawfully and riotously assembled, pull down, or begin to pull down, or destroy any dwelling-house, building, ship or vessel; or perpetrate any premeditated injury, not a felony, on any person, each shall be punished by imprisonment not more than five years, or by fine not exceeding five hundred dollars; and shall also be answerable to any person injured, in an action of trespass to the full amount of damages by him sustained.

7. When the injury to any property as described in section seven [section above] amounts to fifty dollars or more, the town where such property is situated shall indemnify the owner thereof for three-fourths of the value of such injury, to be recovered in an action on the case, if he uses all reasonable diligence to prevent such injuries, and to procure the conviction of the offenders; and the town paying such sum may recover it in an action on the case against the persons doing the injury.

Liability of towns for injury by mobs, &c.
Ib. § 8.

ORDINANCE.

1. In case of any riot, or unauthorized and tumultuous collection of persons, within the limits of the city, it shall be the duty of the city marshal, deputy marshals, policemen, watchmen and constables of the city, so soon as they are informed of the same, to repair immediately to the place where said riot or tumult may be, and report themselves to the mayor, or in his absence, to the city marshal, and they shall use all the power and authority vested in them by the ordinances of the city, or laws of this State, quickly to separate and disperse said mob or tumultuous collection of persons, or to arrest and bring them to trial for said offense, as the case may require, to protect the persons and property of the citizens from injury, and to do all other matters and things which may be commanded them by the mayor or city marshal.

In case of riot, marshal and other police officers to repair to place of riot.
Rev. Ord., 1855.

To use power and authority to disperse mob.

SALE OF SECOND HAND ARTICLES.

STATUTES.

Mayor and aldermen authorized to grant licenses to persons for certain purposes.
Act, 1861, chap. 63.

1. The mayor and aldermen of the city of Portland, may license such persons as they deem suitable to be keepers of shops for the purchase, sale, or barter of junk, old metals, bones, rags, or of any second hand articles, and to be dealers therein.

— to designate place of business, &c.
Ib.

2. The licenses to such persons shall designate the place where the business is to be carried on, and the persons licensed shall be subject to such conditions, restrictions and regulations as may be prescribed by the mayor and aldermen of said city, and the license shall continue in force for one year, unless sooner revoked.

Persons not licensed, liable.
— license revoked, liable.
Penalty.
— how recovered.
Ib.

3. No person, unless licensed as aforesaid, shall keep any shop or place for the purchase, sale or barter of the articles aforesaid, or for the storage thereof, or be a dealer therein ; nor shall any person so licensed, keep such shop, or be a dealer in said articles, in any other place or manner than as is designated in his license or after notice to him that said license has been revoked, under the penalty of twenty dollars for each offense, to be recovered by complaint in the municipal court for said city or by indictment.

SCHOOLS.

STATUTES.

1. Towns may choose school agents; vacancies, how filled.
2. School committee may appoint one of their number to perform certain duties.
3. Towns may choose committees of three or more.
4. Penalty for not choosing committee or supervisor.
5. Towns to make by-laws concerning truants, and certain children not attending school, to be approved by judge of supreme court. Penalty for breach thereof.
6. Shall appoint persons to make complaints of violation of by-laws.
7. Truant children may be placed in suitable institutions.

POWERS AND DUTIES OF SCHOOL COMMITTEES.

8. Committees, &c., must be sworn.
9. " their term of office.
10. " same subject.
11. " their duties.
12. " shall make annual statements.
13. " to furnish books if parents or guardians neglect. Delinquents may be taxed.
14. Committees, &c., may be paid for their services.
15. Blank school returns, when and how distributed.
16. School returns, when to be made.
17. Delinquent towns, when notified. Duty of secretary of State.
18. Amount to be raised in cities for schools.
19. School fund, when withheld.
20. Agent to return lists to school committee.
21. Duty of committee, if agent neglect to act.
22. Committee to return list to assessors.
23. Graded schools, money raised for.

DUTIES AND QUALIFICATIONS OF INSTRUCTORS.

PENAL PROVISIONS AFFECTING SCHOOLS.

ORDINANCES.

STATUTES.

Towns may choose agents. Vacancies how filled. R. S., chap. 11, § 4.

1. A town, at its annual meeting, may choose its school agents ; and vacancies may be filled as in case of other town officers not chosen by ballot.

S. S. committee may appoint one of their number to perform certain duties. Act, March 16, 1862.

2. The superintending school committee may appoint one of their number, who shall have all the power, and perform all the duties specified in the fifth and twelfth items of the forty-ninth section of chapter 11, revised statutes.

Towns may choose a committee with powers of agents. R. S., chap. 11, § 10.

3. Any town may choose a committee consisting of not less than three, all or one-third each year, and invest them with the rights, powers and obligations of superintending school committee and school agents, including the power of determining the age and qualifications of scholars to be admitted into the several schools, of transferring scholars from school to school, of employing teachers, and expending money raised for school purposes.

Penalty for towns failing to choose committees or supervisor. Ib. § 11.

4. Any town failing to elect either of the committees aforesaid, or supervisor for any year, shall forfeit not less than thirty, nor more than two hundred dollars.

5. Towns may make such by-laws, not repugnant to the laws of the State, concerning habitual truants, and children between six and seventeen[1] years of age not attending school, without any regular and lawful occupation, and growing up in ignorance, as are most conducive to their welfare and the good order of society; and may annex a suitable penalty, not exceeding twenty dollars, for any breach thereof; but said by-laws must be first approved by a judge of the supreme judicial court. [See chapter on TRUANTS.]

Towns to make by-laws concerning truants. Ib. § 12, as amended by Act, 1861, chap. 5.

Penalty for breach thereof.

6. Such towns shall appoint, at their annual meeting, one or more persons, who alone shall make complaints for violations of said by-laws to the magistrate having jurisdiction thereof by said by-laws, and execute his judgments.

Shall appoint persons to make complaint of violation of by-laws. Ib. as amended by Act, 1861, chap. 5.

7. Said magistrate, in place of the fine aforesaid, may order children proved to be growing up in truancy, and without the benefit of the education provided for them by law, to be placed for such periods of time as he thinks expedient, in the institution of instruction, house of reformation, or other suitable situation provided for the purpose, under the authority conferred by section twelve of chapter 11 of the revised statutes. [See chapter on TRUANTS.]

Truant children placed in suitable institutions.

POWERS AND DUTIES OF SUPERINTENDING SCHOOL COMMITTEES.

8. Members of superintending school committees and supervisors shall be duly sworn.

Officers to be sworn. Ib. § 46.

9. Superintending school committees, at their first meeting, shall designate by lot one of their number to hold office three years, and another, two years, and certify such designation to the town clerk to be by him recorded. The third member shall hold office one year; and each member elected to fill the place of one whose term expires, shall hold office three years. They shall fill all vacancies

Sup. sch. committee first chosen, term of office. Ib. § 47.

[1] Truants between the age of eight and sixteen years may be sent to the reform school. See chapter on TRUANTS.

in their number until the next annual town meeting. Two members shall constitute a quorum; but if there is but one in office, he may fill vacancies.

Same of com. under sec. ten. Ib.

10. Committees elected under section ten [of chapter 11, revised statutes,] unless chosen for one year only, shall hold office and determine their terms of office, as provided in the preceding section.

Sup. sch. com., duties of. Ib. § 49.

11. Superintending school committees shall perform the following duties:

First.—They shall appoint suitable times and places for the examination of candidates proposing to teach in town, and give notice thereof.

Examine candidates for instructors.

Second.—On satisfactory evidence that a candidate possesses a good moral character, and a temper and disposition suitable to be an instructor of youth, they shall examine him in reading, spelling, writing, English grammar, geography, history, arithmetic, and other branches usually taught in public schools, and particularly in the school for which he is examined, and also as to capacity for the government thereof.

Give certificate. 27 Maine, 266.

Third.—They shall give to each candidate found competent, a certificate that he is qualified to govern said school, and instruct in the branches above named, and such other branches as are necessary to be taught therein.

Direct course of instruction. Uniform system of text books, by whom selected. —notice. Text books, when and how changed. Ib. as amended by Act, March 15, 1862.

Fourth.—Direct the general course of instruction, and what books shall be used in the schools. And it shall be the duty of superintending school committees to select a uniform system of text-books to be used in the schools of the town, due notice of which selection shall be given; and any text-book hereafter introduced into the schools of any town, shall not be changed for five years from the date of its introduction unless by a vote of the town.

Examine schools.

Fifth.—Examine the several schools, and inquire into the regulations and discipline thereof, and the proficiency of the scholars therein, for which purpose one or more of the committee shall visit each school at least twice in summer, and twice in winter, and use their influence to secure the regular attendance at school of the youth in their town.

Sixth.—After due notice and investigation, they shall dismiss any teacher, although having the requisite certificate, who is found incapable or unfit to teach, or whose services they deem unprofitable to the school, and give to said teacher a certificate of dismissal and of the reasons therefor, a copy of which they shall retain, and immediately notify the district agent of such dismissal, which shall not deprive the teacher of compensation for previous services.

May dismiss teachers for sufficient cause.

Give certificate in such cases.

3 Greenl., 450. 16 Maine, 184.

Seventh.—Expel from school any obstinately disobedient and disorderly scholar, after a proper investigation of his behavior, if found necessary for the peace and usefulness of the school, and restore him on satisfactory evidence of his repentance and amendment.

May expel disorderly scholars.

Eighth.—Exclude from the public schools, if they deem expedient, any person who is not vaccinated, though otherwise entitled by law to admission thereto.

May expel scholars not vaccinated.

Ninth.—Direct or approve in writing the expenditure of school money apportioned to inhabitants not included in any district.

Direct expenditures.

Tenth.—Prescribe the sum, on the payment of which persons of the required age resident on territory, the jurisdiction of which has been ceded to the United States, included in or surrounded by a school district, shall be entitled to attend school in such district; and when such territory adjoins two or more districts, they shall designate the one where they may attend.

Prescribe sums to be paid in certain cases.

Eleventh.—Determine what description of scholars shall attend each school, classify them, and transfer them from school to school, in districts where more than one school is kept at the same time, and no district committee is elected.

May classify scholars.

To make annual report. As amended by Act, March 16, 1861.

Twelfth.—At the annual town meeting, they shall make a written report of the condition of the schools for the past year, the proficiency made by the pupils, and the success attending the modes of instruction and government of the teachers; and they shall transmit a copy thereof to the superintendent of common schools.

Shall make annual statement. Ib. § 50. Particulars.

12. They shall annually make out a statement, containing the following particulars:

First.—The amount of money raised and expended for the support of schools, designating what part is raised by taxes, and what part from other funds, and how such funds accrued.

Second.—The number of school districts, and parts of districts in their town.

Third.—The number of children between four and twenty-one years of age, belonging to their town in each district, on the first day of April preceding.

Fourth.—The number of such children who reside on islands, or in any other part of the town not in any district.

Fifth.—The whole number, and the average number of scholars attending the summer schools; the whole number, and the average number of scholars attending the winter schools.

Sixth.—The average length of the summer schools in weeks; the average length of the winter schools in weeks; the average length of the schools for the year.

Seventh.—The number of male teachers and the number of female teachers employed in the public schools during any part of the year.

Eighth.—The wages of male teachers per month, and the wages of female teachers per week, exclusive of board.

Ninth.—They shall give in their returns, full and complete answers to the inquiries contained in the blank forms furnished them under the provisions of law; certify that such statement is true and correct, according to their best knowledge and belief; and transmit it to the office of the secretary of State, on or before the first day of April in each year. When by reason of removal, resignation or death, but one member of the committee remains, he shall make said returns.

Return to secretary of State.

13. If any parent, master or guardian, after notice from the teacher of a school that a child under his care is deficient of the necessary school books, refuses or neglects to furnish such child with the books required, the superintending school committee, on being notified thereof by the teacher, shall furnish them at the expense of the town; and such expense may be added to the next town tax of the parent, master or guardian.

Committee to furnish books, if parents or guardians neglect.

Ib. § 51.

Delinquents may be taxed.

14. Superintending school committees and supervisors shall be paid for their services, on satisfying the municipal officers that they have made the returns to the secretary of State required by law, one dollar and fifty cents a day and all necessary traveling expenses, and no more unless ordered by the town.

Compensation for sup. sch. com. and supervisors.

Ib. as amended by Act, Feb. 18, 1867.

15. The secretary of State shall, on the first day of March in each year, forward to the clerk of the several cities, towns and plantations, blanks for the annual school return, and registers for the school year commencing on the first day of April following; and said clerk shall forthwith deliver the same to the superintending school committee of his respective city, town and plantation.

Blank school returns, when and how distributed.

Act, Feb. 18, 1867, chap. 82, § 1.

16. The superintending school committees or supervisors of the several cities, towns and plantations, shall make their annual school returns now required by law, into the office of the secretary of State, on the first day of May, and shall give the number of scholars as they existed on the first day of April, preceding.

School returns to be made May first.

Act, Feb. 15, 1859, chap. 55, § 1.

Scholars numbered April first.

17. The secretary of State shall, on the first day of June, notify the school committees of any towns whose returns were not received at his office in May, and shall annually ascertain on the first day of July, the number of

Delinquent towns notified June first.

Ib. § 2.

children between four and twenty-one years of age, in the towns from which returns are received, and furnish a list thereof to the State treasurer, and the treasurer shall immediately after the first day of July apportion to the towns all State school funds for the year, according to such list, and in the manner prescribed in section twenty-five, chapter eleven of the revised statutes.

List to be furnished State treasurer July first, and funds apportioned.

Amount to be raised in cities, &c., for support of schools.

R. S., chap. 11, § 5, amended by Act, Feb. 22, 1865, chap. 304, § 1.

18. Every city, town and plantation shall raise and expend annually for the support of schools therein, a sum of money, exclusive of the income of any corporate school fund, or of any grant from the revenue or funds from the State, or of any voluntary donation, devise or bequest, or of any forfeiture accruing to the use of schools, not less than seventy-five cents for each inhabitant, according to the census of the State, by which representatives to the legislature were last apportioned.

School fund, when withheld.

Ib. § 2.

19. No town which neglects to raise the amount of money required to be raised by section one of this act, shall during the year in which such neglect occurs, receive any part of the State school fund, required to be apportioned to the several towns by the treasurer of State; *provided, however*, that all plantations shall be entitled to receive their part of the State school fund, when the inhabitants of such plantations shall have paid their part of all State and county taxes, and not otherwise.

Agents to return lists of persons from 4 to 21 years of age to S. S. committee.

Ib. § 3.

20. Each school agent shall return to the superintending school committee, in the month of April, annually, a certified list of the names and ages of all persons in his district, from four to twenty-one years, as they existed on the first day of said month, leaving out of said enumeration, all persons coming from other places to attend any college or academy, or to labor in any factory, or at any manufacturing or other business.

If agent neglects, S. S. committee to make enumeration of scholars.

Ib. § 4.

21. If any school agent neglects to return the scholars of his district, as provided in section three of this act, the superintending school committee shall immediately make

such enumeration in such district and be paid a reasonable sum for the service, and the sum thus paid shall be taken from the amount to be apportioned to the district of such delinquent agent.

22. The superintending school committee shall return to the assessors on or before the fifteenth day of May, annually, the number of scholars in each school district, according to the enumeration provided for in sections three and four of this act.

S. S. committee to make return of list of scholars in each district to assessors.

Ib. § 5.

23. Any school district maintaining graded schools, may raise for the support of schools therein a sum of money not exceeding that which it receives from the town in addition thereto.

Districts having graded schools may raise money.

Ib. § 6.

DUTIES AND QUALIFICATIONS OF INSTRUCTORS.

24. Every teacher of a public school shall keep a school register containing the names of all the scholars who enter the school, their ages, the date of each scholar's entering and leaving, the number of days each attended, the length of the school, the teacher's wages, a list of text books used, and all other facts required by the blank form furnished under the provisions of law ; such register shall at all times be open to the inspection of the school committee, and be returned to them at the close of the school. No teacher shall be entitled to pay for his services, until the register of his school properly filled up, completed, and signed, is deposited with the school committee or with a person designated by them to receive it.

Teachers to keep school register.

R. S., chap. 11, § 56.

Not to be paid till register is completed.

25. The presidents, professors, and tutors of colleges, the preceptors and teachers of academies, and all other instructors of youth, in public or private institutions, shall use their best endeavors to impress on the minds of the children and youth committed to their care and instruction, the principles of morality and justice, and a sacred regard for truth ; love of country, humanity, and a universal benevolence ; sobriety, industry, and frugality ; chastity,

Instructors of colleges, &c., to inculcate morality, justice and patriotism.

Ib. § 57.

moderation, and temperance ; and all other virtues, which are the ornaments of human society ; and to lead those under their care, as their ages and capacities admit, into a particular understanding of the tendency of such virtues to preserve and perfect a republican constitution, and secure the blessings of liberty, and promote their future happiness ; and the tendency of the opposite vices to slavery, degradation, and ruin.

PENAL PROVISIONS AFFECTING SCHOOLS.

Penalty for disturbing schools. 35 Maine, 195. Ib. § 71.

26. If any person, whether he is a scholar or not, enters any school-house or other place of instruction during or out of school hours, while the teacher or any pupil is there, and wilfully interrupts or disturbs the teacher or pupils by loud speaking, rude or indecent behavior, signs, or gestures ; or wilfully interrupts a school by prowling about the building, making noises, throwing missiles at the school-house, or in any way disturbing the school, he shall forfeit not less than two, nor more than twenty dollars.

Parents or guardians liable. Ib. § 72.

27. If a minor injures or aids in injuring any school-house, out-buildings, utensils or appurtenances belonging thereto ; defaces the walls, benches, seats, or other parts of said buildings by marks, cuts or otherwise ; or injures or destroys any property belonging to a school district, such district by its agent or committee, may recover of his parent or guardian, in an action of debt, double the amount of damages occasioned thereby.

ORDINANCES.

School committee to elect and remove instructors, and determine their salaries, &c. Rev. Ord., 1855.

1. The school committee are authorized to elect all such instructors as they may think necessary for the public schools, and to determine the amount of their respective salaries ; also to remove any instructor from said schools, when in their discretion it may be proper ;

and generally to execute all the powers which the selectmen of towns or school committees are authorized by the laws of this State to exercise.

2. The school committee are authorized to distribute the annual sum which shall be appropriated by the city council for salaries of instructors in the public schools, fixing the salary of each instructor in accordance with the specifications of said committee on which the aggregate amount of salaries may have been predicated, and on which the appropriations shall have been made by said city council.

To apportion salaries of instructors, so as not to exceed the appropriations made by city council.
Ib.

3. No person who has not been vaccinated or otherwise secured against any contagion of small pox, shall be permitted to attend any of the city schools.

Persons not vaccinated not permitted to attend public schools.
Ib.

4. The school committee may cause any scholar of any of the city schools to be vaccinated by the city physician, at the expense of the city; and it shall be their duty to carry into effect the provisions of this and the preceding section, and for that purpose to make such rules and regulations as they may deem proper.

School committee may cause scholars to be vaccinated at expense of city.
Ib.

SEAL OF THE CITY.

ORDINANCE.

Seal of the City.

Seal of the city. Rev. Ord. 1855. The design hereto annexed shall be the device of the city seal; and the motto shall be as follows, to wit:— "*Resurgam, Sigillum Civitatis Portlandiæ.*"

SIDEWALKS.

[See chapter on STREETS.]

SINKING FUND.

ORDINANCES.

1. Committee on reduction of city debt.
2. Appropriations for payment of city debt.
3. Duty of auditor.
4. Committee may loan to city treasurer.

1. The mayor, the chairman of the board of aldermen and the president of the common council, shall be a committee to be called the Committee on reduction of the city debt, whose duty it shall be to cause all moneys passed to their credit in the books of the auditor of accounts, to be applied to the purchase or payment of the capital of the debt of the city, in the manner they may from time to time deem expedient; and it shall be the duty of the auditor, and of the treasurer of the city, to conform to all orders in writing in this respect, which shall be made and signed by all the members of said committee.

Committee on reduction of city debt.
Ord., July 1, 1861.

2. All balances of money unappropriated remaining in the treasury at the end of any financial year; all excesses of income over the original estimated income; all balances of appropriations original, or by additions remaining on the books of the auditor; all receipts for premiums on city notes issued; all receipts in money on account of the sale of any real estate of any description now belonging, or which may hereafter belong to the city, excepting the sale of burial lots in the cemeteries of the city; all receipts on account of the principal sum of any stocks, bonds or notes now owned,

Appropriations for payment of city debt.
Ib. as amended by Ord., Feb. 7, 1865.

or which may hereafter be owned by the city; and also of the annual city tax, such a sum as the city council of each year shall fix and determine not less than five per cent. of the then existing city debt; shall be and the same hereby is appropriated to the payment or the purchase of the principal of the city debt.

Duty of auditor.

Ord., July 1, 1861.

3. It shall be the duty of the auditor, annually, to pass to the credit of the committee on the reduction of the city debt, all receipts, the proceeds of either of the sources before mentioned, and the said amount out of the annual tax; and the sums so passed to the credit of said committee shall be drawn from the treasury of the city for the payment, or the purchase of the capital of the city debt, in the manner before mentioned, and for no other purpose whatever.

Committee may loan to city treasurer.

Ib.

4. The committee on the reduction of the city debt are hereby authorized to lend on interest to the treasurer of the city any amount so passed to their credit as aforesaid, which may not be immediately wanted for the purchase or redemption of said debt.

SOLICITOR.

ORDINANCES.

1. City solicitor to be chosen. His qualifications.
2. His duties.
3. To commence and prosecute suits. To defend suits against city. To appear before the legislature and committees thereof. To furnish legal opinions.
4. To make annual report to city council of unfinished business. Report to be published.

1. In the month of March, annually, and whenever a vacancy in the office shall occur, there shall be chosen by the city council, a solicitor for the city of Portland, who shall have been admitted an attorney and counsellor of the courts of the State, and he shall be removable at the pleasure of the city council.

City solicitor to be chosen. Rev. Ord., 1855, as amended by city charter. His qualifications.

2. It shall be the duty of said city solicitor, by himself or by some person by him duly authorized, for whose conduct, skill and faithfulness he shall be accountable, to draft all bonds, deeds, obligations, contracts, leases, conveyances, agreements, and other legal instruments of whatever nature, which may be required of him by any ordinance or order of the mayor and aldermen, or of the city council, or which by any ordinance or order may be requisite to be done and made by the city of Portland, and which by law, usage and agreement, the city is to be at the expense of drawing.

His duties. Rev. Ord., 1855.

3. It shall be the duty of said city solicitor to commence and prosecute all actions and suits to be commenced by the city, before any tribunal in this State, whether in law or equity, and also to appear and defend and

To commence and prosecute suits. Ib.

To defend suits against city.

advocate the rights and interests of the city, or any of the officers of the city, in any suit or prosecution for any act or omission in the discharge of their official duties, wherein any estate, right, privilege, ordinances or acts of the city government, or any breach of any ordinance may be brought into question. And said solicitor shall also appear before the legislature of this State, or any committee thereof, and there in behalf of the city, represent, answer for, defend and advocate the interests and welfare of said city, whenever the same may be directly or incidentally affected, whether to prosecute or defend the same; and he shall in all matters do all and every professional act, incident to the office, which may be required of him by the city government, or by any joint or special committee thereof, or by any ordinance or order; and he shall, when required, furnish the mayor and aldermen, the common council, or any joint or special committee of either branch thereof, and to any officer of the city government, who may require it in the official discharge of his duties, with his legal opinion on any subject touching the duties of their respective offices.

To appear before the legislature and committees thereof.

To furnish legal opinions.

To make annual report to city council of unfinished business.

4. It shall be the duty of said city solicitor, annually, in the month of February, to report in writing, to the city council, all the unfinished business in his department, including the names, grounds, and stages of progress, of all suits pending, in which the city is a party or is interested; with the names and results of such suits, affecting the city, as may have been decided or adjusted during the year, and such other information as to the business of his department as he may think important, or the city council may direct; which report shall be published with the other annual reports to be made to the city council.

Ib.

To be published.

STEAM ENGINES.

[See chapter on NUISANCES.]

STREETS.

STATUTES.

1. Authority of city council over streets. Land damages. Appeal.
2. Original location of streets to be ascertained by city engineer. Persons may object.
3. Obstruction of streets on public occasions.
4. Portland Gas Company may lay pipes, &c. Liability for damages.
5. Excavations near streets, how to be made ; responsibilities.

ORDINANCES.

1. Names of streets to be continued.
2. Committee on laying out new streets to be appointed.
3. Committee to lay out, &c., new streets. To estimate damages. To report to city council.
4. Commissioner of streets to be elected. To be sworn. Compensation. May be removed.
5. Duties of commissioner. Shall not change the grade of streets, without, &c. To make contracts. To have charge of teams, &c.
6. Powers of street commissioners given to commissioner of streets. To pay damages sustained in consequence of neglect of duty.
7. Commissioner shall be acquainted with lines, &c., of streets. To remove obstructions. To perform duties prescribed by mayor and aldermen or city council. To make arrangements for supply of labor.
8. Commissioner shall discharge all bills once a month. To render account to board of aldermen. To keep account of receipts and expenditures. To present annual account.
9. To cause stone monuments to be erected when, &c. To be recorded.

10. Monuments not to be removed without, &c. Penalty.
11. Dangerous lots of land to be fenced. Penalty. Street commissioner shall cause lots to be fenced.
12. Streets not to be dug up, or gravel removed from, without license, &c. Penalty.
13. Street broken up shall be repaired. Penalty.
14. No drain or aqueduct to be opened or repaired without license. Penalty.
15. When license is granted to open a drain, &c., street to be repaired to satisfaction of commissioner. One-half of street to be kept open. Railing to be kept up. To be lighted. Penalty.
16. Notice to be given of intention to build. Portion of street to be allotted. Portion allotted to be used for building materials, &c. Rubbish, &c., to be carried away. In case of neglect, to be removed at expense of person. To be lighted. Penalties.
17. Lumber, stones, and building materials not to be placed in streets to remain over six hours. Penalty. May be removed at expense of owner.
18. Proceedings when owners refuse to remove them. To be sold at auction.
19. No person to blast rocks within fifty rods of street, without license. Penalty.
20. Persons not to play at bat and ball. Not to throw snow balls. Penalties.
21. Not to shoot with bow and arrow. Penalty.
22. Not to fly kites. Not to coast on sleds or skate. Penalty.
23. Gaming tables or devices not to be exposed in streets. No person to play at unlawful games in street.
24. No person to swim or bathe in exposed situations. Penalty.
25. Manure not to be taken from streets without permission.
26. Streets shall not be obstructed by moving of buildings. Building obstructing streets to be removed at expense of owner.
27. Penalties.
28. No goods or merchandise to be placed so as to project into street. Penalty.
29. Awnings may be placed. Proviso. Regulations.
30. Signs, &c., not to project into street. Penalty.
31. Making noises in streets forbidden.
32. Grinding cutlery, &c., in the streets, forbidden, unless license.
33. Porticoes, porches, &c., not to project into street. Penalty.
34. Cellar doors, &c. Not to remain open, unless lighted. Light to be kept at entrance. Penalties.
35. Entrance and steps to be secured with railings or chains. Light to be placed. Penalties.

36. Apertures and coal holes not to be made without license. Penalty. Not to be left open. Penalty.
37. Gratings in sidewalks not to extend more than eighteen inches. Penalties.
38. Mayor and aldermen may authorise the construction of coal holes, and gratings. Not to extend more than three feet.
39. Horses shall not be driven in streets at a faster rate than six miles an hour. Penalty.
40. Horses, cattle and swine, not to run at large. Penalty.
41. Horses or animals not to be frightened. Penalty.
42. Speed of trains in Commercial street regulated.
43. Bells of locomotives to be rung.
44. Brakemen to be attached to brakes.
45. Penalties.
46. Articles to be unloaded on southeast side of railroad track. Not to obstruct streets leading to, or passage ways. Proviso.
47. Engines,, &c., not to obstruct streets or passage ways.
48. Side tracks, or turn-outs not to be laid without permit of mayor. Street commissioner to superintend the same.
49. Vessels or boats not to be made fast to sea-wall or coping stones; not to lay so as jib-boom, &c., may project. Articles not be shipped or landed over coping stones.
50. Penalties.
51. Width of sidewalk regulated. Sidewalk may be accepted after put in repair.
52. City to maintain sidewalks relinquished. Proviso.
53. Bricks and sand to be furnished to lay sidewalks. To be laid under direction of street commissioner.
54. When city council require sidewalks to be paved.
55. City assume one-half the expense.
56. Names of streets to be recorded. Sidewalks and descriptions to be entered.
57. Alteration in sidewalks. Posts and trees not to be set without consent, &c.
58. Carriages, hand-carts, &c., not to go on sidewalks. Horses or animals not to stand upon.
59. Wood not to be sawed or split upon.
60. Persons not to stand in a group upon side or cross walks so as to obstruct, &c. Penalty. To move on. Penalty.
61. Goods not to be placed upon foot or sidewalk, to obstruct, &c. Penalty. Penalty for suffering to remain after notice. Proviso.
62. Snow to be removed from foot way or sidewalk. Penalty.
63. To apply to snow falling from buildings.
64. Ice to be removed from sidewalks, or to be covered with sand, &c. Penalty.

STATUTES.

Authority of city council over streets.

City charter, 1863, § 9.

1. The city council shall have exclusive authority to lay out, widen or otherwise alter, or discontinue any and all streets or public ways in the city of Portland, without petition therefor, and as far as extreme low water mark; and to estimate all damage sustained by the owners of land taken for that purpose; but all locations below high water mark shall be subject to the provisions of the laws relating to the commissioners of Portland harbor. A joint standing committee of the two boards shall be appointed, whose duty it shall be to lay out, alter, widen, or discontinue any street or way in said city, first giving notice of the time and place of their proceedings to all

parties interested, by an advertisement in two daily papers printed in Portland, for one week at least previous to the time appointed. The committee shall first hear all parties interested, and then determine and adjudge whether the public convenience requires such street or way to be laid out, altered or discontinued; and shall make a written return of their proceedings, signed by a majority of them, containing the bounds and descriptions of the street or way, if laid out or altered, and the names of the owners of the land taken, when known, and the damages allowed therefor; the return shall be filed in the city clerk's office at least seven days previous to its acceptance by the city council. The street or way shall not be altered or established until the report is accepted by the city council, and the report shall not be altered or amended before its acceptance. A street or way shall not be discontinued by the city council, excepting upon the report of said committee. The committee shall estimate and report the damages sustained by the owners of the lands adjoining that portion of the street or way which is so discontinued; their report shall be filed with the city clerk seven days at least before its acceptance. Any person aggrieved by the decision or judgment of the city council in establishing, altering, or discontinuing streets, may, so far as relates to damages, appeal therefrom to the next court having jurisdiction thereof, in the county of Cumberland, which court shall determine the same by a committee or reference under a rule of court, if the parties agree, or by a verdict of its jury, and shall render judgment and issue execution for the damages recovered, with costs to the party prevailing in the appeal. Such appeal shall be made to the term of the supreme judicial court, which shall first be holden in the county of Cumberland, more than thirty days from and after the day the street is finally established, altered or discontinued, excluding the day of commencement of the session of said court. The appel-

Land damages.

Appeal.

lants shall serve written notice of such appeal upon the mayor or city clerk, fourteen days at least before the session of the court, and shall at the first term file a complaint setting forth substantially the facts of the case. On the trial, exceptions may be taken to the rulings of the court, as in other cases. Co-tenants who are appellants shall join in their appeal or shall not recover their costs. If a street or way is discontinued before the damages are paid or recovered for the land taken, the land owner shall not be entitled to recover such damages, but the committee in their report discontinuing the same, shall estimate and include all the damages sustained by the land owner, including those caused by the original location of the streets; and in such cases, if an appeal has been regularly taken, the appellant shall recover his costs. The city shall not be compelled to construct or open any street or way thus hereafter established, until in the opinion of the city council the public good requires it to be done; nor shall the city interfere with the possession of the land so taken by removing therefrom materials or otherwise, until they decide to open and construct said street. The city council may regulate the height and width of sidewalks in any public square, places, streets, lanes or alleys in said city; and may authorize posts and trees to be placed along the edge of side walks. Nor shall the city be answerable for damages occasioned by telegraph poles and wires erected in its streets.

Original location of streets to be ascertained by city engineer, how often.

Ib. § 21.

2. The original location of all streets and ways in said city shall, once in ten years, or oftener, be ascertained by the city engineer, under the direction of the city council, as accurately as practicable—the location of different streets being ascertained by him from time to time, when expedient. He shall make a written report of his doings to the committee on new streets, which shall give twenty days notice, by advertisement in two or more public papers in the city, of the time and place at which it will act upon

said report. Any person may appear and object to the report; and after a full hearing of all parties interested, the committee may accept, alter or amend the report as it shall think right, and shall report their proceedings to the city council, who shall thereupon determine the lines of such streets and ways in said city, according to the original location thereof, and shall order the same to be designated anew by fixed and permanent boundaries, as, and for, the original boundaries; and a record of the location thereof to be made upon the city records; and a copy of the last record of such proceedings respecting any street, with evidence of the location of the boundaries therein designated, shall in all judicial proceedings, be *prima facie* evidence of the place of the original location of said street. Persons may object.

3. The mayor and aldermen of said city may on public occasions, by their order, forbid the passing, temporarily, of horses, carriages or other vehicles, over or through such streets or ways in said city, as they may deem expedient. Nothing in any city charter, or in acts additional thereto, shall be so construed as to deprive county commissioners of the power to lay out, alter or discontinue county roads, within the limits of such cities. Obstruction of streets on public occasions. Ib. § 22. Powers of county commissioners to include cities. Act, Feb. 23, 1866, chap. 47.

4. The Portland Gas Company are authorized to lay down, in and through the streets of the city, and to take up, replace, and repair all such pipes and fixtures as may be necessary for the objects of their incorporation, first having obtained the consent of the city council therefor, and under such restrictions and regulations as said city council may see fit to prescribe. And any obstruction in any street of the city, or taking up or displacement of any portion of any street, without such consent of the city council or contrary to the restrictions or regulations that may be prescribed as aforesaid, shall be considered a nuisance. And said company shall be liable to indictment therefor, and to all the provisions of law applicable thereto. Portland Gas company authorized to lay down pipes, &c., in streets. Act, 1849, chap. 288, § 3.

Liability for damages.

And said company shall in all cases be liable to pay to said city all sums of money that said city may be obliged to pay, on any judgment recovered against said city, for damages occasioned by any obstructions or taking up or displacement of any street by said company, whether with or without the consent of the city council, together with counsel's fees and other expenses incurred by said city in defending any suit to recover damages as aforesaid with interest on the same, to be recovered in an action for money paid to the use of said company.

Excavations near streets, how to be made. Responsibilities. R. S., chap. 18, § 75.

5. Persons desirous of making an excavation near a street or public way, may make written application to the municipal officers setting forth its nature and extent, and requesting their direction thereon ; and they shall in writing direct whether it may or not be made, and if permitted, the manner of making it; and when so made, no liability is incurred thereby. If not so made, the person making it is liable to pay to the town, in an action on the case, all damages occasioned by the repair of the way, or paid to persons injured by defects therein, caused by such excavation.

ORDINANCES.

Names of streets to be continued. Rev. Ord., 1855.

1. The several streets of the city shall continue to be called and known by the names given to them respectively by the selectmen of the town of Portland, the mayor and aldermen of the city, or the city council, until the same shall be altered by the city council.

Committee on laying out new streets to be appointed. Ib.

2. There shall be appointed, annually, by the city council, a joint committee to be called the committee on laying out new streets, to consist of three members of the board of mayor and aldermen, and three members of the common council.

Committee to lay out, &c., new streets.

3. Said committee, when thereto directed by vote of the city council, shall lay out, widen or otherwise alter any street or public way, and estimate the damages any

individual may sustain thereby; and they shall report to the city council, the laying out or alteration of such street or way, with the boundaries and admeasurements thereof, together with names of the parties to whom damages have been assessed therefor.

To estimate damages.

To report to city council.

Ib.

4. There shall annually be elected by the city council in convention, an able and discreet person, to be styled the commissioner of streets, who shall continue in office until removed, or until a successor be appointed, and he shall be sworn to the faithful performance of his duty. He shall receive such compensation for his services as the city council shall establish, and shall be removable at their pleasure; and in case said office shall become vacant by death, resignation, or otherwise, a successor shall be forthwith elected in the manner prescribed.

Commissioner of streets to be elected.

Ib.

To be sworn.

Compensation.

May be removed.

5. It shall be the duty of the commissioner of streets to keep all streets within the city safe and convenient for travelers, to superintend the general state of the streets, sidewalks, lanes, alleys, public walks and squares of the city, to attend to the widening, alteration and repairs of the same; but he shall not be authorized to change the grade of any street, or make any permanent repairs thereon, without having first obtained therefor the sanction in writing of the committee on highways, sidewalks, and bridges. He shall make all contracts for the supply of labor and materials for the same, take general care of the carts and teams owned by the city, and make all necessary arrangements for cleaning the streets, disposing of manure, and removing house dirt.

Duties of commissioner.

Ib.

Shall not change the grade of streets, without, &c.

To make contracts.

To have charge of teams, &c.

6. All the powers given to, and all the duties required from the street commissioners of the town of Portland, as defined and declared by an act of the legislature, passed on the nineteenth day of February, in the year eighteen hundred and thirty-one, are in like manner given to and required from the commissioner of streets, and any damages or expenses which the city may legally sustain in

Powers of street commissioners given to commissioner of streets.

Ib.

To pay damages sustained in consequence of neglect of duty.

consequence of any neglect of duty on his part shall be paid by him.

Commissioner shall be acquainted with lines, &c., of streets. Ib. To remove obstructions. To perform duties prescribed by mayor and aldermen or city council. To make arrangements for supply of labor.

7. The commissioner of streets shall make himself acquainted with the lines and bounds of streets, and remove any fences or other obstructions in the lanes, alleys and squares, and he shall perform generally such duties relative to the same, as the mayor and aldermen or city council may require. He shall make such arrangements with the overseers of the alms-house for the purpose of procuring labor and materials, as the interests of the city seem to require, and may have the teams owned by the city, kept at the city farm, under such regulations as may be agreed upon by him and the overseers of the poor, or whoever may have charge of the farm.

Commissioner shall discharge all bills once a month. Ib. To render account to board of aldermen. To keep account of receipts and expenditures. To present annual account.

8. The commissioner of streets shall as often as once in every month, discharge all bills by him contracted as commissioner, by funds to be supplied to him from the money received and appropriated for that purpose, and also render to the board of aldermen a regular and complete account of the expenditures by him incurred, which account shall be audited monthly by said board, and he shall also keep an accurate account of all his receipts and expenditures, and present the same to the committee of accounts for their examination and approbation, annually, that the same may be laid before the city council.

To cause stone monuments to be erected, when, &c. Ib. To be recorded.

9. It shall be the duty of the commissioner of streets to cause stone monuments to be erected at suitable places in any street, alley, square, or public place, when thereto directed by the committee on laying out streets, or the city engineer; and all monuments so erected shall be recorded in the street books.

Monuments not to be removed without, &c. Ib. Penalty.

10. No person shall remove, or cause to be removed, any monument placed at the corner of any street, or on the line of any street, to mark the width or course of such street, without the permission, in writing, of the mayor and aldermen first obtained, under a penalty of twenty-five dollars for each offense.

11. Owners and lessees of any lot of land abutting on any street, lane, or private way in this city, which for want of a fence or rail shall be dangerous, shall place, or cause to be placed in front of said lot, upon or near the line of said street, lane, or private way, a fence, rail, or guard, which in the opinion of the street commissioner shall be a sufficient guard or protection to the public from danger, by reason of the situation of such lot. And if any owner or lessee of such lot shall refuse or neglect compliance with the requirements of this section, he shall on conviction pay a penalty of not less than one dollar nor more than five dollars for every day during which such lot shall remain unfenced; and if the owners or lessees aforesaid shall neglect or refuse for two days after notice in the premises, from the city marshal or any police officer, to build or cause to be built such fence or guard, the street commissioner shall forthwith cause a proper fence or rail to be constructed in front of such lot, at the cost of the owners or lessees thereof.

Dangerous lots of land to be fenced.
Ib.

Penalty.

Street commissioner shall cause lots to be fenced.

12. No person or persons shall break or dig up, or assist in breaking or digging up, any part of any street, or remove any gravel or other similar thing therefrom, without having first obtained the license of the mayor and aldermen in writing, or of some person by them authorized for that purpose, under a penalty of not less than five nor more than twenty dollars; and a like sum for every day that he shall neglect or refuse to repair the same, to the satisfaction of the mayor and aldermen.

Streets not to be dug up, or gravel removed from, without license, &c.
Ib.

Penalty.

13. Whosoever shall, by virtue of such license, break or dig up, or cause to be dug or broken up, any part of any street, shall, within such time as the mayor and aldermen, or some person by them authorized, may order, cause the same to be repaired and amended, to the satisfaction of the mayor and aldermen, under a penalty of not less than five nor more than twenty dollars for each and every day that he or they shall neglect or refuse so to do after such order.

Streets broken up shall be repaired.
Ib.

Penalty.

No drain or aqueduct to be opened or repaired without license.

Ib.

14. No person shall open or make any drain or aqueduct, or repair the same, by digging up the ground in any street, court, alley, or other public place in the city, without first obtaining a license therefor from the mayor and aldermen, or from some person by them authorized, in writing, specifying in what street, court, alley, or public place the drain or aqueduct is to be made or repaired. And the person who shall dig, make or repair, or cause to be dug, made or repaired, any drain or aqueduct than as above stated, shall for each offense forfeit and pay a sum not less than five nor more than twenty dollars, and a like penalty for every day that the same shall continue open.

Penalty.

When license is granted to open a drain, &c., streets to be repaired to satisfaction of commissioner.

Ib.

15. When any person has obtained a license to open or make or repair a drain or aqueduct, he shall complete and finish the same with all possible dispatch, and shall in filling and covering up the same, do it to the satisfaction of the commissioner of streets; and in case of neglect so to do, the said commissioner shall cause the same to be done in suitable manner, at the expense of the person to or for whom said license was granted, and one-half of the street shall be kept constantly open for the passing of teams or carriages, and the person who shall dig, make or repair any drain or aqueduct, shall keep a good and sufficient fence or railing around the same during the whole time of making or repairing thereof, except when the laborers are actually at work; and a lighted lantern or some other proper and sufficient light, shall be fixed into some part of such fence, or in some other proper manner, over or near such open drain or aqueduct, from twilight in the evening until daylight in the morning, during all the time such drain or aqueduct shall be open, or in a state of repair; and whosoever shall be guilty of a breach of any part of this section shall be liable to a penalty for each offense of not less than ten nor more than fifty dollars.

One-half of street to be kept open.

Railing to be up.

To be lighted.

Penalty.

Notice to be given of intention to build.

16. Every person intending to erect or repair any building upon land abutting on any of the streets, shall

make the same known to the mayor, who shall have power and authority to allot such portion of the street, thereto adjoining, as he shall deem expedient and necessary, on which to deposit materials for the work provided, that not more than one-half of the width of the street shall be so occupied. And the part or portion so allotted, and no other part of said street shall be used for laying the materials for any such building or repairing, and for receiving the rubbish arising therefrom. And all the rubbish arising therefrom or thereby shall be carried away by the person or persons so building or repairing, at such convenient time as the mayor as aforesaid, may direct, and in case of neglect or refusal so to do, it shall be removed by the commissioner of streets, or other person authorized as aforesaid, at the expense of such person or persons. And in all cases the portion so allotted shall be enclosed and lighted as prescribed in the preceding section. Every person offending against any of the provisions of this section shall be liable to a penalty for each offense of not less than five nor more than twenty dollars, and a like sum for every day such offense shall be continued or repeated.

Portion of street to be allotted.

Portion allotted to be used for building materials, &c.

Rubbish, &c., to be carried away.

In case of neglect, to be removed at expense of person.

To be lighted.

Penalties.

Ib., as amended by city charter, § 10.

17. No person shall place or cause to be placed in any of the streets, alleys, squares, or other public places of the city, any lumber, stone, or building materials of any kind, and suffer the same to remain over six hours, without the permission of the mayor and aldermen, or of some person by them authorized, and every person offending against either of the provisions of this section shall be liable to a penalty of not less than five nor more than twenty dollars for each offense, and the city marshal may remove any such lumber or other materials at the expense of the owner or owners thereof.

Lumber, stones and building materials not to be placed in streets to remain over six hours.

Penalty.

Ib.

May be removed at expense of owner.

18. When the owner or owners of any such articles mentioned in the preceding section, shall be unknown, or being known, after notice by the city marshal, shall neglect or refuse to remove the same within the space of twenty-

Proceedings when owners refuse to remove them.

Ib.

four hours, unless the mayor and aldermen or some person by them authorized shall give permit that the same may longer remain, it shall be the duty of the city marshal, or deputy marshals, to cause the same to be advertised, and unless such articles or things shall be duly removed, within forty-eight hours after the same shall be so advertised, and the cost thereof paid, he shall cause the same to be sold at public auction, and after deducting the reasonable expenses and charges of such sale, he shall pay the balance into the city treasury.

To be sold at auction.

No person to blast rocks within fifty rods of street, without license. Ib.

19. No person shall blast any rock or other substance with gunpowder at any place within fifty rods of any street or public place in the city, without license of the mayor and aldermen, in writing, specifying the terms and conditions on which said license is granted, under a penalty of not less than twenty dollars for each offense; provided, however, that the remedy of any person injured by the blasting of rocks shall not be affected by this section.

Penalty. Persons not to play bat and ball. Not to throw snow balls. Ib. Penalties.

20. No person shall play at bat and ball, or foot ball, or throw stones, brick bats, clubs, or snow balls within any of the streets, alleys, squares, or other public places of the city, under a penalty of not less than one nor more than twenty dollars for each offense.

Not to shoot with bow and arrow. Penalty. Ib.

21. No person shall shoot with or use a bow or arrow, in any street, alley, or square within the city, under a penalty of not less than one nor more than twenty dollars for each offense.

Not to fly kites. Ib. Not to coast on sleds or skate. Penalty.

22. If any person shall in any street, alley, or public place set or fly a kite, or shall course or coast upon a sled or skate on any side walk in the city, such person shall forfeit and pay for each offense a sum not less than one nor more than ten dollars.

Gaming tables and devices not to be exposed in streets. Ib.

23. No person shall expose in any street, alley, square, or other public place, any table or device of any kind whatsoever, upon or by which, any game of hazard or chance can be played, and no person shall play at any

such table or device, or at any unlawful game in any street, alley, square or other public place, or on any of the wharves, under a penalty of not less than five nor more than twenty dollars for either of said offenses.

No person to play at unlawful games in street.

24. No person shall swim or bathe in the waters surrounding the city, which are adjacent to any of the wharves, bridges, avenues, or railroads leading into the same, so as to be exposed to view of spectators, under a penalty of not less than five nor more than twenty dollars for each offense.

No person to swim or bathe in exposed situations. Ib.

Penalty.

25. No person shall take or carry away any street dirt or manure, collected from any street or public place in the city, without permission of the commissioner of streets first obtained, under a penalty for every offense of not less than three nor more than ten dollars.

Manure not to be taken from streets without permission. Ib.

26. No person shall obstruct any street, or any part thereof, by placing therein any house, barn, stable, shop, or other building, and no person shall remove or draw through or upon any street, any house, barn, stable, shop, or other building, without first obtaining permission of the mayor and aldermen, and filing a bond with sufficient sureties, approved by the mayor, with the treasurer of the city, conditioned to indemnify the city for all damages sustained by drawing or moving such building; and if any building shall remain in any street or place, beyond the time allowed by such permit, it shall be the duty of the city marshal, when directed by the mayor and aldermen, to cause such building to be taken down or removed out of the street at the expense of the owner thereof.

Streets shall not be obstructed by moving of buildings. Ib.

Building obstructing streets to be removed at expense of owners.

27. Any person offending against either of the provisions of the preceding section shall forfeit and pay for each offense a penalty of not less than fifty dollars, and shall further be liable to indemnify the city for all damages to which it may be subjected in consequence of such violation.

Penalties. Ib.

No goods or merchandise to be placed so as to project into street.

Ib.

Penalty.

28. No person shall place, or cause to be placed, or shall suspend or cause to be suspended from any house, shop, store, lot, or place, over any street, any goods, wares or merchandise whatsover, or any other thing, so that the same shall extend or project from the wall or front of said house, store, shop, lot, or place, more than one foot towards or into the street, under a penalty of not less than three nor more than twenty dollars for each offense.

Awnings may be placed.

Regulations.

Ib.

29. It shall be lawful to place, or continue to maintain awnings and shades before any house, shop or store, in any street, upon the terms and under the regulations mentioned in this section, and not otherwise; provided that the mayor and aldermen, as to particular buildings or streets, may order that no awnings or shades shall be erected. Such awnings or shades shall be safely fixed and supported, in such manner as not to interfere with passengers, and so that the lowest part thereof shall never be less than eight feet in height, above the sidewalk or street, and in no case to extend beyond the line of the sidewalk; and the person so placing or continuing to maintain the same, shall in all respects conform to any directions in relation to the materials, the construction and maintenance thereof, which shall be given by the mayor and aldermen. Any person violating any of the provisions of this section, or such directions of the mayor and aldermen, shall be liable to a penalty of not less than three nor more than twenty dollars, and to a like penalty for every day that such awning or shade shall be continued in violation of such provision or direction.

Signs, &c., not to project into streets.

Ib.

Penalties.

30. No person shall hang, erect or fasten any sign, show-bill, lantern, or show-board of any description whatever, which shall project into any street more than one foot, under a penalty of not less than five nor more than twenty dollars for each offense, and a like penalty for every day such sign, show-bill, lantern, or other board

shall be continued after an order to remove the same, given by the mayor and aldermen, or any person authorized by them.

31. No person shall in any street or other public place make any loud and unusual noises, by shouting, sounding horns, drums, or any instrument or thing, nor sing, nor utter any obscene and indecent songs or words, nor shall in any other unruly or boisterous manner disturb the peace, quiet and good order of the city, under a penalty of not less than five nor more than twenty dollars for each offense.

Making noises in streets forbidden.

Ib.

32. No person shall stand in any street or on any sidewalk for the purpose of grinding cutlery, or for the sale of any article, or for the exercise of any other business or calling, unless duly licensed by the mayor and aldermen, under a penalty of not less than three nor more than twenty dollars for each offense.

Grinding cutlery, &c., in streets forbidden, unless licensed.

Ib.

33. No person shall construct or place, or cause to be constructed or placed, any portico, porch, door, window, or step which shall project into any street, under a penalty of not less than twenty dollars for each offense, and a like penalty for each day that the said portico, porch, door, window, or step, shall be continued as aforesaid, after notice to remove the same from the mayor and aldermen, or some person by them authorized.

Porticos, porches, &c., not to project into street.

Penalty.

Ib.

34. It shall not be lawful to construct or to continue to maintain any cellar door, or cellar door-way, in any sidewalk, or projecting into any street, for the purpose of being kept open as a common entrance, except as herein provided. No occupant or other person having the care of any building, shall suffer any cellar door, or cellar doorway, connected with such building, which projects into any street to remain open, or the platform thereof to be removed more than fifteen minutes during any part of the night time, or for more than two hours in the whole during the day time, unless duly licensed so to do by the mayor and

Cellar doors, &c.

Ib.

Not to remain open, unless licensed.

aldermen, and in all cases whenever any such cellar door or door-way shall be open in the night time as aforesaid, a good and sufficient light shall be kept at the entrance of such door or door-way. Every person offending against any of the provisions of this section shall forfeit and pay a penalty of not less than five nor more than twenty dollars for each offense.

Light to be kept at entrance.

Penalties.

35. Every entrance or flight of steps descending immediately from any street, into any cellar or basement story of any building, where such entrance or flight of steps shall not be safely and securely covered, shall be enclosed with a railing on each side, permanently put up, at least three feet high from the top of the sidewalk or pavement, together with either a gate to open inwardly, or two iron chains across the front of the entrance way, one near the top and the other half way to the top of the railing; and such gate or chains shall, unless there be a light over the steps to prevent accidents, be closed during the night. And any person who shall be guilty of a violation of any of the provisions of this section, shall be liable to a penalty of not less than five, nor more than twenty dollars, and a like penalty for each and every day during which such violation continues, which penalty may be recovered of the owner, occupant or other person having charge of such building.

Entrance and steps to be secured with railings or chains. Ib.

Light to be placed.

Penalties.

36. No person shall make, or cause to be made, any aperture in or under any street or sidewalk, for the purpose of constructing coal-holes, or receptacles for any other article, or for light or air, or for an entrance, or for any other purpose, extending more than eighteen inches into the street, without the license of the mayor and aldermen, under a penalty of not less than two nor more than twenty dollars for each offense, and a like penalty for every day the same shall remain after notice to securely fill up and close the same, given by the mayor, or city marshal, or deputy marshal; and no person shall leave

Apertures and coal-holes not to be made without license. Ib.

Penalty.

such coal-hole or other aperture open or unfastened after sunset, nor in the day time unless while actually in use, with a person or persons by the same, under a penalty of not less than two nor more than ten dollars for each offense.

Not to be left open.

Penalty.

37. No person shall affix or place, or cause to be affixed or placed, or continue in any street or sidewalk, any grating, extending more than eighteen inches into the street, without the license of the mayor and aldermen, under a penalty of not less than two nor more than twenty dollars for each offense, and a like penalty for every week the same shall remain after notice to remove the same given by the mayor, city marshal, or deputy marshal.

Gratings in sidewalks not to extend more than eighteen inches.

Penalties.

Ib.

38. The mayor and aldermen, upon application therefor, may authorize the construction of coal-holes or apertures for the purposes herein before mentioned, and gratings therefor, to extend more than eighteen inches into the street, in such manner as they deem suitable, and under the direction of the commissioner of streets, or some person by him authorized, at the expense of the applicant; and they may also authorize the continuance of any grating already constructed, provided that in no case shall any grating be authorized to extend more than three feet into the street.

Mayor and aldermen may authorize the construction of coal-holes and gratings.

Ib.

Not to extend more than three feet.

39. No person having for the time being the care or use of any horse or other beast of burden, carriage or draught, shall ride or drive or cause the same to be driven through any part of the city at a faster rate than six miles an hour, under a penalty of not less than five dollars nor more than twenty dollars for each offense.

Horses shall not be driven in street at a faster rate than six miles an hour.

Ib.

Penalty.

40. No owner or person having the charge of any horse, kine, swine, sheep, goat, or other grazing animal, shall turn into nor permit the same to go at large in any street, or public place, under a penalty of not less than five dollars nor more than twenty dollars for each offense.

Horses, cattle, and swine not to run at large.

Ib.

Penalty.

Horses or animals not to be frightened.
Ib.
Penalty.

41. No person shall, within any of the streets, alleys, squares, or public places of the city, by means of any words, noises, gestures, or any other act, wantonly frighten or drive any horse, or other animal, under a penalty of not less than five dollars nor more than twenty dollars for each offense.

COMMERCIAL STREET.

Speed of trains in Commercial street regulated.
Ib.

42. No railroad engine, car or cars, whether separately, or in connection with any train, shall be allowed to pass on or over any part of Commercial street, in this city, at a speed exceeding the rate of six miles per hour. And all railroad corporations are hereby restricted and prohibited from passing on or over said street, with any locomotive engine, or car, or cars, as aforesaid, at a speed exceeding the rate aforesaid.

Bells of locomotives to be rung.
Ib.

43. Every railroad corporation shall cause the bell of each locomotive engine to be rung, and kept ringing, during the whole time of its passing on or over said street, except when, to prevent accident, it may be necessary to break up or stop, in which case notice thereof shall be given by the steam whistle.

Brakemen to be attached to brakes.
Ib.

44. Every railroad corporation shall cause a suitable number of brakemen to be attached to the brakes of the several cars, and shall cause all such brakemen to attend to, and promptly perform their appropriate duties, at their respective brakes, and to continue at said brakes while passing in said street.

Penalties.

45. If any railroad corporation, or their agents or servants, shall neglect or refuse to comply with any or either of the provisions contained in the three preceding sections, such corporation shall forfeit for every such neglect or refusal the sum of fifty dollars, to the use of the city.

46. All articles brought by railroad, to be landed in Commercial street, shall be unloaded on the southeast side of the railroad track. And every article landed in the street, either from or for the purpose of being loaded upon the cars shall be so placed as not to obstruct any street or passage-way crossing Commercial street, or connecting with it, and so as to leave a clear space not less than fourteen feet in width from the coping stone, and shall not be allowed to remain in the street over six working hours after they are landed. *Provided, however*, that cars may be unloaded into stores, and loaded from stores, on the northwesterly side of said railroad track, after five o'clock in the evening, from the first day of April to the first day of October, and after four o'clock in the evening during the other six months of the year.

Articles to be unloaded on southeast side of railroad track.

Not to obstruct streets leading to, or passage ways.

Proviso.

Ib., as amended by Ord., 1864.

47. No railroad engine, tender, or car, whether separately or in a train, shall be allowed to stop on Commercial street, in such a manner as to obstruct any street or passage way crossing Commercial street, or connected with it, nor to remain standing on any part of the street any longer time than is actually necessary for unloading or taking in the freight of such car or train.

Engines, &c., not to obstruct streets or passage ways.

Rev. Ord., 1855.

48. No side track or turn-out shall be laid in Commercial street, except by permission from the mayor in writing, and under such restrictions in regard to its construction as he may prescribe; and whenever such permission is granted, it shall be the duty of the street commissioner to superintend the work, and he shall be authorized and required immediately to remove any side-track or turn-out laid or maintained in violation of this section.

Side tracks or turn-outs not to be laid without permit of mayor.

Ib.

Street commissioner to superintend the same.

49. No vessel or boat of any description shall be allowed to be made fast to the sea-wall or coping-stone, or any other part of Commercial street, nor lay at the head of any dock along said street, so that the jib-boom or bowsprit, or any other fixture of the vessel or boat shall

Vessels or boats not to be made fast to sea wall or coping stones.

Ib.

Not to lay so as jib-boom, &c., may project. Articles not to be shipped or landed over coping stones.

project over the line of the street, so as to obstruct the passage way, nor shall any article be landed from, or be shipped on board any vessel or boat, on or over the coping-stone of said street.

Penalties. Ib.

50. Any person, or corporation, master, or owner of any vessel or boat, violating any of the provisions of the four preceding sections, shall incur a penalty to the use of the city, of not less than five nor more than twenty dollars, according to the nature and degree of the offense.

SIDEWALKS.

Width of sidewalks regulated. Ib.

51. The joint standing committee on highways, sidewalks and bridges, are hereby empowered so to regulate the width and height of the sidewalks of any of the streets, as shall, in their judgment, be most conducive to the convenience and interest of the city, and the city council may accept such sidewalks, after the same shall be put in good and perfect repair by the abutters on such streets, and after the same shall be relinquished in writing to the said city, by such abutters.

Sidewalks may be accepted after put in repair.

City to maintain sidewalks relinquished. Proviso. Ib.

52. After such relinquishment and acceptance, such sidewalks shall be maintained at the expense of the city, *provided* that when any sidewalk shall require repair, in consequence of any defect in the cellar door, curb, step or steps, cellar window, coal-hole, cellar wall, or from any other cause, within the control of the owner or occupant of the estate to which such sidewalks adjoin, then and in that case such repairs shall be made at the expense of the owner or occupant.

Bricks and sand to be furnished to lay sidewalks. Ib.

53. The commissioner of streets is authorized, whenever approved of by the committee on highways, &c., to furnish at the expense of the city, good bricks and sand at the rate of five and one-half bricks for every superficial square foot of sidewalk, to any owner or occupant of any estate, adjoining which a sidewalk is necessary; and in cases where bricks are thus furnished, the sidewalk shall

be laid down under the direction of the commissioner of streets, and in all cases the person to whom the bricks are thus furnished, shall furnish such curb stone as shall be approved of by the commissioner of streets, and shall pay the expense of setting the same and for laying the bricks.

To be laid under the direction of street commissioner.

54. Whenever the city council may require the sidewalk or foot way in front of any lot of ground, fronting on any street or way, in the city of Portland, to be paved, it shall be the duty of the commissioner of streets to notify the owner or tenant of such lot, in writing, of such requirement. And if the owner of such lot shall refuse, or neglect to pave the same as aforesaid, to the satisfaction and approval of the committee on streets, for the space of twenty days after notice as aforesaid, it shall be the duty of said commissioner to pave such sidewalk or footway in such manner as said committee may direct.

When city council require sidewalks to be paved.

Ord., June 2, 1863.

55. The city council shall assume one-half part of the cost or expense of paving the sidewalks or footways of the streets of said city, as provided for in the preceding section, said cost or expense to be estimated and determined by the committee on streets; and the city will cause said proportion of the cost or expense of said sidewalk or footway to be paid in money or materials, as the committee on streets shall determine and elect.

City assume one-half the expense.

Ib.

56. The city clerk shall keep a book in which the names of the streets shall be alphabetically arranged, and in which all the sidewalks which now are, or may hereafter be accepted as aforesaid, shall be entered with the date of such acceptance, the length and width of each sidewalk, and the names of the owner or owners of the adjoining estates.

Names of streets to be recorded.

Rev. Ord., 1865.

Sidewalks and description to be entered.

57. No person shall make any alteration in any sidewalk, or set any posts or trees on any of the sidewalks, or in any part of the street, without the consent of the mayor and aldermen, or some person by them authorized,

Alteration in sidewalks.

Ib.

Posts and trees not to be set without consent, &c.

under a penalty of not less than five nor more than twenty dollars for each offense.

Carriages, hand carts, &c., not to go on sidewalks. Ib.

Horses or animals not to stand upon.

58. No person shall drive, wheel or draw, any coach, cart, hand-cart, hand-barrow, or other carriage of burthen or pleasure, except children's hand carriages, and drawn by hand; or drive or permit any horse or other animal under his care to go or stand upon any foot-path or sidewalk in the city, under a penalty of not less than five nor more than twenty dollars.

Wood not to be sawed or split upon. Ib.

59. No person shall saw or split any firewood upon any footwalk or sidewalk of any street, nor place the same thereon, and no person shall stand on any such foot or sidewalk, with a woodsaw or horse, so as to obstruct a free passage for foot passengers, under a penalty of not less than one nor more than twenty dollars.

Persons not to stand in a group upon side or cross-walks, so as to obstruct, &c.

Penalty.

To move on.

Penalty.

Ib., as amended by Ord., May 18, 1867.

60. Three or more persons shall not stand in a group, or near to each other, on any sidewalk or crosswalk or in any street or public way in such a manner as to obstruct a free passage thereon or therein, after a request from any person to make way, under a penalty of not less than two nor more than ten dollars. And if three or more persons, standing in a group or near to each other, on any sidewalk or cross-walk, or in any street or public way in this city, so as to obstruct the walk, street, or way in any manner, shall refuse or neglect to pass on immediately, on being directed so to do by the mayor, any alderman, city marshal or deputy, or any policeman, constable, or watchman, they shall each and severally be liable to a fine of not less than five nor more than fifty dollars. And if any persons shall be found standing in groups of three or more persons, on any sidewalk or crosswalk, or on any street or public way in this city, after having been once directed to pass on by the mayor, any alderman, city marshal or deputy, or any policeman, constable or watchman, he shall be liable to a fine of not less than five nor more than twenty dollars for each offense.

61. No person shall place or cause to be placed upon any foot-path or sidewalk in the city, any lumber, iron, coal, trunk, bale, box, crate, cask, package, or article or thing whatsoever, so as to obstruct a free passage for foot passengers, for more than ten minutes, under a penalty of not less than three nor more than twenty dollars; and if such person shall suffer such obstruction to foot passengers to remain more than one hour after it is first placed there, or more than ten minutes after notice to remove the same, given by the city marshal, deputy marshal or any police officer, the person or persons so offending shall be liable to a penalty of not less than five nor more than ten dollars for every such offense; and for each and every hour thereafter that the same shall be suffered to remain, the person or persons so offending shall be liable to a penalty of not less than five nor more than ten dollars. *Provided*, that nothing contained in this section shall be deemed to extend to such goods, wares or merchandise as shall in conformity with such rules, regulations and orders, as shall be made by the mayor and aldermen upon the subject, be placed in any street, alley, square, or place, for the purpose of being sold at public auction.

Goods not to be placed upon foot or side-walks, to obstruct, &c.

Penalty.

Penalty for suffering to remain after notice.

Rev. Ord., 1855.

Proviso.

62. The tenant or occupant, and in case there should be no tenant, the owner, or any person having the care of any building or lot of land bordering not more than one hundred and fifty feet on any street, lane, court, square, or public place within the city, where there is any footway or sidewalk, shall, after the ceasing to fall of any snow, if in the day time within three hours, and if in the night time, before ten of the clock of the forenoon succeeding, cause such snow to be removed from such footway or sidewalk, and, in default thereof, shall forfeit and pay a sum not less than two dollars, nor more than ten dollars; and for each and every hour thereafter that the same shall remain on such footway or sidewalk, such tenant, occupant, owner or other person, shall forfeit and

Snow to be removed from footway or sidewalk.

Penalty.

Ib., as amended by Ord., Jan. 22, 1857.

pay a sum not less than one dollar, nor more than ten dollars. And if such building or lot should extend more than one hundred and fifty feet, on any street or land, it shall be the duty of such tenant or occupant, owner or other person, to remove such snow from the footway or sidewalk for the space of one hundred and fifty feet, according to the provisions and subject to the penalties aforesaid.

To apply to snow falling from buildings.

Ib.

63. The provisions of the preceding section shall also apply to the falling of snow from any building.

Ice to be removed from sidewalks, or to be covered with sand, &c.

Ib.

64. Whenever the sidewalk, or any part thereof adjoining any building or lot of land on any street, shall be encumbered with ice, it shall be the duty of the occupant, and in case there is no occupant, the owner, or any person having the care of such building or lot, to cause such sidewalk to be made safe and convenient, by removing the ice therefrom, or by covering the same with sand or some other suitable substance; and in case such owner or occupant, or other person, shall neglect so to do, for the space of six hours during the day time, he shall forfeit and pay not less than two nor more than five dollars, and a like sum for every day that the same shall continue so encumbered.

Penalty.

Ice thrown into streets to be placed evenly, and to be broken into small pieces.

Ib.

65. Every person who shall lay, throw, or place, or cause to be laid, thrown or placed, any ice or snow into any street within the city, shall cause the same to be broken into small pieces, and spread evenly on the surface of such street, and in default thereof shall be liable to a penalty of not less than two dollars, nor more than five dollars for every offense.

Word streets to include alleys, lanes, &c., unless, &c.

Ib.

66. Whenever the word street or streets is mentioned in this or any other ordinance, it shall be understood as including alleys, lanes, courts, public squares, and public places, and it shall also be understood as including the sidewalks, unless the contrary is expressed, or such construction would be inconsistent with the manifest intent of the city council.

67. The foregoing provisions shall not be taken or construed as limiting in any manner the legal rights and duties of the commissioner of streets to make any alterations and repairs in the streets, which he may deem the safety and convenience of the inhabitants to require.

Provisions of preceding sections not to limit rights and duties of street commissioner.

Ib.

[See city charter, section 23.]

STREETS ON BACK COVE FLATS.

68. The city council upon the petition of the proprietors of Back Cove flats, will accept and lay out any necessary and desirable streets of suitable courses and widths in said Back Cove, from Tukey's bridge to Deering's bridge, and from the shore line to the line of the harbor commissioners, over flats now or hereafter filled up by said proprietors; *provided*, that said streets shall be filled to such a grade as may be established from time to time by the city, and are properly protected by solid filling or grebble walls; and *provided*, that in all such cases the city shall not be called upon to pay a compensation exceeding four cents per superficial foot of the filling of said streets, which is to be accepted by said proprietors for cost of filling and for damages: and also *provided*, that the committee on laying out and widening streets shall decide that the interests and convenience of the city require such streets to be so accepted and laid out.

Of streets on Back Cove flats.

Ord., Nov. 2, 1863.

LINES AND GRADES OF STREETS.

69. The first section of the ordinance on buildings is so amended, that the notice therein provided, shall be given to city engineer instead of the mayor and aldermen; and the same is further amended, so that, on request, the city engineer shall give the party so notifying, the line and grade of the street, without fee.

Amendment of first section of Ord. on buildings.

Ord., March 24, 1862.

70. It shall be the duty of the city marshal, street commissioner and city engineer, to give notice to the

Encroachments on streets.

Ib.

mayor, of all encroachments made or threatened, upon the streets and other public places in the city, or upon the property of the city, forthwith upon obtaining information thereof, and the mayor shall cause the provisions of this ordinance to be enforced against all persons violating the same.

No new grades fixed, or old ones changed, except by vote of city council. Ib.

Of petitions for grades.

Notice.

71. Hereafter, no new grade shall be fixed for any street, and no old grade shall be changed, except by vote of the city council. All petitions, orders, and other propositions for new grades, or changes of grades, shall be referred to some committee, who shall investigate the case, hear all parties interested, first giving all said parties notice of said hearing by advertising in one of the newspapers of this city, and shall report thereon to the city council. Said report shall in all cases be accompanied by the written opinion of the city engineer on the proposed action, and shall be subject to such action as to the city council seems proper.

PAVING STREETS.

Special appropriations for paving.

Ord., March 31, 1862.

72. In every future year, one-fifth part of the whole annual appropriation for streets, sidewalks and bridges, shall be expended in paving streets and portions of streets not then paved.

Committee to submit plans and estimates for paving.

Ib.

73. In all cases, before paving streets or portions thereof not paved, the committee on highways, sidewalks and bridges shall submit their plans and estimates for such proposed paving to the city council for approval. This ordinance does not apply to the paving of gutters and side drains.

REGULATIONS RESPECTING THE LAYING OF GAS PIPES IN STREETS.

Regulations and restrictions in relation to the laying down and taking up of pipes and fixtures in and through the streets of the city by the Portland Gas Light Company, prescribed and established pursuant to the provisions of section third of the charter of said company, January 25, 1855.

1. Said company before digging up the ground in any street, for the purpose of laying down, taking up, or repairing any gas pipes or fixtures, shall give notice in writing to the commissioner of streets of said city, of their intention so to do, specifying the street or streets, and the points of commencement and termination of their proposed works; and when said work is completed they shall give notice thereof in writing to said commissioner, who shall proceed immediately to examine into the manner said work has been done, and if the same has been done to his satisfaction, he shall certify the same to said company.

Company to give notice to the commissioner of streets of commencement of work.

Of completion. Street commissioner to examine same.

2. No street or sidewalk, or any part thereof, shall be dug up or broken into, for the purpose of laying service pipe, or setting lamp posts, between the first day of December and the fifteenth day of April of each year, without the permission of the mayor and aldermen, in writing, under a penalty of twenty dollars and a further penalty of twenty dollars for each and every day or part of a day, that the work is in progress. Nor shall the streets, nor any part thereof, be dug up or broken into for the laying of main pipes, between the first day of November and the first day of May in each year, under a penalty of twenty dollars for each offense, and a further penalty of twenty dollars for every day or part of a day that the work shall be in progress, or the street remain broken as aforesaid. Nor shall any street or any part thereof be dug up or broken into before the gas pipes are prepared and placed in the vicinity ready to be laid down.

Streets not to be dug up, &c., without consent of mayor and aldermen.

Penalties.

Streets not to be dug up, &c., before pipes are ready to be laid down.

3. Said company shall be liable for all damages occasioned by the digging up and opening any street, or obstructions therein by said company, as follows, viz:— For all or any such works, done before the first day of November, they shall be liable for all damages occasioned

Liability of company for damages.

thereby, for the space of sixty days from and after the approval certified as aforesaid by said commissioner, and for all or any such works done after said first day of November, they shall be so liable until the fifteenth day of June next following, of each year.

Trenches made to be fenced and lighted.

4. All trenches left open after dark, shall, by said company, be safely railed or fenced in, and be sufficiently lighted to protect the public from damage or accident therefrom.

Work to be done with convenient dispatch.

Streets to be repaired.

Materials, rubbish, &c., to be removed.

Company to repair streets to satisfaction of commissioner.

In case of refusal, to be repaired at expense of company.

5. Whenever any street, or any part thereof, is taken up for the purposes aforesaid, said company shall perform the work proposed to be done, with all convenient dispatch, and as soon as the same is done they shall repair such street and put the same in as good condition as it was in before such taking up, and shall cause all surplus earth, stones, materials, and rubbish to be immediately removed from the street ; and whenever such street, or any part thereof, or any pavement thereon, shall thereafter and within the time specified in section two, settle or become out of repair by reason of the works aforesaid, the said company shall thoroughly and completely repair the same, to the satisfaction of said commissioner of streets. In case said company refuse or neglect to repair the same, after one day's notice therefor by said commissioner, he shall proceed to repair the same at the expense of said company.

Restrictions respecting pipes laid in contact with drains or sewers.

Course of drain, &c., may be changed.

6. Whenever any of said pipes, in laying them down, shall come in contact or interfere with any drain or sewer, said pipes shall be laid under or over such drain or sewer, unless in the opinion of the committeee on drains and sewers, it shall be necessary to change the direction of such drain or sewer, in which case the same shall be done by said company under the direction and to the satisfaction of said committee.

SUPERINTENDENT OF BURIALS.

[See chapters on CEMETERIES and HEALTH.]

SURVEYOR OF STONE.

ORDINANCE.

1. There shall annually be elected by the city council, one or more suitable persons as surveyors of granite, marble and free stone, who shall be sworn to the faithful performance of the duties of said office, and who shall continue in office until removed or until a successor is elected and qualified.

One or more surveyors of stone to be appointed. To be sworn.

Ord., May 30, 1859, § 1.

2. It shall be the duty of said surveyors to measure and inspect all granite, marble, free stone and other stone, for building or any other purposes, which they shall be requested to measure or inspect.

Duties.

Ib. § 2.

3. Said surveyors shall be entitled to demand and receive in full for their services the following rates, viz: Ten cents for each ton of marble, granite or free stone, thus measured or inspected by them.

Fees.

Ib. § 3.

TAXES.

STATUTES.

ORDINANCES.

STATUTES.

Election of assessors. Their duties.

City charter, § 8.

1. The assessors shall continue to be elected on the second Monday in March. At the first election thereof under this act, three persons shall be elected assessors, one of whom shall be elected for one year, one for two years, and one for three years; and at each subsequent election one assessor shall be elected for three years, each of whom shall continue in office until some other person shall have been elected and qualified in his place. The city council shall elect an assistant assessor in each ward, whose duty it shall be to furnish the assessors with all the necessary information relative to persons and property taxable in his ward; he shall be sworn or affirmed to the

faithful performance of his duty. All taxes shall be assessed, apportioned and collected in the manner prescribed by the laws of this State relative to town taxes, except as herein modified; and the city council may establish further or additional provisions for the collection thereof and of interest thereon. Interest.

2. The treasurer of the city of Portland shall also be the collector for said city, with all the powers of collector of taxes under the laws of this State. All warrants directed to him by the assessors and municipal officers shall run to him and his successors in office, and shall be in the form prescribed by law, changing such parts only as by this act are required to be changed. The method of keeping, vouching and settling his accounts, shall be subject to such rules and regulations as the city council may establish. Said treasurer and collector shall collect all such uncollected taxes and assessments in whatever year assessed as may be collected during his term of office; and at the expiration of said term, his powers as collector shall wholly cease; all sales, distresses, and all other acts and proceedings, lawfully commenced by him as such treasurer and collector, may be as effectually continued and completed by his successor in office as though done by himself; and all unreturned warrants, which would otherwise be returnable to him, shall be returned to his successor in office.

Treasurer shall be collector of taxes. Ib. § 20.

3. A collector of taxes shall have the same authority to distrain property and arrest the body in any part of the State, which he now has in the place where such tax is assessed.

Collectors may distrain and arrest in any part of the State. Act, March 24, 1863.

4. Treasurers of towns shall be entitled to demand and receive thirty cents from each purchaser of real estate sold for non-payment of taxes, whether of resident or non-resident owners, as compensation for receiving and paying out the proceeds of the sale.

Treasurer may receive compensation, when. Act, March 10, 1863.

ORDINANCES.

Advertisement of sale of real estate.
Ord., March 24, 1862.

1. All notices of advertisements of sales of real estate for non-payment of taxes, by the treasurer and collector, or his deputies, in addition to the notices now required by law, shall be published in one of the daily papers of the city, three times successively, previous to the day of sale.

Treasurer and collector to publish list of unpaid taxes over $20.
Rev. Ord., 1855, as amended by Ord., Feb. 20, 1865.

2. It shall be the duty of the city treasurer and collector, between the first and tenth day of March, annually, to publish in one of the daily newspapers in the city, a list of all the taxes assessed upon residents amounting to twenty dollars and upwards, then remaining unpaid in the bills committed to him, together with the names of the persons assessed therefor.

Assessors to deliver to treasurer tax bills.
Ord., Aug. 14, 1865.

3. It shall be the duty of the assessors to make out and deliver to the treasurer and collector, at the time of the commitment of the warrant for the collection of taxes in each year, tax bills for all taxes assessed upon all resident persons and estates with the name and residence of the same marked thereon.

Duty of treasurer.
Ib.

4. The treasurer and collector shall immediately issue the tax bills, and if the same are not paid within four months thereafter, he shall issue a summons to each delinquent person assessed, and if such person shall not pay his taxes within ten days after the receipt of such summons, or after the service thereof in the usual form, the said treasurer and collector shall issue his warrant for the collection of said taxes according to law.

Interest on unpaid taxes.
Ib.

5. On all taxes assessed, interest shall be charged at the rate of six per cent. per annum, commencing sixty days after the commitment of said bills to the treasurer and collector.

Discount on taxes.
Ib.

6. On all taxes paid within sixty days from the date of the commitment thereof, a discount of five per cent. on the amount will be allowed.

TREES.

STATUTES.

1. Cities may make by-laws relating to trees.
2. Trees may be planted in public places.
3. Injury to trees. Penalty.

ORDINANCES.

1. Ornamental trees in streets, &c., not to be removed, except, &c. If horses, &c., mutilate or destroy, penalty.
2. Trees not to be injured, except by consent. Animals not to be fastened to trees. Penalties.
3. Duty of city marshal to prosecute. Fines collected to constitute a fund for replanting.

STATUTES.

1. Cities may make such by-laws or ordinances as they think proper, not inconsistent with the laws of the State, and enforce them by suitable penalties, for planting and preserving trees by the side of streets.

Cities may make by-laws relating to trees in streets. R. S., chap. 3, § 27.

2. A sum not exceeding five per cent. of the amount committed to him, may be expended by a surveyor, under the direction of the municipal officers, in planting trees about public burying grounds, squares, and ways within his district, if the town by vote authorizes it.

Trees may be planted. Ib., chap. 18, § 46.

3. Whoever wilfully and maliciously cuts down, destroys, or otherwise injures any tree for ornament or use, shall be punished by imprisonment less than one year, and by fine not exceeding one hundred dollars.

Injury to trees. Ib. chap. 127, § 5. Penalty.

ORDINANCES.

Ornamental trees on streets, &c., not to be removed, &c., without consent of mayor and aldermen.

Rev. Ord., 1855.

1. If any person shall remove, mutilate, or destroy any ornamental tree planted, or that may hereafter be planted, in any of the streets, alleys, squares, or other public places within the limits of the city, without a permit in writing from the mayor and aldermen, he shall pay a penalty of not less than five nor more than fifty dollars for each offense, according to the degree and aggravation of the offense, and if any owner or driver of any horse or other animal, shall suffer them to mutilate or destroy any tree as aforesaid, such owner or driver shall pay a like penalty for such offense.

Penalty if horses, &c., mutilate or destroy.

Trees shall not be injured without consent of mayor and aldermen.

Ib.

2. No person, except by permission of the mayor and aldermen, shall climb, break, peel, cut, deface, either by posting bills of any description, or otherwise, remove, injure, or destroy any of the trees growing, or which shall hereafter be planted, on the walks or promenades, or in the streets or public places of the city; and no person shall in any way fasten any horse or other animal to any of said trees, or allow any animal owned by him or under his control, to stand so near to the same that they may be gnawed or otherwise injured by any horse or other animal so fastened or permitted to stand. Any person violating any of the provisions of this section, shall be liable to a penalty of not less than five nor more than fifty dollars for each offense.

Horses and animals shall not be fastened to.

Shall not injure.

Penalties.

Duty of city marshal to prosecute.

Ib.

Fines, &c., collected to constitute fund for replanting trees.

3. It shall be the duty of the city marshal to prosecute all violations of this ordinance, and the fines and forfeitures thus collected, shall constitute a fund for replanting of such trees as have been thus removed or destroyed.

TRUANTS.

STATUTES.

1. Truants may be sent to reform school.
2. Cities authorized to make laws concerning truants, &c.
3. Persons authorized to make complaints.

ORDINANCES.

1. Children between eight and sixteen required to attend school.
2. Punishment for not attending school.
3. Truant officer to be appointed.
4. What provided as suitable places of punishment.
5. Habitual truants, how punished.
6. Same subject.

STATUTES.

1. When any boy between the ages of eight and sixteen years is convicted of truancy, the court may sentence him to the reform school, or to the other punishment provided for the same offense.

Truants may be sent to reform school. Act, March 16, 1861, chap. 57. § 3.

2. Towns may make such by-laws not repugnant to the laws of the State, concerning habitual truants, and children between six and seventeen years of age not attending school, without any regular or lawful occupation, and growing up in ignorance, as are most conducive to their welfare and the good order of society, and may annex a suitable penalty not exceeding twenty dollars for any breach thereof; but said by-laws must be first approved by a judge of the supreme judicial court.

Cities and towns authorized to make laws concerning truants. R. S. 11, § 12, as amended by Act, Feb. 14, 1861.

Persons appointed to make complaint. Ib.

3. Such towns shall appoint at their annual meeting, one or more persons, who alone shall make complaints for violations of said by-laws to the magistrate having jurisdiction thereof by said by-laws, and execute his judgments.

ORDINANCES.

Children between the ages of six and seventeen, required to attend school unless, &c. Rev. Ord., 1855.

1. All children between the ages of six and seventeen years, residing in the city of Portland, without any regular and lawful occupation, growing up in ignorance, shall be required, unless there be some sufficient reason to the contrary, to attend some public or private school, or suitable place of instruction.

Punishment for not attending school. Ib., as amended by Ord., May 27, 1861.

2. Every child in the city of Portland between the ages of six and seventeen years, who shall not attend school, and not be engaged in any regular and lawful occupation, and growing up in ignorance, shall be punished by a fine not exceeding twenty dollars, to be recovered to the use of the city, on complaint before the municipal court in said Portland, or by being placed in the house of correction in said city, for such period of time as the judge of said court may deem expedient.

Truant officer to be appointed. Ord., May 27, 1861.

3. The city council of the city of Portland, shall annually appoint one or more persons, who alone are authorized to make the complaints as specified in this ordinance, and it shall be their duty to arrest all such children as are described in the 1st, 4th, 5th and 6th sections of this ordinance, who may be found during school hours, in any of the streets, alleys, lanes, squares or other public places of resort or amusement, and to take them to such schools as they are accustomed or entitled to attend, where they shall be detained during school hours, by the teacher thereof, and written notice of such arrest and detention shall be forthwith sent to the parent, or guardian of such child, by the officer by whom the arrest is made, and every child who shall have been three times thus arrested, shall be proceeded against by complaint as an habitual truant.

4. The house of correction connected with the alms house, in the city of Portland, or State reform school, is hereby assigned and provided as the institution of instruction, house of reformation or other suitable situation, mentioned in section fourteen of chapter eleven of the revised statutes.

What provided as suitable places of punishment.
Ib.

5. Every child in the city of Portland, between the ages of eight and sixteen years, who shall become an habitual truant, shall be punished by a fine not exceeding twenty dollars, to be recovered to the use of the city, on complaint before the municipal court of said Portland, or by being placed in the house of correction, in said city, or State reform school, for such period of time as the judge of said court may deem expedient.

Habitual truants, how punished.
Ib.

6. Every child in the city of Portland, between the ages of eight and sixteen years, who shall not attend school, and not be engaged in any regular and lawful occupation, and growing up in ignorance, shall be punished by a fine not exceeding twenty dollars, to be recovered to the use of the city, on complaint before the municipal court, in said city, or by being placed in the house of correction in said city, or the State reform school, for such period of time as the judge of said court may deem expedient.

Children between the ages of eight and sixteen not attending school, how punished.
Ib.

WARDS.

STATUTES.

ORDER OF CITY COUNCIL.

STATUTES.

City divided into seven wards. City charter, § 11.

1. The city shall remain divided into seven wards; and it shall be the duty of the city council, once in ten years or oftener, to revise, and if it be needful, to alter such wards, in such manner as to preserve, as nearly as may be, an equal number of voters in each. In each of said wards, at the annual municipal election, there shall be chosen by ballot, a warden and clerk, who shall hold their offices for one year from the Monday following their election, and until others shall have been chosen and qualified in their places. Said warden and clerk shall be sworn or affirmed to the faithful performance of their respective duties by any justice of the peace of the city;

Wardens and clerks.

and a certificate of such oaths or affirmations having been administered, shall be entered by the clerk on the records of the ward. The warden shall preside at all ward meetings with the powers of moderators of town meetings. If at any meeting the warden shall not be present, or shall refuse to preside, the clerk of such ward shall call the meeting to order and preside until a warden *pro tem.* shall be chosen. If both are absent, or shall refuse to act, a warden and clerk *pro tem.* shall be chosen. The clerk shall record all proceedings, and certify the votes given, and deliver over to his successor in office all such records and journals, together with all other documents and papers held by him in said capacity. The voters of each ward may choose two persons to assist the warden in receiving, sorting and counting the votes.

All regular ward meetings shall be notified and called by warrant from the mayor and aldermen, in the manner prescribed by the laws of this State for notifying and calling town meetings by the selectmen of the several towns.

Ward meetings how called.

2. In addition to the seven wards, the several islands within the city of Portland are so far constituted a separate ward as to entitle the legal voters thereon to choose a warden, ward clerk, and one constable, who shall be residents on such islands. They shall hold their ward meetings on any one of the islands which a majority of the qualified voters residing on said islands may designate, and may, on the days of election, vote at the place designated for all officers named in the warrant calling the meeting. The warden shall preside at all meetings, receive the votes of all qualified electors present whose names are borne on the lists; shall sort, count and declare the votes in open meeting and in the presence of the clerk, who shall make a list of the persons voted for, with the number of votes for each person, and a fair record thereof, in presence of the warden and in open meeting,

Island Ward.

Ib. § 15.

and a copy of the list shall be attested by the warden and clerk, sealed up in open meeting, and delivered to the clerk of ward number one, within eighteen hours after the close of the polls, to become a part of the record of said ward; and all votes thus thrown shall be deemed as thrown in and belonging to ward number one. All meetings of the voters of said island ward, for choice of municipal officers, shall, after the business of the meeting is transacted, stand adjourned for two days to determine whether an election has been effected; and adjournments may be had, not exceeding two days at any one time, until the election has been effected. If the warden or clerk of said island ward shall be absent at any election, a warden or clerk may be chosen *pro tempore*. Or in case of a failure or omission to elect a warden or clerk, said officers may be chosen at any legal meeting duly called in said ward.

Wards in cities, change or alteration in the limits of, how to be made.

Act, 1861, chap. 1.

3. No change or alteration, in the limits of any ward in any city in this State by any action or proceedings of the city council, shall be of any force or effect, unless the same shall be submitted to the legal voters in such city, for their approval, at the election for city officers, that shall be holden next after such action of the city council; the warrants for the ward meetings shall contain an article for that purpose; if a majority of the votes given on the question of the approval of such change or alteration, shall be in favor thereof, the same shall take effect, and not otherwise.

ORDER OF CITY COUNCIL.

[*Passed March* 10, 1862.]

1. *Ordered*, That the present divisions of the wards of the city, made January 27th, 1851, be changed, and that the following described lines be the boundaries of the same:

Ward 1. Commencing at the harbor, at a point parallel with the line of the centre of Mountfort street, thence on such line to the centre of Mountfort street across Congress street, through the centre of Washington street and Back Cove bridge to the channel of Back Cove, comprising all the city territory northeast of this line. Ward one.

Ward 2. Commencing at the harbor, at foot of Franklin street, thence through the centre of Franklin to Fore street, thence through the centre of Fore to Hampshire street, thence through the centre of Hampshire to Congress street, thence through the centre of Congress to Franklin street, thence through the centre of Franklin to Cumberland street, thence through the centre of Cumberland to Boyd street, thence through the centre of Boyd to Lincoln street, thence on a line parallel with the centre of Boyd street to the channel of Back Cove, comprising all the territory between this line and the before mentioned line of ward one. Ward two.

Ward 3. Commencing at the harbor, at the foot of Silver street, thence through the centre of Silver to Middle street, thence through the centre of Middle to Lime street, thence through the centre of Lime to Congress street, thence through the centre of Congress to a line parallel with the southwest line of the lot of land on which the city and county buildings are located, thence on the southwest and northwest lines of said lot to Myrtle street, thence through the centre of Myrtle to Lincoln street, thence on a line parallel with the centre of Myrtle to the channel of Back Cove, comprising all the territory between this line and the before mentioned line of ward 2. Ward three.

Ward 4. Commencing at the harbor, at the foot of Maple street, thence through the centre of Maple to Pleasant street, thence through the centre of Pleasant to South street, thence through the centre of South to Free street, thence through the centre of Free to Brown street, thence through the centre of Brown to Cumberland street, Ward four.

thence through the centre of Cumberland to Preble street, thence through the centre of Preble street, and on a line parallel with the centre of Preble street to the channel of Back Cove, comprising all the territory between this line and the before mentioned line of ward 3.

Ward five. *Ward* 5. Commencing at the harbor, at the foot of High street, thence through the centre of High to Congress street, thence through the centre of Congress to Green street, thence through the centre of Green and Deering's bridge to the channel of Back Cove, comprising all the territory between this line and the before mentioned line of ward 4.

Ward six. *Ward* 6. Commencing at the channel at Portland bridge, thence through the centre of said bridge and on a line parallel to Brackett street, thence through the centre of Brackett street, to the southeast line of the lot on which the Brackett street school house is located, thence on the southeast, northeast and northwest lines of said lot to Brackett street, thence through the centre of Brackett street to Walker's Lane, thence through the centre of Walker's Lane across Congress street to Mellen street, thence through the centre of Mellen street across Portland street, and in a line parallel with the centre of Mellen street to the Creek that divides Portland and Westbrook, comprising all the territory between this line and the before mentioned line of ward 5.

Ward seven. *Ward* 7. Comprising all the territory southwest of the before named line of ward 6.

When to take effect. 2. *Ordered*, That the foregoing division of the city into seven wards shall be of force and take effect from and after the time that it shall have been approved by the legal voters of this city at ward meeting held for the election of city officers.

[The division as above was approved by the legal voters, April 9, 1862.]

WATCH.

[See Revised Statutes, chapter 25.]

WATERING TROUGHS.

STATUTES.

1. A town, at its annual meeting, may authorize its assessors to abate three dollars from the tax of any inhabitant, who shall construct, and during the year keep in repair a watering trough beside the highway, well supplied with water, the surface of which shall be two and a half feet or more above the level of the ground, and easily accessible for horses and carriages, if the assessors think such watering trough for the public convenience. If more than one person in a surveyor's district claim to furnish it, the municipal officers are to decide where it shall be located.

Watering troughs, abatement for.

R. S., chap. 18, § 52.

WEIGHERS AND GAUGERS.

ORDINANCES.

One or more weighers and gaugers to be appointed. To be sworn. Rev. Ord., 1855.

1. There shall annually be elected by the city council, in the month of March, one or more city weighers and gaugers, who shall be sworn to the faithful performance of the duties of said office, and who shall continue in office until removed, or until a successor is elected and qualified.

Duties. Ib.

2. It shall be the duty of said weighers and gaugers when thereto requested by the owner, to weigh or gauge, as the case may be, the contents or capacity of any pipe, hogshead, tierce, barrel, cask, box and other vessel or article, and mark the contents and tare, and outs, as the case may be, and the initials of his name and office on each such vessel or article he shall so weigh or gauge.

Fees. Ib.

3. Said weigher and gauger shall be entitled to charge and receive in full for his services aforesaid, the following fees for weighing, viz: seventeen cents for each pipe or hogshead, twelve cents for each tierce or box, eight cents for each barrel, twenty cents per ton for other articles, and the following fees for gauging, viz: ten cents for each pipe or hogshead, eight cents for each tierce, four cents

for each barrel or cask, and three cents for ascertaining and marking the outs of each cask, when the same is not gauged at the same time.

4. Weighers and gaugers shall pay to the city treasurer, to the use of the city, as compensation for the use of the city scales, one and a half cents for each pipe or hogshead ; one cent for each tierce or box ; one-half cent for each barrel ; and two cents per ton for all other articles weighed with said scales.

Weighers and gaugers shall pay for use of city scales. Ord., May 21, 1858.

5. Any person, not duly authorized as city weigher and gauger, who shall exercise that office by weighing or gauging any cargo or parts of cargo of any foreign merchandize, requiring a city weigher or gauger, or shall exercise or perform the duties of weigher or gàuger in any manner for fees or hire, shall for every such violation of this ordinance, forfeit and pay a sum not exceeding thirty dollars to the use of the city.

Persons not authorized, acting. Penalty. Ord., Aug. 7, 1866.

WEIGHTS AND MEASURES.

STATUTES.

Town seal and standard of beams, weights and measures to be kept by treasurers, &c.

R. S., chap. 43, § 4.

1. The treasurers of towns, at the expense thereof, shall constantly keep a town seal, and, as town standards, a complete set of beams, weights, and copper and pewter measures, conformable to the State standards, except that the bushel measure, and the half bushel, peck and half peck measures may be of wood instead of copper or pewter, but of the same dimensions, and except also a nest of troy weights other than those from the lowest denomination to eight ounces; they shall cause all beams, weights and measures, belonging to their towns, to be proved and

sealed by the State or county standards once in ten years, computing from July first, eighteen hundred and forty; and for every neglect of duty as aforesaid they shall forfeit one hundred dollars, half to the use of the town, and half to the use of the person suing therefor.

2. The municipal officers of each town shall annually appoint a sealer of weights and measures therein, removable at pleasure and have power to fill any vacancy that occurs; and for each month's neglect of this duty, they shall severally forfeit ten dollars, to be appropriated as in the preceding section. Any city may purchase and keep for use scales for weighing hay and other articles, appoint weighers and fix their fees.

Appointment of sealers, &c. Ib. § 5.

3. If any person, so appointed and notified thereof, refuses for seven days to accept the office and be sworn, he shall forfeit five dollars; but when sworn, he shall receive the standards and seal from the treasurer, giving a receipt therefor, describing them and their condition, and therein engaging to re-deliver them at the expiration of his office in like good order; and he shall be accountable for their due preservation while in his possession.

Penalty for sealer not accepting office, &c. Ib. § 6.

4. Every such sealer shall annually, in the month of May, post notices in different parts of his town stating the times and places at which he will attend to the proof and sealing of weights and measures; shall deface or destroy all weights and measures that are not or cannot by him be made conformable to the standard; shall visit the houses of innholders, the warehouses and stores of merchants, and the dwelling houses of such other inhabitants, as neglect to send to him their weights and measures, and there prove and seal the same; and every sealer neglecting any duty herein required of him, and every person neglecting or refusing to have his weights and measures proved and sealed as aforesaid, shall forfeit ten dollars.

Duty of town sealer; penalty for neglect, how appropriated. Ib. § 7.

5. In all cases of weighing, the vibrating steelyard invented by Benjamin Dearborn, or the vibrating steel-

What scales may be used, &c. Ib. § 8.

yard invented by Benjamin Dearborn and improved by Samuel Hills, or the Fairbanks' scale, may be used; but before being offered for sale, or used, each beam and the poises thereof shall be sealed by a public sealer of weights and measures, appointed according to law.

Measures, for articles sold by heaped measure, shall be conformable to standard.

Ib. § 9.

6. All measures, by which fruit and other things, usually sold by heaped measures, are sold, shall be conformable in capacity and breadth, to the public standard; and if any person otherwise sells and exposes to sale any such fruit or other thing, any goods or commodities whatever by any other beams, weights, or measures than those proved and sealed as aforesaid, he shall forfeit for each offense not less than one dollar nor more than ten dollars; one-half to the use of the town, and the other to the sealer, or to him who prosecutes therefor.

Twenty-five pounds shall be a quarter, &c.

Ib. § 10.

7. Such articles as are sold or exchanged in any market or town in this State by gross or avoirdupois weight, shall be sold or exchanged as follows: twenty-five avoirdupois pounds constitute one quarter; four quarters, one hundred; and twenty hundreds, one ton; and all other articles, usually sold by tale, shall be sold by decimal hundred.

WEIGHER OF HARD COAL.

STATUTES.

1. Coal to be sold by weight, &c.
2. Weighers to be appointed and sworn.
3. Coal to be weighed by sworn weighers before sale, when not sold by cargo. Parties may agree upon weight.

ORDINANCES.

1. Weigher of hard coal to be chosen.
2. Duties.
3. To examine and prove scales used by him.
4. To give public notice of scales not sealed.
5. Not to use scales unless sealed. Penalty.
6. Penalty for dealer in coal, refusing weigher to prove his scales.
7. Compensation.

STATUTES.

1. Anthracite, bituminous, or other mineral coal, shall be sold by weight, and two thousand pounds avoirdupois shall be the standard for the ton by which the same shall be weighed.

Coal to be sold by weight, &c.

Act., Feb. 25, 1867, chap. 98, § 1.

2. The municipal officers of cities and towns may annually appoint weighers of such coal, who shall be duly sworn, and receive such fees as said officers may establish to be paid by the buyer.

Weighers of coal to be appointed and sworn.

Ib. § 2.

3. The seller of such coal, when not sold by the cargo, shall cause the same to be weighed by a sworn weigher, who shall make a certificate of the weight thereof, and the seller shall not be entitled to recover or commence

Coal to be weighed by sworn weigher before sale, when not sold by cargo.

Ib. § 3.

any action for the price of such coal until he shall deliver, or cause to be delivered, to the buyer such certificate; *provided, however*, that it shall be competent for the parties to agree upon the quantity of coal without such survey or liability.

Parties may agree upon weight.

ORDINANCES.

Weigher of coal to be chosen.
Rev. Ord., 1855.

1. There shall be chosen, annually, by the city council in convention, a suitable person as weigher of hard coal, who shall be sworn to the faithful discharge of the duties of said office, and who shall be removable by vote of the city council; and in case of a vacancy in said office, the city council shall choose a suitable person to fill the same.

Duties.
Ib.

2. It shall be the duty of the weigher of hard coal, when thereto requested, carefully to weigh or superintend the weighing of hard coal, sold in the city, and deliver to the driver or person taking away such coal, for each load he may weigh or superintend, as aforesaid, a ticket by him signed, certifying the quantity such load contains, and the names of seller and purchaser; and he shall keep an office in some convenient place in the vicinity of the principal coal yards in the city, where he can be found, for the performance of the duties of his office.

To examine and prove scales used by him.
Ib.

3. The weigher of hard coal shall, from time to time, as often as once a month carefully examine, try and prove all scales used by him or under his superintendence for weighing hard coal; and if upon any examination and trial, it shall be found that such scales are not conformable to the legal standard, he shall give immediate notice thereof, in writing, to the owner or keeper of said scales, therein requesting him to have the same regulated and sealed forthwith.

To give public notice of scales not sealed.

4. In case said owner or keeper shall refuse or neglect to have the same tried, proved, and sealed by the public sealer of weights and measures, for the space of twenty-four hours after such notice, it shall be the duty

of said weigher forthwith to give public notice thereof, in two of the city daily papers, published in this city.

5. Said weigher is hereby forbidden from using said scales, or certifying the weight of coal weighed therewith, until the same shall have been tried, proved and sealed as aforesaid; and for any neglect of duty aforesaid, or violations of the provisions of this ordinance, said weigher shall forfeit and pay not less than two dollars for each load of coal he shall weigh therewith, until the same shall be sealed as aforesaid, one-half of said penalty to enure to the prosecutor, and the other half to the city.

Not to use scales unless sealed.
Ib.

Penalty.

6. If any dealer in hard coal in this city, after being requested by any person purchasing coal of him, shall refuse permission to said weigher to weigh said coal upon his scales, he shall forfeit and pay five dollars for each time he refuses such permission to said weigher, one-half thereof to the city and the other half to the complainant.

Penalty for dealer in coal, refusing weigher to prove his scales.
Ib.

7. Said weigher of hard coal shall receive such fees for his services as shall be from time to time established by the mayor and aldermen, to be paid by the person requesting his services.

Compensation.
Ib.

WEIGHER OF PLASTER.

ORDINANCES.

1. Weigher of plaster to be elected.
2. His compensation.
3. City to provide scales.
4. Bonds to be given.

Weigher of plaster to be elected. Rev. Ord., 1855.

1. There shall annually be elected, by the city council, a suitable person as weigher of plaster, who shall be sworn to the faithful discharge of the duties of his office.

Compensation. Ib.

2. The weigher of plaster shall receive for and in full compensation for weighing plaster, seven cents per ton, to be paid by the purchaser for whom the services are performed.

City to provide scales. Ib.

3. Scales suitable for weighing plaster shall be provided by the city, for the use of which, the weigher of plaster shall pay the city treasurer one-seventh part of all monies received by him for weighing.

Bonds to be given. Ib.

4. The weigher of plaster shall give a bond in the sum of one hundred dollars, to be approved by the mayor and aldermen, for the faithful performance of his duty, and for the payment of such sums as shall be due to the city for the use of the scales.

WELLS AND PUMPS.

ORDINANCES.

1. If any person shall wilfully or carelessly break, injure or deface any pump in a well, partly or wholly made at the expense of the city, he shall forfeit and pay a sum not less than one nor more than ten dollars for each offense, and shall be further liable to the action of the city for all damages done by him to such pump.

Penalty for injury to pumps.

Rev. Ord., 1855.

2. No person shall at any time take more water from any of the wells aforesaid than he may want for immediate use, nor shall take water from such well, unless it be into some cask or other vessel, nor shall in any manner waste the water of such well, under a penalty of not less than one nor more than ten dollars for each offense.

Penalty for taking water from pump or well, or wasting the same.

Ib.

WHARVES.

STATUTES.

ORDER.

STATUTES.

Wharves not to extend below low water mark, without consent.
City charter, § 22.
Not to be extended beyond harbor commissioners' line.

1. No existing wharf in Portland shall be extended in the harbor a greater distance below low water mark than the same now exists, and hereafter no such new wharf shall be extended below low water mark into the harbor, without, in either case, the written assent of the mayor and aldermen. No wharf or incumbrance shall hereafter be erected or extended into said harbor beyond the harbor commissioners' line.

Notice for construction of wharves required.
R. S., chap. 17, § 21.

2. When the construction or extension of a wharf in tidal waters in any city is desired by the permission of the city authorities, they shall require the applicant to give fourteen days notice thereof by publication in two newspapers, before acting upon it.

WHARVES.

ORDER.

IN BOARD OF ALDERMEN,
October 11, 1854.

1. *Ordered*, That the following described line be, and the same hereby is fixed and established as the wharf line or limit of construction on the north side of Portland harbor, beyond which no wharf shall hereafter be constructed or extended in said harbor, within the limits bounded by said line, to wit: Wharf tablish Rev. Or 7 Cush,

Commencing at the eastern corner of the Gas Company's wharf, next above Portland bridge, in a straight line to the southern corner of the end of Robinson's wharf, and along the end of it to the eastern corner, thence in a straight line to the southern corner of the end of Central wharf, and along the end of it to the eastern corner; thence in a straight line to the southern corner of the end of Custom House wharf, and along the end of it to the eastern corner; thence in a straight line to the southern corner of the end of Railway wharf, and along the end of it to the eastern corner; thence in a straight line to the southerly corner of the end of St. Lawrence wharf, and along the end of it to the eastern corner; thence parallel to the straight portion of the outside railroad track, to the shoals to the southward of Fish point, as defined in a copy of a plan of Portland harbor, made by the United States coast survey, in 1853.

[See chapter on HARBOR OF PORTLAND.]

WOOD, BARK AND CHARCOAL.

STATUTES.

WOOD.

1. Dimensions of a cord of wood.
2. Penalty for selling without survey.
3. How wood, brought by water, shall be measured.
4. Ticket required.
5. Penalty for fraudulent stowage.

CHARCOAL.

6. How charcoal may be measured and sold.
7. Coal baskets to be sealed; dimensions.
8. Penalty.
9. Seizure of unlawful baskets.
10. Penalty for refusing to give certificate.

ORDINANCES.

1. Measurers of firewood and bark to be chosen. To be sworn. Vacancies to be filled.
2. Measurement to be in two branches. Of wood and bark brought into the city by carts, &c. Of same by water or railroad. City divided into two districts.
3. Duties of measurers. To give tickets certifying measure, &c. To keep record of tickets issued. To make annual report to city council.
4. Teams with wood or bark not to stand in streets longer than ten minutes. Cattle not to be fastened to post, &c. Team not to be fed in streets. Wood not to be unloaded or piled in market, if any.
5. Penalties.
6. Mayor and aldermen to appoint person to seize charcoal baskets.

STATUTES.

WOOD AND BARK.

1. Towns may, by ordinance, regulate the measure and sale of wood, coal, and bark therein, and the location of teams hauling the same; and enforce it by reasonable penalties. All cord wood exposed to sale shall be four feet long including half the scarf; and well and closely laid together; a cord of wood or bark shall measure eight feet in length, four feet in width, and four feet in height, or otherwise contain one hundred and twenty-eight cubic feet; and the measurer shall make due allowance for refuse or defective wood, and bad stowage.

Dimensions of a cord of wood.

14 Maine, 404.

R. S., chap. 41, § 1.

2. If any firewood or bark, brought into any town by land, is sold and delivered, unless otherwise agreed to by the purchaser, before it is measured by a sworn measurer, and a ticket signed by him and given to the driver, stating the quantity the load contains, the name of the driver, and the town in which he resides, such wood or bark shall be forfeited, and may be libeled and disposed of according to law.

Penalty for selling wood or bark before survey.

Ib. § 2.

3. All cord wood, brought by water into any town for sale, shall be corded on the wharf or land, on which it is landed, in ranges, making up in height what is wanting in length; then it shall be so measured and a ticket given to the purchaser, who shall pay the stated fees; and no such wood shall be carried away by any wharfinger or carter, before it has been so measured, under a penalty of one dollar for every load.

How cord wood, brought by water, shall be measured, &c.

Ib. § 3.

4. Every person, carrying any firewood from a wharf or landing for sale, shall be furnished by the owner or seller of it with a ticket stating the quantity and name of the driver; and if such firewood is carried away without such ticket, or any driver refuses to exhibit such ticket to any sworn measurer on demand, or does not consent to have the same measured, if in the opinion of the measurer

Ticket stating quantity and name of driver, required, &c.

Ib. § 4.

the ticket certifies a greater quantity of wood than the load contains, such wood shall be forfeited, and may be seized, and libeled by said measurer according to law.

Penalty for fraudulent stowage.
Ib. § 5.

5. When any wood, bark, or charcoal, is sold by the cord, foot, or load, which is stowed in such a manner as to prevent the surveyors from examining the middle of the load, and it appears on delivery, that it was stowed with a fraudulent intent of obtaining payment for a greater quantity than there was in fact, the seller or owner thereof shall pay ten dollars for the use of the county, with costs of prosecution.

CHARCOAL.

How charcoal may be measured and sold.
Ib. § 6.

6. Any charcoal brought into a town for sale, may be measured and sold by the cord or foot, estimating the cord at ninety-six bushels, when the purchaser and seller may agree to the same; and the measurers before named shall be measurers of charcoal also.

Coal baskets to be sealed; dimensions.
Ib. § 7.

7. All baskets for measuring charcoal brought into a town for sale, shall be sealed by the sealer of the town where the person using them usually resides, and shall contain two bushels and be of the following dimensions, viz.; nineteen inches in breadth in every part thereof, and seventeen inches and a half deep, measuring from the top of the basket to the highest part of the bottom; and in measuring charcoal for sale the basket shall be well heaped.

Penalty.
Ib. § 8.

8. Whoever measures charcoal for sale, in any basket of less dimensions, or not sealed, shall forfeit, for each offense, five dollars.

Seizure of unlawful baskets.
Ib. § 9.

9. The municipal officers of towns may appoint some suitable person to seize and secure all the baskets used for measuring coal, not according to the provisions hereof.

Penalty for refusing to give certificate, &c.
Ib. § 10.

10. If any measurer of wood, bark, or charcoal, neglects or refuses to give to the owner or purchaser a certificate of the contents of any load, he shall forfeit five dollars for each offense; and all the penalties herein

before provided, may be recovered by action of debt or complaint, one-half to the town where the offense is committed, and the other to the prosecutor.

ORDINANCES.

1. There shall be chosen annually by the city council in convention, two or more measurers of fire-wood and bark, brought into the city for sale, who shall be sworn to the faithful performance of their office,—and shall hold their office during the municipal year, and until others are appointed in their stead, unless sooner removed by vote of the city council. In case of a vacancy in said office by resignation, removal or otherwise, the city council shall proceed to fill the same by a new election for the residue of the year.

Measurers of firewood and bark to be chosen.

Rev. Ord., 1855.

To be sworn.

Vacancies to be filled.

2. In order to prevent competition in the survey of firewood and bark, this department shall be divided into two branches, one of which shall embrace the survey of all firewood and bark brought into the city on carts, wagons or sleds, and the other shall embrace the survey of firewood and bark brought by water or railroad conveyance; and each measurer shall be independent of the other, and shall attend personally and exclusively to the duties of that branch of the survey to which he is chosen. In order still further to prevent competition, the number of measurers of firewood and bark, brought into the city by water or railroad conveyance, shall be limited to two, and the city shall be divided into two districts for the measurement of the same, to each of which districts one measurer shall be designated; and all wood and bark brought as aforesaid into either district, shall be measured as provided in section three of this ordinance, exclusively by the measurer appointed to said district. So much of the city as lies westerly of a line drawn through the centre of Wilmot street, to Congress street; thence through the centre of Congress to Exchange street; thence through

Measurement divided into two branches.

Of wood and bark brought into city by carts, &c.

Of same by water or railroad.

City divided into two districts.

Ib., as amended by Ord., May 29, 1856.

the centre of Exchange to Long wharf, and including Long wharf, shall constitute district number one; and so much as lies to the easterly of said lines shall constitute district number two. The measurer first elected by the city council shall be the measurer for district number one, during the municipal year, unless the district of each measurer shall be designated at the time of said election.

Duties of measurers. Rev. Ord., 1855.

3. It shall be the duty of each measurer, carefully and accurately to measure all firewood and bark which he may be requested to measure in his branch of survey, on payment of the fees allowed for such service, and deliver to the driver, or person having the care of the wood or bark, a ticket under his hand for each load he may measure, certifying in words at length, written in ink, the quantity the load contains, with the name of the driver, or person having the charge of the wood or bark, and the town in which he resides. Each measurer shall keep an accurate record of all tickets by him issued, in a book to be by him provided and kept for that purpose, and shall report annually, to the city council, the number of cords of firewood and bark measured by him during the preceding year, and the amount of fees received therefor.

To give tickets certifying measure, &c.

To keep record of tickets issued.

To make annual report to city council.

Teams with wood or bark not to stand in street longer than ten minutes. Ib.

Cattle not to be fastened to post, &c.

Team not to be fed.

Wood not to be unloaded or piled in market.

4. No team having firewood or bark for sale, shall be suffered to stand in any street, alley, square, or other public place, for a longer time in any one day, than ten minutes, nor shall the driver of any team which has brought firewood or bark as aforesaid, hitch or fasten his cattle to any post, tree, or fence, in any street or lane; nor shall any driver of such team feed his cattle, or suffer the same to be fed, in any street, alley, square, or other public place; nor shall any person unload or pile any firewood or bark upon or within the wood market, if any.

Penalties. Ib.

5. Every person offending against any of the preceding sections, or unreasonably neglecting to perform any of the duties therein required, shall forfeit and pay, for the

use of the city, a sum not less than five dollars for each offense.

CHARCOAL.

6. The mayor and aldermen may annually appoint one or more suitable persons to seize and secure all baskets used for measuring charcoal that shall not be of the dimensions prescribed by the laws of the State, and to prosecute all persons who shall be guilty of a breach of said laws.

Mayor and aldermen to appoint person to seize charcoal baskets.
Ib.

WORK HOUSES.

[See Revised Statutes, chapter 21.]

CITY OF PORTLAND.

IN THE YEAR ONE THOUSAND EIGHT HUNDRED AND SIXTY-EIGHT.

AN ORDINANCE IN RELATION TO THE REVISED ORDINANCES.

Be it ordained by the mayor, aldermen, and common council of the city of Portland, in city council assembled, as follows:

SECTION 1. All the ordinances printed and contained in the preceding pages, that is to say, in a certain book prepared and printed under the direction of Gilbert L. Bailey, Charles M. Rice, Samuel H. Colesworthy, Frederick N. Dow, and Henry H. Burgess, a committee duly appointed and authorized for that purpose by a vote of the city council of the city of Portland, passed on the first day of April, in the year eighteen hundred and sixty-seven, shall be deemed and are declared to be ordinances of the said city, and shall have the force thereof.

The ordinances in this book declared to be the ordinances of the city.

SEC. 2. All orders, ordinances and parts of orders and ordinances, inconsistent with any of the preceding ordinances, are hereby repealed.

Repeal of inconsistent ordinances.

SEC. 3. The repeal in the preceding section shall not affect any act done, or any right accruing or accrued, or established, or any suit or proceeding had or commenced in any civil case before the time when such repeal shall take effect, nor any offense committed, nor

Saving of rights accrued, suits pending, &c.

23

any penalty or forfeiture incurred, nor any suit or prosecution pending at the time of such repeal, for any offense committed or for the recovery of any penalty or forfeiture incurred, under any of the provisions so repealed and in all cases where any provisions of the preceding ordinances made, are to go into operation at any time hereafter, the corresponding provisions, if any, of the said repealed ordinances or orders shall continue in force until the said new provisions shall go into operation; subject, however, to any express regulations relating thereto which may be contained in the preceding ordinances; and no ordinance, order, or part of an ordinance or order which has been heretofore repealed, shall be revived by the repeal in the preceding section.

How copies of revised ordinances shall be kept, &c.

SEC. 4. All copies of the revised ordinances, not otherwise disposed of, shall be deposited with the city clerk, subject to the direction and control of the city council, and shall be on sale at such price as shall be determined by the mayor and aldermen.

Copies for city council.

SEC. 5. Every member of the city council shall be entitled to one copy of the revised ordinances.

IN BOARD OF MAYOR AND ALDERMEN,
January 20, 1868.

This bill having been read twice, passed to be ordained.

AUGUSTUS E. STEVENS, *Mayor.*

IN COMMON COUNCIL,
Jan. 20, 1868.

This bill having been read twice, passed to be ordained.

FRED. N. DOW, *President pro tem.*

Approved January 21, 1868.

AUGUSTUS E. STEVENS, *Mayor.*

APPENDIX.

APPENDIX.

AN ACT

TO AUTHORIZE THE CITY OF PORTLAND TO AID THE CONSTRUCTION OF THE ATLANTIC AND ST. LAWRENCE RAILROAD.

[Statutes 1848, Chapter 135.]

Be it enacted by the Senate and House of Representatives in Legislature assembled, as follows :

City of Portland authorized to loan its credit to the Atlantic and St. Lawrence Railroad Co.

SEC. 1. The city of Portland is hereby authorized to loan its credit to the Atlantic and St. Lawrence Railroad Company, in aid of the construction of their railroad, subject to the following terms and conditions.

This act to be accepted by the directors of said company, and by the inhabitants of said city.

SEC. 2. This act shall not take effect, unless it shall be accepted by the directors of said railroad company, and by the vote of the inhabitants of said city, voting in ward meetings duly called, according to law ; and at least two-thirds of the votes cast at such ward meetings shall be necessary for the acceptance of the act. The returns of such ward meetings shall be made to the aldermen of the city, and by them counted and declared, and the city clerk shall make record thereof.

City treasurer authorized to make and issue the scrip of the city.

SEC. 3. Upon the acceptance of the act as aforesaid, the city treasurer is authorized to make and issue from time to time, for the purposes contemplated in this act, the scrip of said city, in convenient and suitable sums, payable to the holder thereof, on a term of time not less than twenty, nor more than thirty years, with coupons for interest attached, payable semi-annually, or yearly, as may be agreed.

When $550,000 have been received from assessments and expended on said road, the city treasurer authorized to deliver the directors scrip to the amount of $200,000.

SEC. 4. When the railroad company shall have received from assessments upon the shares of the private stockholders therein, and shall have expended upon the construction of the road, and its necessary equipment, the sum of five hundred and fifty thousand dollars, the city treasurer shall then deliver to the directors of the company, the scrip aforesaid to the amount of two hundred thousand dollars. When the company shall have expended that sum in the further construction and equipment of the road, and shall have received from the assessments upon the shares of private stockholders, the further amount of one hundred thousand dollars, the city treasurer shall deliver of the scrip, a further amount of three hundred thousand dollars.

When $300,000 more may be delivered.

When further portions may be delivered.

SEC. 5. When the company shall have expended in the further construction and equipment of the road, at least one-half the proceeds of the scrip last named, further portions of the scrip shall be from time to time delivered thereafter, in such amounts and proportions, that the aggregate of all the scrip delivered shall at no time exceed the whole amount of the assessments paid in and expended. But the whole amount of the scrip to be issued and delivered shall never exceed one million of dollars.

Whole amount not to exceed $1,000,000.

Certain pre-requisites to be complied with.

SEC. 6. Before the delivery of any of the scrip, in any of the cases provided in the preceding sections, the directors of the company shall furnish satisfactory evidence to the mayor and aldermen of the city, that all the pre-requisites therein prescribed in the several cases have been respectively complied with, and shall file with the city treasurer a certificate of such compliance, signed by the president and treasurer of the company, to which certificate they shall severally make oath. In all cases, the scrip shall bear date from the delivery thereof, and

Date of scrip.

the proceeds thereof shall be applied by the directors of the company, exclusively to the construction and necessary furniture and equipment of the Atlantic and St. Lawrence railroad.

Proceeds applied exclusively to the construction of said road, &c.

SEC. 7. Upon the delivery of each and every portion of the scrip aforesaid, the directors shall execute and deliver to the city treasurer, the bond of the company, in an equal amount, payable to the city, conditioned that the company will duly pay the interest on said scrip, and will provide for the reimbursement of the principal thereof, and hold the city harmless on account of the issue of the same, according to the provisions of this act.

Bond to be given treasurer on delivery of scrip.

SEC. 8. The directors shall also transfer to the city, upon the delivery of any portion of the scrip as aforesaid, an equal amount in the shares of the company, to be held as collateral security for the bond of the company, required to be given in such case. And the shares so held as collateral shall be credited on the stock books of the company as fully paid up, and no assessments shall ever be required thereon, nor shall any dividends be paid on the same, nor any right of acting or voting at the meetings of the company be claimed or exercised by reason of said shares, so long as the same shall be held as collateral as aforesaid.

Collateral security.

SEC. 9. From and after the issue and delivery to the directors of any portion of the scrip aforesaid, the city shall have a lien upon the said railroad, and upon all the property and franchise of the company, to secure the performance of the conditions of all the bonds of the company, executed and delivered under the provisions of this act.

Lien created on the railroad for said bond.

SEC. 10. For the purpose of providing for the reimbursement of the principal of the scrip, authorized to be issued by this act, there shall be established a sinking fund, and commissioners shall be appointed to manage the same. One of said commissioners shall be appointed by

Sinking fund.

Commissioners.

the mayor and aldermen of the city, and one by the directors of the company, and in case of a vacancy in the place of either, the same shall be supplied by the mayor and aldermen, or by the directors, respectively. Both of said commissioners shall be appointed, and qualified before the delivery to the directors of any of the scrip. The commissioners shall severally be sworn to the faithful discharge of the duties enjoined upon them by this act, in presence of the city clerk, who shall make a certificate and record thereof, as in the case of the qualification of city officers. Each of the commissioners shall give a bond to the city, with satisfactory sureties, in the penal sum of ten thousand dollars, conditioned for the faithful discharge of his duty as commissioner. They shall receive such compensation as may be established by the directors, which shall be paid to them by the company, and shall not be diminished during their continuance in office.

Bond.

Compensation.

Sinking fund, how constituted.

SEC. 11. Whenever the directors shall receive any portion of the scrip, authorized as aforesaid to be delivered to them, they shall pay to the city treasurer, two per cent. of the amount of the scrip so delivered, which amount shall be, by the city treasurer, placed to the credit of the commissioners of the sinking fund, and shall constitute a part of said fund. The directors shall also, annually, in the month of April, pay to the city treasurer, from the income of the road, one per cent. of the whole amount of scrip which shall have been, before that time, issued and delivered, and shall be then outstanding; but after the expiration of five years from the time of the delivery and receipt of the first portion of scrip as aforesaid, the said annual payments from the income of the road shall be increased to one and a half per cent. of the amount of the scrip, then outstanding as aforesaid, and the said annual payments of one per cent. for five years, and one and a half per cent. annually thereafter, shall be successively placed to the credit of the commissioners of the sinking fund, and shall constitute a part of said fund.

SEC. 12. The commisioners shall have the care and management of all the moneys and securities at any time belonging to said fund; but the moneys uninvested, and the securities, shall be in custody of the city treasurer, who shall be, by virtue of his office, treasurer of the sinking fund, and shall be responsible, on his official bond to the city, for the safe keeping of the moneys and securities of the fund. He shall pay out and deliver any of the said moneys and securities only upon the warrant of the commissioners.

Duty of commissioners.

Treasurer.

SEC. 13. The commissioners shall from time to time, at their discretion, invest the moneys on hand, securely, so that they shall be productive, and the same may be loaned on mortgage of real estate, or to any county, or upon pledge of the securities of any county in this State, or invested in the stock of this State, or of the United States, or in the stock of any railroad company in New England, whose road is completed, and whose capital has been wholly paid in. Any portion of the fund may be invested in the city scrip authorized by this act, and such scrip shall not thereby be extinguished, but shall be held by the commissioners, like their other investments, for the purposes of the fund. An amount not exceeding ten per cent. of the fund may be loaned on pledge of the stock of any bank, or of any stock insurance company in this State. And the commissioners may from time to time sell and transfer any of said securities.

Moneys belonging to said fund, how invested.

SEC. 14. The sinking fund, and all the sums which shall be added thereto by accumulation upon the investments thereof, shall be reserved and kept inviolate for the redemption and reimbursement of the principal of said scrip at the maturity thereof, and shall be applied thereto by the commissioners.

To be reserved for the redemption of the principal of said scrip.

SEC. 15. Any of the shares in the stock of the railroad company, held by the city as collateral, may be sold and transferred by direction of the commissioners of the sinking fund, with the consent of the directors of the rail-

When the shares held as collateral may be sold or transferred.

road company, whenever an exchange thereof can be advantageously made for any of the city scrip, authorized by this act, or whenever the said scrip can be advantageously purchased with the proceeds of any such sale of such collateral shares. And the scrip so purchased or taken in exchange, shall be thereupon cancelled and extinguished, and the amount thereof shall be endorsed on the respective bonds of the railroad company given on the issue and delivery of such scrip. But no part of the sinking fund, or of its accumulations, shall be applied at any time or in any manner to the redemption and extinguishment of the scrip before maturity thereof.

If directors fail to pay into the sinking fund, per centage on income of road.

SEC. 16. If the directors of the railroad company shall, at any time, fail to pay to the city treasurer, for the sinking fund, the amount aforesaid of one per cent. or of one and a half per cent. required to be paid into the sinking fund, out of the income of the road, the commissioners are authorized, at their discretion, upon such notice to the company as they shall deem suitable, to sell so many of such collateral shares as may be necessary to produce the amount of such deficiency, and the proceeds of such sale shall thereupon be paid into the sinking fund, and shall be applied to the purposes thereof. And all conveyances and transfers of such collateral shares shall be made by the city treasurer, under the direction of the commissioners of the fund, in pursuance of the provisions of this act.

Commissioners authorized to sell collateral shares.

Conveyances and transfers.

Commissioners to keep a record of proceedings.

SEC. 17. The commissioners shall keep a true record of all their proceedings and an account of all the sums paid into the fund, and of the investments made of the same, and shall, annually, in the month of July, report to the mayor and aldermen, and to the directors of the railroad company, their proceedings for the year, the amount and condition of the fund, and the income of the several parts thereof. And their records, and the accounts of the fund, and the securities belonging thereto, shall at all times be open to inspection by such committee as may be appointed

Annual report.

for that purpose by the mayor and aldermen, or by the directors of the company.

Power of supreme judicial court, on complaint against said commissioners.

SEC. 18. To secure the faithful discharge of the several trusts confided to the said commissioners under this act, the supreme judicial court is hereby empowered, upon the complaint of the mayor and aldermen, or of the directors of the railroad company, against the said commissioners, or either of them, concerning any of said trusts and duties, by summary process according to the course of proceedings in equity, to hear and adjudge upon the matter of such complaint, and to issue thereon, any suitable writ or process, and make any proper decree to compel the appropriate discharge and performance of such trusts and duties, and to remove the said commissioners, or either of them; and in case of such removal, the vacancy shall be immediately supplied, as provided in the tenth section of this act.

If sinking fund at any time exceed the amount of scrip unredeemed.

SEC. 19. If the said sinking fund with its accumulations, shall at any time exceed the amount of the scrip unredeemed and outstanding, all such excess shall be annually paid over to the railroad company; and if any surplus of the fund shall remain after the redemption and reimbursement of all the scrip, such surplus shall be paid over to the company.

When to take effect.

SEC. 20. This act shall take effect and be in force, from and after its approval by the governor, so far as to empower the directors of the railroad company, and the inhabitants of the city to act upon the question of accepting the same, as provided in the second section of this act. And the several ward meetings of the inhabitants for that purpose, shall be called and holden within thirty days after such approval. And if the act shall be accepted as aforesaid, then, after such acceptance, and record thereof, all the parts of the act shall take effect and be in full force.[1]

[1] Accepted August 16, 1848. See city records, vol. 4, page 50.

AN ACT

TO AUTHORIZE THE CITY OF PORTLAND TO GRANT FURTHER AID IN THE CONSTRUCTION OF THE ATLANTIC AND ST. LAWRENCE RAILROAD.

[Statutes 1850, Chapter 335.]

Be it enacted by the Senate and House of Representatives in Legislature assembled, as follows:

City of Portland authorized to loan its credit.

SEC. 1. The city of Portland is hereby authorized to make a further loan of its credit to the Atlantic and St. Lawrence Railroad Company, in aid of the construction of their railroad—subject to the following terms and conditions.

Act when to take effect.

SEC. 2. This act shall not take effect, unless it shall be accepted by the directors of said railroad company, and by the vote of the inhabitants of said city, voting in ward meetings duly called according to law; and at least two-thirds of the whole number of votes cast at such ward meetings shall be necessary for the acceptance of the act. The returns of such ward meetings shall be made to the aldermen of the city, and they shall count and declare the votes returned, and the city clerk shall make record thereof.

Scrip to be issued, &c.

SEC. 3. Upon the acceptance of the act as aforesaid, the city treasurer is authorized to make and issue from time to time, for the purposes contemplated in this act, the scrip of said city, in convenient and suitable sums payable to the holder thereof, on a term of time not less than twenty nor more than thirty years, with coupons for interest attached, payable semi-annually or yearly.

SEC. 4. The whole amount of the scrip to be issued and delivered under this act, shall not exceed five hundred thousand dollars, and the same shall be delivered by the city treasurer to the directors of the railroad company from time to time as may be required, subject to the several provisions of this act. In all cases the scrip shall bear date from the delivery thereof, and the proceeds of the same shall be applied by the directors of the company, exclusively to the construction and necessary furniture and equipment of the Atlantic and St. Lawrence railroad.

Amount not to exceed $500,000.

Date of scrip and how applied.

SEC. 5. Upon the delivery of each and every portion of the scrip aforesaid, the directors shall execute and deliver to the city treasurer, for the city, the bond of the company in an equal amount, payable to the city, conditioned that the company will duly pay the interest on said scrip, and will provide for the reimbursement of the principal thereof, and hold the city harmless on account of the issue of the same, according to the provisions of this act.

Bond of the company to be given for the scrip.

SEC. 6. The directors shall also, if required by the mayor and aldermen of the city, transfer to the city, upon the delivery of any portion of the scrip as aforesaid, an equal amount in the shares of the company, to be held as security for the faithful performance of all the obligations of the company mentioned in the preceding section, and the certificate of such shares shall be delivered to the city treasurer. The shares so transferred shall be credited in the stock books of the company as fully paid up. But the city shall not be taken and held as a stockholder in the company by reason of the transfer of shares for the purposes aforesaid, under the provisions of this act, or of an act passed August first, one thousand eight hundred and forty-eight, nor shall any assessment ever be required on the shares hereby authorized to be transferred as aforesaid, nor shall any dividends be paid on the same, nor any right of acting or voting at the meetings of the

Security to be given if required.

City not to be considered a stockholder.

company be claimed or exercised by reason of said shares, so long as the same shall be held as security as aforesaid.

Additional lien.

SEC. 7. From and after the issue and delivery to the directors of any portion of the scrip issued under this act, the city shall have, in addition to the lien which it now has by virtue of the act passed as aforesaid August first, one thousand eight hundred and forty-eight, a further lien upon said railroad, and upon all the property and franchise of the company, to secure the performance of the conditions of all the bonds, executed and delivered under the provisions of this act, which lien may be enforced in the manner hereinafter provided.

Sinking fund.

SEC. 8. For the purpose of providing for the reimbursement of the principal of the scrip, authorized to be issued by this act, a sinking fund shall be established, and shall be under the management of commissioners. The same persons who shall from time to time, be the commissioners of the sinking fund created under the act aforesaid, passed August first, one thousand eight hundred and forty-eight, shall be the commissioners of the sinking fund, created under this act. They shall severally be sworn to the faithful discharge of the duties enjoined upon them by this act, before the delivery of any portion of the scrip hereby authorized, which oath shall be taken in presence of the city clerk, who shall make record thereof, as in the case of the qualification of city officers.

Sinking fund, how raised.

SEC. 9. Whenever the directors shall receive any portion of the scrip, authorized as aforesaid to be delivered to them, they shall pay to the city treasurer two per cent. of the amount of the scrip so delivered, which amount shall be by the city treasurer placed to the credit of the commissioners of the sinking fund, and shall constitute a part of the fund established by this act. The directors shall also annually, in the month of April, pay to the city treasurer, from the income of the road, one per cent. of the whole amount of scrip which shall have been before that time issued and delivered under this act, and which shall be then outstanding; but after the expiration of five years from the time of the delivery and receipt of the first portion of scrip as aforesaid, the said annual payments from the income of the road shall be increased to one and a half per cent. of the amount of the scrip so issued and then outstanding as aforesaid, and the said annual payment of one per cent. for five years, and one and a half per cent annually thereafter, shall be successively placed to the credit of the commissioners of the sinking fund, and shall constitute a part of said fund established by this act.

Sinking fund, how managed.

SEC. 10. The commissioners shall have the care and management of all the moneys and securities at any time belonging to said fund; but the moneys uninvested, and the securities, shall be in the custody of the city treasurer, who shall be, by virtue of his office, treasurer of the sinking fund established by this act, and shall be responsible in his official bond to the city, for the safe keeping of the moneys and securities of the fund. He shall pay out and deliver any of said moneys and securities only upon the warrant of the commissioners.

Investment of sinking fund.

SEC. 11. The commissioners shall, from time to time, at their discretion, invest the moneys on hand, securely, so that they shall be productive, and the same may be loaned on mortgage of real estate, or to any county, or upon pledge of the securities of any county in this State, or invested in the stock of this State, or of the United States. And any portion of the fund may be invested in the scrip authorized by this act, or by the aforesaid act of August first, one thousand eight hundred and forty-eight, and such scrip shall not thereby be extinguished, but shall be held by the commissioners, like their other investments, for the purposes of the fund. An amount not exceeding twelve per cent. of the fund may be loaned on pledge of the stock of any bank, or of any stock insurance company in this State, and the commissioners may, from time to time, sell and transfer any of said securities.

Sinking fund to be reserved for a specific purpose.

SEC. 12. The sinking fund aforesaid, and all the sums which shall be added thereto by accumulation upon the investments thereof, shall be reserved and kept inviolate for the redemption and reimbusement of the principal of the scrip authorized by this act at the maturity thereof, and shall be applied thereto by the commissioners.

Shares in the stock may be exchanged for scrip.

SEC. 13. Any of the shares in the stock of the company, held by the city for security, as provided in the sixth section of this act, may be sold and transferred by the commissioners of the sinking fund, with the consent of the directors of the company, whenever an exchange thereof can be advantageously made for any of the scrip authorized by this act, or whenever the said scrip can be advantageously purchased with the proceeds of any such s ale of such collateral shares. And the scrip so purchased and taken in exchange, shall be thereupon cancelled and extinguished, and the amount thereof shall be endorsed on the respecttive bonds of the company given on the issue and delivery of such scrip. But no part of the sinking fund established by this act, or of its accumulations, shall be applied at any time or in any manner to the redemption and extinguishment of the scrip, before the maturity thereof.

Commissioners authorized to sell stock in certain cases.

SEC. 14. If the directors of the company shall at any time fail to pay to the city treasurer for the sinking fund created by this act, the amount aforesaid of one per cent. or of one and a half per cent. required to be paid into the sinking fund, out of the income of the road, the commissioners are authorized, at their discretion, upon such notice to the company as they shall deem suitable, to sell so many of the shares held by the city for security, as may be necessary to supply the amount of such deficiency, and the proceeds of such sale shall thereupon be paid into the sinking fund, and shall become a part thereof. All such conveyances and transfers of shares, which may be sold as aforesaid, shall be made by the city treasurer, under the direction of the commissioners.

Record, how kept.

SEC. 15. The commissioners shall keep a true record of all their proceedings, and an account of all the sums paid into the fund, and of the investments of the same, and shall, annually in the month of July, report to the mayor and aldermen of the city, and to the directors of the railroad company, their proceedings for the year, the amount and condition of the fund, and the income of the several parts thereof. Their records, and the accounts of the fund, and the securities belonging thereto shall at all times be open to the inspection of any committee appointed for that purpose by the mayor and aldermen, or by the directors of the company.

Matters of complaint between the city and commissioners, how adjusted.

SEC. 16. To secure the faithful discharge of the several trusts confided to the said commissioners under this act, the supreme judicial court is hereby empowered, upon the complaint of the mayor and aldermen of the city, or of the directors of the railroad company, against the said commissioners or either of them, concerning any of their said trusts and duties, by summary process, according to the course of proceedings in equity, to hear and adjudge upon the matters of such complaint, and to issue thereon, any suitable writ or process, and make any lawful decree to compel the proper discharge and performance of such duties and trusts, and to remove the said commissioners or either of them.

Excess of sinking fund, how applied.

SEC. 17. If the said sinking fund with its accumulations shall at any time exceed the amount of the scrip unredeemed and outstanding, issued under this act, all such excess shall be annually paid over to the railroad company; and if any surplus of the fund shall remain after the redemption and reimbursement of all the said scrip, such surplus shall be paid over to the company. And the mayor and aldermen may from time to time, cause to be reconveyed to the railroad company, such parts of the stock transferred to the city under this act, or the act aforesaid, passed August first, one thousand eight hundred and forty-eight, as they may deem not to be required for the securities herein provided. Upon the final completion of all the duties enjoined upon the commissioners under this act, their records and accounts shall be deposited with the railroad company.

Lien to be secured by mortgage.

SEC. 18. For the purpose of securing and enforcing the lien granted to the city by the seventh section of this act, and by the ninth section of the act aforesaid, passed August first, one thousand eight hundred and forty-eight, the directors of the company are hereby authorized, and it shall be their duty whenever thereby directed by the mayor and aldermen, to execute and deliver to the city of Portland a mortgage of said railroad and of all its property real and personal, and of the franchise of the company. Such mortgage shall be signed by the president of the company in his official capacity, and shall be executed according to the laws of the several States through which the railroad shall pass, and shall be of due and legal form, and shall contain apt and sufficient terms for the security of the city against any liabilities then existing, or which may thereafter be incurred in pursuance of this act, and of the act aforesaid, passed August first, one thousand eight hundred and forty-eight. The record of such mortgage in the registry of deeds for Cumberland county shall be a sufficient registry thereof to all intents and purposes, within this State. If any portion of the railroad shall not have been completed at the time of the execution of such mortgage, the directors shall be held whenever thereto requested, as aforesaid, to execute and deliver other like mortgages of any other portion of the road and property, as may be from time to time required, and such further mortgage shall be subject to like provisions, and shall have like operation as is hereinbefore prescribed.

Mortgage, how executed, &c.

SEC. 19. If the directors of the company shall neglect or refuse to execute and deliver any such mortgage, after request as aforesaid, the mayor and aldermen may cause a suit in equity to be instituted in the name of the city to compel the due execution and delivery thereof. The supreme judicial court for the county of Cumberland, shall have jurisdiction of such suit, and shall hear and determine the same, by summary process, in their discretion, and shall make such decree therein as may be suitable to effect the purposes herein required. Neglect of duty, &c.

SEC. 20. For the purpose of foreclosing any such mortgage upon the property and franchise of the company within this State, it shall be sufficient for the mayor and aldermen to give notice according to the mode prescribed in the fifth section of the one hundred and twenty-fifth chapter of the revised statutes, which notice may be published in a newspaper printed in the city of Portland, and record thereof may be made within thirty days after the date of the last publication, in the registry of deeds for the county of Cumberland, which publication and record shall be sufficient for the purposes of such foreclosure. Upon the expiration of three years from and after such publication, if the conditions of such mortgage shall not within that time have been performed, the foreclosure shall be complete, and shall be sufficient to make the title to all the property and franchise aforesaid, absolute in the city of Portland. And any transfer of any of the personal property of the company, made after publication of such notice to foreclose, without the consent of the mayor and aldermen, shall be wholly void; but lawful transfers and changes of any of the personal property of the company, not including the franchise, and the rails actually laid, and the right of way, may be made notwithstanding such mortgage, before publication of notice to foreclose as aforesaid; and all personal property acquired by the company, by purchase, exchange or otherwise, after the execution and Foreclosure of mortgage.

delivery of any such mortgage, shall be covered and held thereby.

City of Portland to take possession of the road in case the company omit to pay the interest.

SEC. 21. If the directors of the company shall at any time neglect or omit to pay the interest which may become due upon any portion of the scrip issued and delivered under the provisions of this act, or of the act aforesaid, passed August first, one thousand eight hundred and forty-eight, or to make the annual payments thereby required for the sinking fund, the city of Portland may take actual possession in the manner hereinafter provided, of the railroad, of all the property real and personal of the company and of the franchise thereof, and may hold the same and apply the income thereof to make up and supply such deficiencies of interest and amounts payable for the sinking fund and all further deficiencies that may occur, while the same are so held, until such deficiencies shall be fully made up and discharged. A written notice signed by the mayor and aldermen, or by a majority of their number, and served upon the president or treasurer, or any director of the company, or if there are none such, upon any stockholder in the company, stating that the city thereby takes actual possession of the railroad, and of the property and franchise of the company, shall be a sufficient actual possession thereof, and shall be a sufficient legal transfer of all the same for the purposes aforesaid to the city, and shall enable the city to hold the same against any other transfers thereof, and against any other claims thereon, until such purposes have been fully accomplished. Such possession shall not be considered as an entry for foreclosure, under any mortgage hereinbefore provided, nor shall the rights of the city or of the company under such mortgage be in any manner affected thereby.

Notice, how given.

All money accruing from the road after said notice to belong to the city.

SEC. 22. All moneys received by or for the railroad company, after notice as aforesaid, from any source whatever, and by whomsoever the same may be received, shall belong to and be held for the use and benefit of the city, in the manner, and for the purposes herein provided, and shall, after notice given to persons receiving the same respectively, be by them paid to the city treasurer, which payment shall be an effectual discharge from all claims of the company therefor; but if any person, without such notice, shall make payment of moneys so received to the treasurer of the company, such payment shall be a discharge of all claims of the city therefor. All moneys received by the treasurer of the company, after such notice, or in his hands at the time such notice may be given, shall be by him paid to the city treasurer, after deducting the amount expended, or actually due for the running expenses of the road, for the salaries of the officers of the company, and for repairs necessary for conducting the ordinary operations of the road. Such payments to the city treasurer shall be made at the end of every calendar month, and shall be by him applied to the payment of the interest due as aforesaid, and placed to the credit of the commissioners of the sinking fund, in the amounts required by the provisions of this act, and the act aforesaid, passed August first, one thousand eight hundred and forty-eight. And any person who shall pay or apply any moneys received as aforesaid in any manner contrary to the foregoing provisions, shall be personally liable therefor, and the same may be recovered in an action for money had and received, in the name of the city treasurer, whose duty it shall be to sue for the same, to be by him held and applied as is herein required.

Penalty, &c.

SEC. 23. For the purpose of effecting the objects prescribed in the two preceding sections, the mayor and aldermen may cause a suit in equity to be instituted in the name of the city, in the supreme judicial court in the county of Cumberland, against the railroad company, its directors, and any other person, as may be necessary for the purpose of discovery, injunction, account or other relief under the provisions of this act. And any judge

A writ of injunction may be issued.

of the court may issue a writ of injunction or any other suitable process on any such bill, in vacation or in term time, with or without notice, and the court shall have jurisdiction of the subject matter of such bill, and shall have such proceedings and make such orders and decrees, as may be within the powers and according to the course of proceedings of courts of equity, and as the necessities of the case may require.

Directors to be appointed by the city of Portland in case the company neglect or refuse.

SEC. 24. If the railroad company shall, after notice of possession as aforesaid, neglect to choose directors thereof, or any other necessary officers, or none such shall be found, the mayor and aldermen of the city shall appoint a board of directors, consisting of not less than seven persons, or any other necessary officers, and the persons so appointed shall have all the power and authority of officers chosen or appointed under the provisions of the act establishing said company, and upon their acceptance of such offices, shall be subject to all the duties and liabilities thereof.

Act, when to take effect.

SEC. 25. This act shall take effect from and after its approval by the governor, so far as to empower the directors of the railroad company, and the inhabitants of the city to act upon the question of accepting the same. The several ward meetings of the inhabitants for that purpose, shall be called and holden within thirty days after such approval. And if the act shall be accepted as aforesaid, then, after such acceptance, and record thereof, all the parts of the act shall take effect and be in full force.[1]

[1] Accepted August 22, 1850. See city records, vol. 5, page 352.

AN ACT

TO AUTHORIZE THE CITY OF PORTLAND TO GRANT FURTHER AID IN THE CONSTRUCTION OF THE ATLANTIC AND ST. LAWRENCE RAILROAD.

[Statutes 1852, Chapter 475.]

Be it enacted by the Senate and House of Representatives, in Legislature assembled, as follows:

SEC. 1. The city of Portland is hereby authorized to make a further loan of its credit to the Atlantic and St. Lawrence Railroad Company, for the purpose of aiding the final completion and equipment of the railroad of said company, subject to the following terms and conditions.

Loan authorized.

SEC. 2. This act shall not take effect, unless it shall be accepted by the directors of said railroad company, and by the vote of the inhabitants of said city, voting in ward meetings duly called according to law; and at least two-thirds of the whole number of votes cast at such ward meetings shall be necessary for the acceptance of the act. The returns of such ward meetings shall be made to the aldermen of the city, and they shall count and declare the votes returned, and the city clerk shall make record thereof.

Act not to take effect unless accepted by company and city of Portland.

Return of votes how made.

SEC. 3. Upon the acceptance of the act as aforesaid, the city treasurer shall make and issue for the purposes contemplated in this act, the scrip of said city, in convenient and suitable sums, payable to the holder thereof, on a term of time not less than twenty nor more than thirty years, with coupons for interest attached, payable semi-annually or yearly. The whole amount of said scrip shall

City scrip, how issued and amount.

not exceed the sum of five hundred thousand dollars, and the same shall be delivered by the city treasurer to the directors of the railroad company, subject to the several provisions of this act. The proceeds of the same shall be applied by the directors of the company, exclusively to the construction and necessary equipment of the Atlantic and St. Lawrence Railroad.

How applied.

To be secured by penal bond.

SEC. 4. Upon the delivery of the scrip aforesaid, the directors of the railroad company shall execute and deliver to the city treasurer, for the city, the bond of the company in a suitable penal sum, conditioned that the company will duly pay the interest and the principal of said scrip, and will hold the city harmless and free from all expenditure, damage or loss, on account of the issue and delivery of the same.

Mortgage bonds issued and secured by deed of trust and mortgage of road.

SEC. 5. As a further security for the issue and delivery of said scrip, the directors of the company shall also deliver to the city treasurer the mortgage bonds of said company issued and bearing date on the first day of April, eighteen hundred and fifty-one, and secured by a deed of trust and mortgage of said railroad and the franchise and property of the company, of the same date, heretofore executed and delivered by said company, to trustees for the benefit of the holders of the mortgage bonds aforesaid. The amount of said mortgage bonds, so delivered to the city treasurer, shall be equal to the amount of the scrip issued and delivered under this act, and the same shall be held by the city treasurer for the time being, as collateral security to the obligation and bond given by the company as aforesaid, to hold and save the city harmless on account of the issue and delivery of said scrip. Upon the payment by the company of the interest which shall from time to time accrue upon the said scrip, the city treasurer shall cancel and surrender to the company an amount of the interest warrants attached to said mortgage bonds, equal to, and corresponding as nearly as

Amount of bonds equal to the amount of scrip.

Interest warrants canceled on payment of interest.

may be in date, to the amount of interest so paid on said scrip.

Trustees authorized, on non-payment of scrip, to convey title to city of Portland.

SEC. 6. At the maturity of the mortgage bonds herein provided to be delivered as collateral security, and after the payment of all the other mortgage bonds issued under said deed of trust and mortgage, if any portion of the scrip hereby authorized to be issued shall be unredeemed and outstanding, the trustees for the time being under said deed of trust and mortgage shall be authorized to release, assign and convey to the city of Portland, all the title and interest, which they may then have in the estate, property and franchise of the company by virtue of said deed, and of any other conveyances made in pursuance of the covenants therein contained, which conveyance shall be a discharge of said trustees from all the trusts created and declared in said deed, and the city shall, by such conveyance, take and hold the said estate, property and franchise, as in mortgage, for the security and indemnity of the city, on account of the issue and delivery of its scrip as herein authorized, until the final redemption and reimbursement of said scrip, and the interest accruing thereon.

City to hold the property conveyed as security.

Act when to take effect.

SEC. 7. This act shall take effect and be in force from and after its approval by the governor, so far as to authorize the directors of the company, and the inhabitants of the city, to act upon the question of accepting the same. The several ward meetings of the inhabitants for that purpose shall be holden within three months after such approval. And if the act shall be accepted as aforesaid, then after such acceptance and record thereof, all the parts of the act shall take effect and be in force.[1]

[1] Accepted February 24, 1852. See city records, vol. 6, page 64.

AN ACT

TO AUTHORIZE THE CITY OF PORTLAND TO GRANT FURTHER AID IN THE CONSTRUCTION OF THE ATLANTIC AND ST. LAWRENCE RAILROAD.

[Statutes 1853, Chapter 4.]

Be it enacted by the Senate and House of Representatives in Legislature assembled, as follows:

Loan authorized.

SEC. 1. The city of Portland is hereby authorized to make a further loan of its credit to the Atlantic and St. Lawrence Railroad Company, in aid of the construction and furnishing of their railroad, subject to the following terms and conditions.

Acceptance of act, conditions of, &c.

SEC. 2. This act shall not take effect, unless it shall be accepted by the directors of said railroad company, and by the vote of the inhabitants of said city, voting in ward meetings duly called according to law; and at least two-thirds of the whole number of votes cast at such ward meetings shall be necessary for the acceptance of the act. The returns of such ward meetings shall be made to the aldermen of the city, and they shall count and declare the votes returned, and the city clerk shall make record thereof.

Returns of ward meetings, how made.

Acceptance of act, loan how made, &c.

SEC. 3. Upon the acceptance of the act as aforesaid, the city treasurer is authorized to make and issue, on demand made by the said directors, for the purposes contemplated in this act, the scrip of said city in convenient and suitable sums, payable to the holder thereof, on a term of time not less than twenty nor more than thirty years, with coupons, for interest, attached.

SEC. 4. The whole amount of the scrip to be issued and delivered under this act, shall not exceed three hundred and fifty thousand dollars, and the same shall be delivered by the city treasurer to the directors of the railroad company as they may require the same. The proceeds of such scrip shall be applied by the directors of the company exclusively to the construction and necessary furniture and equipment of the Atlantic and St. Lawrence Railroad.

Scrip or loan, amount authorized.

Scrip, proceeds of, how applied.

SEC. 5. Upon the issue and delivery of the scrip aforesaid, the directors of the railroad company shall cause a mortgage to be executed and delivered to the city, in the name of the company, conveying to the city, subject to any mortgages existing before the passage of this act, all the estate, property and franchise of the company, conditioned that the company will duly pay the interest accruing from time to time on the scrip issued under this act, and will pay the principal of the same at the maturity thereof. Such mortgage shall be executed according to the laws of the several States through which the railroad shall pass. The record thereof in the registry of deeds in Cumberland county, shall be a sufficient registry of the same to all intents and purposes within this State.

Road mortgaged to secure payment of scrip.

Mortgage, how executed and recorded.

SEC. 6. Upon failure to perform any of the conditions of said mortgage, the city shall be authorized to take possession of the estate, property and franchise thereby conveyed, and the proceedings under such possession, and all proceedings for the foreclosure of said mortgage, and the rights, liabilities and remedies of the parties, under such possession and entry for foreclosure, shall be governed, regulated, limited and controlled in the manner that is provided in the twentieth, twenty-first, twenty-second, twenty-third and twenty-fourth sections of an act passed on the twenty-seventh day of July, eighteen hundred and fifty, entitled "An Act to authorize the city of Portland to grant further aid in the construction of the Atlantic

Mortgage, failure to perform conditions of, &c.

and St. Lawrence Railroad," in respect to the mortgage therein mentioned.

Act when to take effect.

SEC. 7. This act shall take effect from and after its approval by the governor, so far as to empower the directors of the company, and the inhabitants of the city, to act upon the question of accepting the same. The several ward meetings of the inhabitants for that purpose, shall be called and holden within thirty days after such approval. And if the act shall be accepted as aforesaid, then, after such acceptance, and record thereof, all the parts of the act shall take effect and be in force.[1]

[1] Accepted February 24, 1853. See city record, vol. 6, Page 244.

AN ACT

RESPECTING CONVEYANCES TAKEN BY THE COMMISSIONERS OF THE SINKING FUNDS OF THE ATLANTIC AND ST. LAWRENCE RAILROAD.

[Statutes 1853, chapter 14.]

Be it enacted by the Senate and House of Representatives in Legislature assembled, as follows:

Conveyances in cases of vacancy, to vest in remaining commissioner, &c.

SEC. 1. If the commissioners of the sinking funds created under the several acts authorizing the city of Portland to aid the construction of the Atlantic and St. Lawrence Railroad, passed respectively, August first, eighteen hundred and forty-eight, and July twenty-seventh, eighteen hundred and fifty, shall at any time have or take any conveyance to themselves in their capacity as commissioners of said funds, their successors and assigns, for the purpose of securing any of the investments of said funds, all the title and estate of said commissioners under such conveyance, shall, in case of a vacancy in the place of either of them, vest in the remaining commissioner, and shall pass to and be upheld in their successors, as the same shall be lawfully appointed from time to time, and such survivor and successors shall take and hold the said title and estate, with all the powers necessary to effect the objects of the conveyance.

Commissioners, right of succession, &c.

SEC. 2. This act shall take effect from and after its approval by the governor.

[See city ordinance, *ante*, on FINANCE, sections 8 and 9, relating to the surrender of the certificates of the city debt by the Atlantic and St. Lawrence Railroad Company.]

AN ACT

TO INCORPORATE THE PORTLAND GAS LIGHT COMPANY.

[Statutes 1849, Chapter 288.]

Be it enacted by the Senate and House of Representatives in Legislature assembled, as follows:

Corporators.

SEC. 1. Charles Q. Clapp, A. W. H. Clapp, John Neal, Abner Lowell, Francis O. J. Smith, Horace V. Bartol, and Henry B. McCobb, their associates and successors, are hereby constituted a body politic and corporate by the name of the Portland Gas Light Company, and by that name shall have and enjoy all the necessary powers and privileges to effect the objects of their association, and shall be subject to such duties, liabilities and exemptions as are or may be provided by the general laws of this State in case of manufacturing corporations.

Corporate name.

Powers and duties.

Capital stock.

SEC. 2. The capital stock of said company shall be not less than thirty thousand dollars nor more than one hundred thousand dollars, and shall be divided into shares of one hundred dollars each. The said capital stock shall be applied exclusively to the manufacture and distribution of gas for the purpose of lighting the city of Portland; *provided*, that said company shall not have power to erect, establish or continue any works for the manufacture of gas at any place within the limits of said city of Portland, without the previous assent of the city council, and a specific assignment of the boundaries of such establishment, and such erection, establishment or continuance without such previous consent, shall be con-

How applied.

Proviso.

sidered a nuisance, and said company shall be liable to indictment therefor, and to all the provisions of law applicable thereto. And nothing contained in this act shall be construed to affect or diminish the liabilities of said company for any injury to private property, by depreciating the value thereof, or otherwise, but said company shall be liable therefor in an action on the case.

Liability for injury to private property.

Regulations for laying down pipes, fixtures, &c.

SEC. 3. The said company are hereby authorised to lay down in and through the streets of said city, and to take up, replace, and repair all such pipes and fixtures as may be necessary for the objects of their incorporation, first having obtained the consent of the city council therefor, and under such restrictions and regulations as said city council may see fit to prescribe. And any obstruction in any street of said city, or taking up or displacement of any portion of any street, without such consent of the city council, or contrary to the restrictions or regulations that may be prescribed as aforesaid, shall be considered a nuisance. And said company shall be liable to indictment therefor and to all the provisions of law applicable thereto. And said company shall in all cases be liable to repay to said city all sums of money that said city may be obliged to pay on any judgment recovered against said city, for damages occasioned by any obstructions, or taking up or displacement of any street by said company whatever, with or without the consent of the city council, together with counsel fees and other expenses incurred by said city in defending any suit to recover damages as aforesaid, with interest on the same, to be recovered in an action for money paid to the use of said company.

Liability to city for damages.

Obstruction to public travel in laying down, erecting or repairing works.

SEC. 4. Whenever the company shall lay down any pipes, or erect any fixtures in any street, or make any alterations or repairs upon their works in any street, they shall cause the same to be done with as little obstruction to the public travel as may be practicable. And shall at their own expense without unnecessary delay cause the earth and pavements removed by them, to be replaced in proper condition. They shall not be allowed in any case to obstruct or impair the use of any public or private drain, or common sewer or reservoir, but said company shall have the right to cross, or where necessary to change the direction of any private drain, in such manner as not to obstruct or impair the use thereof, being liable for any injury occasioned by any such crossing or alteration to the owner thereof, or any other person, in an action upon the case.

Not to obstruct or impair the use of any drain, &c.

City council authorized to contract for lighting the streets and public buildings.

SEC. 5. The city council of the city of Portland, are hereby authorized to contract with said company for lighting the streets and public buildings of said city, and the moneys necessary to be expended therefor, shall be assessed and collected in the same manner as taxes for other purposes.

Exclusive privileges granted under certain conditions.

SEC. 6. If the said company shall be duly organized within two years from the passage of this act, and shall within that time, have raised and expended at least ten thousand dollars for the objects of their incorporation, and shall have actually commenced the lighting of the city with gas, they shall then have and enjoy the franchise and privileges granted them by this act, exclusively, for the term of thirty years from the date of their organization, subject to the terms and limitations hereinafter prescribed, and subject to all such regulations and control as may, by law, be exercised over corporations by the judicial tribunals of this State; *provided*, and this grant is upon the condition, that said company should at all times, and within a reasonable time after request by the city council of Portland, supply with gas, to such an extent and in such a manner as may be required, any street, or public buildings, at a fair and reasonable rate of payment therefor; and in case said parties cannot agree upon the rate of payment, said company shall be obliged to furnish said gas at a rate to be fixed by three disinterested

Proviso.

persons, to be selected one by each of said parties, and a third by the two thus selected, who shall be paid for their services by said parties equally, and if said company shall at any time refuse, or unreasonably neglect to comply with this condition, the exclusive privilege herein granted shall be of no effect.

Directors.

SEC. 7. The management of the affairs of the company, and all expenditures made for the purposes authorized by this act, shall be directed by a board of directors, to be chosen annually, of such number as may be prescribed by the by-laws of the company. The accounts of the company shall be kept by a treasurer, who shall be chosen by the directors. The directors shall severally be sworn before the clerk of the corporation to make true and faithful exhibits in their records, of all expenditures directed or allowed by them for the purposes authorized by this act. The treasurer shall in like manner be sworn to make and keep true and distinct accounts of all expenditures authorized by the directors, and paid by him from the funds of the company.

Treasurer.

City of Portland authorized to take and hold stock in said company.

SEC. 8. At any time after the organization of the company, the city of Portland shall be authorized, upon a vote of the city council to that effect, to take and hold in the capital stock of the company, an amount not exceeding one-half thereof, upon paying to the company a like proportional part of the cost, up to such time, of all their buildings, works, fixtures, pipes, and other property, and ten per cent. of such proportional part in addition thereto. The amount so received by the company for the proportional part so taken by the city shall be distributed and paid over to the other stockholders, in proportion to their several interests, and the par value of the several shares held by them shall be reduced accordingly. The company shall, at the same time, create and issue to the city such a number of shares of the same par value, together with a fractional share, if necessary, as shall

Amount received for such stock to be paid over to other stockholders.

Value of the shares reduced accordingly.

Shares created and issued to city.

represent the whole amount paid by the city for the proportional part of the capital stock so taken. At all meetings of the stockholders of the company, the shares held by the city shall be represented by such agent as the city council may by vote, from time to time appoint, who shall be entitled to cast one vote for every share held by the city. And if said company shall neglect to comply with the provisions of this section for the space of one month after an offer and request from the mayor to that effect, all the rights and privileges of said company shall wholly cease and be of no effect.

How represented.

Rights and privileges void if company neglect to comply within one month.

SEC. 9. At the expiration of the term of thirty years named in the seventh section of this act, the city of Portland shall be authorized, upon the vote of the city council to that effect, to pay to said company the appraised value of their said buildings, works, pipes, fixtures, and other property, and upon such payment, may take and hold all said property, without any right, privilege or franchise remaining to said company, and may dispose of said property in such manner as the city council shall determine. For the purpose of making the valuation aforesaid, the city council shall, within three months before the expiration of the thirty years aforesaid, give notice to the company and appoint two disinterested persons, and the company shall appoint two other disinterested persons, to be appraisers, and the four persons so appointed, shall appoint a fifth disinterested person to be one of the appraisers. If the company shall neglect or omit, for two months after the notice aforesaid, to appoint appraisers on its part, then the two appraisers appointed by the city council shall be authorized to make the apprisal, and the decision of the appraisers in either case, shall be final. And if said company shall neglect or refuse for the space of one month after an apprisal shall have been made in pursuance of the provisions of this section, and after said city shall have notified said company of its readiness to take

Authority of city to take the property of said company at its appraised value after thirty years.

Appraisers, how appointed.

Provision in case said company should neglect or refuse to deliver its aforesaid property to city.

said property at such apprisal, to deliver all its aforesaid property to said city, and to execute good and sufficient conveyances thereof, then said city may take possession of said property and hold the same as is hereinbefore provided, being responsible to said company to pay the appraised value aforesaid, and no sale of said property, at any time by said company, in derogation of the rights of said city herein specified, shall be valid, and the rights and privileges of said company as a corporation shall wholly cease from and after their refusal as aforesaid.

Exclusive privileges continued to said company for twelve years, in case said city should not take the property.

SEC. 10. If the city of Portland shall not so pay for and take the property of the company, at the apprisal so made, then the franchise and privileges hereby granted to said company, shall be continued to them and shall be held and enjoyed by them exclusively, for a further term of twelve years after the expiration of the thirty years aforesaid, subject to the limitation prescribed in the ninth section of this act.

Liability of company for wilfully or negligently leaving obstructions in any street.

—or for neglecting to repair any street, &c.

Fine, how collected and applied.

Liable for personal injury by reason of said negligence, &c.

SEC. 11. If the said company or any of their servants or officers employed in effecting the objects of the company, shall wilfully or negligently place or leave any obstructions in any of the streets of Portland, beyond what is actually necessary in laying down, taking up and repairing their fixtures, or shall wilfully or negligently omit to repair and put in proper condition any street, in which the earth or pavements may have been removed by them, the company shall be subject to indictment therefor, in the same manner that towns are subject to indictment for bad roads, and shall be holden to pay such fine as may be imposed therefor, which fine shall be collected, applied and expended in the same manner as is provided in case of the indictments aforesaid against towns, or may be ordered to be paid into the treasury of the city. If any person shall suffer injury in his person or property by reason of any such negligence, wilfulness or omission, he shall be entitled to recover damages of the company therefor, by an action on the case, in any court of competent jurisdiction.

Rights of mayor and aldermen in certain cases.

SEC. 12. The mayor and aldermen for the time being, shall at all times have the power to regulate, restrict and control the acts and doings of said corporation, which may in any manner affect the health, safety or convenience of the inhabitants of said city.

SEC. 13. This act shall be taken and deemed to be a public act, and shall be in force from and after its approval by the governor.

[Approved, August 14, 1849.]

AN ACT

TO INCREASE THE CAPITAL STOCK OF THE PORTLAND GAS LIGHT COMPANY.

[Statutes 1854, Chapter 203.]

Be it enacted by the Senate and House of Representatives in Legislature assembled, as follows :

Capital stock, increase of.

SEC. 1. The Portland Gas Light Company is hereby authorized to increase its capital stock to the extent of one hundred thousand dollars, so that the whole capital stock of said company shall be two hundred thousand dollars, instead of the amount now established. The said additional capital shall be divided into shares of fifty dollars each, which shall be the established par value of the same.

Shares.

—how disposed of.

SEC. 2. Whenever the directors of the company shall vote to issue any part of such additional shares, the same shall be first offered to and may be taken by the existing shareholders, in proportion to their several amounts of stock. The balance of any such issue not taken by existing shareholders, may be sold and disposed of by the directors, in such manner as they may deem most for the interest of the company. The said additional capital and shares shall be issued subject to the rights of the city of Portland, as herein provided.

Rights of city of Portland.

Same subject.

SEC. 3. If the city of Portland shall not, at the time of any issue of such capital stock, take its proportional number of shares thereof, the city council may at any time thereafter, by vote, determine to take for the city, so many of the additional shares aforesaid, as may be required to constitute the city the owner of one-half of all the said additional capital stock of the company.

Shares to be numbered.

SEC. 4. For the purpose of effecting the object provided by the last preceding section, the directors of the company, whenever they shall issue any of the additional stock aforesaid, shall cause the shares thereof to be numbered consecutively, and the numbers of all the shares so issued to be expressed in the several certificates representing the same, and in the several shareholders' accounts on the stock books of the company. The certificates of such additional stock shall also express that the shares therein represented are issued and held subject to the provisions of this act.

Stock issued subject to the provisions of this act.

City council authorized to take a certain number of shares.

SEC. 5. Whenever the city council shall determine by vote as aforesaid, to take additional shares, as provided in the third section of this act, the city shall be entitled to take and become the owner of all the new shares issued as aforesaid, which are numbered by the even numbers, and shall thereupon pay to the treasurer of the company, the sum of fifty-five dollars for every share so taken. The vote of the city council as aforesaid, shall be certified to the directors of the company, and they shall cause the same to be recorded in their record. The treasurer shall receive the amount so paid by the city, and shall hold the same, subject to be paid to the order or receipt of the several persons from whom the said shares shall be so taken. He shall issue to the city, certificates of the shares so taken and paid for by the city, and shall adjust the stock accounts of the several shareholders from whom the same are so taken accordingly, and issue to them, if required, new certificates representing the balance of their shares.

Amount per share.

Vote of city council to be certified to directors of company, &c.

Treasurer authorized to receive and pay over purchase money.

—shall issue certificates of shares.

SEC. 6. This act shall take effect from and after its approval by the governor.

[Approved, March 8, 1854.]

AN ACT

TO INCREASE THE CAPITAL STOCK OF THE PORTLAND GAS LIGHT COMPANY.

Be it enacted by the Senate and House of Representatives in Legislature assembled, as follows :

SEC. 1. The Portland Gas Light Company is hereby authorized to increase its capital stock, to the extent of two hundred thousand dollars, so that the whole capital stock of said company shall be four hundred thousand dollars, instead of the amount now established. The said additional capital stock shall be divided into shares of fifty dollars each, which shall be the established par value of the same.

Capital stock increased.

Shares, par value of.

SEC. 2. Whenever the directors of the company shall vote to issue any part of such additional shares, the same shall be first offered to, and may be taken by the existing shareholders, in proportions to their several amounts of stock. The balance of any such issue not taken by existing stockholders, after twenty days' notice given in one of the daily newspapers published in the city of Portland, to the stockholders, may be sold and disposed of by the directors, in such manner as they may deem most for the interest of the company. The said additional capital and shares shall be issued, subject to the rights of the city of Portland as herein provided.

Stock first offered to existing shareholders.

Balance how disposed of.

City of Portland, rights of.

SEC. 3. If the city of Portland, at the expiration of the twenty days' aforesaid, shall not have taken its proportional number of shares thereof, the city council may, at any time thereafter, by vote, determine to take for the

City council may make the city joint owner of stock.

city, so many of the additional shares aforesaid, as may be required to constitute the city the owner of one-half of all the said additional stock of the company.

Directors, duties of.

SEC. 4. For the purpose of effecting the object provided by the last preceding section, the directors of the company, whenever they shall issue any of the additional stock aforesaid, shall cause the shares thereof to be numbered consecutively, and the numbers of all the shares so issued, to be expressed in the several certificates representing the same, and in the several shareholders' accounts on the stock books of the company. The certificates of such additional stock shall also express that the shares therein represented are issued and held subject to the provisions of this act.

Ownership, conditions of.

SEC. 5. Whenever the city council shall determine, by vote as aforesaid, to take additional shares as provided in the third section of this act, the city shall be entitled to take and become the owner of all the new shares issued as aforesaid, which are numbered by the even numbers, and shall thereupon pay to the treasurer of the company, the sum of fifty-five dollars for every share so taken. The vote of the city council as aforesaid, shall be certified to the directors of the company, and they shall cause the same to be recorded in their record. The treasurer shall receive the amount so paid by the city, and shall hold the same, subject to be paid to the order or receipt of the several persons from whom the said shares shall be so taken. He shall issue to the city certificates of the shares so taken and paid for, and shall adjust the stock accounts of the several shareholders from whom the same are so taken accordingly, and issue to them, if required, new certificates representing the balance of their shares.

Shares, value of.

Treasurer, duties of.

[Approved February 5, 1856.]

AN ACT

TO INCORPORATE THE PORTLAND AND FOREST AVENUE RAILROAD COMPANY.

Be it enacted by the Senate and House of Representatives, in Legislature assembled, as follows:

SEC. 1. Eliphalet Clark, John B. Coyle, John W. Adams, Newell A. Foster and Warren Sparrow, their associates and successors, are hereby constituted a corporation by the name of the Portland and Forest Avenue Railroad Company, with authority to construct, maintain and use a railroad to be operated by horse power, with convenient single or double tracks, from such point or points in the city of Portland, upon and over such streets therein, as shall from time to time be fixed and determined by the municipal officers of said city of Portland, and assented to in writing by said corporation, to the boundary line between said city and the town of Westbrook, and thence upon and over such streets, town and county roads in said town of Westbrook as from time to time, may be fixed and determined by the municipal officers of said town, and assented to in writing by said corporation, to some point at or near the entrance to Evergreen Cemetery, and to such other point or points in said town of Westbrook, as may in like manner from time to time be fixed and determined by the municipal officers of said town, and assented to in writing by said corporation; said corporation shall also have authority to construct, maintain and use said railroad over and upon any lands where the land damages have been mutually settled by said corporation

Corporators.

Corporate name.

Construction.

Location, how determined.

Act, 1860, as amended by act, 1861.

Authorized to construct, when land damages have been settled, &c.

and the owners thereof; but said corporation shall make no erections within any of the tide waters of Back Cove without the written approval of the harbor commissioners; *provided, however*, that all tracks of said railroad shall be laid at such distances from the sidewalks of said city of Portland and town of Westbrook, as the municipal officers thereof, respectively, shall in their order fixing the routes of said railroad determine to be for public safety and convenience. The written assent of said corporation to any vote or votes of the municipal officers of either said city or town, prescribing from time to time the routes of said railroad, shall be filed with the respective clerks of said city or town, and shall be taken and deemed to be the locations thereof. Said corporation shall have power from time to time, to fix such rates of compensation for transporting persons or property, as it may think expedient, and generally shall have all the powers and be subject to all the liabilities of corporations, as set forth in the forty-sixth chapter of the revised statutes. Rails shall not be laid down in said city or town without the assent of the municipal officers thereof, respectively. The original location of the route when granted shall be for the term of twenty-five years. The same may be renewed from time to time for a term not exceeding fifty years at any one time, by said municipal officers, upon such terms as they may deem expedient. No such renewal shall be granted prior to two years before the expiration of the location then established. No location shall be granted or renewed, except upon reasonable prior notice to all parties interested. If at the expiration of any of said terms, the use of the streets, roads or highways, occupied by said company's railroad, is granted by the municipal officers of either said city or town, or both, to any other corporation or person, it shall be upon condition that such corporation or person shall purchase of said company all its property of every description in necessary use for the purposes of said railroad upon such terms as may be

Proviso.

Vote or votes of city or town, assent of corporation, shall be filed with clerks, &c.

Powers, &c.

Original location, term of.

— may be renewed.

— when to be renewed.

Notice.

If at expiration of terms, use of streets, &c., is granted any other corporation, &c.

— said corporation shall purchase, &c.

agreed upon by the parties, or determined by persons selected by them; and if they are unable to agree, the value of the same shall be determined by three disinterested persons, appointed by a judge of the supreme judicial court, on application of either party, and hearing thereon. Said appraisers shall be sworn, give notice of the time and place of their meeting to examine and appraise said property, and shall make to each party a written award; and their services shall be paid in equal proportions by the parties. If the municipal officers of either said city or town, or both, determine, that at the expiration of any of said terms, the use of the streets, roads or highways occupied by said company's railroad, shall be granted to any person or corporation, for the purposes of a horse railroad, on the payment of any sum of money, yearly or in any other manner, said company shall have the preference, and such use shall be granted or renewed to said company, provided it will pay as much therefor as any other corporation or person. Any similar corporation hereinafter incorporated which shall construct its road from Cape Elizabeth, or Westbrook, where the Portland and Forest Avenue Railroad Company have no track, may enter upon and connect with and use the track of the Portland and Forest Avenue Railroad Company for such rates of compensation as may be agreed upon, or in case of disagreement of the directors of the two companies, three disinterested persons shall be appointed by a judge of the supreme court, on application of either party, and a hearing thereon shall be had before said commission. Said commissioners shall be sworn, give notice of the time and place of their meeting to determine the matter in dispute, and shall make to each party a written final decision of the points submitted, and their services shall be paid in equal proportions by the parties.

— terms, how determined.

Appraisers, duties of.

— services of, how paid.

Connection of similar corporation.

Compensation, how determined.

As amended by Act, 1861.

SEC. 2. Said railroad shall be operated and used by said corporation with horse power only. The municipal

Railroad, how to be used.

City and town may make regulations, &c.

Act, 1860.

officers of said city of Portland, and of said town of Westbrook, respectively, shall have power at all times to make all such regulations, as to the rate of speed and removal of snow and ice from the streets, roads and highways by said company at its expense, and mode of use of the track of said railroad within said city or town, as the public convenience and safety require.

Corporation shall keep in repair, streets, &c.

Ib.

SEC. 3. Said corporation shall keep and maintain in repair, such portion of the streets, town or county roads, as shall be occupied by the tracks of its railroad, and shall make all other repairs of said streets or roads, which, in the opinion of the municipal officers of said city or town respectively, may be rendered necessary by the occupation of the same by said railroad, and if not repaired upon reasonable notice, such repairs may be made by said city or town respectively, at the expense of said corporation. And said corporation shall be liable for any loss or damage which any person may sustain by reason of any carelessness, neglect or misconduct of its agents or servants.

— liability.

Obstructions in use of roads, &c.

Ib.

Penalty.

SEC. 4. If any person shall wilfully and maliciously obstruct said corporation in the use of its road or tracks, or the passing of the cars or carriages of said corporation thereon, such person and all who shall aid and abet therein, shall be punished by a fine not exceeding two hundred dollars, or may be imprisoned in the county jail for a period not exceeding sixty days.

Capital stock.

Ib. as amended by act, 1863.

Shares.

SEC. 5. The capital stock of said corporation shall not exceed one hundred thousand dollars, to be divided into shares of one hundred dollars each, and no share shall be issued for less than the par value.

May hold real and personal estate.

Act, 1860.

SEC. 6. Said corporation shall have power to purchase and hold such real estate as may be necessary and convenient for the purposes and management of said railroad.

SEC. 7. Said railroad shall be constructed and maintained in such form and manner, and with such rail, and upon such grade as the municipal officers of said city of Portland, and of said town of Westbrook, respectively, shall from time to time prescribe and direct; and whenever in the judgment of said corporation it shall be necessary to alter the grade of any street, town or county road, occupied by its railroad, said alterations may be made at the sole expense of said corporation; *provided*, the same shall be assented to by the municipal officers of said city and town respectively. If the tracks of said company's railroad cross any other railroad of any kind, in either said city or town, and a dispute arises in any way in regard to the manner of crossing, said municipal officers of the town or city in which said proposed crossing is to be made, shall, upon hearing, decide and determine in writing in what manner the crossing shall be made, which shall be constructed accordingly.

Railroad to be constructed, &c., under direction of city and town.

Ib.

— alterations in grade.

Proviso.

Crossings.

— manner of, how determined.

SEC. 8. Nothing in this act shall be construed to prevent the proper authorities of said city or town respectively from entering upon and taking up any of the streets, town or county roads occupied by said railroad, for any purpose for which they may now lawfully take up the same.

Streets or roads, in relation to.

Ib.

SEC. 9. This act shall be void unless the same shall be accepted by said corporation, and ten per cent. of the capital stock thereof, be paid within five years from its passage.

Act, acceptance of, &c.

Ib.

SEC. 10. Said corporation is hereby authorized to issue bonds for the purpose of constructing its railroad, or for money which it may borrow for any purpose sanctioned by law; but the bonds so issued shall not exceed the amount of capital stock paid in by the stockholders. Said bonds may be issued in sums not less than one hundred dollars each, payable in not more than twenty years from their date, with interest at the rate of six per cent., payable semi-annually.

Bonds, issue of, &c.

Ib.

— approval of, &c. Ib.

SEC. 11. Such bonds shall be approved by a majority of the finance committee of said corporation, who shall certify that each of said bonds is properly issued and recorded upon the books of the corporation. All bonds and notes which shall be issued by said corporation shall be binding and collectable in law, notwithstanding such bonds or notes may be negotiated and sold by said corporation or its agents at less than their par value.

— how secured. Ib.

SEC. 12. Said bonds shall be secured by a conveyance of the corporate property to three trustees, by a suitable instrument of mortgage to secure the payments of said bonds.

Sinking fund. Ib.

— trustees to have management of, &c.

SEC. 13. Said corporation shall pay semi-annually to said trustees, a sum equal to one per cent. on the amount of said bonds for the purpose of creating a sinking fund. Said trustees shall have the care and management of all the moneys, funds and securities belonging to said sinking fund, and they shall from time to time, at their discretion, invest the moneys on hand securely, and so that the same shall be productive ; and the same may be invested in the bonds of said corporation, secured as aforesaid, or loaned on interest to any county, city or town, or any bank in this State, or the same may be loaned on interest, well secured by a first mortgage of real estate to an amount not exceeding one-half the value thereof, or by pledge of the scrip or stock of any of the New England States, or of any city, county or town as aforesaid, and the said fund with the accruing interest shall constitute a sinking fund for the payment and redemption of said bonds.

Certain acts made applicable to bonds, &c. Ib.

SEC. 14. The provisions of the fifty-third section of the fifty-first chapter of the revised statutes, and of the nine sections of said chapter next following, are hereby made applicable to said bonds and to said mortgage made to secure the same, but said corporation shall not be subject to the other general provisions of law relating to railroads.

SEC. 15. This act shall take effect when approved by the governor.

[Approved March 19, 1860.]

AN ACT

ADDITIONAL TO AN ACT ENTITLED "AN ACT TO INCORPORATE THE PORTLAND AND FOREST AVENUE RAILROAD COMPANY."

[Approved, March nineteen, eighteen hundred and sixty.]

Be it enacted by the Senate and House of Representatives in Legislature assembled, as follows:

SEC. 1. The Portland and Forest Avenue Railroad Company is hereby authorized to extend its railroad over either or both of the bridges which connect the city of Portland with Cape Elizabeth, and to construct and maintain the same in said town, with all the rights and privileges, and subject to all the conditions specified in the act to which this is additional, upon condition that said corporation shall locate and build so much of said road as lies within the limits of the town of Cape Elizabeth, within two years after the passage of this act.

Railroad may be extended, &c.

Act, 1865.

Rights, privileges, &c.

Ib.

SEC. 2. Section one of said act is hereby amended so as to require the assent of the directors only, where that of the corporation is required.

Ib. as amended by Act, 1866.

SEC. 3. The capital stock of said corporation is hereby increased to the sum of three hundred thousand dollars.

Capital stock increased $300,000.

Ib. as amended by act, 1866.

SEC. 4. Said corporation is hereby authorized to operate its road in either or both of said towns of Westbrook and Cape Elizabeth, or in said city of Portland, with dummy engines, with the consent of the municipal officers thereof.

Dummy engines, use of, authorized, &c.

SEC. 5. The title of said corporation is hereby amended by striking out the words "and Forest Avenue."

Corporate name changed.

[Approved, February 24, 1865.]

CATALOGUE

OF THE

GOVERNMENT OF THE CITY OF PORTLAND,

IN CHRONOLOGICAL ORDER OF THEIR SERVICE,

FROM ITS

INSTITUTION, APRIL 1832, TO MARCH 1867.

CATALOGUE OF CITY GOVERNMENT,

FROM 1832 TO 1867.

VOTES FOR MAYOR AT THE SEVERAL ELECTIONS HELD FROM 1832 TO 1867.

1832—(1st trial.)

Emerson,	621
Richardson,	278
Clapp,	333
Churchill,	141
Total,	1374

(2d trial.)

Emerson,	737
Churchill,	699
Scattering,	7
Total,	1442

[Emerson resigned before the year expired, and Jonathan Dow was elected to fill the vacancy.]

1833.

Jonathan Dow,	709
Anderson,	783
Scattering,	10
Total,	1492

1834.

Cutter,	1232
Anderson,	835
Total,	2067

1835.

Cutter,	964
Harris,	558
Total,	1522

1836.

Cutter,	980
Clapp,	962
Total,	1942

1837.

Cutter,	940
Boody,	380
Scattering,	94
Total,	1414

1838.

Cutter,	1245
Mitchell,	985
Total,	2230

1839.

Cutter,	1044
Clapp,	686
Scattering,	12
Total,	1742

1840—(1st trial.)

Greely,	497
Cutter,	509
Southgate,	702
Scattering,	9
Total,	1717

(2d trial.)

Cutter,	776
Southgate,	700
Scattering,	105
Total,	1581

[No choice. Mr. Cutter was elected by city council.]

1841—(1st trial.)

Churchill,	710
Southgate,	680
Scattering,	137
Total,	1527

(2d trial.)

Churchill,	577
Cutter,	269
Southgate,	787
Scattering,	38
Total,	1671

[No choice. The city council elected Churchill.]

1842.

Churchill,	863
Anderson,	963
Scattering,	23
Total,	1849

1843—(1st trial.)

Greely,	691
Anderson,	904
Cutter,	311
Scattering,	12
Total,	1918

(2d trial.)

Greely,	547
Anderson,	745
Cutter,	240
Scattering,	36
Total,	1568

[There being no choice the city council elected Greely.]

1844—(1st trial.)

Greely,	771
Emery,	583
Appleton,	458
Scattering,	10
Total,	1822

(2d trial.)

Greely,	855
Greenough,	598
Scattering,	14
Total,	1467

1845—(1st trial.)

Greely,	817
Clapp,	666
Winslow,	316
Scattering,	19
Total,	1818

(2d trial.)

Greely,	950
Clapp,	636
Scattering,	6
Total,	1592

1846—(1st trial.)

Greely,	764
Holden,	515
Adams,	514
Scattering,	6
Total,	1799

(2d trial.)

Greely,	941
Holden,	849
Scattering,	6
Total,	1796

1847.

Greely,	1018
Wells,	687
Scattering,	20
Total,	1725

1848—(1st trial.)

Greely,	811
Howard,	720
Scattering,	116
Total,	1647

[Of the scattering, 93 for Clapp.]

(2d trial.)

Greely,	922
Howard,	715
Clapp,	103
Scattering,	13
Total,	1753

1849—(1st trial.)

Cahoon,	957
Clapp,	1016
Scattering,	95
Total,	2068

(2d trial.)

Cahoon,	1066
Clapp,	1022
Scattering,	84
Total,	2182

[There being no choice, Cahoon was elected by the city council.]

1850.

Cahoon,	1013
McCobb,	674
Scattering,	23
Total,	1710

1851—(1st trial.)

Neal Dow,	1184
Shepley,	972
Noyes,	225
Scattering,	5
Total,	2386

(2d trial.)

Dow,	1331
Shepley,	975
Scattering,	2
Total,	2308

1852.

Dow,	1496
Parris,	1900
Scattering,	3
Total,	3399

1853.

Cahoon,	1313
Dow,	353
Fox,	611
Fessenden,	75
Scattering,	59
Total,	2511

1854.

Cahoon,	1590
Dow,	1487
Scattering,	34
Total,	3111

1855.

Dow,	1894
McCobb,	1819
Scattering,	29
Total,	3742

1856.

McCobb	2115
Willis,	1837
Scattering,	3
Total,	3955

1857.

Willis,	1964
Cummings,	1547
Scattering,	3
Total,	3514

1858.

Jewett,	1757
Shepley,	1490
Scattering,	53
Total,	3390

1859.

Jewett,	2017
Holden,	1812
Scattering,	4
Total,	3833

1860.

Howard,	2420
Jewett,	2323
Scattering,	16
Total,	4759

1861.

Thomas,	2431
Howard,	2281
Scattering,	9
Total,	4619

1862.

Thomas,	1821
McLellan,	1687
Scattering,	6
Total,	3514

1863.

McLellan,	2166
Carroll,	1950
Scattering,	21
Total,	4139

1864.

McLellan,	1941
Carroll,	805
Scattering,	7
Total,	2753

1865.

McLellan,	1765
Sturdivant,	689
Scattering,	505
Total,	2959

1866.

Stevens,	2029
Shurtleff,	934
Scattering,	192
Total,	3155

1867.

Stevens,	1903
Shurtleff,	755
Scattering,	2
Total,	2660

1832.

MAYOR.

ANDREW L. EMERSON.*

ALDERMEN.

Ward 1.—Thomas Hammond,
2.—John Williams,
3.—John Patten,
4.—Charles Mussey,
Ward 5.—Seth Bird,
6.—Nathan Cummings,
7.—Ebenezer Webster.

COMMON COUNCIL.

SAMUEL FESSENDEN, PRESIDENT.

Ward 1.—Samuel Fessenden,
James Mountfort,
Ansyl Clark.

Ward 2.—William Cammett,
Daniel Winslow,
John T. Walton.

Ward 3.—Moses Hall,
Eliphalet Greely,
George Jewett.

Ward 4.—David Dana,
John W. Appleton,
Simeon Hall.

Ward 5.—Oliver Everett,
Isaac Smith,
Elisha Trowbridge.

Ward 6.—George Bartol,
William Cutter, Jr.,
James B. Cahoon.

Ward 7.—Job Randall,
Isaac Sparrow,
Ezra Holden.

CHARLES HARDING, *Clerk.*

* Resigned previous to expiration of office, and Jonathan Dow was chosen to fill the vacancy, December 31, 1832.

1833.

MAYOR.

JOHN ANDERSON.

ALDERMEN.

Ward 1.—Ansyl Clark,
2.—John Williams,
3.—Moses Hall,
4.—Simon Greenleaf,
Ward 5.—Nathaniel Shaw,
6.—Charles Q. Clapp,
7.—William T. Vaughan.

COMMON COUNCIL.

DANIEL WINSLOW, PRESIDENT.

Ward 1.—James Mountford,
William W. Thomas,
Steph. Frothingham.

Ward 2.—George W. Pierce,
Daniel Winslow,
David Burbank.

Ward 3.—Eliphalet Greely,
Thomas Warren,
Moses Plummer.

Ward 4.—Simeon Hall,
Andrew P. Mason,
Thomas Chadwick.

Ward 5.—Thomas Bolton,
Jeremiah Leavett,
Nathaniel Hamlin.

Ward 6.—Martin Gore,
Benjamin Larrabee,
George Bartol.

Ward 7.—Ezra Holden,
James Townsend,
Robert Knight.

BENJAMIN C. FERNALD, *Clerk.*

1834.

MAYOR.

LEVI CUTTER.

ALDERMEN.

Ward 1.—Phillip Greely,
2.—William Cammett,
3.—Thomas Warren,
4.—John Purington.
Ward 5.—Alpheus Shaw,
6.—James B. Cahoon,
7.—William T. Vaughan.

COMMON COUNCIL.

ELIPHALET GREELY, PRESIDENT.

Islands.—John Starling.

Ward 1.—Steph. Frothingham,
James Mountfort.

Ward 2.—Lemuel Dyer, 2d,
Marshall French,
Charles M. Davis.

Ward 3.—Eliphalet Greely,
Moses I. Plummer,
Benj. Knight.

Ward 4.—Thomas Chadwick,
Simeon Hall,
Andrew P. Mason.

Ward 5.—Joseph Noble,
Asa Hanson,
Edward D. Preble.

Ward 6.—Benjamin Larrabee,
Nathaniel Warren,
John Dow.

Ward 7.—Ezra Holden,
Alden Pierce,
Nathaniel Hasty, Jr.

CHARLES HARDING, *Clerk.*

1835.

MAYOR.

LEVI CUTTER.

ALDERMEN.

Ward 1.—Phillip Greely,
2.—William Cammett,
3.—Thomas Warren,
4.—John Purington,
Ward 5.—John Fox,
6.—James B. Cahoon,
7.—Nathaniel Ilsley.

COMMON COUNCIL.

ELIPHALET GREELY, President.

Ward 1.—Steph. Frothingham,
James Mountfort.

Ward 2.—Marshall French,
Hosea Harford,
Seba Smith.

Ward 3.—Eliphalet Greely,
Benjamin Knight,
Samuel Chase.

Ward 4.—Thomas Chadwick,
Nathaniel Sweetsir,
Benjamin Ilsley.

Ward 5.—Asa Hanson,
Edward D. Preble,
Phineas Varnum.

Ward 6.—Oliver B. Dorrance,
Henry B. Hart,
Solomon H. Mudge.

Ward 7.—James Hall,
Nathaniel Hasty,
Ira Bradford.

Charles Harding, *Clerk.*

1836.

MAYOR.

LEVI CUTTER.

ALDERMEN.

Ward 1.—Phillip Greely,
2.—Wm. W. Woodbury,
3.—Charles M. Davis,
4.—Mark Harris,
Ward 5.—Asa Hanson,
6.—James B. Cahoon,
7.—William T. Vaughan.

COMMON COUNCIL.

PHINEAS VARNUM, President.

Ward 1.—James Mountfort,
Steph. Frothingham.

Ward 2.—Enoch Moody,
William Capen,
William Robinson.

Ward 3.—Charles Rogers, Jr.
Benj. Knight,
William Boyd.

Ward 4.—Samuel Hale,
Horace Ward,
Freeman Bradford.

Ward 5.—Phineas Varnum,
John Edmond,
Elisha Trowbridge.

Ward 6.—Oliver B. Dorrance,
Henry B. Hart,
Seth Paine, Jr.

Ward 7.—Nathaniel Hamblin,
Ira Bradford,
James Hall.

Charles Harding, *Clerk.*

1837.

MAYOR.

LEVI CUTTER.

ALDERMEN.

Ward 1.—Steph. Frothingham,
2.—Eleazer Wyer,
3.—Charles Rogers, Jr.,
4.—Charles C. Mitchell,
Ward 5.—Asa Hanson,
6.—James B. Cahoon,
7.—Albert Smith.

COMMON COUNCIL.

JOHN D. KINSMAN, President.

Ward 1.—James Mountfort,
Joseph R. Thompson.

Ward 2.—Enoch Moody,
Charles Blanchard,
William Capen.

Ward 3.—William Boyd,
Thomas Cummings,
Nathaniel Ellsworth.

Ward 4.—Andrew T. Dole,
Rufus Read,
James L. Merrill.

Ward 5.—John D. Kinsman,
Elisha Trowbridge,
Winslow H. Purinton.

Ward 6.—Oliver B. Dorrance,
Ezra F. Beal,
John L. Meserve.

Ward 7.—Nathaniel Hamblin,
Ira Bradford,
Stephen W. Eaton.

Charles Harding, *Clerk.*

1838.

MAYOR.

LEVI CUTTER.

ALDERMEN.

Ward 1.—Steph. Frothingham,
2.—Eleazer Wyer,
3.—Eliphalet Greely,
4.—Charles C. Mitchell,
Ward 5.—George Clark,
6.—Oliver B. Dorrance,
7.—Albert Smith.

COMMON COUNCIL.

JOHN D. KINSMAN, President.

Ward 1.—James Mountfort,
George Pearson,
Simeon Skillings.

Ward 2.—William Capen,
William Robinson,
Hall J. Little.

Ward. 3.—William Boyd,
Thomas Cummings,
John B. Cross.

Ward 4.—Charles Kimball,
Ebenezer Owen,
George Worcester.

Ward 5.—John D. Kinsman,
Elisha Trowbridge,
Charles Davidson.

Ward 6.—John L. Meserve,
Nathaniel F. Deering,
Clement Pennell.

Ward 7.—Stephen W. Eaton,
Alfred Randall,
Samuel Elder.

Charles Harding, *Clerk.*

1839.

MAYOR.

LEVI CUTTER.

ALDERMEN.

Ward 1.—Steph. Frothingham,
2.—Eleazer Wyer,
3.—Eliphalet Greely,
4.—Charles C. Mitchell,
Ward 5.—George Clark,
6.—Nathaniel F. Deering,
7.—Joseph Howard.

COMMON COUNCIL.

ELISHA TROWBRIDGE, PRESIDENT.

Ward 1.—George Pearson,
Joshua B. Osgood,
Simeon Skillings.

Ward 2.—William Robinson,
Hall J. Little,
Alexander Hubbs.

Ward 3.—William Boyd,
Thomas Cummings,
Charles E. Barrett.

Ward 4.—Charles Kimball,
Ebenezer Owen,
George Worcester.

Ward 5.—Elisha Trowbridge,
St. John Smith,
Nahum Libby.

Ward 6.—Clement Pennell,
Nathaniel Blanchard,
William E. Greely.

Ward 7.—Stephen W. Eaton,
Alfred Randall,
John Sweetsir.

CHARLES HARDING, *Clerk.*

1840.

MAYOR.

LEVI CUTTER.

ALDERMEN.

Ward 1.—Joshua B. Osgood,
2.—Hall J. Little,
3.—William Boyd,
4.—John Purinton,
Ward 5.—Joseph M. Gerrish,
6.—Nathaniel F. Deering,
7.—Joseph Howard.

COMMON COUNCIL.

CHARLES E. BARRETT, PRESIDENT.

Ward 1.—Harrison Brazier,
Ezekiel Thurston,
John Brackett.

Ward 2.—William Robinson,
Edward Fernald,
Joseph Brooks.

Ward 3.—Charles E. Barrett,
Seward Merrill,
Edmund Winship.

Ward 4.—Samuel Chadwick,
Henry B. Hart,
Joseph L. Kelly.

Ward. 5.—St. John Smith,
Nahum Libby,
Theophilus C. Hersey.

Ward 6.—Nathaniel Blanchard,
William E. Greely,
John B. Brown.

Ward 7.—Ira Bradford,
Joseph R. Matthews,
Levi Bolton.

CHARLES HARDING, *Clerk.*

1841.

MAYOR.

JAMES C. CHURCHILL.

ALDERMEN.

Ward 1.—Joshua B. Osgood,
2.—Hall J. Little,
3.—Samuel Chase,
4.—John Purinton,
Ward 5.—Joseph M. Gerrish,
6.—William Goodenow,
7.—Joseph Howard.

COMMON COUNCIL.

HENRY B. HART, President.

Ward 1.—Harrison Brazier,
Ezekiel Thurston,
John Brackett.

Ward 2.—Edwin Fernald,
Joseph Brooks,
Elias Mountfort.

Ward 3.—Edmund Winship,
William D. Little,
William C. Beckett.

Ward 4.—Henry B. Hart,
Joseph L. Kelly,
George Worcester.

Ward 5.—St. John Smith,
Rufus Horton,
Eleazer McKenney.

Ward 6.—Nathaniel Blanchard,
John B. Brown,
Benjamin Larrabee.

Ward 7.—Levi Bolton,
Joseph R. Matthews,
Joseph S. Sargent.

Charles Harding, *Clerk.*

1842.

MAYOR.

JOHN ANDERSON.

ALDERMEN.

Ward 1.—John Yeaton,
2.—John Williams,
3.—Samuel Chase,
4.—James Todd,
Ward 5.—Parker McCobb,
6.—James Appleton,
7.—Joseph Howard.

COMMON COUNCIL.

CHARLES HOLDEN, President.

Ward 1.—Samuel Clark,
Peter Mugford,
John Brackett.

Ward 2.—Charles Holden,
Benjamin Fogg,
John Dela.

Ward 3.—Edmund Winship,
William D. Little,
William C. Beckett.

Ward 4.—Eliphalet Clark,
George W. Smith,
Zenas Libby.

Ward 5.—Henry Trickey,
William P. Stodder,
Byron Greenough.

Ward 6.—Charles Blake,
William W. Thomas,
Calvin Edwards.

Ward 7.—James Meserve,
William Budd,
Elisha Hasty.

John G. Sawyer, *Clerk.*

1843.

MAYOR.

ELIPHALET GREELY.

ALDERMEN.

Ward 1.—John Yeaton,
2.—John Williams,
3.—Samuel Chase,
4.—Thomas R. Jones,
Ward 5.—Elisha Trowbridge,
6.—John Dow,
7.—Joseph Howard.

COMMON COUNCIL.

WILLIAM D. LITTLE, President.

Ward 1.—Judah Chandler,
John B. Hudson,
Islands.— John Brackett.

Ward 2.—Benjamin Fogg,
Edward Waite,
Ebenezer C. Stevens.

Ward 3.—William D. Little,
William Hammond,
Nathan Chapman.

Ward 4.—George W. Smith,
Zenas Libby,
Abel M. Baker.

Ward 5.—Byron Greenough,
William P. Stodder,
Hanson M. Hart.

Ward 6.—Calvin Edwards,
Clement Pennell,
Alvah Conant.

Ward 7.—William Budd,
Alvah Libby,
John W. Munger.

John G. Sawyer, *Clerk.*

1844.

MAYOR.

ELIPHALET GREELY.

ALDERMEN.

Ward 1.—Steph. Frothingham,
2.—John Williams,
3.—Samuel Chase,
4.—Thomas R. Jones,
Ward 5.—Elisha Trowbridge,
6.—John Dow,
7.—Stephen W. Eaton.

COMMON COUNCIL.

WILLIAM D. LITTLE, President.

Ward 1.—Judah Chandler,
John B. Hudson,
Islands.— Charles York.

Ward 2.—Ebenezer C. Stevens,
Edward Waite,
Samuel R. Leavitt.

Ward 3.—William D. Little,
Edmund Winship,
William Hammond.

Ward 4.—Abel M. Baker,
Henry B. Hart,
Benjamin Ilsley, Jr.

Ward 5.—Hanson M. Hart,
W. C. Osborne,
Wm. E. Edwards.

Ward 6.—Alvah Conant,
Clement Pennell,
Rufus Horton.

Ward 7.—Alvah Libby,
Daniel Brazier,
Lewis J. Sturdivant.

S. B. Beckett, *Clerk.*

1845.

MAYOR.

ELIPHALET GREELY.

ALDERMEN.

Ward 1.—Steph. Frothingham,
2.—James C. Churchill,
3.—Charles E. Barrett,
4.—Thomas R. Jones,
Ward 5.—Elisha Trowbridge,
6.—William Goodenow,
7.—George F. Shepley.

COMMON COUNCIL.

WILLIAM D. LITTLE, PRESIDENT.

Ward 1.—George Pearson,
Joseph Hay,
Franklin C. Moody,

Ward 2.—William E. Kimball,
Solomon Crockett,
Josh. W. Waterhouse.

Ward 3.—William D. Little,
William Hammond,
Joseph R. Thompson.

Ward 4.—Benjamin Ilsley, Jr.
Henry B. Hart,
Joseph L. Kelly.

Ward 5.—Ezra Carter,
Freeman S. Clark,
Elbridge Tobie.

Ward 6.—Rufus Horton,
Horace V. Bartol,
Clement Pennell.

Ward 7.—Samuel Rolfe,
David J. True,
Jeremiah Proctor.

S. B. BECKETT, *Clerk.*

1846.

MAYOR.

ELIPHALET GREELY.

ALDERMEN.

Ward 1.—Harrison Brazier,
2.—John Yeaton,
3.—Charles E. Barrett,
4.—Edward Howe,
Ward 5.—Henry B. Hart,
6.—John Dow,
7.—P. Fox Varnum.

COMMON COUNCIL.

WILLIAM D. LITTLE, PRESIDENT.

Ward 1.—George Pearson,
Joseph Hay,
Franklin C. Moody.

Ward 2.—Harris C. Barnes,
Hosea Harford,
Solomon Crockett.

Ward 3.—William D. Little,
Joseph R. Thompson,
Reuben Kent, Jr.

Ward 4.—Benjamin Ilsley, Jr.
Solomon T. Corser,
Nahum Libby.

Ward 5.—Wm. E. Edwards,
Robert F. Green,
Thomas F. Tolman.

Ward 6—Clement Pennell,
Rufus Horton,
Horace V. Bartol.

Ward 7.—George T. Hedge,
Samuel Rolfe,
Jeremiah Proctor.

JOHN H. WILLIAMS, *Clerk.*

1847.

MAYOR.

ELIPHALET GREELY.

ALDERMEN.

Ward 1.—Harrison Brazier,
2.—Jona. O. Bancroft,
3.—Samuel Chase,
4.—Edward Howe.
Ward 5.—Simon Merrill,
6.—Nathaniel F. Deering,
7.—P. Fox Varnum.

COMMON COUNCIL.

WILLIAM D. LITTLE, PRESIDENT.

Ward 1.—George Pearson,
Franklin C. Moody,
Jacob T. Lewis.

Ward 2.—Hosea Harford,
Solomon Crockett,
Eliphalet Webster.

Ward 3.—William D. Little,
Reuben Kent, Jr.,
Alfred M. Dresser.

Ward 4.—Solomon T. Corser,
Edward Wheeler, Jr.,
Nathan Barker.

Ward 5.—George Worcester,
John Edwards,
(One vacancy.)

Ward 6.—Clement Pennell,
Horace Bartol,
Charles Baker.

Ward 7.—Moody F. Walker,
Samuel Rolfe,
James Meserve.

JOHN H. WILLIAMS, *Clerk*.

1848.

MAYOR.

ELIPHALET GREELY.

ALDERMEN.

Ward 1.—Steph. Frothingham,
2.—Lemuel Cobb, Jr.,
3.—Geo. W. Woodman,
4.—John Purinton,
Ward 5.—Byron Greenough,
6.—Nathaniel F. Deering,
7.—Edward Fox.

COMMON COUNCIL.

WILLIAM D. LITTLE, PRESIDENT.

Ward 1.—Jacob T. Lewis,
Elisha Hinds,
Abner Lowell.

Ward 2.—Rufus W. Thaxter,
Harris C. Barnes,
John C. Tukesbury.

Ward 3.—William D. Little,
Thomas Cummings,
Joseph R. Thompson.

Ward 4.—Solomon T. Corser,
Charles W. Child,
William E. Kimball.

Ward 5.—Hezekiah Winslow,
James T. McCobb,
Elbridge Tobie.

Ward 6.—James B. Cahoon,
Rufus Horton,
Martin Gore.

Ward 7.—Alvah Libby,
Peter Bolton,
Hiram Brooks.

JOHN H. WILLIAMS, *Clerk*.

1849.

MAYOR.

JAMES B. CAHOON.

ALDERMEN.

Ward 1.—Robert Dresser,
2.—E. C. Stevens,
3.—W. W. Woodbury,
4.—John Purinton,
Ward 5.—S. R. Lyman,
6.—Alvah Conant,
7.—Edward Fox.

COMMON COUNCIL.

WILLIAM D. LITTLE, President.

Ward 1.—Joshua Dyer,
Daniel M. Thurston,
Peter Mugford.

Ward 2.—Moses Russell,
Hosea Harford,
James Crie.

Ward 3.—William D. Little,
Caleb S. Carter,
Thomas Cummings.

Ward 4.—William E. Kimball,
Joseph R. Lufkin,
Moses Merrill.

Ward 5.—Eleazer McKenney,
George Worcester,
Eli Webb.

Ward 6.—John Bradford,
Nathaniel O. Cram,
Edwin A. Norton.

Ward 7.—Alvah Libby,
Hiram Brooks,
Peter Bolton.

John H. Williams, *Clerk.*

1850.

MAYOR.

JAMES B. CAHOON.

ALDERMEN.

Ward 1.—Steph. Frothingham,
2.—E. C. Stevens,
3.—Charles E. Barrett,
4.—J. B. Cummings,
Ward 5.—S. R. Lyman,
6.—Alvah Conant,
7.—Edward Fox.

COMMON COUNCIL.

WILLIAM D. LITTLE, President.

Ward 1.—Simeon Skillings, 3d,
Eliphalet Webster,
William G. Kimball.

Ward 2.—Hosea Harford,
James Crie,
Moses Russell.

Ward 3.—William D. Little,
Thomas Cummings,
Thomas Warren.

Ward 4.—Moses Merrill,
William E. Kimball,
Calvin Gilson.

Ward 5.—George Worcester,
Eleazer McKenney,
Charles Blake.

Ward 6.—N. O. Cram,
John Bradford,
Jedediah Jewett.

Ward 7.—Thomas W. O'Brien,
Hiram Brooks,
Nathan Mayhew.

John H. Williams, *Clerk.*

1851.

MAYOR.

NEAL DOW.

ALDERMEN.

Ward 1.—Steph. Frothingham,
2.—George Pearson,
3.—Samuel Chase,
4.—J. B. Cummings,
Ward 5.—Charles Jones,
6.—Wm. W. Thomas,
7.—Hiram Brooks.

COMMON COUNCIL.

WILLIAM G. KIMBALL, PRESIDENT.

Ward 1.—Simeon Skillings, 3d,
William Hoit,
S. B. Beckett.

Ward 2.—William I. Cross,
Joseph R. Brazier,
Moses Russell.

Ward 3.—Bradbury Dearborn,
Henry Nowell,
Daniel Plummer.

Ward 4.—Moses Merrill,
Joseph Ring,
William Cammett.

Ward 5.—James E. Robinson,
Veranus C. Hanson,
Hanson M. Hart.

Ward 6.—Jedediah Jewett,
John Bradford,
William G. Kimball.

Ward 7.—John W. Rand,
Nathaniel Walker,
J. S. Palmer.

JOHN H. WILLIAMS, *Clerk.*

1852.

MAYOR.

ALBION K. PARRIS.

ALDERMEN.

Ward 1.—Robert Dresser,
2.—George Pearson,
3.—W. P. Smith,
4.—James Furbish,
Ward 5.—Hezekiah Winslow,
6.—Jacob McLellan,
7.—J. S. Palmer.

COMMON COUNCIL.

CHARLES B. SMITH, PRESIDENT.

Ward 1.—John Chase,
John H. Short,
L. D. Mason.

Ward 2.—H. Bailey,
Joseph Hay,
J. R. Brazier.

Ward 3.—John Yeaton,
C. C. Harmon,
Charles Holden.

Ward 4.—Joseph Ring,
Calvin Gilson,
Charles D. Bearce.

Ward 5.—P. Fox Varnum,
Charles B. Smith,
Ezra Russell.

Ward 6.—Nathaniel Warren,*
Edwin Churchill,
Abial Somerby,
Charles H. Haskell.

Ward 7.—John W. Rand,
Charles H. Lovejoy,
F. Seymour Nichols.

JOHN H. WILLIAMS, *Clerk.*

---

* Resigned, and Mr. Haskell elected to vacancy.

1853.

MAYOR.

JAMES B. CAHOON.

ALDERMEN.

Ward 1.—Samuel L. Carleton,
2.—George Pearson,
3.—Geo. W. Woodman,
4.—Rufus E. Wood,
Ward 5.—O. L. Sanborn,
6.—Jacob McLellan,
7—Jonas H. Perley.

COMMON COUNCIL.

EDWARD P. GERRISH, PRESIDENT.

Ward 1.—Emery Cushing,
Moses G. Dow,
Sewall Mitchell.

Ward 2.—Samuel Blanchard,
Joseph Hay,
Thomas P. Sweetsir.

Ward 3.—William E. Kimball,
William C. Means,
Daniel Green.

Ward 4.—Joseph Ring,
James Todd,
George Lord.

Ward 5.—Ezra Russell,
Albion Witham,
Charles B. Merrill.

Ward 6.—Rufus Horton,
Nathaniel Ross,
Edward P. Gerrish.

Ward 7.—N. P. Cushman,
Marshall Rood,
Charles H. Green.

JOHN H. WILLIAMS, *Clerk.*

1854.

MAYOR.

JAMES B. CAHOON.

ALDERMEN.

Ward 1.—Samuel L. Carleton,
2.—Henry A. Jones,
3.—Geo. W. Woodman,
4.—Rufus E. Wood,
Ward 5.—O. L. Sanborn,
6.—N. Cummings,
7.—Hiram Brooks.

COMMON COUNCIL.

HENRY C. BABB, PRESIDENT.

Ward 1.—Henry Robinson,
Sewall Mitchell,
Henry C. Babb.

Ward 2.—Samuel Blanchard,
Rufus Beal,
George W. Brown.

Ward 3.—Wm. C. Means,
N. J. Gilman,
Daniel Green.

Ward 4.—James Todd,
Joseph Ring,
James S. Marrett.

Ward 5.—Ezra Russell,
Charles B. Merrill.
Albion Witham.

Ward 6.—Daniel L. Choate,
George Worcester,
Augustus E. Stevens.

Ward 7.—Sewall C. Chase,
Charles H. Green,
Denney M. C. Dunn.

JOHN T. HULL, *Clerk.*

1855.

MAYOR.

NEAL DOW.

ALDERMEN.

Ward 1.—Samuel L. Carleton,
2.—Henry A. Jones,
3.—Joseph Libby,
4.—Joseph Ring,
Ward 5.—S. J. Anderson,
6.—Wm. W. Thomas,
7.—Hiram Brooks.

COMMON COUNCIL.

HEZEKIAH PACKARD, PRESIDENT.

Ward 1.—Moses G. Dow,
Henry Robinson,
Joseph York.

Ward 2.—R. C. Webster,
Paul Hall,
George W. Brown.

Ward 3.—N. J. Gilman,
Wm. C. Means,
George F. Ayer.

Ward 4.—James Todd,
James S. Marrett,
Stephen Emerson.

Ward 5.—Eli Webb,
Ira P. Farrington,
Wm. P. Stodder.

Ward 6.—Daniel L. Choate,
John B. Carroll,
Hall J. Little.

Ward 7.—Hezekiah Packard,
Thomas Starbird,
Charles H. Green.

JOHN T. HULL, *Clerk.*

1856.

MAYOR.

JAMES T. McCOBB.

ALDERMEN.

Ward 1.—S. R. Leavitt,
2.—J. R. Brazier,
3.—C. C. Harmon,
4.—R. E. Wood,
Ward 5.—S. J. Anderson,
6.—N. O. Cram,
7.—J. S. Palmer.

COMMON COUNCIL.

CHARLES HOLDEN, PRESIDENT.

Ward 1.—D. W. Fessenden,
William V. Bowen,
Joshua F. Weeks.

Ward 2.—Joshua Dyer,
W. H. Purinton,
Charles H. Warren.

Ward 3.—Charles Holden,
Wm. D. Little,
J. W. Russell.

Ward 4.—Stephen Emerson,
James Todd,
C. H. Adams.

Ward 5.—A. K. Shurtleff,
William P. Stodder,
I. P. Farrington.

Ward 6.—T. A. Roberts,
C. H. Haskell,
Hall J. Little.

Ward 7.—Willard Brackett,
C. H. Stuart,
Daniel Garland.

M. F. WHITTIER, *Clerk.*

1857.

MAYOR.

WILLIAM WILLIS.

ALDERMEN.

Ward 1.—S. R. Leavitt,
2.—D. W. Fessenden,
3.—N. J. Miller,
4.—R. E. Wood,
Ward 5.—E. Trowbridge,
6.—Rensalear Cram,
7.—Samuel E. Spring.

COMMON COUNCIL.

H. B. HART, PRESIDENT.

Ward 1.—William V. Bowen,
J. F. Weeks,
Moses Gould.

Ward 2.—Jonathan M. Heath,
Samuel Waterhouse, Jr.,
George M. Elder.

Ward 3.—Benjamin Fogg,
Francis Blake,
D. D. Akerman.

Ward 4.—James Todd,
Stephen Emerson,
C. H. Adams.

Ward 5.—H. B. Hart,
Nathaniel Walker,
Henry Willis.

Ward 6.—Stephen Patten,
Frederic Hatch,
Aretus Shurtleff.

Ward 7.—J. N. Morrill,
L. B. Smith,
John P. Lowell.

M. F. WHITTIER, *Clerk.*

1858.

MAYOR.

JEDEDIAH JEWETT.

ALDERMEN.

Ward 1.—William V. Bowen,
2.—D. W. Fessenden,
3.—N. J. Miller,
4.—James Todd,
Ward 5.—Mark P. Emery,
6.—E. McKenney,
7.—Samuel E. Spring.

COMMON COUNCIL.

LEWIS B. SMITH, PRESIDENT.

Ward 1.—Moses Gould,
Emery Cushing,
George W. Beal.

Ward 2.—Jonathan M. Heath,
Samuel Waterhouse, Jr.,
George M. Elder.

Ward 3.—Benjamin Fogg,
Francis Blake,
D. D. Akerman.

Ward 4.—C. H. Adams,
Stephen Emerson,
J. D. Seavey.

Ward 5.—Stevens Smith,
N. A. Foster,
J. S. Boothby.

Ward 6.—Frederic Hatch,
A. Shurtleff,
E. P. Banks.

Ward 7.—J. N. Morrill,
Lewis B. Smith,
Levi Weymouth.

J. T. HULL, *Clerk.*

1859.

MAYOR.

JEDEDIAH JEWETT.

ALDERMEN.

Ward 1.—William Curtis,
2.—Daniel W. Fessenden,
3.—J. R. Thompson,
4.—James Todd,
Ward 5.—Mark P. Emery,
6.—Eleazer McKenney,
7.—Hiram Brooks.

COMMON COUNCIL.

LEWIS B. SMITH, PRESIDENT.

Ward 1.—George W. Beal,
Emery Cushing,
William A. Winship.

Ward 2.—Charles M. Plummer,
William C. How,
Samuel Waterhouse.

Ward 3.—D. D. Akerman,
Samuel W. Larrabee,
William L. Alden.

Ward 4.—James D. Seavey,
B. F. Chadbourn,
Samuel S. Webster.

Ward 5.—Stevens Smith,
N. A. Foster,
John Lynch.

Ward 6.—William W. Thomas,
John W. Lane,
G. A. Churchill.

Ward 7.—Levi Weymouth,
Lewis B. Smith,
John W. Rand.

CYRUS NOWELL, *Clerk.*

1860.

MAYOR.

JOSEPH HOWARD.

ALDERMEN.

Ward 1.—Emery Cushing,
2.—J. W. Dyer,
3.—J. R. Thompson,
4.—Samuel Trask,
Ward 5.—Charles P. Kimball,
6.—H. J. Libby,
7.—J. S. Palmer.

COMMON COUNCIL.

O. M. MARRETT, PRESIDENT.

Ward 1.—George W. Beal,
George Trefethen,
H. C. Lovell.

Ward 2.—John Barbour,
E. D. Choate,
Samuel Rounds.

Ward 3.—S. W. Larrabee,
John Lynch,
Otis Cutler.

Ward 4.—W. L. Putnam,
Thomas Parker,
B. F. Chadbourn.

Ward 5.—E. G. Bolton,
Ezra Russell,
O. M. Marrett.

Ward 6.—William W. Thomas,
John W. Lane,
George A. Churchill.

Ward 7.—R. M. Richardson,
Simeon Shurtleff,
Charles H. Stuart.

D. H. INGRAHAM, *Clerk.*

1861.

MAYOR.

WILLIAM W. THOMAS.

ALDERMEN.

Ward 1.—Moses Gould,
2.—John E. Donnell,
3.—S. W. Larrabee,
4.—Samuel Trask,
Ward 5.—Charles P. Kimball,
6.—Edward Hamblen,
7.—Levi Weymouth.

COMMON COUNCIL.

HENRY FOX, PRESIDENT.

Ward 1.—George Trefethen,
William A. Winship,
Daniel Brown.

Ward 2.—Dorville Libby,
Charles H. Osgood,
Rufus Beal.

Ward 3.—John Lynch,
James Bailey,
John True.

Ward 4.—W. L. Putnam,
George H. Chadwick,
Sewell Waterhouse.

Ward 5.—Orland M. Marrett,
Gardner Ludwig,
Charles W. Strout.

Ward 6.—Thomas A. Roberts,
Henry Fox,
Benjamin Stevens, Jr.

Ward 7.—Jonathan H. Fletcher,
Rishworth Rich,
William H. Stewart.

IRA J. BATCHELOR, *Clerk*.

1862.

MAYOR.

WILLIAM W. THOMAS.

ALDERMEN.

Ward 1.—Moses Gould,
2.—R. C. Webster,
3.—S. W. Larrabee,
4.—William L. Putnam,
Ward 5.—A. K. Shurtleff,
6.—Thomas R. Jones,
7.—D. H. Furbish.

COMMON COUNCIL.

HENRY FOX, PRESIDENT.

Ward 1.—William A. Winship,
Increase Pote,
Daniel Brown.

Ward 2.—C. H. Osgood,
Rufus Beal,
Dorville Libby.

Ward 3.—James Bailey,
John True,
Charles Holden.

Ward 4.—George H. Chadwick,
James McGlinchy,
Sewall Waterhouse.

Ward 5.—Gardner Ludwig,
E. H. Davies,
Henry Trickey.

Ward 6.—Henry Fox,
Benjamin Stevens, Jr.,
T. E. Twitchell.

Ward 7.—William H. Stewart,
Samuel E. Spring,
J. H. Fletcher.

IRA J. BATCHELOR, *Clerk*.

1863.

MAYOR.

JACOB McLELLAN.

ALDERMEN.

Ward 1.—George W. Beal,
2.—F. C. Moody,
3.—S. W. Larrabee,
4.—Benjamin Larrabee, 2d,
Ward 5.—Stevens Smith,
6.—F. G. Messer,
7.—William H. Stewart.

COMMON COUNCIL.

THOMAS E. TWITCHELL, President.

Ward 1.—Increase Pote,
William Brown,
J. D. Snowman.

Ward 2.—S. Whittimore,
Henry L. Paine,
Samuel Waterhouse.

Ward 3.—Charles Holden,
John True,
James Bailey.

Ward 4.—James McGlinchy,
J. H. Harmon,
C. H. Fling.

Ward 5.—Gilbert L. Bailey,
Edmund Phinney,
George L. Storer.

Ward 6.—T. E. Twitchell,
J. R. Hamlen,
T. E. Stewart.

Ward 7.—C. K. Ladd,
Joseph Johnson,
Brown Thurston.

Ira J. Batchelor, *Clerk.*

1864.

MAYOR.

JACOB McLELLAN.

ALDERMEN.

Ward 1.—George W. Beal,
2.—Franklin C. Moody,
3.—John E. Donnell,
4.—John G. Hayes,
Ward 5.—Stevens Smith,
6.—F. G. Messer,
7.—Wm. H. Stewart.

COMMON COUNCIL.

JAMES H. HAMLEN, President.

Ward 1.—Increase Pote,
Wm. Brown,
J. D. Snowman.

Ward 2.—S. Whittemore,
Jere Howe,
Wm. G. Soule.

Ward 3.—John T. Gilman,
C. H. Burr,
Cyrus Nowell.

Ward 4.—A. P. Morgan,
C. A. Gilson,
Edwin Clemens.

Ward 5.—G. L. Storer,
Gilbert L. Bailey,
Edmund Phinney.

Ward 6.—J. H. Hamlen,
T. E. Stewart,
Eben Corey.

Ward 7.—C. K. Ladd,
Joseph Johnson,
Brown Thurston.

Ira J. Batchelor, *Clerk.*

1865.

MAYOR.

JACOB McLELLAN.

ALDERMEN.

Ward 1.—Thomas S. Jack,
2.—Stephen Whittemore,
3.—John E. Donnell,
4.—A. P. Morgan,
Ward 5.—Edmund Phinney,
6.—Wm. L. Southard,
7.—George F. Foster.

COMMON COUNCIL.

GILBERT L. BAILEY, PRESIDENT.

Ward 1.—Joseph S. York,
Charles Bailey,
John J. Gerrish.

Ward 2.—Jere Howe,
George G. Soule,
C. M. Rice.

Ward 3.—Cyrus Nowell,
C. H. Burr,
Daniel Plummer.

Ward 4.—Charles A. Gilson,
W. C. Robinson,
Joseph Bradford.

Ward 5.—Gilbert L. Bailey,
Thomas F. Cummings,
A. P. Fuller.

Ward 6.—Eben Corey,
E. P. Gerrish,
Charles Staples, Jr.

Ward 7.—Ambrose Giddings,
F. W. Clark,
John M. Brown.

IRA J. BATCHELOR, *Clerk.*

1866.

MAYOR.

AUGUSTUS E. STEVENS.

ALDERMEN.

Ward 1.—Thomas S. Jack,
2.—Stephen Whittemore,
3.—Charles Holden,
4.—A. P. Morgan,
Ward 5.—Edmund Phinney,
6.—Wm. L. Southard,
7.—Ambrose Giddings.

COMMON COUNCIL.

CHARLES M. RICE, PRESIDENT.

Ward 1.—J. J. Gerrish,
J. S. York,
J. W. Brackett.

Ward 2.—C. M. Rice,
D. W. Fessenden,
S. H. Colesworthy.

Ward 3.—Daniel Plummer,
J. B. Matthews,
Augustus D. Marr.

Ward 4.—C. A. Gilson,
W. C. Robinson,
Joseph Bradford.

Ward 5.—A. P. Fuller,
Wm. Gray,
W. P. Files.

Ward 6.—E. P. Gerrish,
Charles Staples, Jr.,
C. R. Milliken.

Ward 7.—F. W. Clark,
Wm. H. Phillips,
Elias Chase.

IRA J. BATCHELOR, *Clerk.*

1867.

MAYOR.

AUGUSTUS E. STEVENS.

ALDERMEN.

Ward 1.—Russell Lewis,
2.—Charles M. Rice,
3.—Wm. Deering,
4.—C. A. Gilson,
Ward 5.—Gilbert L. Bailey,
6.—Thomas Lynch,
7.—Ambrose Giddings.

COMMON COUNCIL.

FRANKLIN FOX, PRESIDENT.

Ward 1.—H. H. Burgess,
J. S. Winslow,
James Knowlton.

Ward 2.—S. H. Colesworthy,
Franklin Fox,
George W. Green.

Ward 3.—J. B. Matthews,
Albert Smith,
J. A. Thompson.

Ward 4.—Wm. C. Robinson,
Joseph Bradford,
J. C. Shirley.

Ward 5.—Wm. Gray,
W. P. Files,
A. D. Marr.

Ward 6.—C. R. Milliken,
A. P. Fuller,
Frederic N. Dow.

Ward 7.—Elias Chase,
W. H. Phillips,
Wm. E. Gould.

F. A. GERRISH, *Clerk.*

INDEX.

INDEX.

www.ingramcontent.com/pod-product-compliance
Lightning Source LLC
LaVergne TN
LVHW020918110826
845150LV00004B/712

* 9 7 8 1 4 2 5 5 5 5 2 3 8 *